Illustrated
Microsoft Excel 2.10

Paul L. Schlieve

and

Jon I. Young

Wordware Publishing, Inc.

Library of Congress Cataloging-in-Publication Data

Schlieve, Paul L.
  Illustrated Microsoft Excel.

  Includes index.
  1. Microsoft Excel (Computer program).   2. Business—
  Data processing.   I. Young, Jon I.   II. Title.
  HF5548.4.M523S35   1989   005.36'9   88-33599
  ISBN 1-55622-109-6

ISBN 1-55622-109-6
10 9 8 7 6 5 4 3 2 1
V8903

Apple and Macintosh are registered trademarks of Apple Computer, Inc.
dBase II and dBase III are registered trademarks of Ashton-Tate
IBM is a registered trademark of International Business Machines, Inc.
Lotus and 1-2-3 are registered trademarks of Lotus Development Corporation
Microsoft is a trademark of Microsoft Corporation

All inquiries for volume purchases of this book should be addressed to Wordware Publishing,
Inc., at the above address. Telephone inquiries may be made by calling:

(214) 423-0090

Contents

Module	Title	Page
1	About This Book	1
2	Overview	3
3	Sample Session	7
4	Alignment	11
5	Apply Names	14
6	Arrange All	19
7	Border	22
8	Calculation, Calculate Now	25
9	Cell Protection	29
10	Chart	32
11	Clear	39
12	Close	42
13	Column Width	45
14	Copy, Cut, Paste	50
15	Create Names	56
16	Define Name	59
17	Delete (Database)	65
18	Delete (Edit)	71
19	Delete (File)	74
20	Display	77
21	Exit	81
22	Extract	83
23	Fill Right, Fill Down	91
24	Find (Database)	95
25	Find (Edit)	102
26	Font	106
27	Form	111
28	Format (Chart)	118
29	Freeze Panes/Unfreeze Panes	130
30	Gallery (Chart)	137
31	Goto	143
32	Hide/Unhide	145
33	Insert	150
34	Justify	152
35	Links	156
36	Menus	161
37	Move	166
38	New	169
39	New Window	173
40	Note	176
41	Number	180
42	Open	185

Contents Continued

Module	Title	Page
43	Page Setup	188
44	Parse	193
45	Paste Function	197
46	Paste Link	213
47	Paste Name	222
48	Paste Special	226
49	Print	237
50	Printer Setup	241
51	Protect Document	250
52	Record	255
53	Reference	261
54	Repeat	265
55	Replace	268
56	Row Height	271
57	Run	278
58	Save, Save As, Save Workspace	281
59	Select Special	287
60	Series	291
61	Set Criteria	297
62	Set Database	305
63	Set Page Break/Remove Page Break	310
64	Set Print Area	315
65	Set Print Titles	318
66	Show Info/Show Document	322
67	Size	330
68	Sort	334
69	Split	341
70	Table	344
71	Undo	351
72	Workspace	354
Appendix A	Terms and Definitions	359
Appendix B	Keystroke Commands and Functions	361
Appendix C	Error Messages	365
Appendix D	Excercises	366
Index		374

Recommended Learning Sequence

Sequence		Description	Module	Page
☐	1	About This Book	1	1
☐	2	Overview	2	3
☐	3	Sample Session	3	7
☐	4	Menus	36	161
☐	5	Undo	71	351
☐	6	Close	12	42
☐	7	Exit	21	81
☐	8	Delete (Edit)	18	71
☐	9	Open	42	185
☐	10	New	38	169
☐	11	Save, Save As, Save Workspace	58	281
☐	12	Hide/Unhide	32	145
☐	13	Copy, Cut, Paste	14	50
☐	14	Reference	53	261
☐	15	Goto	31	143
☐	16	Number	41	180
☐	17	Column Width	13	45
☐	18	Alignment	4	11
☐	19	Font	26	106
☐	20	Justify	34	152
☐	21	Row Height	56	271
☐	22	Border	7	22
☐	23	New Window	39	173
☐	24	Size	67	330
☐	25	Move	37	166
☐	26	Arrange All	6	19
☐	27	Clear	11	39
☐	28	Insert	33	150
☐	29	Fill Right, Fill Down	23	91
☐	30	Protect Document	51	250
☐	31	Cell Protection	9	29
☐	32	Printer Setup	50	241
☐	33	Print	49	237
☐	34	Page Setup	43	188
☐	35	Set Page Break/Remove Page Break	63	310
☐	36	Set Print Area	64	315
☐	37	Set Print Titles	65	318
☐	38	Find (Edit)	25	102
☐	39	Replace	55	268
☐	40	Workspace	72	354
☐	41	Gallery (Chart)	30	137

Recommended Learning Sequence (Cont.)

Sequence		Description	Module	Page
☐	42	Chart	10	32
☐	43	Format (Chart)	28	118
☐	44	Calculation, Calculate Now	8	25
☐	45	Paste Function	45	197
☐	46	Define Name	16	59
☐	47	Note	40	176
☐	48	Create Names	15	56
☐	49	Apply Names	5	14
☐	50	Paste Name	47	222
☐	51	Show Info/Show Document	66	322
☐	52	Display	20	77
☐	53	Select Special	59	287
☐	54	Set Database	62	305
☐	55	Form	27	111
☐	56	Sort	68	334
☐	57	Set Criteria	61	297
☐	58	Find (Database)	24	95
☐	59	Delete (Database)	17	65
☐	60	Extract	22	83
☐	61	Series	60	291
☐	62	Table	70	344
☐	63	Parse	44	193
☐	64	Split	69	341
☐	65	Freeze Panes/Unfreeze Panes	29	130
☐	66	Paste Link	46	213
☐	67	Links	35	156
☐	68	Paste Special	48	226
☐	69	Delete (File)	19	74
☐	70	Repeat	54	265
☐	71	Record	52	255
☐	72	Run	57	278

Module 1
ABOUT THIS BOOK

INTRODUCTION

This book describes Microsoft Excel, the state of the art in computerized worksheets. Excel combines all of the functionality of a traditional spreadsheet with integrated database and graphics functions. Because Excel runs with Windows, it offers the ability to cut and paste information among products. This book presents detailed information about Excel, and each command and technique is illustrated with examples.

This book is designed for a broad range of users. It is designed for first-time users of spreadsheets who need a sequential introduction to the system, and for users who are familiar with Excel, but need a reference manual with numerous examples to extract the full benefits of this complex software system.

ORGANIZATION

This book is not designed to be read in page-number order. If you are learning Excel, follow the *Recommended Learning Sequence* printed in the front of the book. This leads you from one command group to another in a simple-to-complex sequence.

Module 2 contains an overview of Excel and the Windows graphics environment. Module 3 is a sample session, designed to provide you with a brief introduction to working with Excel. The remainder of the modules in the book are arranged alphabetically by command. The alphabetical sequence is provided so that in addition to serving as a guide for learning Excel, the book can serve as a convenient command reference.

Appendix A contains terms and definitions to help you with unfamiliar vocabulary. Appendix B contains keystroke commands that serve as shortcuts to the mouse-based interface for some commands. Appendix C contains error messages you may encounter when developing Excel worksheets. Appendix D provides questions that are designed to help you monitor your understanding of Excel as you progress through the learning sequence.

THE WRITING STYLE

Each command module contains three sections. A *Description* section explains the operation of each command. An *Applications* section explains why you would want to use this command, and compares the command to similar or related commands. A *Typical Operation* section provides one or more step-by-step examples using the command.

Understanding several practices followed in the book can make the reading easier for you.

- Discussion of Excel features and procedures is presented in paragraph form. Steps which you perform in the Typical Operations are numbered.
- Keys you type or press are indicated by bold type.
- Selections you pick with the mouse are indicated by bold type.
- Two-key combinations are indicated by a hyphen, such as Ctrl-C. This notation means that you press and hold the key marked "Ctrl," then press and release the key for typing the letter "c," and finally release the key marked "Ctrl."

HARDWARE AND SOFTWARE REQUIREMENTS

Although Microsoft advertises that Excel requires an IBM PC/AT as the minimum hardware platform, Excel runs on any IBM PC, AT, PS/2, or compatible, running MS-DOS or PC-DOS 2.1 or later that has 640K of RAM, a hard disk, and a compatible graphics adapter and monitor. All of the excercises in this book have been tested and found to operate (although slowly) on an original IBM PC-XT with an IBM Color Graphics Adapter (CGA). Although it is possible to operate Excel without a mouse, it certainly isn't practical.

In addition to the hardware required for its operation, Excel takes advantage of additional hardware that may be present in your computer system to improve its performance. Excel automatically detects and uses a numeric co-processor if it is installed in your computer. Excel also makes use of either extended or expanded memory to improve its performance. Excel and/or Windows automatically detect the presence of extended or expanded memory in your system and suggest the appropriate installation options as you install Excel and/or Windows.

WINDOWS

Excel is a graphics-based system that uses Microsoft Windows to communicate with your hardware. Windows has a set of extensions to DOS that allow multiple programs to run on your computer at the same time with a common graphical interface. When you purchase Excel, the package of disks you receive contains a limited version of Windows that allows you full access to all of Excel's features, but does not allow you to run other Windows programs.

You may choose to either use the run-time version of Windows that is packaged with Excel, or to purchase either Windows/286 or Windows/386 as a separate product, allowing Excel to function as part of a group of Windows-based programs. In those few places where it matters which version you use, instructions are included for each Windows version.

Because Windows applications automatically take advantage of the maximum capabilities of your display hardware, there will undoubtably be some differences between the screen displays illustrated in the book and the displays you see on your computer screen as you work through the Typical Operations. Your screen may show more worksheet rows and columns on the display and provide additional options for the use of colors and patterns on your display. This should not, however, affect your ability to successfully complete all of the sample sessions.

Module 2
OVERVIEW

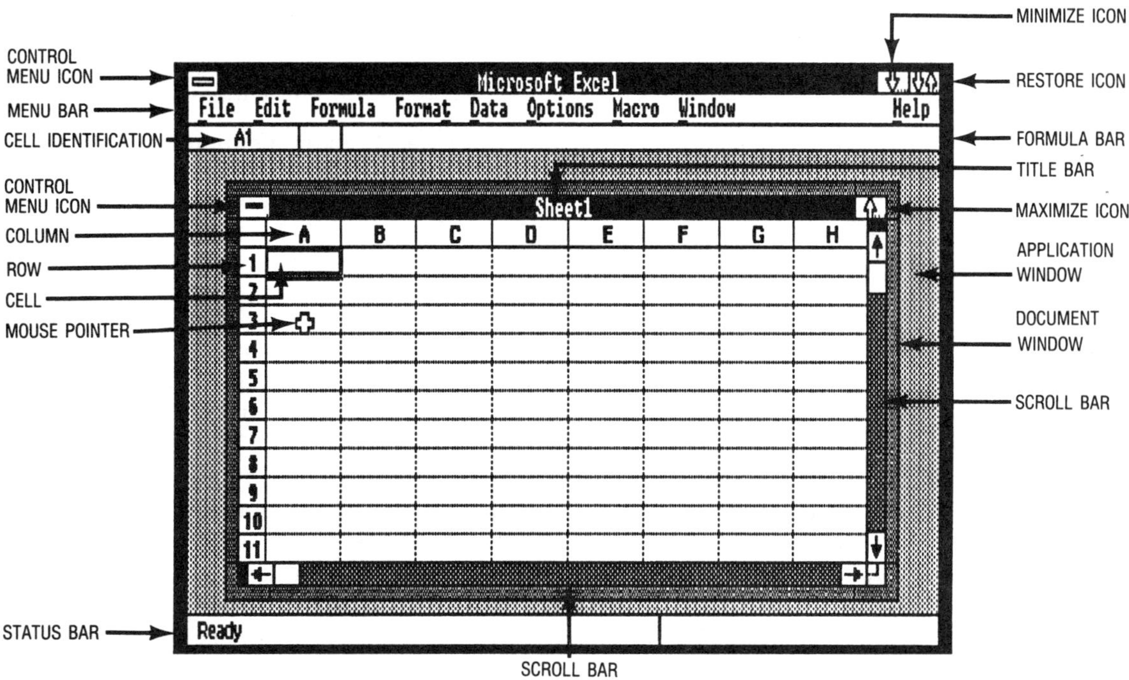

INTRODUCTION

Microsoft Excel is a software application that combines data management procedures, using a spreadsheet format, with a graphics capability. This combination permits you to store, modify, and graphically display a variety of data types. Since the software is based on a spreadsheet presentation, you can manipulate text and numbers with mathematical and statistical formulas and even store the data so that other database management systems can access it.

WINDOWS

A valuable feature of the Excel software is the *windows* concept. The user can open an unlimited number of windows at the same time and move quickly between them. Only one window on the screen is the active window and it can be increased in size until it fills the entire screen, or it can be decreased in size until it becomes a small *icon* at the bottom of the screen. An icon is a little graphic that is used to identify an activity or device, instead of using a word.

A window is best conceptualized by the following analogy. The window permits you to look at (and work with) documents. It is analogous to looking through the window of a house and seeing one or more documents or worksheets on a table. Through this window you can direct Excel to increase the size of a document or worksheet until it fills the window, or you can direct Excel to increase the size of the worksheet until only a portion of it is visible. Excel can move the window to permit you to view different portions of the worksheet. Excel can also arrange several worksheets so that they can be viewed through the window.

Each time you open a window you will be provided with one worksheet. You can direct Excel to provide you with multiple worksheets. You can work with one worksheet and then move to another and back to the first. All of these worksheets together constitute the Excel *workspace*. The workspace includes all of the worksheets you have opened in any window.

The illustration screen at the beginning of this module shows: (1) an application window called Excel, which is an application of the Microsoft Windows program; (2) a document window (Sheet1) which is a worksheet for Excel. The document window is positioned over the application window. Both windows have a Control menu icon in the upper left corner.

WORKSHEETS

The *active* worksheet is always recognized by the Control icon in the upper left corner and the *scroll* bars on the right side and the bottom. In the screen illustration at the beginning of this module you notice that Sheet1 is the active screen and cell A1 is ready to receive information. If you load Excel and an active worksheet is not automatically placed on your screen, it is because the active window is somewhere else. You can activate a window on the screen by clicking with the mouse pointer on the title bar containing the name "Sheet1" or by opening the File menu and starting a new worksheet. If you have more than one worksheet on the screen, you can make any worksheet active by clicking on any portion of the worksheet with the mouse, or by using the Window menu from the keyboard. You will learn how to do these operations later in this book. Once the worksheet on the screen has been defined as the active worksheet, you are ready to begin moving through the worksheet or entering data.

The *worksheet* is the basic spreadsheet format that Excel uses to store and manipulate data; it consists of *rows* and *columns* which together form a grid pattern. The intersections of these rows and columns are called *cells*. Each cell has a distinct address that gives the column designation first and the row designation second. Thus, cell F16 is the sixteenth cell in column F. There are 256 columns and 16,384 rows in each worksheet. You can enter data in any of the cells you choose. At the top of the grid is a "cell identification" space and a "text" line. This space identifies the cell where you are currently working and shows the information you type in a cell. You can increase the size of each cell so that all of the information you put in one can be seen in the cell. Information you type in one cell that is too large to fit in the cell will overlap into the next cells if they are empty. The *menu* bar is also located at the top of the screen, listing the menus that are currently available to you. These menus may be opened by typing the underlined letter in the name or clicking on the name with the mouse. Each menu displays several options from which you may select.

The bars, with arrows on each end, at the bottom of the worksheet and at the right of the worksheet, are called scroll bars. They are used to move the workspace to another section of the worksheet.

Finally, notice that in the upper right corner are two boxes, one with one arrow in it and one with both an up and a down arrow in it. These two boxes are used to minimize or maximize the windows.

SPREADSHEETS

Excel's primary vehicle for data manipulation is the spreadsheet. Spreadsheets can be modified to accommodate a variety of data types and the data can be stored as numbers or characters, manipulated using mathematical formulas, and printed in a variety of graphic presentations. You simply modify the spreadsheet to accommodate the data to be entered and create the appropriate relationships between data. When you change any data, the spreadsheet will automatically adjust all of the other related data.

The spreadsheet format offers significant storage capability. Excel's spreadsheet has 256 columns starting with letter "A" and ending with "IV." There are 16,384 rows for a total of 4,194,304 cells. Cells are referenced by the column and row designation called an *address*. Excel will permit you to move to an address you specify thus permitting you to move through the worksheet rapidly.

In addition, Excel spreadsheets permit cells to be organized into arrays, and the arrays can be treated as a common cell. The spreadsheet format also permits the use of user-programmed "mini-programs" that can be activated at any time to perform a predetermined set of operations. This capability reduces the necessity of recreating commonly used operations.

MENUS

You communicate with Excel through a series of *pull down* menus. Some menus are identified by a name, others by an icon. On your screen the arrows in the upper right corner and the box in the upper left corner are icons. Once you select a name or an icon, using either a mouse or the keyboard, a menu appears. You simply select the option desired from the menu. Excel assists you by inactivating some menu options when they don't apply to the current task. The user-friendly system of menus assists in simplifying the creation, storage, and utilization of various data types.

KEYBOARD/MOUSE

One of the significant features of Excel is that the program permits you to interact with it using either a keyboard or a mouse. Although you will probably find that the mouse is the most useful of the two in moving around the worksheet and accessing the different menus, the keyboard is the main data input device. You can use the keyboard to move through the worksheet, but you will have to either memorize the keystroke commands or develop a system for easy access. What can be accomplished with the click of a mouse button may take two or three keystrokes.

Mouse users will notice that when you are in the worksheet proper, the mouse pointer is in the form of a cross or mathematical plus sign. When the mouse is outside the worksheet, it is in the form of either a double arrow or a single arrow. The double arrow is used to change the size of the worksheet and the single arrow is used to access a menu item.

HELP

Excel supports you with a complete system of help options. The help offered by Excel is *context sensitive* meaning that the help options presented at any particular time are dependent on what task is being performed at that time. In this way you are automatically presented with the most useful help information at any time. Of course, this doesn't prevent you from reading through all of the help options at any time.

OTHER FEATURES

Windows provides some utility and entertainment options as well. These are often very useful and include Calculator, Calendar, Cardfile, Notepad, Write, and Paint. Notepad is a normal ASCII text file that is limited in size. Write is a word processor with a variety of options and Paint is a drawing program that is useful in illustrating.

Continue with Module 3.

Module 3

SAMPLE SESSION

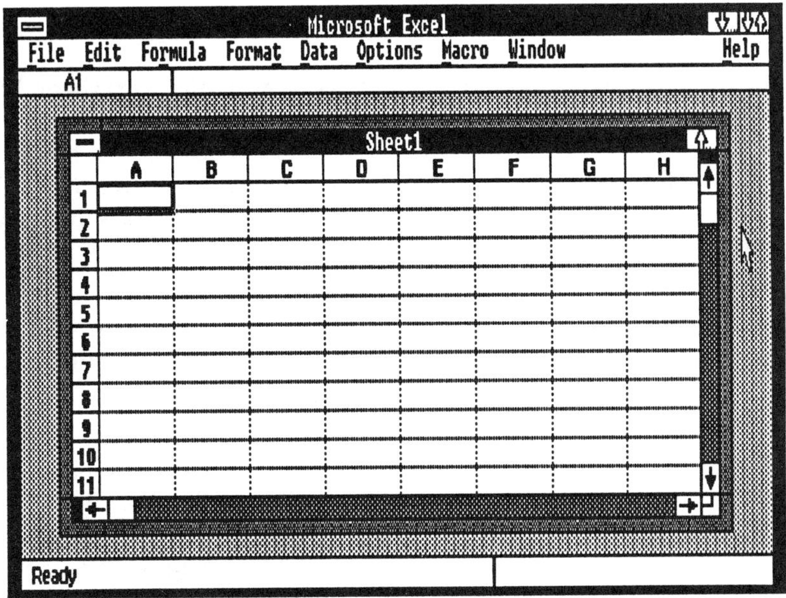

LOADING EXCEL

In this module you will open an Excel spreadsheet and learn how to manipulate the windows and worksheets.

1. From the system prompt, type **CD\windows**, (type **CD\WIN386** if you are using Windows/386), and press **Enter**.

2. Type **Excel** and press **Enter**.

The image on your monitor should look like the illustrated screen above. It shows two windows: the Microsoft Excel application window and the document window called Sheet1.

MOVING AROUND THE WORKSHEET

You are now ready to enter text and numbers in a worksheet, create and use a formula to manipulate the numbers, and save the work. These are the most basic operations that you will use in Excel and will serve to provide you with some understanding of how to use the workspace.

3. Press **Ctrl-Right Arrow** to move to the extreme right-hand edge of the worksheet. The screen should now show you the columns at the end of the worksheet, ending with column IV.

4. Press **Ctrl-Down Arrow** to move to the bottom of the worksheet. The screen should now show you the rows at the bottom of the worksheet, ending with row 16,384.

5. Press **Ctrl-Home** to return to the beginning of the worksheet.

KEYBOARD SCROLLING   The worksheet can be scrolled with the arrow keys or the page keys. Page keys scroll the worksheet up or down. Each arrow key will also scroll the worksheet. The viewing area moves in the direction of the arrow used. For example, to move to the right in the worksheet, use the Right Arrow. Each column or row will move across the screen and continue to do so as long as you maintain pressure on the arrow key.

MOUSE SCROLLING   The mouse uses the *scroll bars* to move the worksheet. Each scroll bar has an arrow at both ends with an empty box immediately behind one of the two arrows. Clicking on the arrows in the scroll bar will move the worksheet in the direction of the arrow each time the mouse is clicked. Clicking and holding the empty box behind the arrow will permit you to drag the box along the scroll bar until the desired position is reached. When using the mouse pointer to scroll or move through the workspace, be sure that the pointer is *not* the double arrow that is used to size the worksheet.

6. Practice using the arrow keys, page keys, and scroll bars to move through the workspace. When you are finished, press **Ctrl-Home** to return the workspace to its original position.

ENTERING DATA

7. Type **Income for the year of 1990** in cell A1. Notice that the text appears in both the cell and the text line. If the text you wish to put in a cell is too large to fit in the cell, you can read it on the text line. Only part of it will appear in the cell. Excel will keep track of what text belongs in what cells. In order to see what is in a cell, simply make that cell the active one and the text will appear in the text line.

8. Press **Backspace** until all the text is erased except for the word Income.

9. Make cell **A3** the active cell and type **Salary**.

10. Type **Expenses** in cell D1.

11. Type **Mortgage** in cell D3.

12. Type **Food** in cell D4.

13. Type **Auto** in cell D5.

14. Type **Clothes** in cell D6.

15. Type **Savings** in cell D7.

16. Type **Taxes** in cell D8 and press **Enter**.

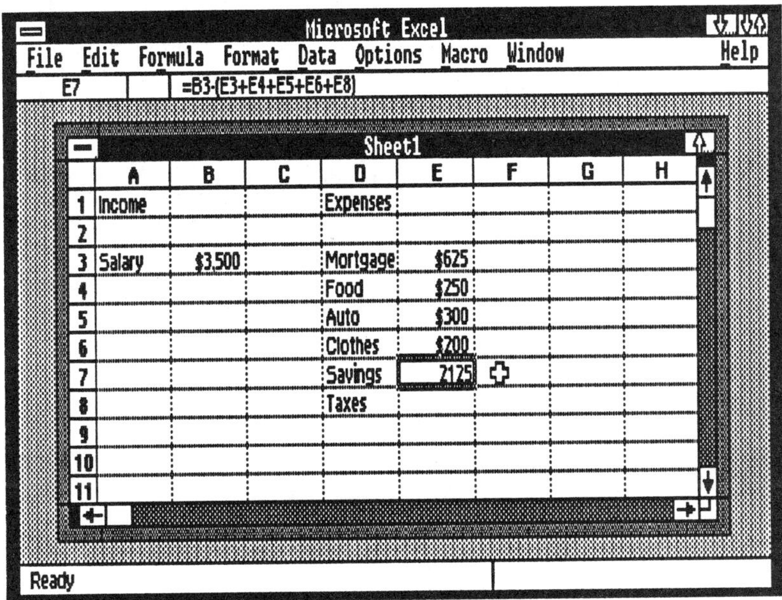

17. Type **$3500** in cell B3.

18. Type **$625** in cell E3.

19. Type **$250** in cell E4.

20. Type **$300** in cell E5.

21. Type **$200** in cell E6.

22. Type **= B3-(E3 + E4 + E5 + E6 + E8)** in cell E7, and press **Enter**.

The result of this formula will be placed in cell E7. The value of 2125 reflects zero amount in cell E8. If you were to make E8 the active cell and press the Spacebar, the formula in E7 would give you "#VALUE" because Excel would interpret the space as a text character.

23. Assume a 20% tax rate and type **=B3∗.20** in cell E8 and press **Enter**. You should now have the value 1425 in cell E7 and the value 700 in cell E8. These are the values that result from the two formulas you typed in those cells.

24. Press **Alt-F** or click on **File** in the menu bar.

25. Type **S** or click on the **Save** command.

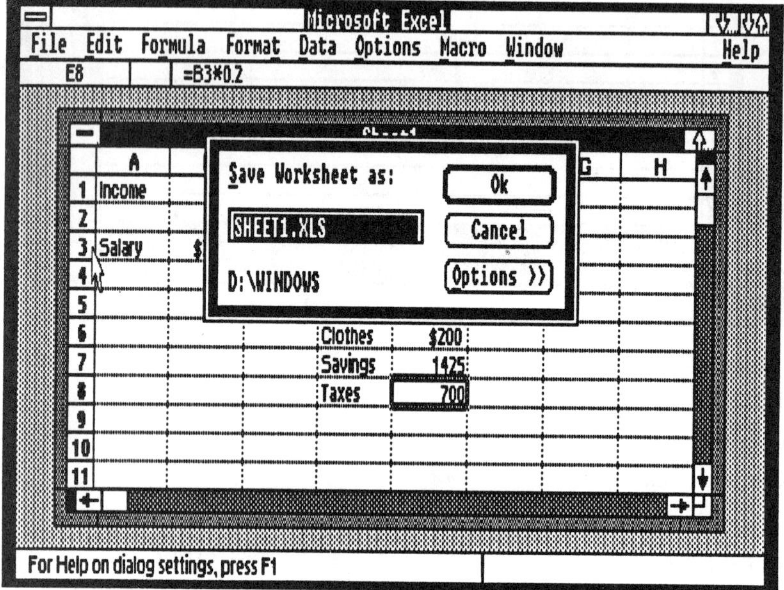

26. Press **Enter** or click on **OK** and the window is saved as SHEET1.XLS.

27. Press **Alt-F** or click on **File** in the menu bar.

28. Type **X** or click on the **Exit** command.

Depending on the version of Windows you are using, you are either at the DOS "C>" prompt, or in the MS-DOS Executive.

29. Turn to Module 36 to continue the learning sequence.

Module 4

ALIGNMENT

DESCRIPTION

Use the Alignment command on the Format menu to specify the placement of the data within each cell. First select the cell, row, column, or region that you want to format, then pick the command with the mouse or press Alt-T A. The following dialog box appears.

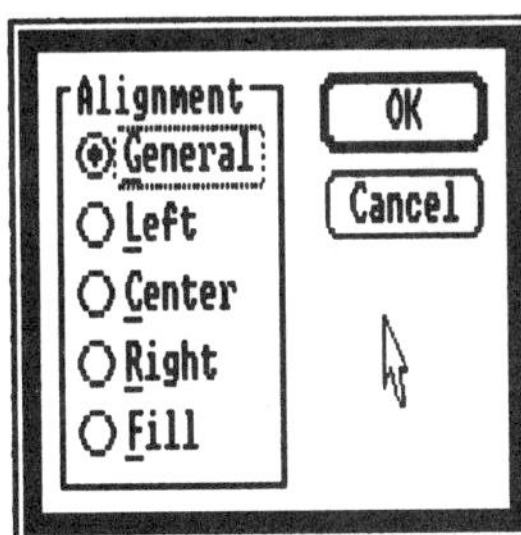

Select the alignment option that best fits the presentation of the data. General alignment left-justifies text and right-justifies numbers. Left, Center, and Right provide their respective forms

Module 5

APPLY NAMES

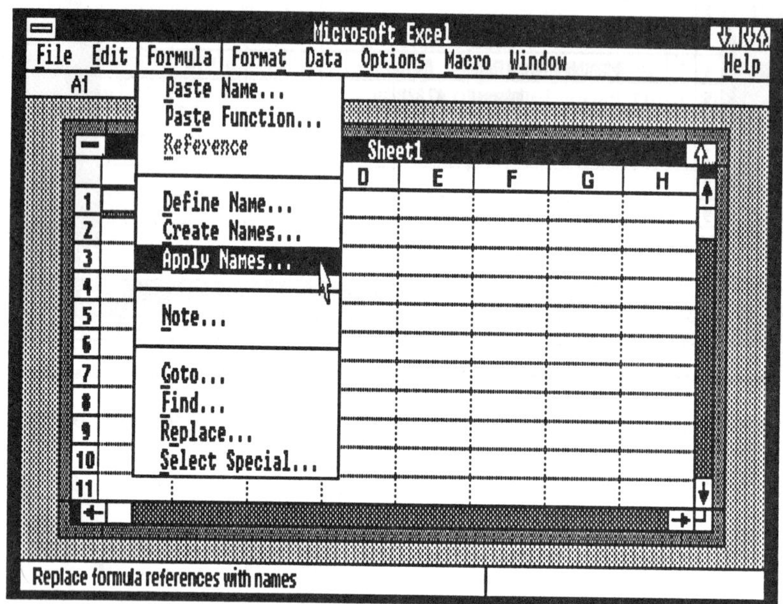

DESCRIPTION

The Apply Names command allows you to convert cell-reference-based formulas and references to name-based references for selected formulas. The Apply Names command is greyed out on the menu until you have defined at least one name using the Define Name or Create Names commands.

If a rectangular region of the worksheet is selected when you begin the Apply Names command, the Apply Names operation is only performed on the selected region. If only a single cell is highlighted, the Apply Names operation is performed on the entire worksheet.

When you select the Apply Names command from the Formula menu, Excel displays a dialog box with basic selections and an Option box. Picking the Option box displays the full dialog box, as follows:

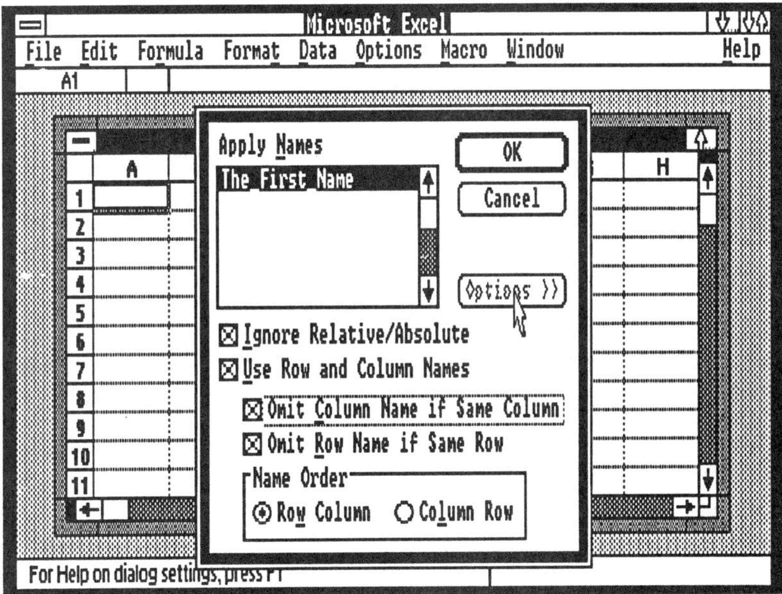

The selection box at the top left shows the names defined for the current worksheet and allows you to pick the name or names you want to have substituted in formulas. When selecting multiple names with the mouse, depress the shift key while picking names with the left mouse button. When selecting multiple names with the keyboard, press and hold the Ctrl key while moving through the selection box with the Up Arrow and Down Arrow keys. Press the Spacebar to add a name to the selection list. The Ignore Relative/Absolute check box allows you to specify how strict Excel is in replacing references with names. When not checked, Excel replaces only relative references with relative names, absolute references with absolute names, and mixed references with mixed names. When checked, Excel ignores the differences between relative and absolute references when applying names. Refer to Module 53 (Reference) for more information on cell reference.

Picking the Options button reveals several advanced options of the Apply Names command that are useful in building sophisticated models. The Omit Column Name if Same Column check box allows you to specify the type of reference used to refer to a referenced cell in a row-oriented named range. When checked, it causes Excel to replace references with the row-oriented name, omitting the column-oriented name. Otherwise both a column and row reference are used. The Omit Row Name if Same Row check box allows you to specify the type of reference used to refer to a referenced cell in a column-oriented named range. When checked, it causes Excel to replace references with the column-oriented name, omitting the row-oriented name. Otherwise both a column and row reference are used. The Use Row and Column Names check box allows you to specify whether row and column names should be used when an exact match is not found. When replacing a cell reference with both a row-oriented name and a column-oriented name, Excel normally refers to the cell by specifying the row first, then the column. You can change that name ordering by picking the "Column Row" option in the Name Order area.

APPLICATIONS

Developing a worksheet is frequently a process of starting small and building, rather than first developing a grandiose master plan. Frequently, prototype worksheets are developed with numerous row/column references to cells in formulas. Later, you may decide to associate a name with the data that already appears in those cells. The Apply Names command allows you to go through your worksheet retroactively and replace those meaningless row and column references with meaningful names.

TYPICAL OPERATION

In this session you create a simple formula on a worksheet, create names for the component parts of the formula, then apply those names to the worksheet, updating the definition of the formula for readability.

1. Start Excel and expand Sheet1 to fill the screen, or continue your work session by creating a new worksheet with the **New** command on the File menu.

2. Type **Fixed Costs** in cell A1.

3. Type **Variable Costs** in cell A2.

4. Type **Total Costs** in cell A3 and press **Enter**.

5. Increase the width of column A to hold the entries.

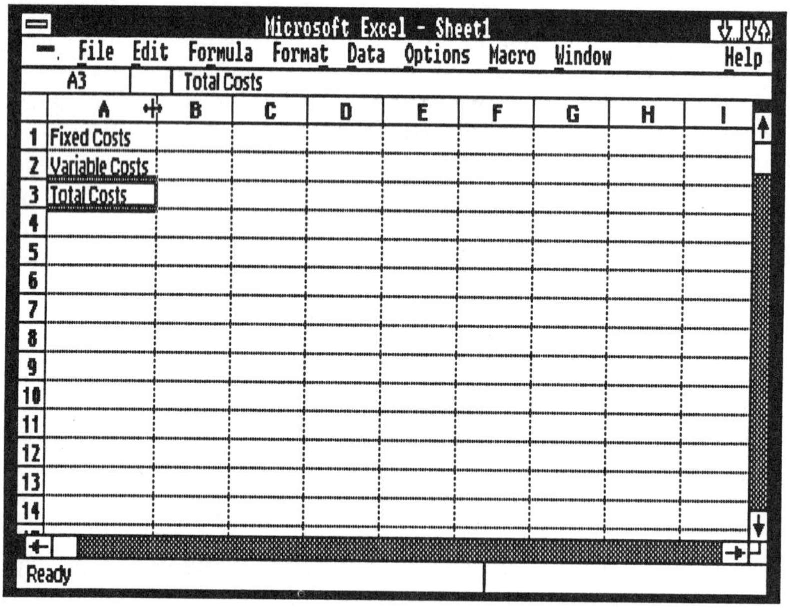

6. Type **125000** in cell B1.

7. Type **250000** in cell B2.

8. Type **=B1+B2** in cell B3 and press **Enter**.

9. If necessary, increase the width of column B to display the results.

10. Select (highlight) the cell range A1 through B2; then select **Create Names** from the Formula menu. Pick **Left Column** to specify that the names are along the left edge of the region.

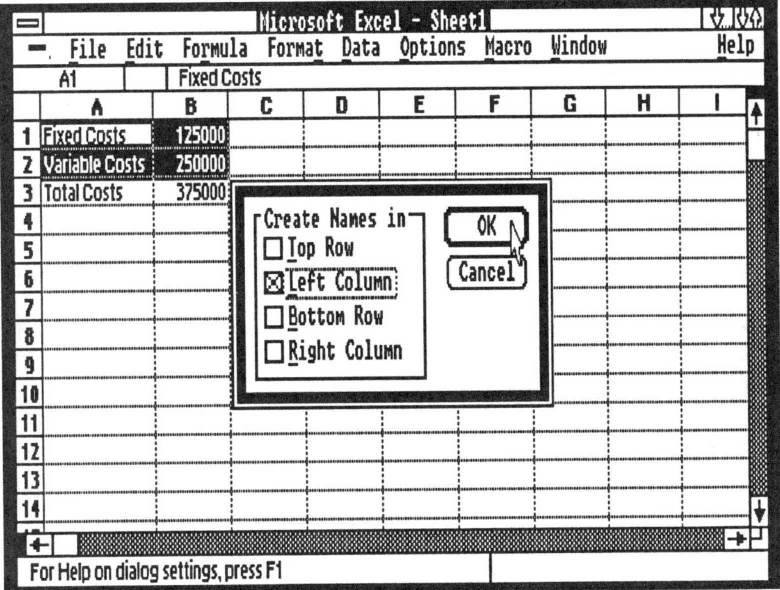

11. Pick the **OK** button in the Create Names dialog box.

12. Select (highlight) the rectangular region A1 through B3.

13. Select **Apply Names** from the Formula menu. Both Fixed_Costs and Variable_Costs are highlighted in the selection box. (If not, select them now so that they are highlighted.)

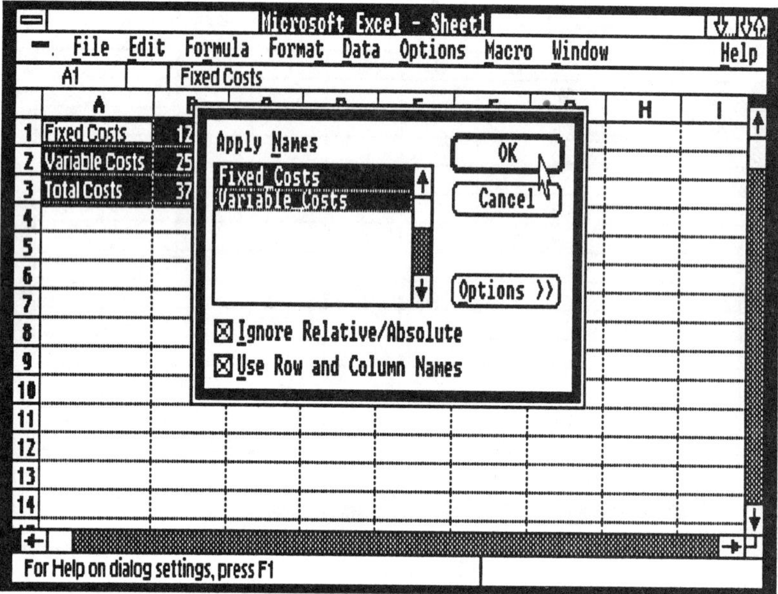

14. Pick **OK**.

15. Select cell B3 and examine the formula definition in the formula bar. Notice that the cell references have been replaced by their respective names.

16. Close the worksheet. It is not necessary to save it.

17. Exit Excel, or continue your work session without a worksheet on the screen.

18. Turn to Module 47 to continue the learning sequence.

Module 6
ARRANGE ALL

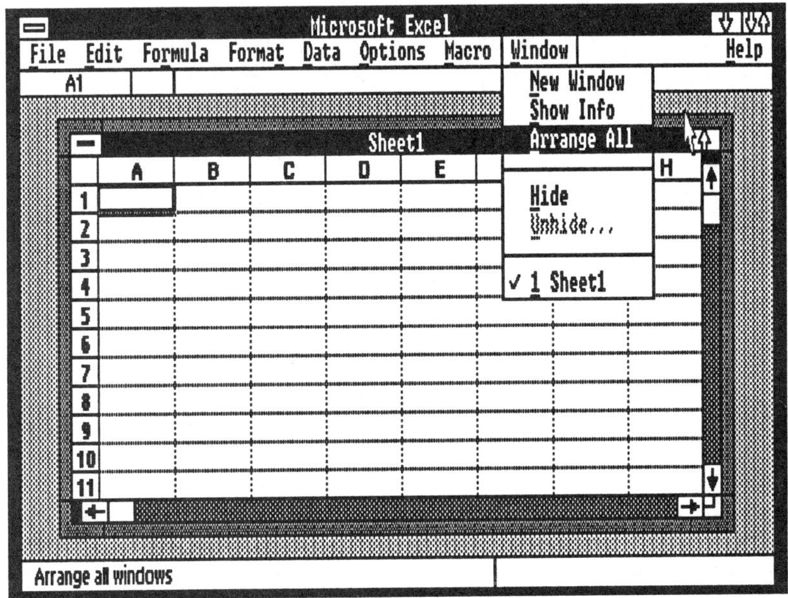

DESCRIPTION

The Arrange All command is located in the Window menu and is used to reorganize the active worksheets on the screen. This command will help you keep track of the available worksheets that you can use at any time. Once you use this command, Excel will organize the worksheets according to a default standard. If you don't like the way Excel organizes the worksheets, you can use the Move command to rearrange them or use the Arrange All command again.

Having reorganized the worksheets with Arrange All, you can move between the worksheets with the Ctrl-F6 keystrokes or by clicking on the desired worksheet with the mouse.

APPLICATIONS

As you create new worksheets and enter data in them, you will need to have some simple method of organizing them to facilitate access to them. If you save several worksheets together as a workspace or open several worksheets to work with, you will need to organize them so that you can easily move between them or see what information is available on each. Sometimes you may even forget what worksheets you have already opened. The Arrange All command will do this for you.

TYPICAL OPERATION

In this operation you use the Arrange All command to organize the open worksheets on the screen. You should have come directly to this module from the Move module. If you didn't, then restore the workspace you saved at the conclusion of that module before continuing with this operation.

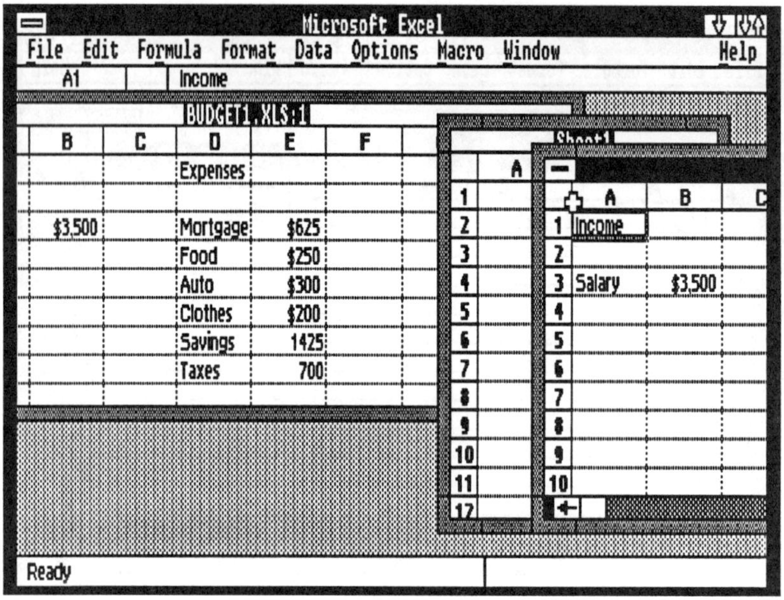

1. Access **Arrange All** from the Window menu.

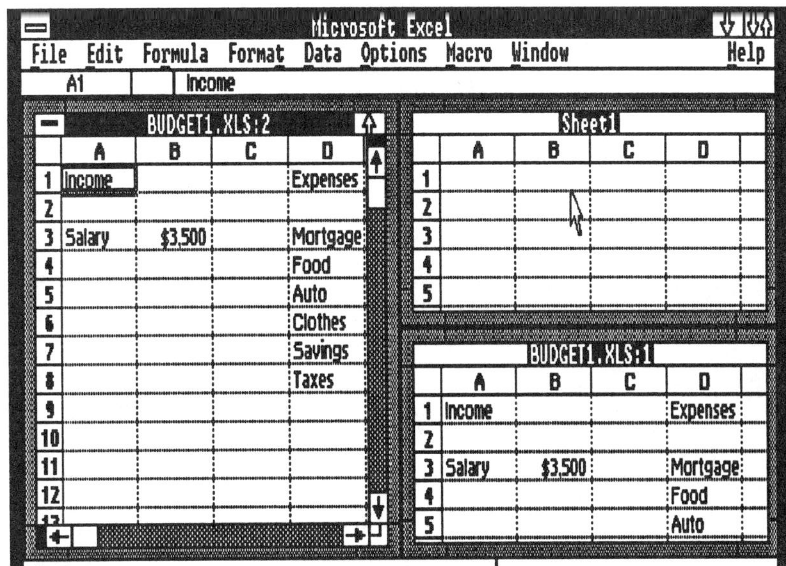

All of the worksheets have been reorganized.

2. Pick on Sheet1, making it the active worksheet.

3. Access **Arrange All** from the Window menu.

Excel has reorganized the worksheets.

4. Close each worksheet and continue your work session, or exit Excel.

5. Turn to Module 11 to continue the learning sequence.

Module 7

BORDER

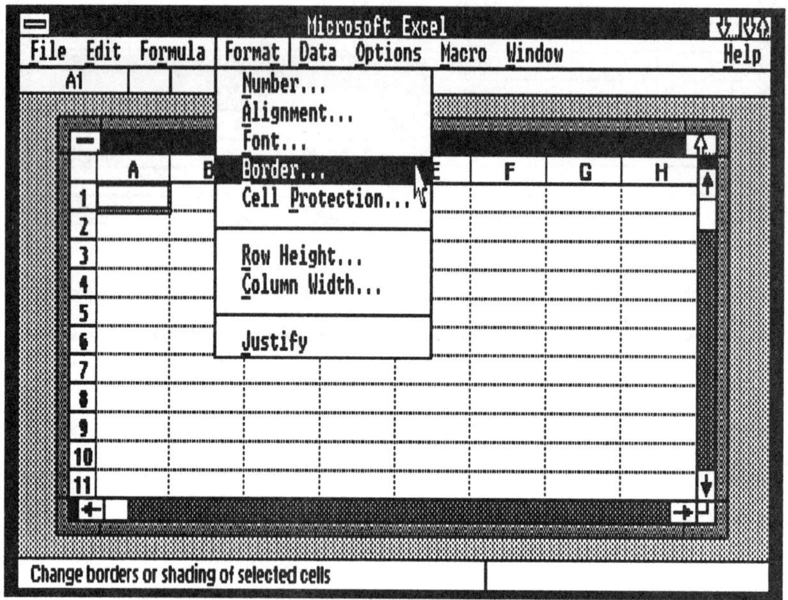

DESCRIPTION

The Border command on the Format menu allows you to specify treatments for cells and their borders. Select the command from the menu with the mouse, or press Alt-T B. The following dialog box appears.

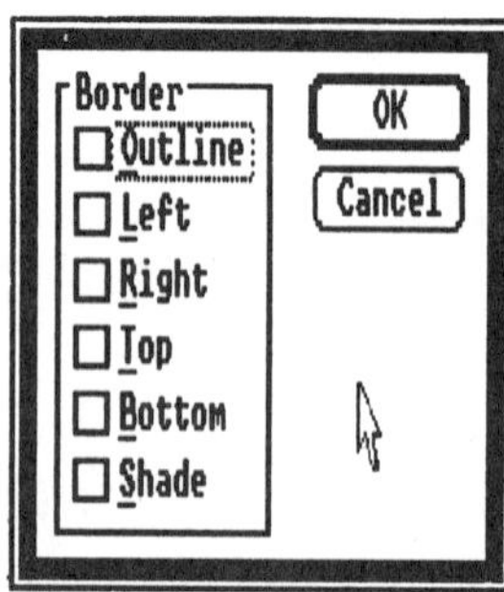

Options on this dialog box allow you to specify the placement of an outline around each cell, or to place a line individually along any side of the cell.

The shade option allows you to provide background shading for cells.

Select the desired option, then pick OK.

APPLICATIONS

The border treatments allow you to place ruling lines either horizontally or vertically at any location in your worksheet. These lines can be used to separate headings from data, to separate expenses from income, or to separate detail information from summary information. You can choose to apply a treatment to a single cell, a group of cells, or an entire row or column.

TYPICAL OPERATION

In this session you use the Border command on the Format menu to place a line on the INTEREST.XLS worksheet that you used most recently in the Row Height module.

1. Start Excel and open INTEREST.XLS, or continue your work session from the previous module.

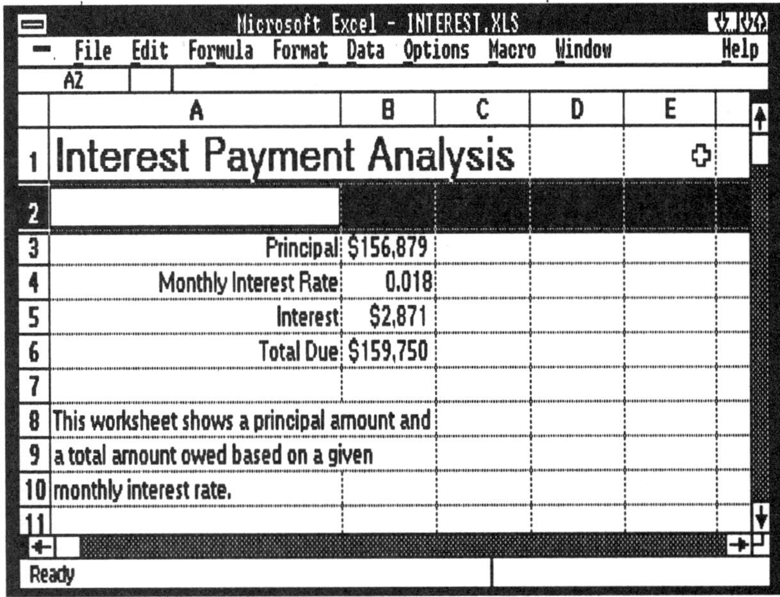

2. Select cell B5, then select **Border** from the Format menu.

3. Pick the **Bottom** check box.

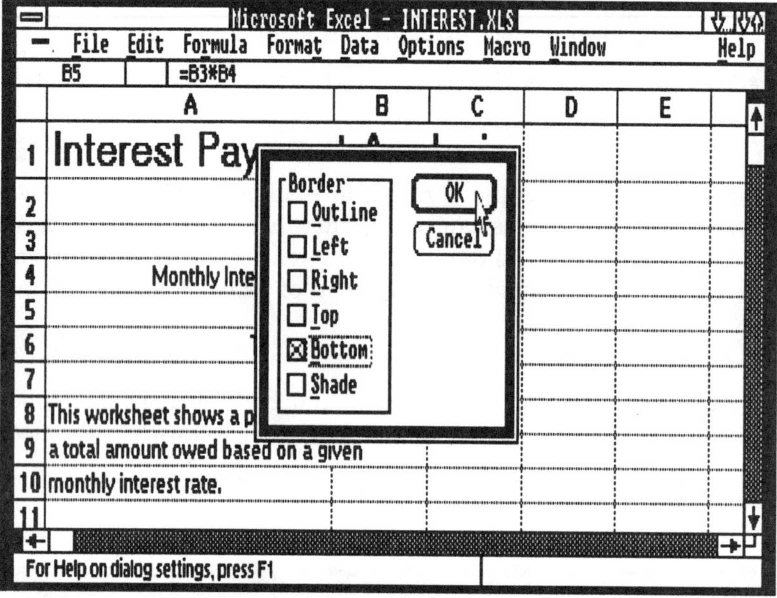

4. Pick **OK**, then pick cell A11. Notice the line under cell B5.

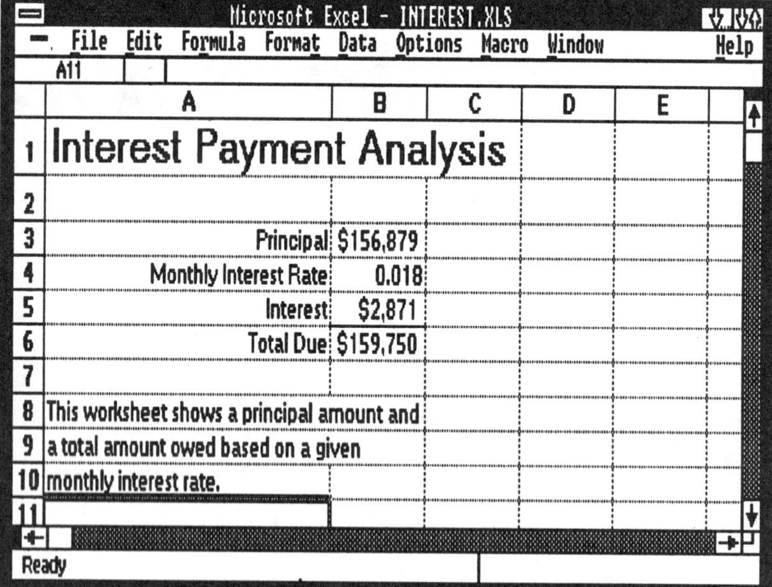

5. Save the worksheet and exit Excel.

6. Turn to Module 39 to continue the learning sequence.

Module 8

CALCULATION, CALCULATE NOW

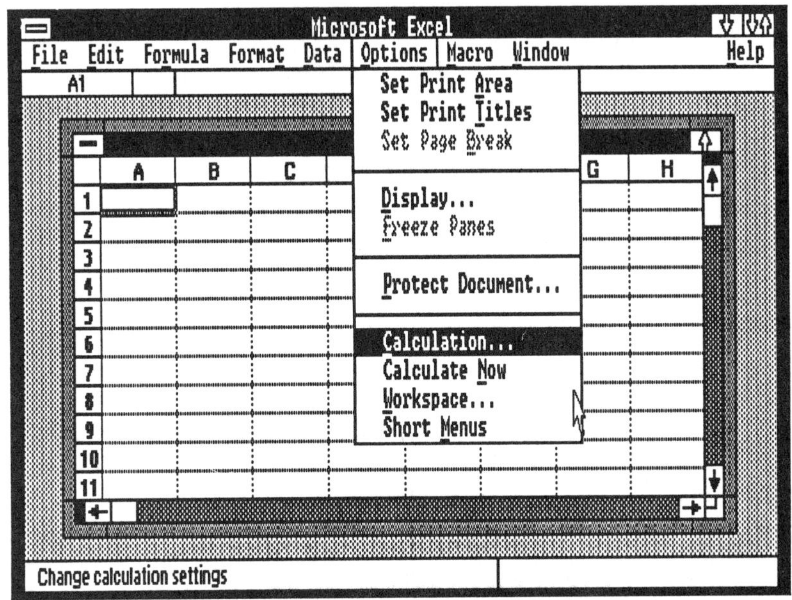

DESCRIPTION

Calculation and Calculate Now commands are used together. They are accessed through the Options menu by Alt-O C and Alt-O N, respectively. The default setting in Excel provides that, whenever you create a formula or change a formula, Excel will automatically perform the calculations for all values associated with that formula in the entire worksheet. It is sometimes appropriate that you take control of all calculations. You can do this by turning off the automatic calculation and making it a manual operation.

When you access the Calculation command you will be shown a dialog box. In the dialog box you can:

1. Make calculations automatic, manual, or leave them automatic except for tables;

2. Specify the number of iterations you want Excel to perform on circular definitions (formulas that refer to themselves) before providing a result;

3. Update any references to the formula that are outside the worksheet, specify the level of precision you require and require that your IBM PC use the same date system as the Apple Macintosh.

APPLICATIONS

Using the automatic calculation means that you don't need to constantly monitor and refigure all the operations associated with a particular calculation. This could become a major undertaking. The automatic feature means that Excel will constantly update all the values associated with any formula throughout the entire worksheet.

The major handicap with using the automatic feature is that as the worksheet grows in size the automatic process of updating can be time consuming. At this point you have the option of turning the automatic calculation off and performing any calculations after all the changes have been made to the various formulas.

Another time you might want to stop the automatic calculation is when you are planning a large number of changes and you are not sure what the final formula will be. In this instance you might elect to turn off the automatic calculation and wait until you are completely finished.

TYPICAL OPERATION

In this operation you use both the automatic and manual calculation operation to compute the results provided by different formulas.

1. Start Excel and open BUDGET1.XLS, or continue directly from Module 28, Format. Scroll the worksheet so that column I is visible on the right.

2. In cell I3 type **= (E4 + E11)/B4** and press **Enter**. This determines what percent of salary is spent on the mortgage and the utilities.

```
 =  Microsoft Excel                                        ▼ ▲
 File  Edit  Formula  Format  Data  Options  Macro  Window            Help
 I3              =(E4+E11)/B4
```

	B	C	D	E	F	G	H	I
1								
2				Expenses				
3				Expected	Jan	Feb	Mar	0.228571
4	$3,500		Mortgage	$625	$625	$625	$625	
5	$500		Insurance	$100	$50	$75	$175	
6	$500		Food	$300	$150	$100	$200	
7	$500		Auto	$300	$0	$700	$0	
8			Clothes	$250	$150	$0	$400	
9			Savings	875	1500	850	1075	
10			Taxes	875	875	875	875	
11			Utilities	$175	$150	$275	$150	

Ready

The result informs you that almost 23% of the salary amount is being spent on the mortgage and utilities payments.

3. Change the amount in cell E4 to **$725** and press **Enter**.

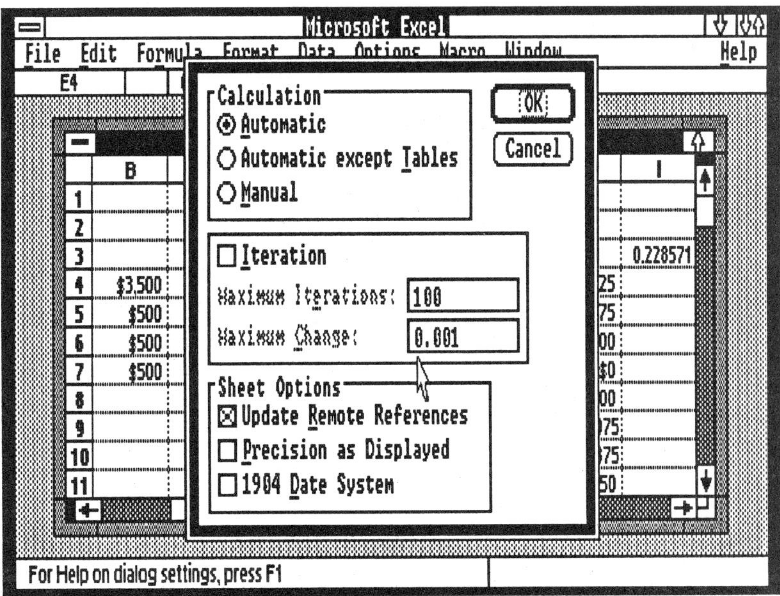

The percentage amount in cell I3 has been changed to almost 26% automatically.

4. Change the amount in E4 back to **$625** and press **Enter**.

5. Open the Options menu and select **Calculation**.

This is the dialog box explained in the Description section.

6. Use the Tab key or mouse to select the Manual option and press **Enter**.

7. Change the value in cell E4 to **$725** and press **Enter**.

The percentage value in cell I3 does not change.

8. Select **Calculate Now** from the Options menu. The percentage value in cell I3 has now been updated. Any references in other worksheets would also have been updated as a result of this command since the Update Remote References in the Calculate command is active.

9. BUDGET1.XLS is not used again in the learning sequence. Close the worksheet and, optionally, quit Excel.

10. Turn to Module 45 to continue the learning sequence.

Module 9

CELL PROTECTION

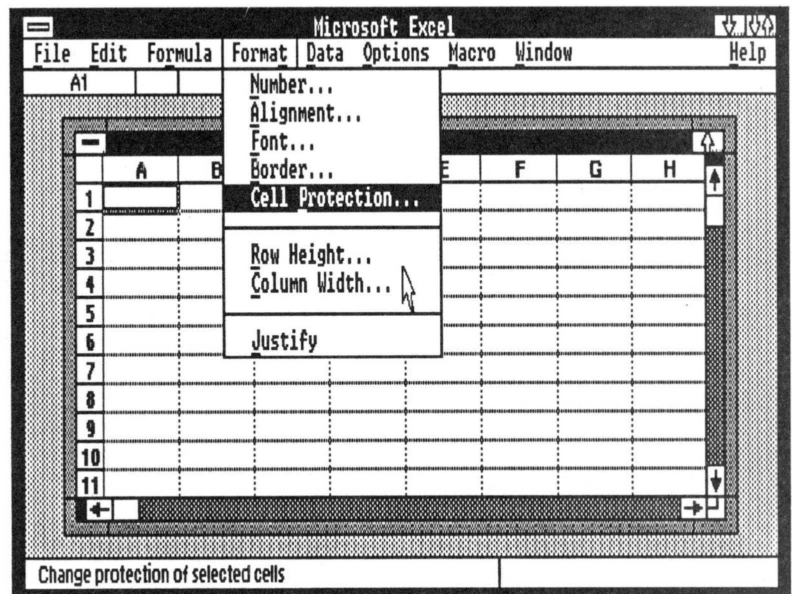

DESCRIPTION

Cell protection allows you to specify that a cell value cannot be changed, or that a cell value (or range of cell values) is hidden. The command is accessed from the Format menu with Alt-T P. When you select Protection, a dialog box appears and you can choose to lock the marked cells so that they are protected under the Protect Document command, or to unlock them so only they can be changed when Protect Document is in force.

The other option you have is to hide the marked cells. Selecting this option removes the marked cell's formula from the screen.

APPLICATIONS

Cell protection permits you to unlock certain cells so that, while the document is protected, those cells can be changed. You are also able to hide from view the formula of a cell with this command. This command is useful when only parts of the document are appropriate to hide or unlock.

Remember you can also hide cells by changing the width of the column or height of the row.

TYPICAL OPERATION

You should begin this module from Module 51, Protect Document. If you haven't, you need to open Budget1 from the library and then open a new window and arrange them like the last illustration in Module 51.

1. Type **= $B$4-(E4 + E5 + E6 + E7 + E8 + E10 + E11)** in cell E9. Notice that the formula appears on the formula line.

2. Select **Cell Protection** from the Format menu.

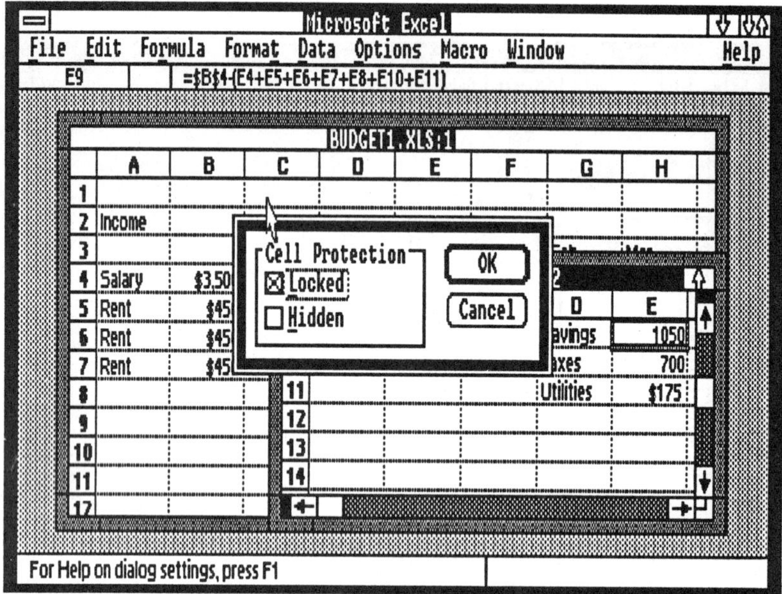

If you remove the "X" on the Locked option, you will be able to change the contents of the cell, even after the document is protected. If you activate the Hidden option, the formula for the cell will be removed from the formula bar.

3. Activate **Hidden** (by pressing Tab and Spacebar or by clicking in the Hidden box with the mouse) and press **Enter**.

4. Select **Protect Document** from the Options menu. Don't write a password, just press **Enter**. The formula has now disappeared from the formula line.

5. Select **Unprotect document** from the Options menu, then activate cell **E4**.

6. Select **Cell Protection** from the Format menu.

7. De-activate **Locked** using the Spacebar or mouse and press **Enter**.

8. Select **Protect Document** from the Options menu.

9. Press **Enter** from the dialog box.

You can now change the value in E4 but you will be prevented from changing any other value until you Unprotect the document. You can save it or you can close it without removing the protection command. Remember that the protection command will remain in effect until you remove it.

10. **Unprotect** the document.
11. Turn to Module 50 to continue the learning sequence.

Module 10
CHART

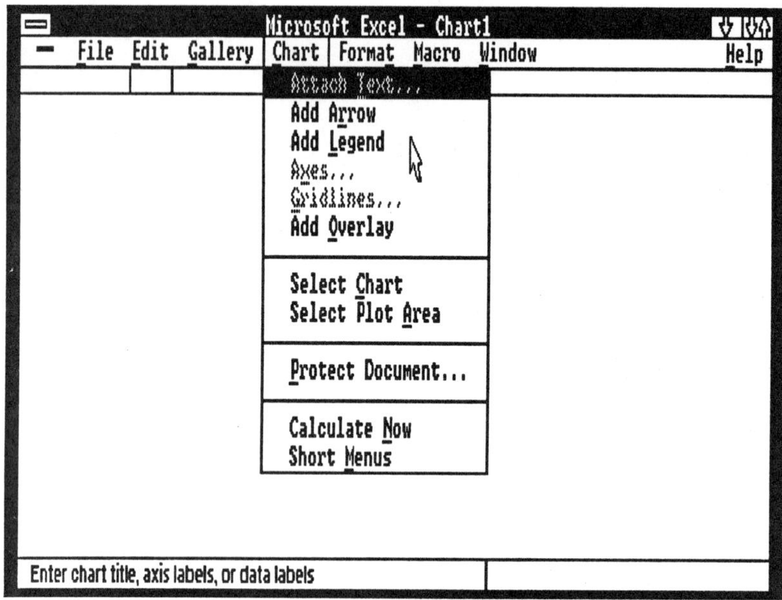

DESCRIPTION

The Chart menu (Alt-C) permits you to add text, arrows, legends, axis and gridlines, and overlays. You can also protect the chart from this menu and perform calculations, as you could in the normal worksheet.

The Attach Text option permits you to attach text to the chart. When you choose this option you will be given a dialog box that allows you to attach the text to the chart title, the value (vertical) axis, or the category (horizontal) axis. In addition, you can attach text to a specific data point. You will need to identify the data to which you want to attach the text. This is done by specifying the number of the data point and the location of the desired data in that data point.

Add Arrow and Add Legend permit these additions to the chart. Axis and Gridlines permit you to change or remove these components. Add Overlay permits you to make part of the chart into a different chart and overlay it on the main chart.

Select Chart and Select Plot Area define the area you want to change. The Select Chart includes all of the area designated and the Select Plot Area is the area between the axes.

APPLICATIONS

Charts are useful to illustrate data. Pictures of how the data looks help to provide explanations and to assist you as you try to understand what the data means. Simple charts can be created by using the standard default options. More complicated charts can be made to meet specific needs.

TYPICAL OPERATION

In this operation you add descriptive information to a chart. You should begin this operation with the chart on the screen from Module 30, Gallery.

1. Select **Add Legend** from the Chart menu.

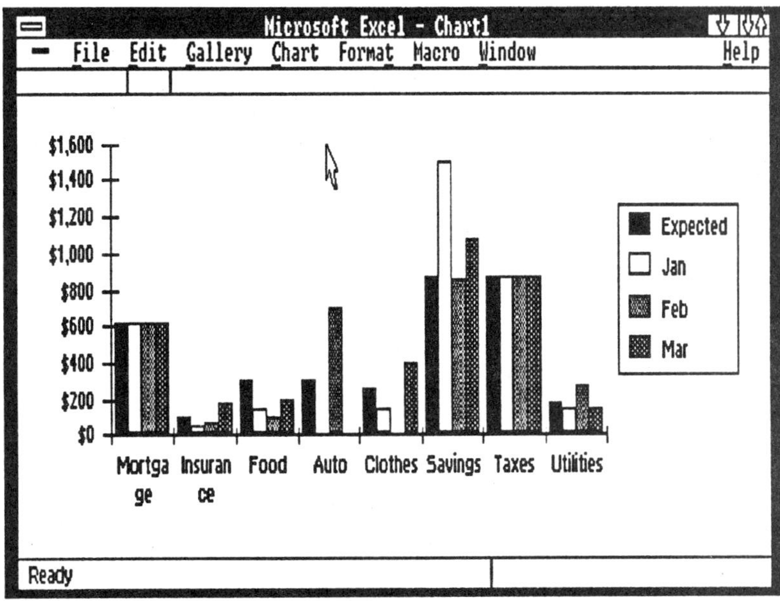

2. Select **Axes** from the Chart menu.

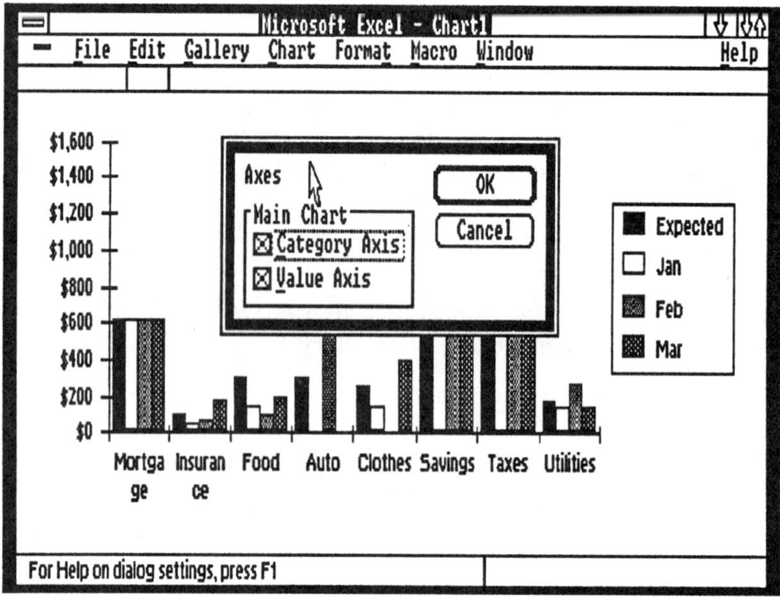

3. Turn **off** both axes and press **Enter**. (If both axis choices are already off, you may want to turn them on to see the difference.)

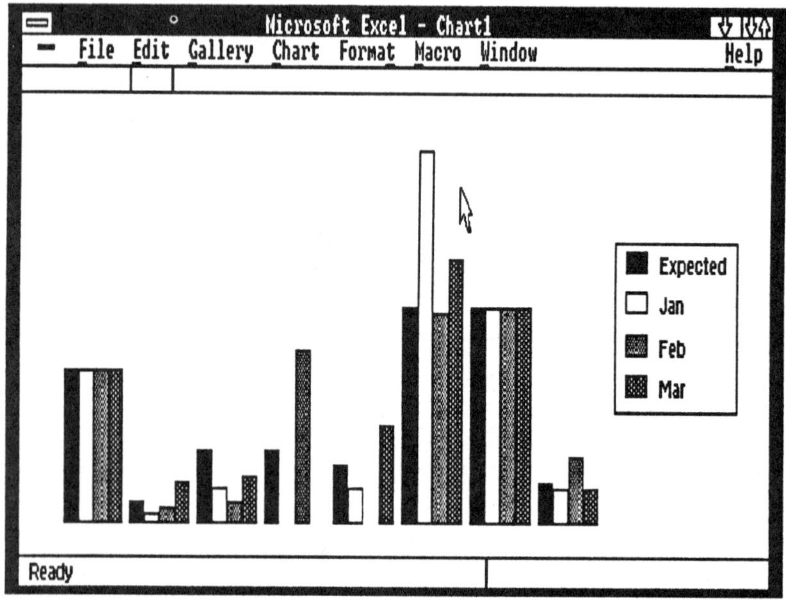

4. Select **Gridlines** from the Chart menu, activate **Major Gridlines** in both categories, and press **Enter**.

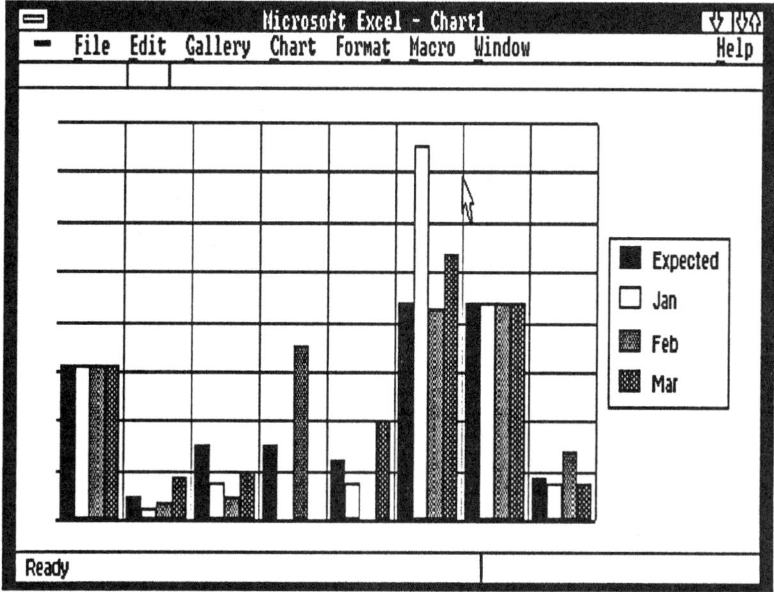

5. Go back into the Chart menu and remove the Gridlines and restore the Axes.

6. Select **Attach Text** from the Chart menu.

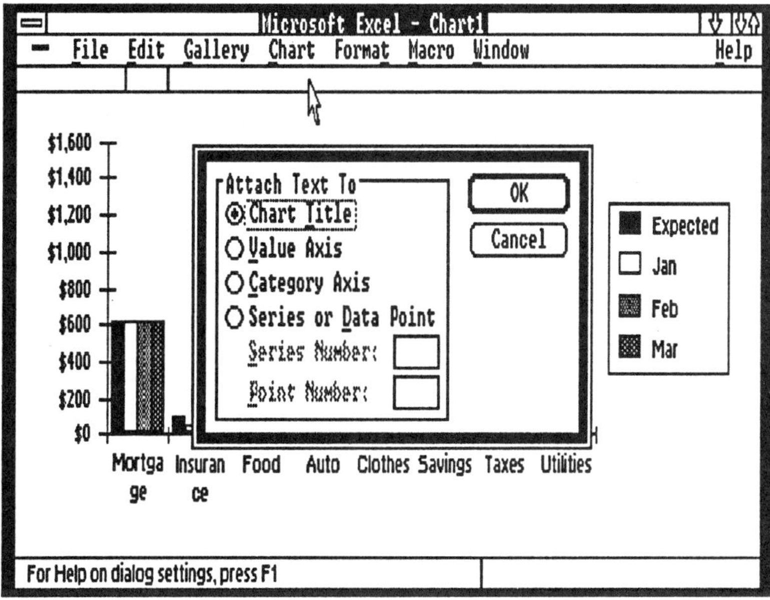

You can now add text to identify Values, Categories, Data Points and Titles.

7. Activate **Series or Data Point**. Attach the text to the second column in the Savings category by typing **2** in the Series Number box, **6** in the Point Number box, and pressing **Enter**.

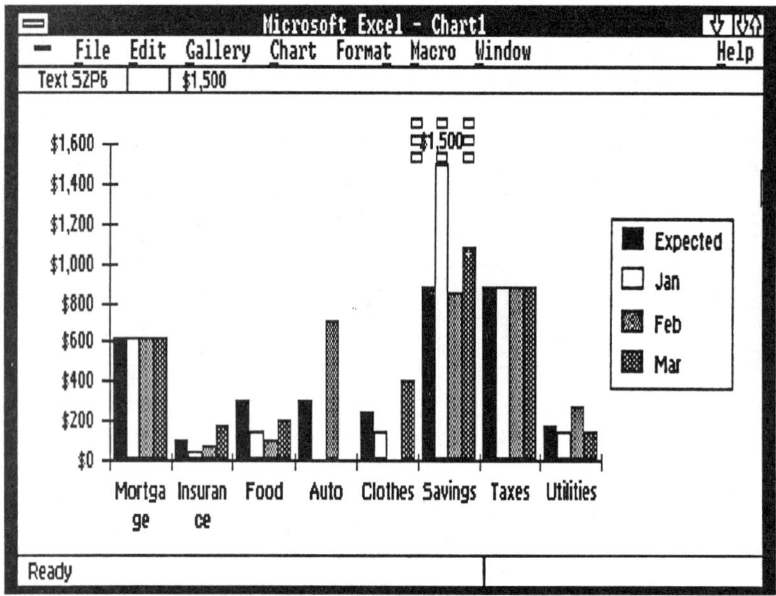

Notice that the text appears on the Text line and on the chart.

8. Delete the text with the Backspace key and press **Enter**.
9. Access **Attach Text**, select **Chart Title**, and press **Enter**.

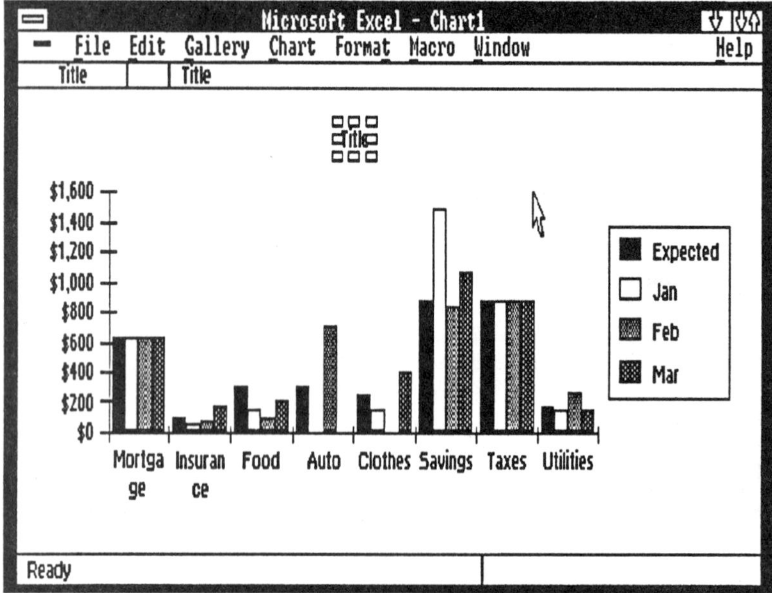

You can now write the title of the chart.

10. Type **Personal Budget** and press **Enter**.

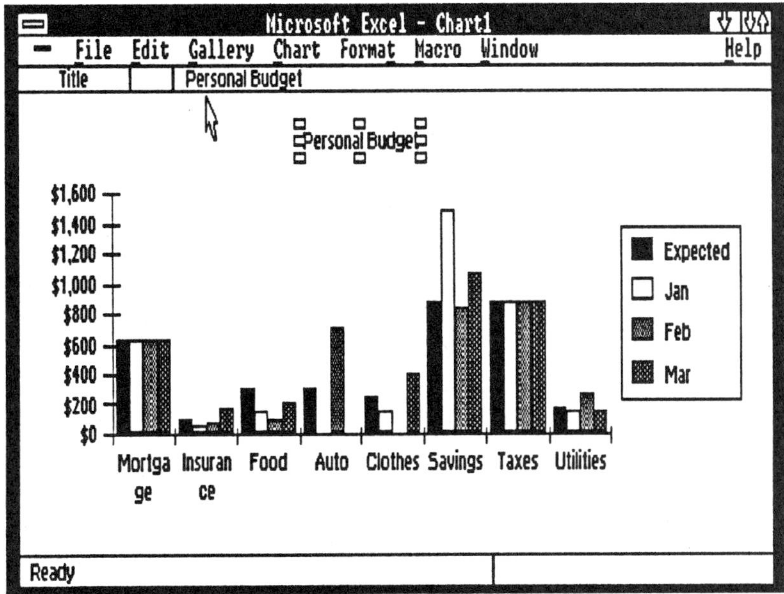

11. Select **Add Overlay** from the Chart menu.

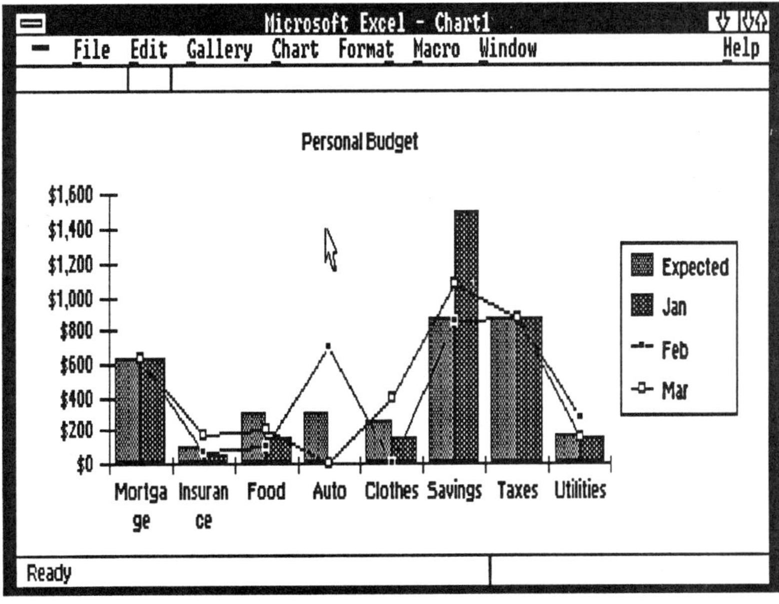

Part of the original chart has been converted to a line chart and overlaid on the bar chart.

12.   Select **Delete Overlay**.

13.   Select **Add Arrow** from the Chart menu.

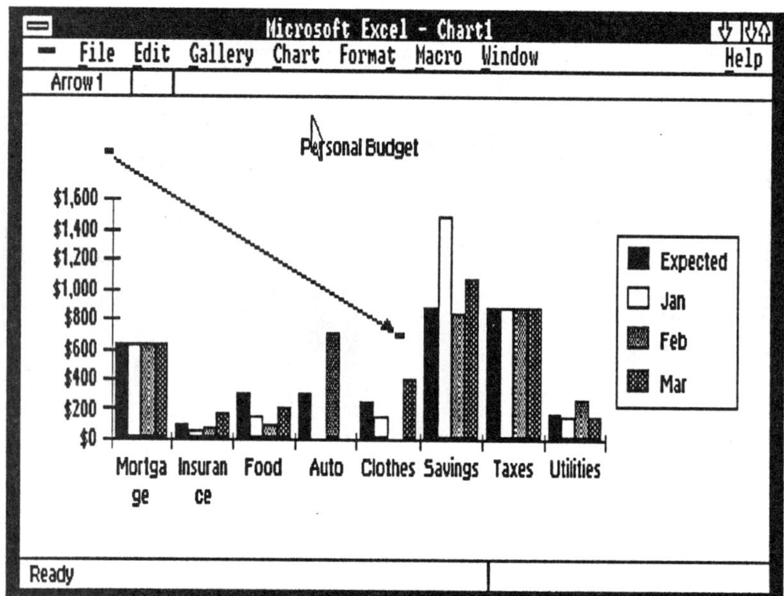

The remaining options in the Chart menu permit you to select the whole chart or just the plotted area to receive any changes you might make from the Format menu. You can also use this menu to protect your chart or to perform calculations to update formulas.

14.   Turn to Module 28 to continue the learning sequence.

Module 11

CLEAR

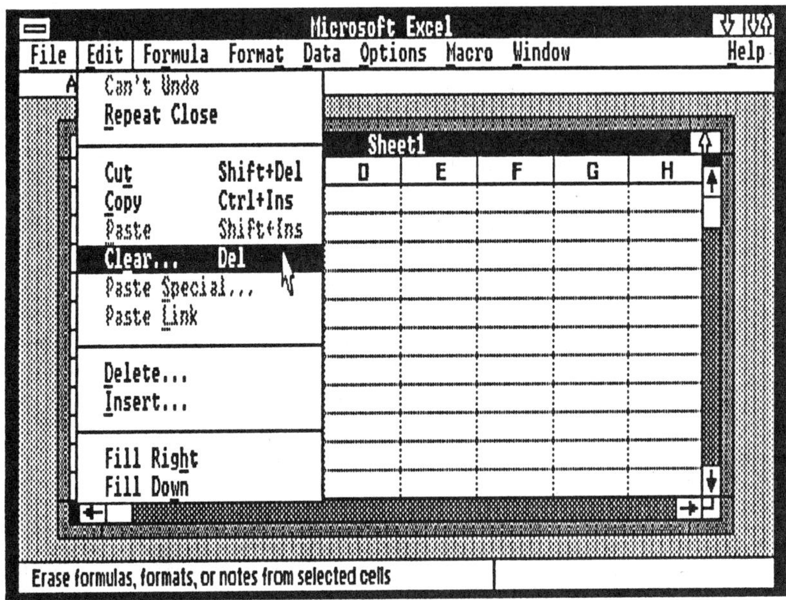

DESCRIPTION

The Clear command allows you to delete specified data in the worksheet. It is accessed from the Edit menu or by pressing Alt-E E or by pressing Del. In order to use the Clear command, you must first mark the area of the worksheet you want to clear. When the Clear command is accessed, you will be presented a dialog box that permits you to select which type of information to delete. You can clear all of the information in the designated area, only the formulas (which includes all of the visible data), only the formats (the specifications you place on the data you enter in the worksheet), or the notes (comments you write about the data that are attached to the worksheet but don't appear on the worksheet).

APPLICATIONS

The Clear command is useful in correcting errors that you might make in the course of working in a worksheet. It also allows you to change your mind after you have cleared a cell or range by accessing the Undo Clear command. Both commands are in the Edit menu. If you are clearing data in an active cell of the worksheet, you need only press the Backspace key on the keyboard. The Clear command is used with more than one cell or after the data has been entered.

TYPICAL OPERATION

In this operation you clear data that has been entered in a worksheet.

1. Start Excel, or continue your work session from the previous module.
2. Open the worksheet SAVINGS.XLS.
3. Copy the data in the worksheet to cells E1 through F6.
4. Select **Clear** from the Edit menu.

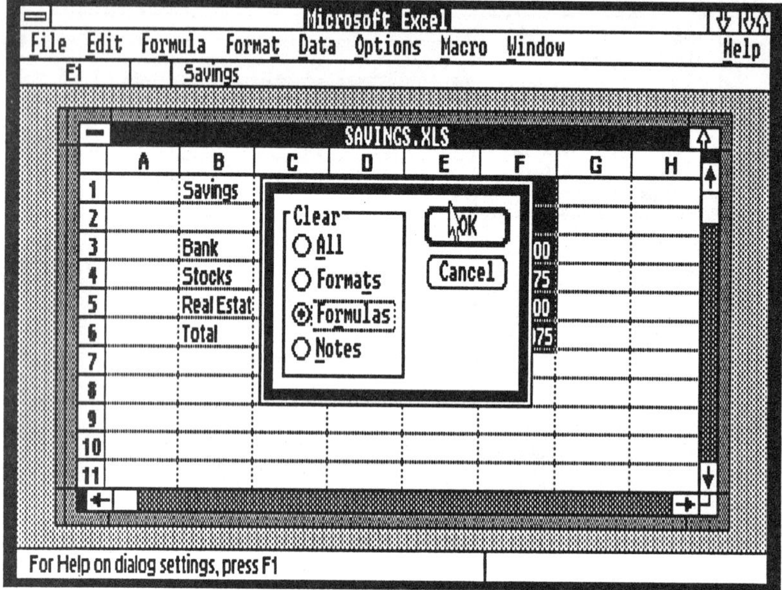

5. Select **Formulas** and press **Enter**.
6. Select **Undo** from the Edit menu and the information is returned.
7. Select **Clear** from the Edit menu.

8. Select **All** and press **Enter**.

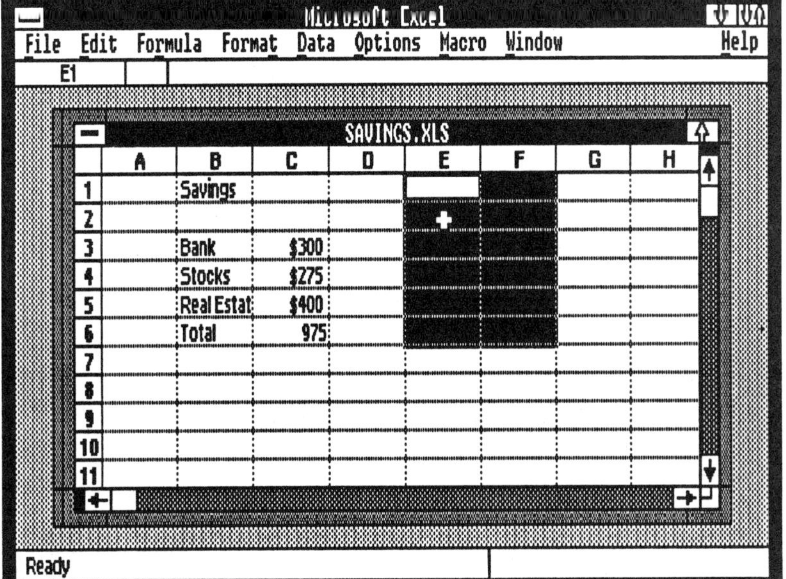

Compare this screen with the first cleared screen. Notice that even the information in the text bar under the menu bar is cleared.

9. Close the worksheet without saving the changes.

10. Exit Excel, or continue your work session with the next module by turning to Module 33.

Module 12
CLOSE

DESCRIPTION

The Close option is accessed either through the File menu (Alt-F C) or the Control icon menu (Alt-Hyphen C). Regardless of the menu you use to locate a Close command, you will accomplish the same action. The Close command closes a window. If you use the Control icon menu from the Excel window and select Close, you will close the application window and the result is leaving Excel. If you use the Close command from either the File menu or the document window Control icon menu; you will close the window but remain in Excel, with the option of opening a new window from the File menu.

APPLICATIONS

The flexibility of opening and closing windows as you work in Excel assists you in the organization of your work. It is unlikely that you will need to use the Close command from the Control icon of the Excel application window unless you want to open other files that might be stored in your MS-DOS Executive window. This window is only available to you if you are running under the full Windows version.

Once you enter data or change data in a worksheet and then attempt to close, Excel will ask whether you want to save the changes you have made or discard them. This will help you avoid closing a window you have modified without saving the modifications. Each time you close a window in which you have been working, you can reopen it from the Open command in the File menu. The Open command is in Module 42, Open.

TYPICAL OPERATION

In this operation you close both a worksheet and a window.

1. Start Excel. From the system prompt type **Excel** and press **Enter**.
2. Type **The rain falls mainly on the plain.** in cell A1 and press **Enter**.
3. Access the **Close** command from either the worksheet Control icon or the File menu.

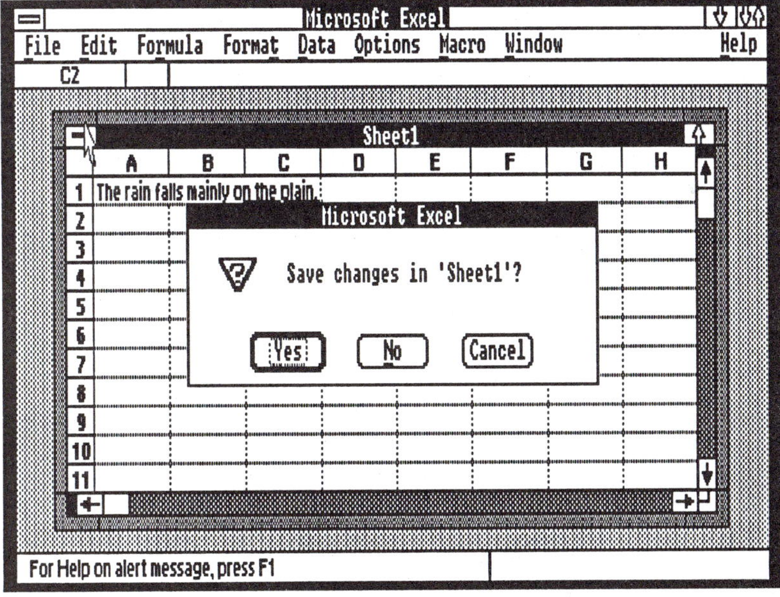

4. Click on **No** or press **Tab** and then press **Enter**.

5. Select the **Close** command from the Control icon menu.

If you are using the full Windows version, you now have the MS-DOS Executive on the screen. If you are using another version of Windows, you will now be at the "C" prompt. If you are at the MS-DOS Executive, complete the next step if you want to return to the DOS prompt.

6. Select the **Close** command from the Control icon menu.

The dialog box warns you that you are about to end your Windows session.

7. Press **Enter** or click on **OK**.

8. Turn to Module 21 to continue the learning sequence.

Module 13

COLUMN WIDTH

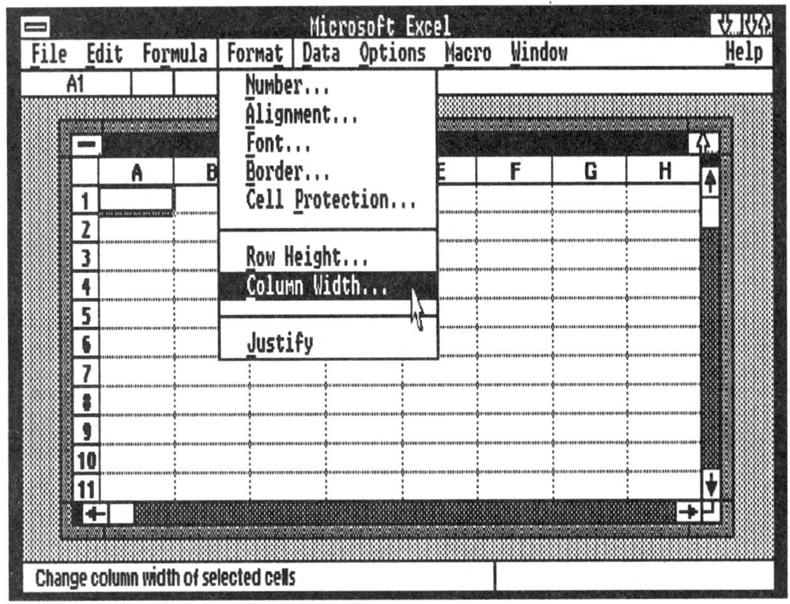

DESCRIPTION

You may specify a width for a single column or for a group of columns. First, select the column or group of columns for which you want to specify the width. Then, select the Column Width command from the Format menu, or press Alt-T C. Excel displays the following dialog box.

You can change the column width by typing a new value, or you may pick the Standard Width check box to restore columns to their default width.

You may also adjust and hide columns on the screen visually through using the mouse. First, place the mouse cursor between two column headings until it forms a cross, as shown between columns C and D in the following screen.

Press the left mouse button and drag the column edge to the left or right, changing the column width. Release the mouse button when the width is correct.

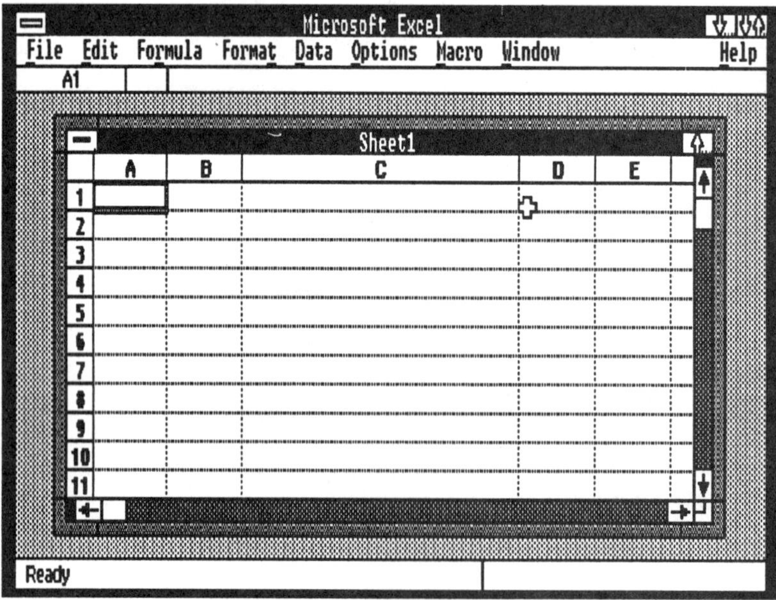

APPLICATIONS

Big numbers and long labels do not fit in the standard width columns that Excel provides as its default. Excessive column width prevents you from seeing as many columns of small numbers as you could see with narrower column widths.

You may also adjust the width of columns to 0 or drag their edges over the top of other columns to hide columns of data that is irrelevant or confidential. A salesperson, for example, can hide columns containing costs and margins, showing only quantities, prices, and available discounts.

TYPICAL OPERATION

In this session you add labels to the INTEREST.XLS worksheet, adjusting the width of the column to contain the full length of the text.

1. Start Excel and open the INTEREST.XLS worksheet, or continue directly from Module 41.

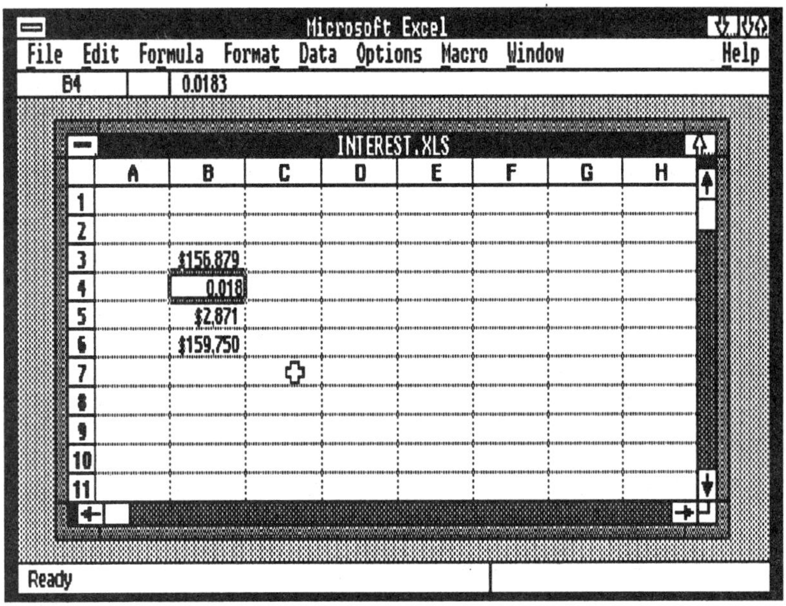

2. Type **Interest Payment Analysis** in cell A1.
3. Type **Principal** in cell A3.
4. Type **Monthly Interest Rate** in cell A4.
5. Type **Interest** in cell A5.

6. Type **Total Due** in cell A6 and press **Enter**.

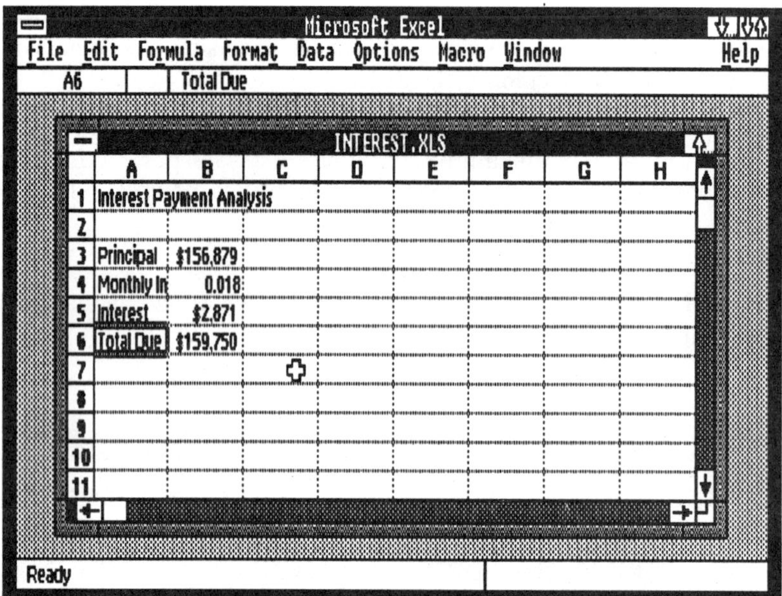

7. Select column A, then select **Column Width** from the Format menu.

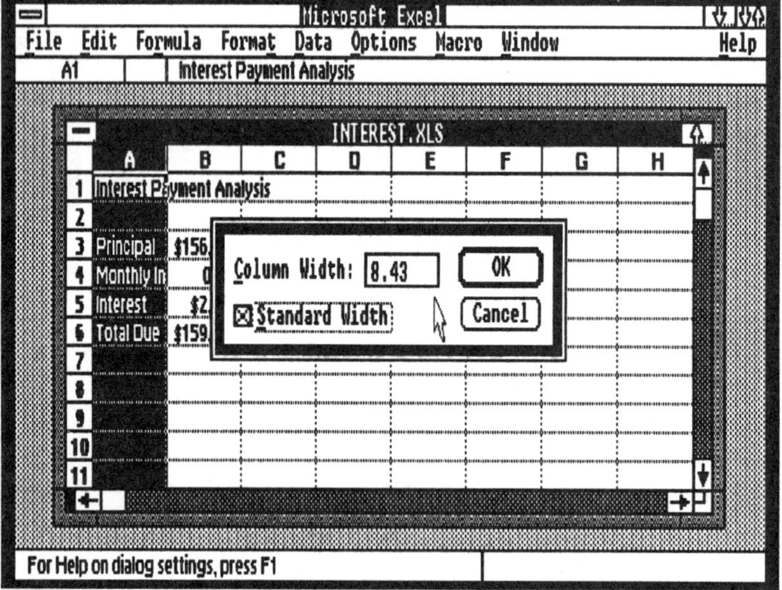

8. Type **50** as the Column Width and pick **OK**. Pick cell A1 to eliminate the row highlighting.

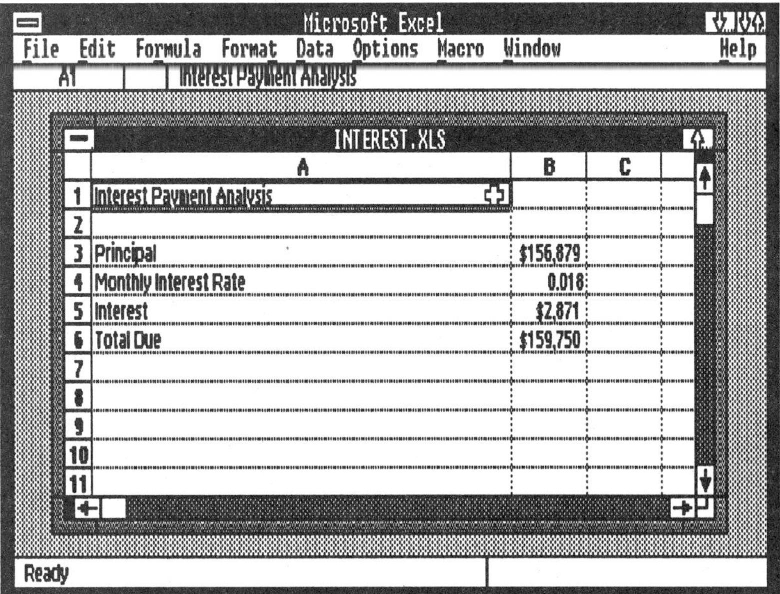

Since the column is now too wide, adjust it visually to a better width.

9. Move the mouse to the border between heading A and B until the cursor becomes a cross. Press the mouse button and drag it to the left to adjust the width of column A until it looks similar to the following screen; then release the mouse button.

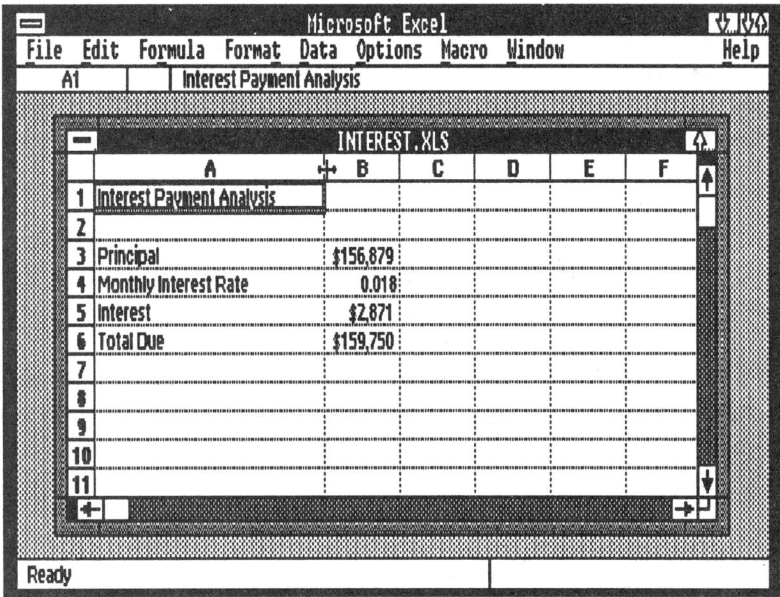

10. Save the worksheet and exit Excel, or continue the learning sequence by turning to Module 4.

Module 14

COPY, CUT, PASTE

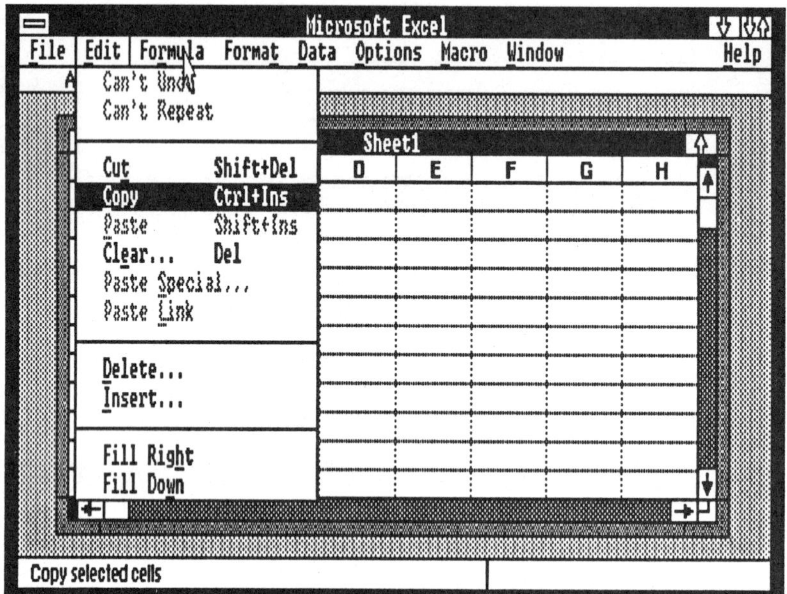

DESCRIPTION

The Copy, Cut, and Paste commands are used together. All three commands are accessed from the Edit menu. The three commands are used to move data in a worksheet from one place to another. The commands can also be used to move information from one worksheet to another. They differ only slightly.

The Copy command (Alt-E C) copies the designated information into memory, where it will reside until you use the Paste command (Alt-E P) to relocate it. Using this command leaves the information in both the old and the new location.

The Cut (Alt-E T) command is used exactly like the Copy command with the difference being in the result. The Cut command removes the designated information and relocates it in the new location.

APPLICATIONS

Using these three commands permits you to reorganize the information on your worksheets without retyping it. Being able to move information from one part of a worksheet to another part or to move it to another worksheet will save you time and help avoid errors.

When using these commands you need to remember some simple rules:

1.   Information cannot be pasted into an area that is smaller than the area it originally occupied.

2.   When copying data that include formulas you may have to adjust the formula if it contains references to certain cells in the worksheet, because Excel automatically adjusts the formula to compensate for the new location.

The Cut command places formulas in the new location without adjusting for the change. If, for example, you had a formula in cell A8 that utilized information in cells B3 and you copied the formula to cell F5, Excel would look in cell G3 for the information. The formula would be adjusted for its new location and produce an erroneous result.

TYPICAL OPERATION

In this operation you use the commands Cut, Copy and Paste to manipulate simple data.

1.   Start Excel, or continue your work session from the previous module.

2.   Select **Open** from the File menu. Recall BUDGET1 to the screen.

3. Activate cell **D3** and use **Shift-Right Arrow** and **Shift-Down Arrow** to mark the Expense information as a block. Notice that the cells that are being marked will change color. Mouse users can click and drag the cursor across the desired cells.

```
 ═                        Microsoft Excel
 File  Edit  Formula  Format  Data  Options  Macro  Window            Help
     D3            Mortgage
 ┌─────────────────────────── BUDGET1.XLS ───────────────────────────┐
 │        A        B       C       D       E       F       G       H  │
 │  1  Income                   Expenses                              │
 │  2                                                                 │
 │  3  Salary    $3,500        Mortgage   $625                        │
 │  4                          Food       $250                        │
 │  5                          Auto       $300                        │
 │  6                          Clothes    $200                        │
 │  7                          Savings    1425                        │
 │  8                          Taxes       700                        │
 │  9                                                                 │
 │ 10                                                                 │
 │ 11                                                                 │
 └───────────────────────────────────────────────────────────────────┘
 Cut (Select destination and press Enter or choose Paste)
```

4. Select **Cut** from the Edit menu.

The area marked to be cut shows a distinctive dotted line around it.

5. Make cell **G3** the active cell.

6. Select **Paste** from the Edit menu.

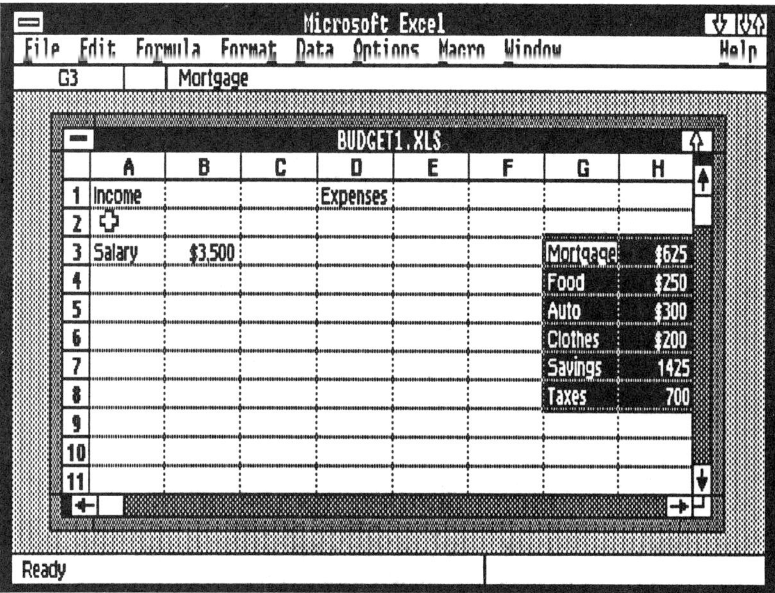

The information in the cut section has been moved to the new location and removed from the old location. If you activate cell H7 you will see that the formula has been adjusted for its new location. Mark the information in its new location as a block.

7. Select **Copy** from the Edit menu.

8. Activate cell **D3**.

9. Select **Paste** from the Edit menu.

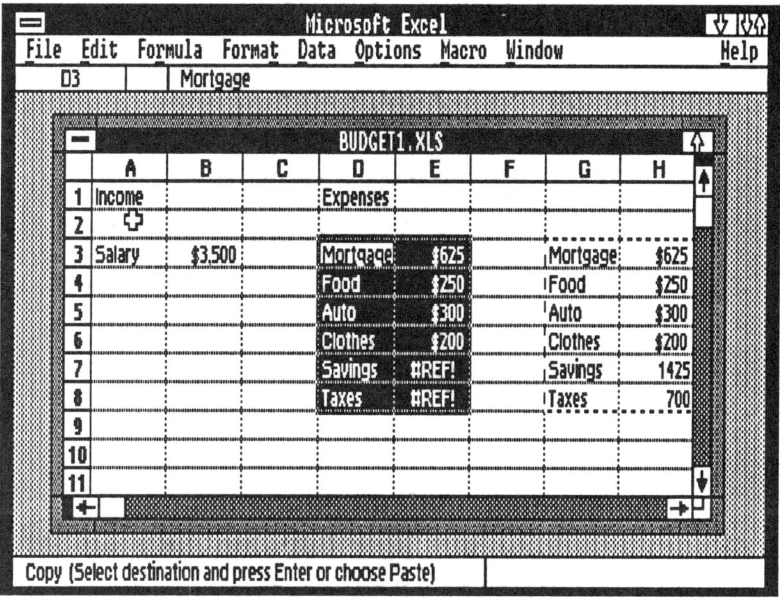

You now have the information in both places. Notice that the values of the formulas in cells E7 and E8 have been replaced with an error message. This problem has to do with the absolute and relative reference to B3. (See Module 53, Reference). To make the reference absolute, add "$" to the formulas.

10. Add **$** to the formulas in cells H7 and H8. Activate each cell and either retype the information or press **F2** (function key), and use the arrow keys to move to the appropriate spot in the formula and then add **$**. The formulas should now look like = **$B$3-(H3 + H4 + H5 + H6 + H8)** and = **$B$3*0.2**.

11. Mark the information in columns G and H as a block.

12. Select the **Copy** command from the Edit menu.

13. Make cell **A6** the active cell.

14. Select the **Paste** command from the Edit menu.

```
┌──────────────────────────────────────────────────────────────────┐
│ ▬                    Microsoft Excel                      ⬆ ⬇⬆    │
│ File  Edit  Formula  Format  Data  Options  Macro  Window   Help  │
│    A6          │    Mortgage                                       │
│  ┌──────────────────────────────────────────────────────────┐    │
│  │ ▬                    BUDGET1.XLS                      ⬆   │    │
│  │     A       B     C     D        E      F     G       H   │    │
│  │ 1 Income               Expenses                          │    │
│  │ 2  ✛                                                      │    │
│  │ 3 Salary  $3,500        Mortgage  $625      Mortgage $625 │    │
│  │ 4                       Food      $250      Food    $250  │    │
│  │ 5                       Auto      $300      Auto    $300  │    │
│  │ 6 Mortgage  $625        Clothes   $200      Clothes $200  │    │
│  │ 7 Food      $250        Savings   #REF!     Savings 1425  │    │
│  │ 8 Auto      $300        Taxes     #REF!     Taxes    700  │    │
│  │ 9 Clothes   $200                                          │    │
│  │10 Savings   1425                                          │    │
│  │11 Taxes      700                                          │    │
│  └──────────────────────────────────────────────────────────┘    │
│ Copy (Select destination and press Enter or choose Paste)         │
└──────────────────────────────────────────────────────────────────┘
```

The new set of information is accurate.

15. Mark the new set of information as a block.

16. Select the **Cut** or **Copy** command from the Edit menu.

17. Select the **New** command from the File menu.

18. Press **Enter** for a new worksheet.

19. Select the **Paste** command from the Edit menu.

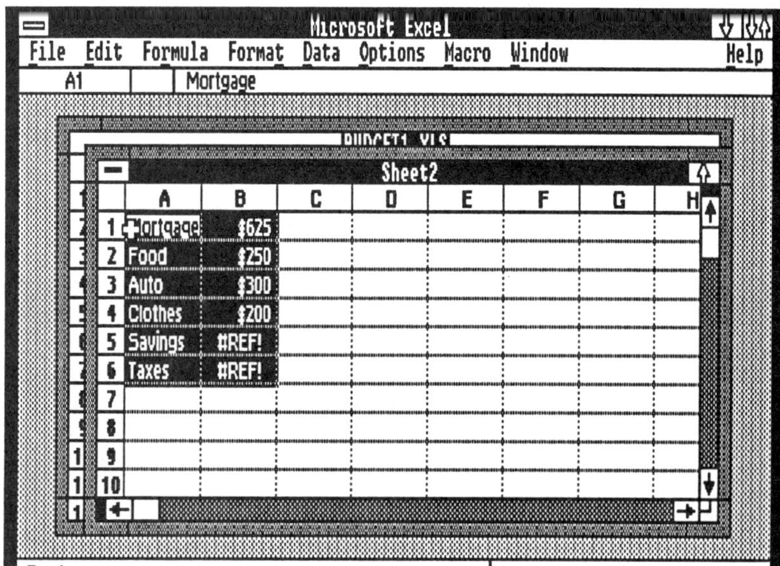

The information has been moved to a new worksheet. The values produced by the formulas are incorrect. You need to use the Paste Link command to move between worksheets. You can learn about this procedure in Module 35, Links.

20. Exit Excel, or close each worksheet without saving any of the changes.

21. Turn to Module 53 to continue the learning sequence.

Module 15

CREATE NAMES

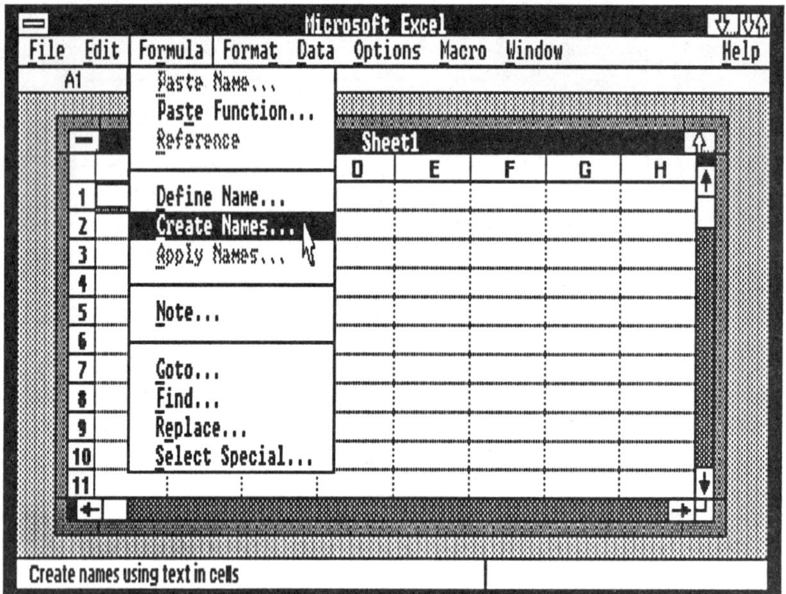

DESCRIPTION

Use the Create Names command to define names in a single operation for a rectangular region of the worksheet containing data and names. First, select the region containing the data and the names. Then select the Create Names command from the Formula menu. The following dialog box appears.

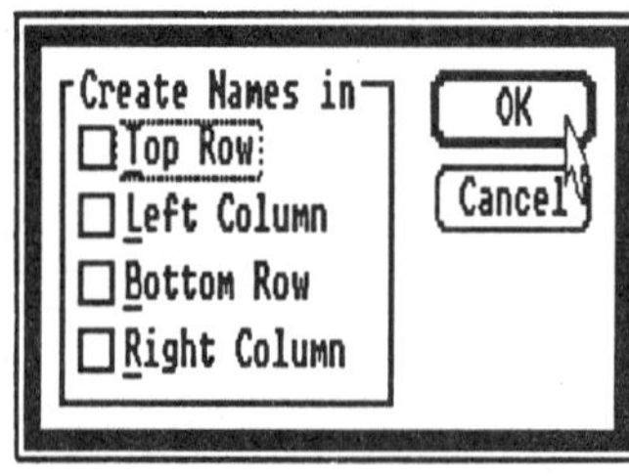

If the region contains only a single row or column of data adjacent to a single row or column of text, the text forms cell names. If the region contains multiple rows or columns of data with the names along an edge, the text becomes a range name. Inform Excel which edge of the region contains the names, then select OK. For example, if you choose Top Row, the text in each cell of the top row is interpreted as the name for the cell or range of cells below it.

APPLICATIONS

When you have a row or column of text representing the desired names for data that is in rows or columns immediately adjacent to the text, using the Define Name command repetitively is tedious. The Create Names command automates the process, allowing you to define names for an entire rectangular region of the worksheet in a single operation.

TYPICAL OPERATION

In this session you use the Create Names command to assign names to each city's gold price in the GOLD.XLS worksheet you created in the Define Name module.

1. Start Excel and open the GOLD.XLS worksheet, or continue your work session from the previous module in the learning sequence.

	Microsoft Excel - GOLD.XLS							
File Edit Formula Format Data Options Macro Window								Help
B11	=(1+(Prime+0.015)/4)*Average							
	A	**B**	**C**	**D**	**E**	**F**	**G**	**H**	**I**
1		Gold Prices							
2	Hong Kong	$403.85							
3	New York	$405.24							
4	London	$403.05							
5	Paris	$401.47							
6	Frankfurt	$404.24							
7	Zurich	$404.25							
8									
9	Average	$403.68							
10	Future	$413.80							
11	Cost	$415.29							
12									
13									
14									
Ready									

2. Select the region with corners at cells A2 and B7, containing the city names and the closing price of gold in each city.

3. Select **Create Names** from the Formula menu.

4. Specify that the data names are along the left boundary by picking the Left Column check box.

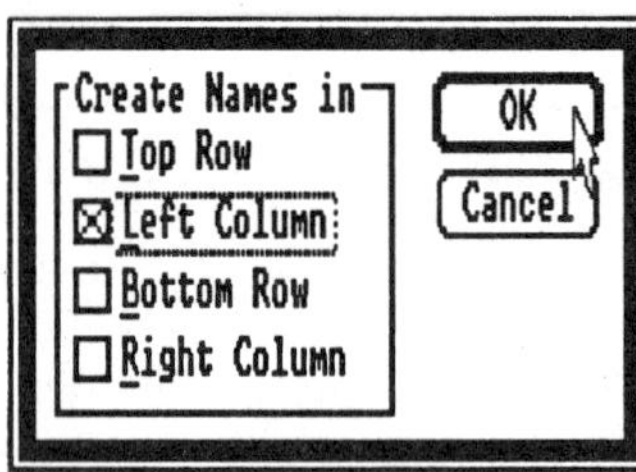

5. Select **OK** or press **Enter**.

6. Type **Continental High** in cell D8 and press **Enter**. Adjust the width of column D to display the entire label.

7. Type **=MAX(Paris,Frankfurt,Zurich)** in cell E8 and press **Enter**, instructing Excel to choose the maximum price of gold in Paris, Frankfurt, and Zurich.

8. Select dollars and cents format for column E.

	A	B	C	D	E	F	G	H
1		Gold Prices						
2	Hong Kong	$403.85						
3	New York	$405.24						
4	London	$403.05						
5	Paris	$401.47						
6	Frankfurt	$404.24						
7	Zurich	$404.25						
8				Continental High	$404.25			
9	Average	$403.68						
10	Future	$413.80						
11	Cost	$415.29						
12								
13								
14								

9. Save and close the worksheet.

10. Exit Excel, or continue to the next module without an active worksheet on the screen.

11. Turn to Module 5 to continue the learning sequence.

Module 16

DEFINE NAME

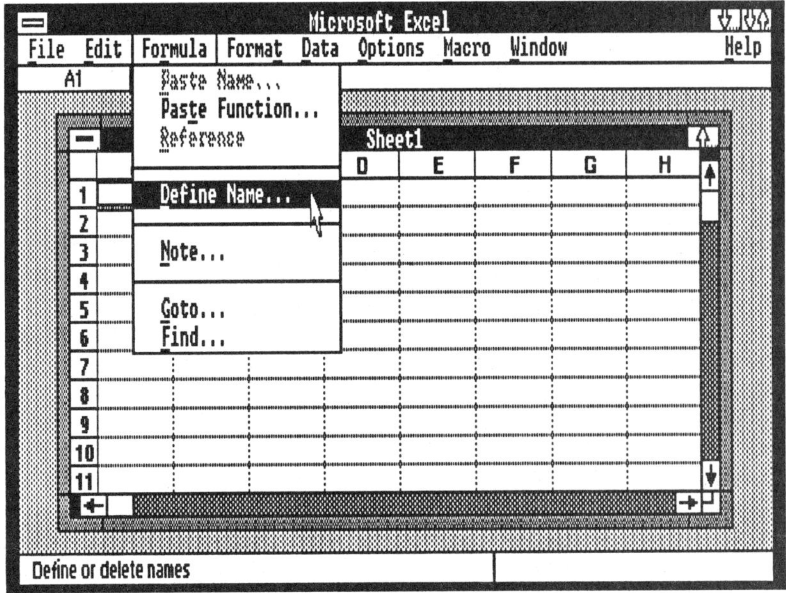

DESCRIPTION

Use the Define Name command on the Formula menu to assign a meaningful name to a value, a cell, or a range of cells. The name can then be used throughout the worksheet, instead of a cryptic reference to a value, a cell, or a range of data. When you want to assign a name to a single cell or a range of cells, first select (highlight) the cell or the range. When you select the Define Name command, the following dialog box appears, using default values as explained in the following paragraph.

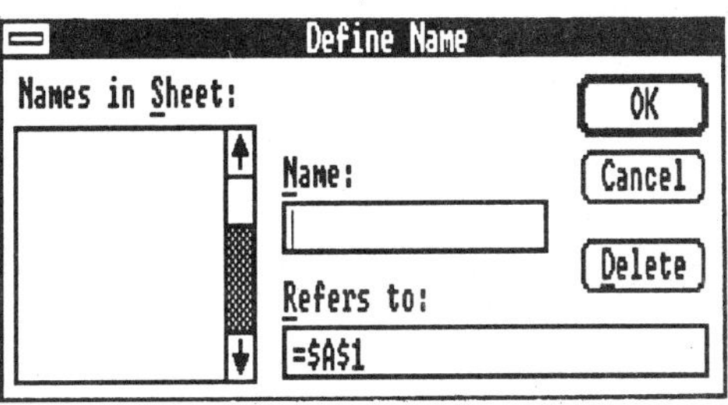

All presently defined names appear in the Names in Sheet selection box at the left of the dialog box. The selected cell or range of cells appears in the Refers to field. If the selected cell contains text, the text appears as the proposed name in the Name field. If the selected cell is blank or contains a value or a formula, then Excel looks first to the left, and then up, to find a candidate for a name. If it finds text in one of those places, the text is proposed as the name.

You can change the name by typing a new name in the Name field, or by picking it from the worksheet. You can also redefine an existing name by picking it from the selection list. You may change the cell or range reference in the Refers to field by typing a new value, or by picking the cell from the screen. In general, the Refers to field can contain any value or formula that could be entered into a cell with the formula bar. You can also use the name facility to create a name for a value not in the worksheet. Typing Prime as the name and 14.75 defines Prime as 14.75, but contains no reference at all to any worksheet cell. You can then use "Prime" anywhere in the worksheet you need it. Use the Define Name command again anytime you need to change the value for "Prime."

APPLICATIONS

Meaningless cell references are a frequent source of confusion in developing spreadsheet models — confusion typically resulting in error. When you make business decisions based on spreadsheet data you want to take every reasonable precaution to assure that the calculations are meaningful. Computing interest payments based on the electric rate instead of the interest rate could mean the difference between profitability and bankruptcy. When you define names for values and ranges in your worksheet, then base your calculations on the names instead of the ranges, your worksheet is far more likely to be free from logical error.

TYPICAL OPERATION

In this session you construct a worksheet to work with gold prices and interest rates. You construct formulas that use defined names for cell references, cell ranges, and values.

1. Start Excel. Expand Sheet1 to fill the screen.

2. Type **Gold Prices** in cell B1.

3. In cells A2 through A7, type the world gold markets, **Hong Kong, New York, London, Paris, Frankfurt**, and **Zurich**.

4. In cells B2 through B7, type the closing gold prices, **403.85, 405.24, 403.05, 401.47, 404.24**, and **404.25**.

5. Select column **B**; then select **Number** from the Format menu and pick a dollars and cents format **$#,##0.00 ;($#,##0.00)**. Select **OK** to confirm your choice.

6. Visually adjust the width of columns A and B to attractively display the data. (Place the mouse cursor between the column headings A and B. When the mouse cursor changes to a narrow cross, depress the left mouse button and drag the border toward the right. Repeat the process to adjust the width of column B.)

7. Select cell B7 to remove the column highlight.

Your screen looks similar to the following one.

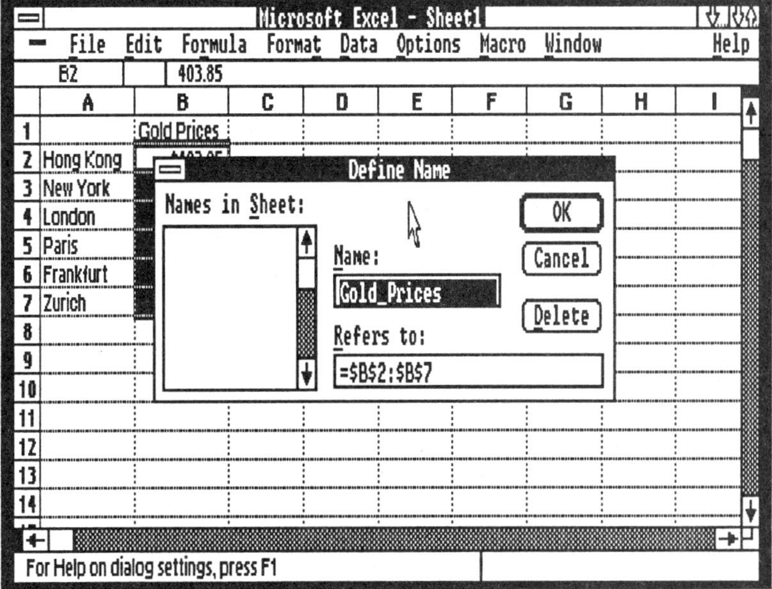

8. Select (highlight) cell range B2 through B7. Select **Define Name** from the Formula menu.

Excel places the selected range in the Refers to field and assumes that the cell immediately above the defined range is the name for the data, proposing Gold_Prices as the name.

NOTE
Notice that names do not contain spaces. Excel
automatically converted the name "Gold Prices"
to "Gold_Prices."

9. Select **OK** to accept the default name for the range. The dialog box disappears.

10. Type **Average** in cell A9.

11. Type **= Average(Gold_Prices)** in cell B9 and press **Enter**.

12. With cell B9 selected, pick **Define Name** from the Formula menu. Notice that "Gold_Prices"
    appears as a previously defined name in this worksheet, and that the text value "Average"
    from cell A9 is proposed as the name for the data in cell B9.

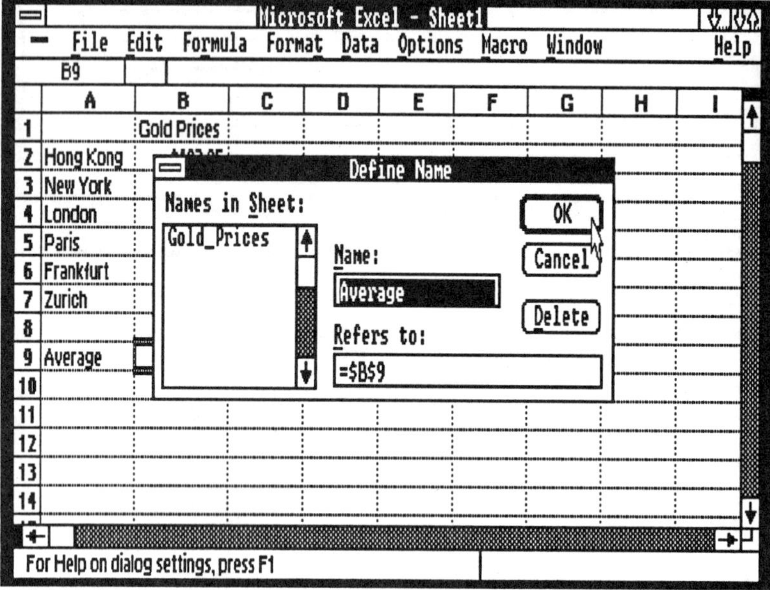

13. Pick **OK** to accept the default selections.

14. Select **Define Name** from the Formula menu. Type **Prime** as the Name, type **0.10** in the Refers to reference box, and pick **OK**.

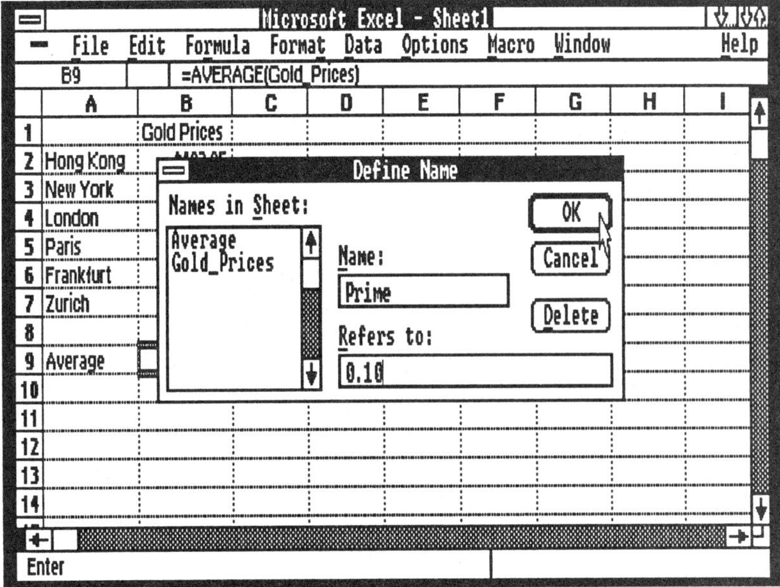

15. Type **Future** in cell A10 and type **413.80** in cell B10, representing the current price of a 90-day futures contract in gold.

Using the gold as collateral, you know that you can borrow money for its purchase at 1.5% above the prime rate on a 90-day single-pay note.

16. Type **Cost** in cell A11.

17. Type **= (1 + (Prime + 0.015)/4)*Average** in cell B11 and press **Enter**.

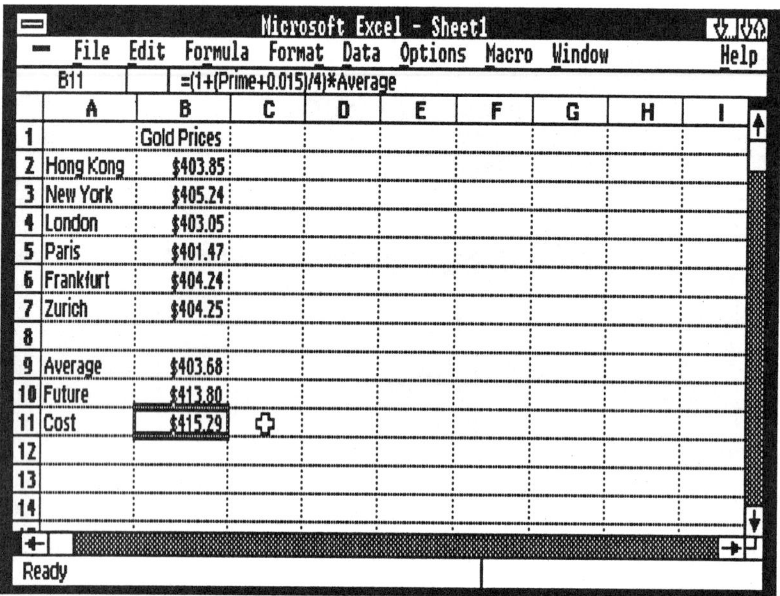

	A	B	C	D	E	F	G	H	I
1		Gold Prices							
2	Hong Kong	$403.85							
3	New York	$405.24							
4	London	$403.05							
5	Paris	$401.47							
6	Frankfurt	$404.24							
7	Zurich	$404.25							
8									
9	Average	$403.68							
10	Future	$413.80							
11	Cost	$415.29							
12									
13									
14									

Ready

The named references are substituted into the formula, computing the correct value.

18. Save the worksheet as GOLD.XLS. You use it again in performing Typical Operations in other modules in the learning sequence.

19. Exit Excel, or continue your work session with the active worksheet on the screen.

20. Turn to Module 40 to continue the learning sequence.

Module 17
DELETE (DATABASE)

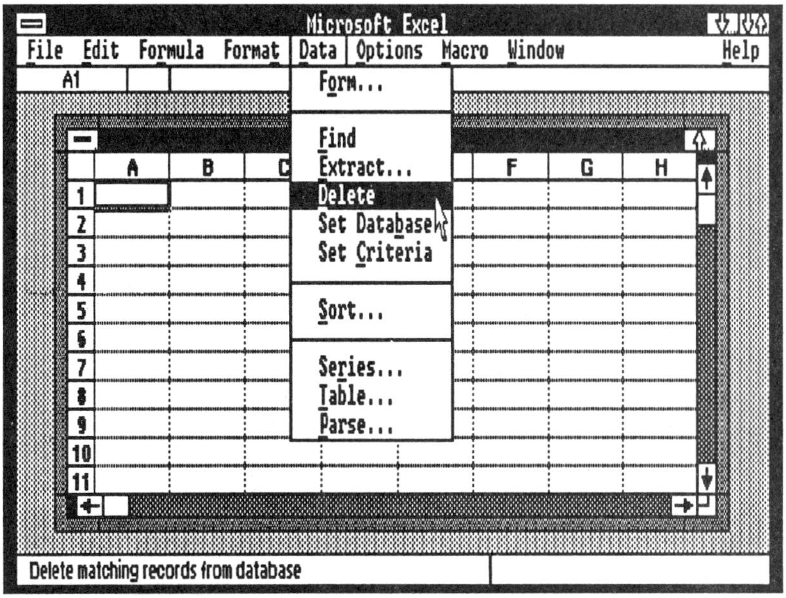

DESCRIPTION

The Delete command on the Data menu is used for removing records from a database. To use the Delete command you must first define the database with the Set Database command, then you must specify the criteria for deletion with the Set Criteria command. Finally, you use the Delete command on the Data menu to delete all database records matching the selection criteria.

When you select the command (with the mouse or by pressing Alt-D D) Excel presents a warning message that matching records will be deleted permantly. You can select OK or cancel the command at that point.

APPLICATIONS

Excel has three Delete commands. One is a general-purpose deletion command to remove a worksheet cell or range of cells. Located on the Edit menu, it is not specifically designed to work with databases, but can be used for that purpose. The Delete command on the Data menu is specifically designed for use with databases. It uses the selection criteria established with the

Set Criteria command to delete all matching database records. It is also possible to delete information from a database through the use of the Delete option of the Form command. Use the following guidelines to help determine which procedure to use:

- Use the Delete command on the Edit menu for deletion of general information in the worksheet.
- Use the Delete option of the Form command on the Data menu for performing interactive delete operations on data organized as a database. This option requires that you view each record in the data form window, performing the deletion one record at a time.
- Use the Delete command on the Data menu to perform a structured deletion of information that meets a deletion criteria (established with the Set Criteria command) from a database, where one use of the command could delete a single record or hundreds of records. You could accomplish the same result through repetitive use of the Delete option of the Form command, but you would have to execute the option for each deleted record.

Because the actions of the Data Delete command are permanant and there is no "undo" operation to reverse an incorrect action, it is important that you take steps to minimize the possibility for disaster. Before you issue the Delete command, use the Find command to examine selected records before allowing the Delete command to do its work. Save the worksheet immediately before issuing the Delete command. If you create a disaster with the delete, you can close the worksheet (without saving) and then open the worksheet again, reverting to the most recently saved version from the disk.

TYPICAL OPERATION

In this session you delete the clothing records from the camping store inventory, last used in the Find (Database) module, for all clothing items costing less than $1.00.

1. Start Excel and open the INVENT.XLS worksheet, or continue your work session from the previous module.

	Microsoft Excel – INVENT.XLS					
—	File Edit Formula Format Data Options Macro Window				Help	
A14		Clothing				
	A	**B**	**C**	**D**	**E**	**F**
10	Dept	Description	Quantity	Cost	Value	
11	Camping	Mountain Tent	6	$330.21	$1,981.26	
12	Clothing	Rain Jacket	12	$45.50	$546.00	
13	Clothing	Red Bandana	144	$0.96	$138.24	
14	Clothing	Blue Bandana	71	$0.96	$68.16	
15	Fishing	Spinning Rod	3	$14.32	$42.96	
16						
17						
18						
19						
20						
21						
22						
23						
Ready						

2. Move the cursor to the selection criteria in the first rows of the worksheet.

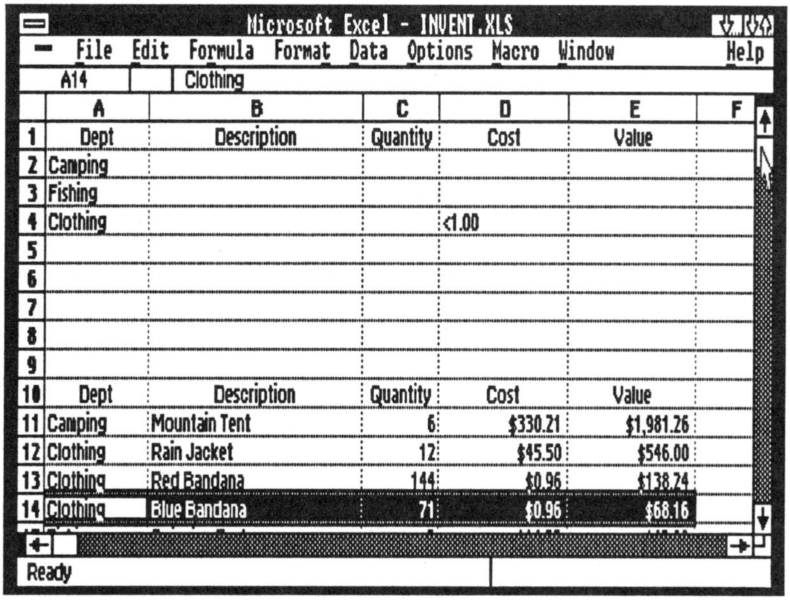

You could either modify the existing set of selection criteria, or create a new selection set. In this case, create a new selection set.

3. Highlight the cell range A1 through E1, then select **Copy** from the Edit menu.

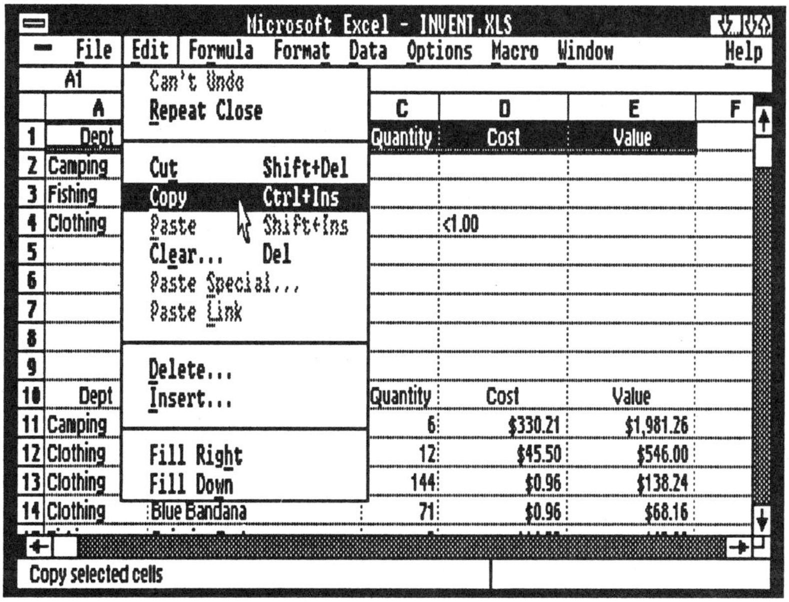

4. Position the screen cursor in cell A6, then select **Paste** from the Edit menu.

Microsoft Excel - INVENT.XLS					
File	Edit	Formula Format Data Options Macro Window			Help

A6		Can't Undo				
	A	Repeat Close	**C**	**D**	**E**	**F**
1	Dept		Quantity	Cost	Value	
2	Camping	Cut Shift+Del				
3	Fishing	Copy Ctrl+Ins				
4	Clothing	Paste Shift+Ins		<1.00		
5		Clear... Del				
6		Paste Special...				
7		Paste Link				
8						
9		Delete...				
10	Dept	Insert...	Quantity	Cost	Value	
11	Camping		6	$330.21	$1,981.26	
12	Clothing	Fill Right	12	$45.50	$546.00	
13	Clothing	Fill Down	144	$0.96	$138.24	
14	Clothing	Blue Bandana	71	$0.96	$68.16	

Place data in selected cells

5. Type <**1.00** in cell D7, type **Clothing** in cell A7, and press **Enter**.

Microsoft Excel - INVENT.XLS					
File	Edit	Formula Format Data Options Macro Window			Help

A7		Clothing				
	A	**B**	**C**	**D**	**E**	**F**
1	Dept	Description	Quantity	Cost	Value	
2	Camping					
3	Fishing					
4	Clothing			<1.00		
5						
6	Dept	Description	Quantity	Cost	Value	
7	Clothing			<1.00		
8						
9						
10	Dept	Description	Quantity	Cost	Value	
11	Camping	Mountain Tent	6	$330.21	$1,981.26	
12	Clothing	Rain Jacket	12	$45.50	$546.00	
13	Clothing	Red Bandana	144	$0.96	$138.24	
14	Clothing	Blue Bandana	71	$0.96	$68.16	

Ready

6. Highlight the range A6 through E7, then select **Set Criteria** from the Data menu.

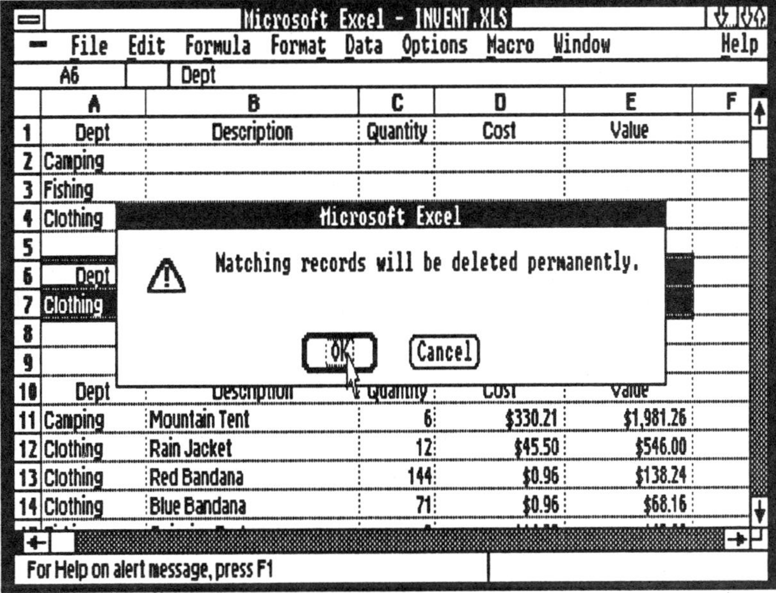

7. Select **Save** from the File menu to save the current state of the worksheet prior to using the Delete command.

8. Select **Delete** from the Data menu to perform the deletion.

9. Select **OK** to confirm the permanent deletion of the matching records.

The two clothing items costing under $1.00 are removed from the database.

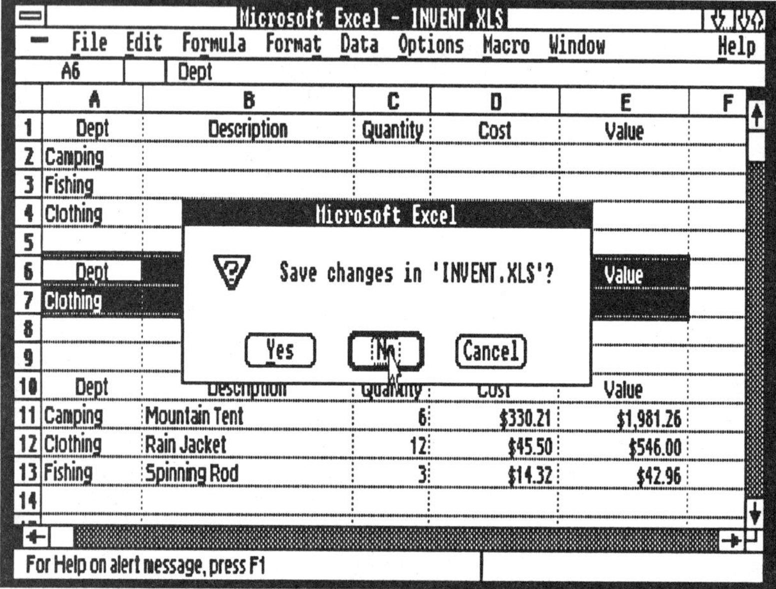

10. Close the INVENT.XLS worksheet but do not save it (in effect, reversing the deletion). You use the worksheet version you saved prior to the Delete operation in Module 22, Extract.

11. Exit Excel, or continue your work session without an active worksheet on the screen.

12. Turn to Module 22 to continue the learning sequence.

Module 18
DELETE (EDIT)

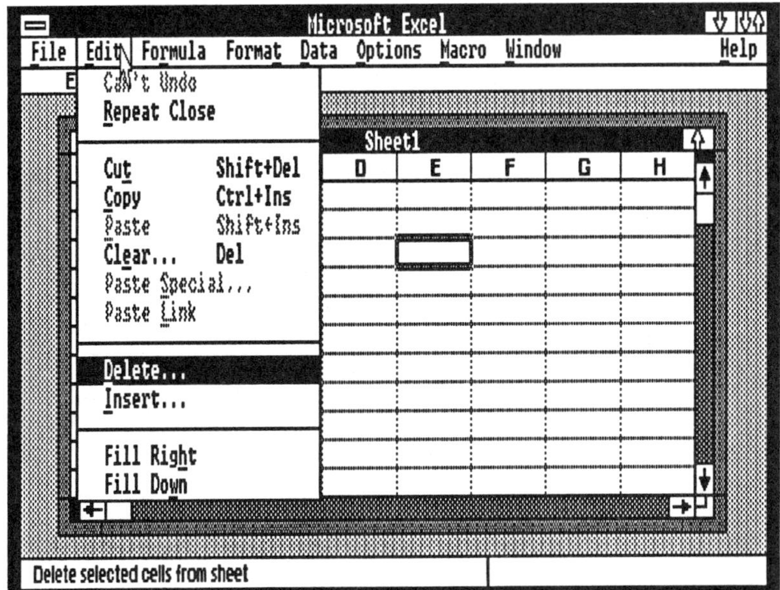

DESCRIPTION

The Delete command in the Edit menu permits you to delete entire rows or columns. The command is accessed with Alt-E D.

APPLICATIONS

The delete command from the Edit menu is useful if you are rearranging the information in the worksheet. Another use of this delete function is to reduce the size of your worksheets. Excel assigns memory space based on the size of the worksheet being used. The worksheets are quite large and, therefore, occupy considerable space. By deleting any unused cells you can provide yourself with additional memory capability.

Once you have entered data in a worksheet, you can eliminate any columns and rows that are before the last cell that contains data. Later, if you decide to add more columns or rows, you can do so using the Insert command in the Edit menu. (See Module 33, Insert).

NOTE

If you delete a row or column that contains a cell
that is referenced by another cell in the
worksheet or in another worksheet, Excel will
warn you with the message "#REF!".

TYPICAL OPERATION

In this operation you delete rows and columns from a worksheet. Begin this operation with a
clean worksheet. First mark the row or column you wish to delete.

1. Start Excel.

2. Type **The rain falls mainly on the plain.** in cell A2.

3. Place the cursor in row 1 and press **Shift-Spacebar** or click on the number **1** as shown
    in the following screen.

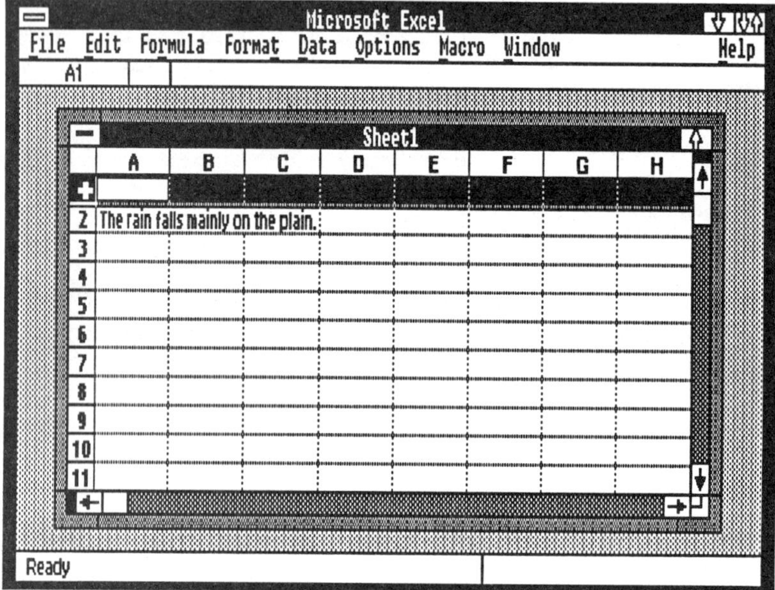

4. Select **Delete** from the Edit menu.

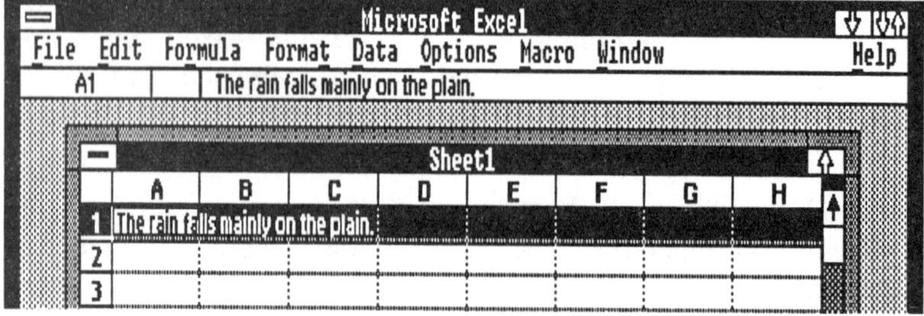

The first row is deleted and the second row is moved up in its place.

5. Select a cell in column A and press **Ctrl-Spacebar** or click on **A** at the top of the column with the mouse.

6. Select **Delete** from the Edit menu.

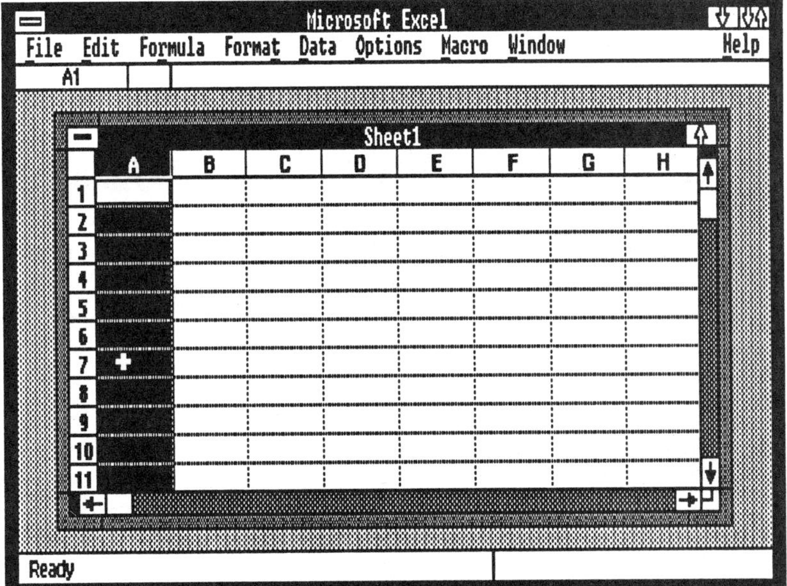

The sentence you entered in cell A2 is deleted with column A. This is an instance when you can use the Undo command in the Edit menu to recover the lost sentence.

7. Select **Exit** from the File menu and click **No** to abandon the worksheet and return to either DOS or the MS-DOS Executive.

8. Turn to Module 42 to continue the learning sequence.

Module 19

DELETE (FILE)

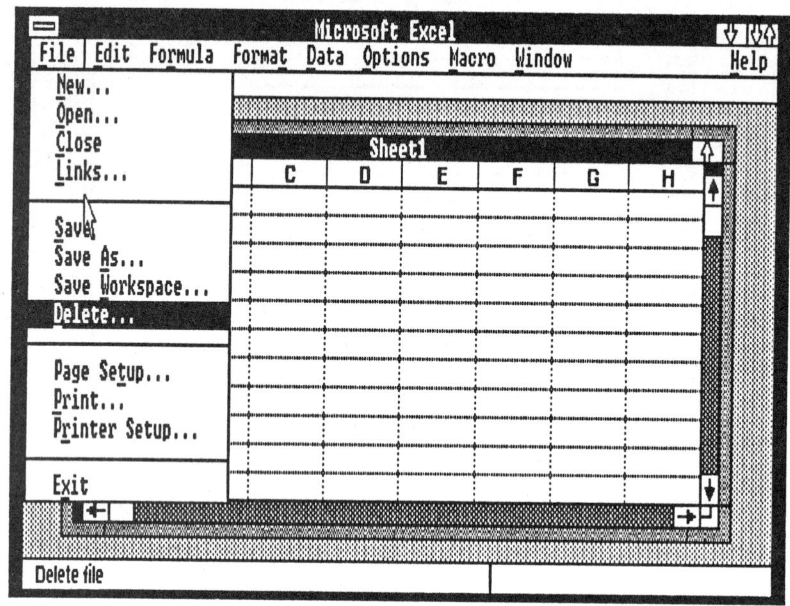

DESCRIPTION

The Delete command for removing files occurs in the File menu. It can be accessed by opening the File menu and selecting the Delete command or by using the keystrokes Alt-F D.

APPLICATIONS

This command is used to remove unnecessary files from the Excel library. After using Excel for a while you will build a library of files, some of which will eventually become old and outdated. Periodically, you will want to remove these files to make room for new files or to reuse a particular filename. Periodic "house cleaning" permits you to keep only those files which are of value to you.

If you are using the full version of Windows, you should also be aware that you can always remove files that are not longer of use by going to the MS-DOS screen and using the Delete command from the File menu associated with that screen.

TYPICAL OPERATION

In this module you remove some files from the Excel library using the Delete command in the File menu.

1. Start Excel, or continue your work session from the previous module.

2. Select **Delete** from the File menu.

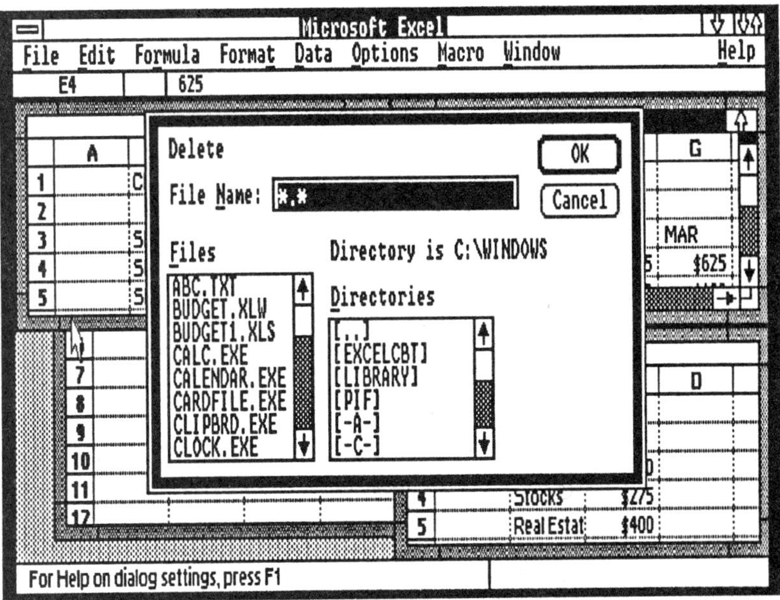

Your screen may not be exactly like the one illustrated, in that you may not have all of the same files listed. There are several methods of selecting the file you wish to delete. Using the mouse you can scroll the files until you locate the one you wish to delete, click on it with the mouse, and click on OK.

You can press Tab to activate the file selector, use the arrow keys to move through the files until you find the file you want to delete, and then press Enter.

The third method is to type the name of the file you want to delete and press Enter.

CAUTION

Once a file is deleted, it *cannot* be recalled. Even
the Undo command will not work.

3. Type **BUDGET1.XLS** and press **Enter**.

4. Press **Enter** or click on **Yes** in the dialog box.

BUDGET1.XLS is removed from the list of files. Be careful when you use this command because there is no way to recall it.

5. Pick **Cancel** or press **Esc** to return to the worksheet.

6. Exit Excel.

7. Turn to Module 54 to continue the learning sequence.

Module 20

DISPLAY

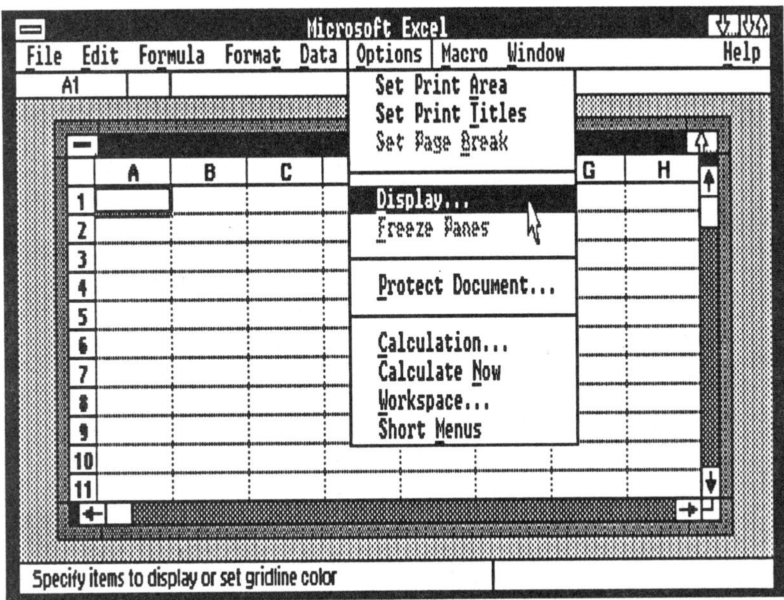

DESCRIPTION

Use the Display command on the Options menu to control the appearance of your worksheets. Each worksheet has a separate set of display options accessed through the Display command. Select it with the mouse, or press Alt-O D. When you select the Display command, the following dialog box appears.

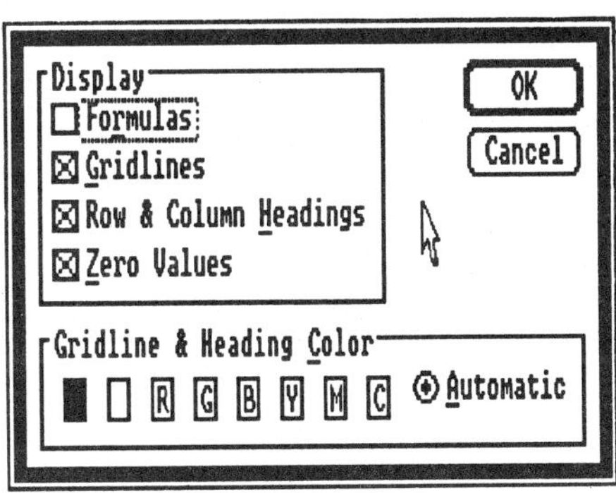

The Formulas check box determines whether the worksheet displays results of formulas or the formulas themselves. The default setting (not checked) is to display results, not formulas.

The Gridlines check box determines whether the row and column grid is visible in the worksheet. The default is to show gridlines.

The Row & Column Headings check box determines whether the labels for the rows and columns are visible on the screen. (The letters are for columns and the numbers for rows.)

The Zero Values check box determines whether zeroes are displayed as 0 or blank.

You may change the color of the gridlines in the Gridline & Heading Color selection area to make a more attractive display.

APPLICATIONS

The Display command helps you accomodate your personal work style and produce worksheets that are visually attractive for use in presentations. Turning off the gridlines and row and column headings can help make a more visually clean display for use with a projection system if you share your worksheets in a meeting.

Use the Formula display option to help in finding errors in worksheets and to recall your strategy in solving problems.

If you elect to display zeroes as blanks, you may find yourself later placing other information in the cells by mistake. Consider using the Protect command to protect these cells to prevent inadvertently overwriting their contents.

TYPICAL OPERATION

In this session you modify the display of a worksheet using the Display command.

1. Start Excel, or continue your work session from the previous module.

2. Open the GOLD.XLS worksheet. Expand the worksheet to fill the screen, and select cell E8 if it is not already selected.

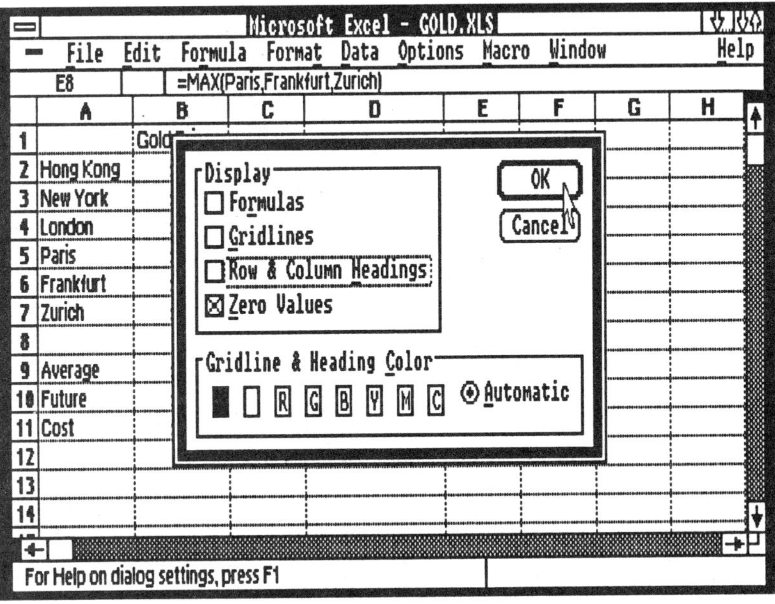

3. Click on **Display** on the Options menu, or press **Alt-O D**.

4. Turn off the Gridlines and the Row & Column Headings by picking the respective check boxes, removing the "X" marks from the boxes.

5. Pick **OK**. The worksheet is displayed without the headings and the gridlines.

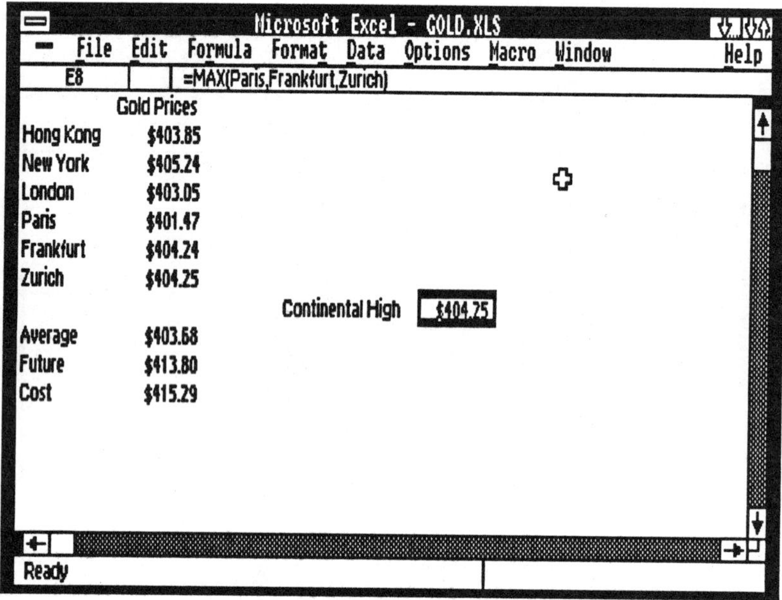

6. Close the worksheet. There is no need to save it.

7. Exit Excel, or continue your work session without an active worksheet on the screen.

8. Turn to Module 59 to continue the learning sequence.

Module 21

EXIT

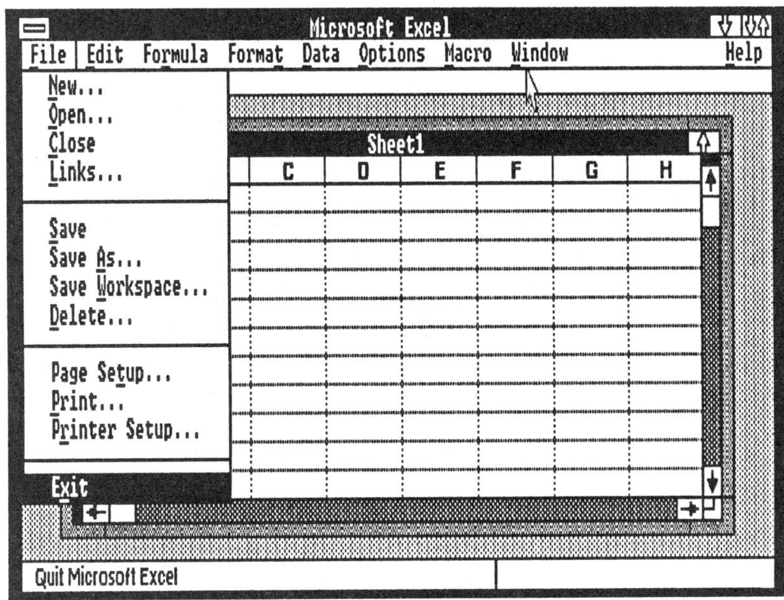

DESCRIPTION

The Exit command is located in the File menu and is accessed with Alt-F X. As in the Close command, the Exit command will close a window. It also will take you out of Excel and place you in the MS-DOS Executive or the "C" prompt.

APPLICATIONS

You would normally use the Exit command when you complete your work with Excel. If you made any changes in your worksheets, Excel will ask whether or not you want to save the changes.

If you are editing an already existing worksheet, Excel will also give you the opportunity to decide if you want to keep the same name or change it. If your action will result in you leaving Excel, it will so inform you.

TYPICAL OPERATION

In this module you use the Exit command to close a window and exit Excel.

1. Start Excel by typing **Excel** at the system prompt.

2. Type **The rain falls mainly on the plain** in cell A1 of your current worksheet and press **Enter**.

3. Select **Exit** from the File menu.

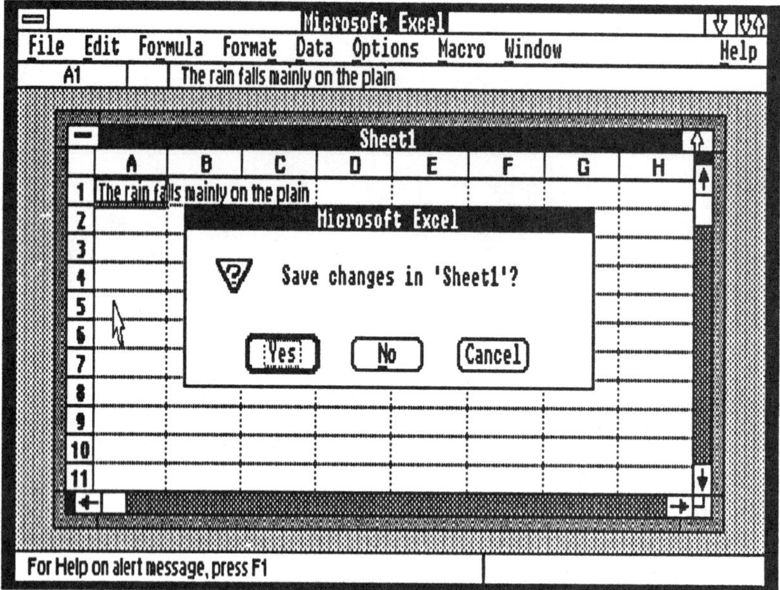

4. Select **NO**.

Depending on the version of Windows you are using, you should either be in the MS-DOS Executive or at the "C" prompt. If you are in the MS-DOS Executive, then continue with the following steps.

5. Select the **Exit** command from the File menu.

You should see a dialog box on your screen that informs you that you are about to end your Windows session.

6. Press **Enter** or click on **OK**.

7. Turn to Module 18 to continue the learning sequence.

Module 22

EXTRACT

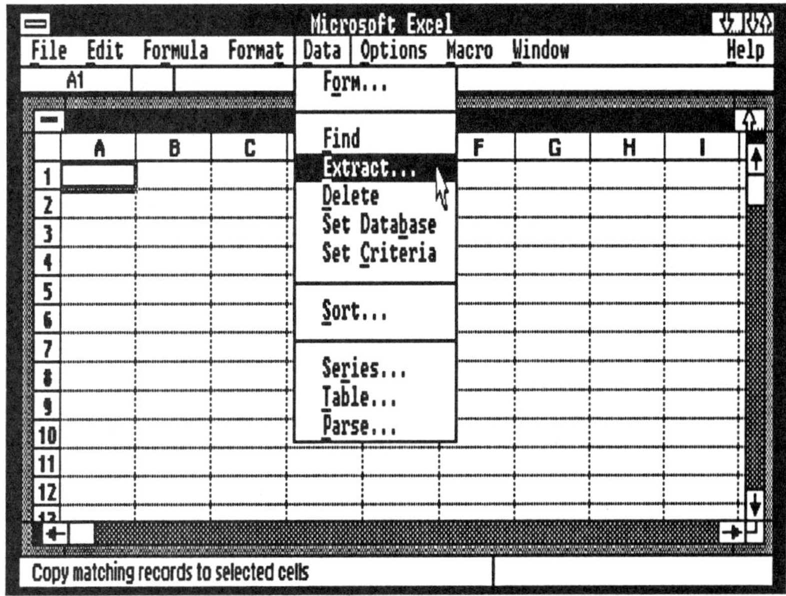

DESCRIPTION

Use the Extract command on the Data menu to copy selected records, or parts of records, from an Excel database to an available portion of the worksheet. To use the Extract command:

1. Define the range of the database with the Set Database command.

2. Define the criteria for record extraction with the Set Criteria command.

3. In an unused area of the worksheet, type the field names for the fields you want to extract, or copy the field names from the top line of the database with the Copy and Paste commands.

4. Highlight a range of cells including and, optionally, beneath the extract field names to contain the extracted database.

5. Select the Extract command from the Data menu. (Select Extract from the Data menu with the mouse or press Alt-D E.)

The spelling of the field names you specify in the extract range must match exactly the field names in the database definition; however, the use of capital letters does not matter. It is not necessary to use all the fields, and it is not necessary to place the fields in the same order as they appear in the database.

If you specify an extract range including both the extract field names and a range of cells below them, the Extract command extracts only as many records as fit in the defined range. If you specify only the single line containing the field titles as the extract range, the Extract command clears all information between the field titles and the bottom of the worksheet for the extract database.

CAUTION

If you elect to specify the single field line as the
extract range, first make certain that you have
not stored any valuable data between the titles
and the bottom of the worksheet. The Extract
command clears all information in this
rectangular region.

When you extract a computed field, only the present value of the field is extracted. The formula is not extracted.

APPLICATIONS

It is often necessary to perform an analysis of information that requires only part of a database. For large databases, the size of the database can be an inconvenience. You end up carrying along a great deal of extra baggage. Other times, you may want to share information with others, but not want them to have access to portions containing confidential or proprietary information. It is also possible that the additional information is irrelevant. In these cases, it is useful to extract the required data from the database into another, smaller database. You then have the choice of either working with the subset in the original worksheet, or possibly copying the extracted information to another worksheet. Excel provides both facilities.

Use the Extract command to produce subsets of databases. To create a smaller database containing only certain *records* meeting your selection criteria: use the Copy command to copy the database titles, use Set Criteria to establish the selection criteria, then perform the Extract command. To create a smaller database containing only specified *fields* of the entire database: create a header line containing only the required field names, use Set Criteria to establish a criteria range containing a blank line, then perform the Extract command. You can also use Extract to produce a subset that contains only specific fields of records meeting specific criteria. It is not necessary that the selection criteria be one of the fields included in the extracted database.

TYPICAL OPERATION

In this session you extract selected inventory records from the camping equipment store inventory, most recently used in the Delete module.

1. Start Excel, or continue your work session from the previous module.

2. Open the worksheet INVENT.XLS and expand the worksheet to fill the screen.

	A	B	C	D	E	F
1	Dept	Description	Quantity	Cost	Value	
2	Camping					
3	Fishing					
4	Clothing			<1.00		
5						
6	Dept	Description	Quantity	Cost	Value	
7	Clothing			<1.00		
8						
9						
10	Dept	Description	Quantity	Cost	Value	
11	Camping	Mountain Tent	6	$330.21	$1,981.26	
12	Clothing	Rain Jacket	12	$45.50	$546.00	
13	Clothing	Red Bandana	144	$0.96	$138.24	
14	Clothing	Blue Bandana	71	$0.96	$68.16	

The worksheet appears as it did when you saved it immediately prior to performing the Delete command in the Module 18 Typical Operation. The current selection criteria specify clothing items costing less than $1.00. As a first extraction from the database, extract these items.

3. Highlight the region A10..E10, the database field titles.

4. Select **Copy** from the Edit menu.

5. Select cell A25. (You may need to use the scroll bars to move through the worksheet—depending on your computer hardware setup.)

6. Select **Paste** from the Edit menu.

7. Select **Extract** from the Data menu.

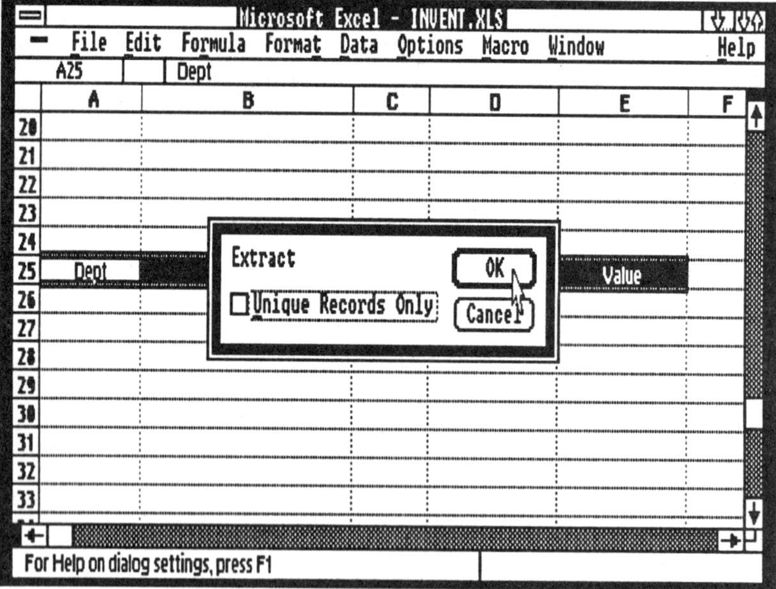

8. Pick **OK** to select all records meeting the criteria, not only unique records. The database of records meeting the criteria appears on the screen.

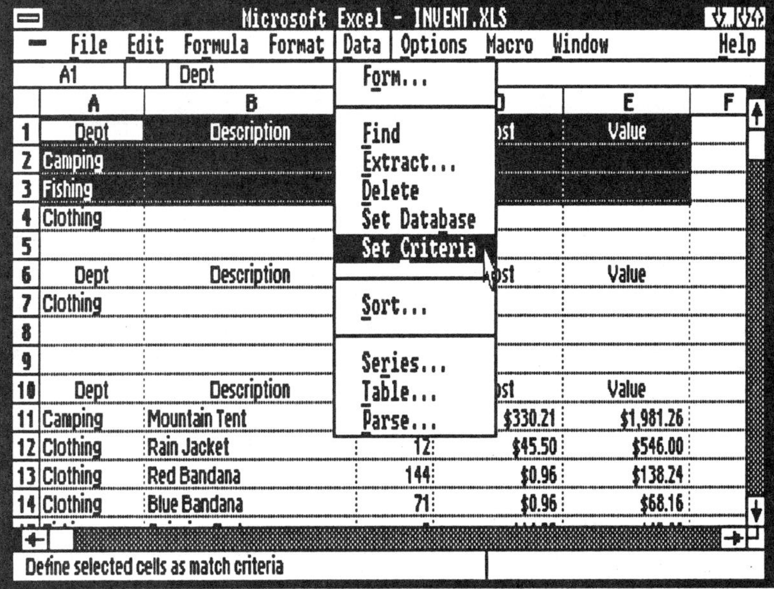

9. Scroll back to the top of the worksheet. Select the range A1 through E3; then select **Set Criteria** from the Data menu.

10. Scroll to row 25 and highlight the range A25 through E25. Select **Extract** from the Data menu. Pick **OK** to extract all matching records.

It is not necessary to extract all the fields when you perform the Extract command.

11. Scroll to the selection criteria at the top of the worksheet.

12. Highlight the cells A6 through A7; then select **Set Criteria** from the Data menu.

```
┌──────────────────────────────────────────────────────────────────────┐
│ ▬            Microsoft Excel - INVENT.XLS                      ▼▲ ▐◤▼▶ │
│ ─   File   Edit   Formula   Format │ Data │ Options   Macro   Window        Help │
│     A6          │  Dept          Form...                                  │
│        A    │      B      │   Find      │st  │     E     │ F │▲           │
│  1    Dept  │  Description │   Extract...│    │   Value   │   │           │
│  2  Camping │             │   Delete    │                                │
│  3  Fishing │             │   Set Database                               │
│  4  Clothing│             │   Set Criteria                               │
│  5          │             │             │                                │
│  6    Dept  │  Description │   Sort...   │st  │   Value   │                │
│  7  Clothing│             │             │                                │
│  8          │             │   Series... │                                │
│  9          │             │   Table...  │                                │
│ 10    Dept  │  Description │   Parse...  │st  │   Value   │                │
│ 11  Camping │  Mountain Tent│          $330.21│ $1,981.26 │               │
│ 12  Clothing│  Rain Jacket │        12 │ $45.50 │  $546.00  │            │
│ 13  Clothing│  Red Bandana │       144 │ $0.96  │  $138.24  │            │
│ 14  Clothing│  Blue Bandana│        71 │ $0.96  │   $68.16  │▼           │
│ Define selected cells as match criteria                                  │
└──────────────────────────────────────────────────────────────────────┘
```

13. Select cell G10 and type **Description**. Type **Value** in cell H10 and press **Enter**. Adjust the column widths for the Description and Value columns visually to appropriate widths as shown.

```
┌──────────────────────────────────────────────────────────────────────┐
│ ▬            Microsoft Excel - INVENT.XLS                      ▼▲ ▐◤▼▶ │
│ ─   File   Edit   Formula   Format   Data   Options   Macro   Window      Help │
│     H10         │  Value                                               │
│       D     │     E      │  F  │       G       │       H    ┼ │ I │▲   │
│  1   Cost   │   Value    │     │               │              │        │
│  2          │            │     │               │              │        │
│  3          │            │     │               │              │        │
│  4  <1.00   │            │     │               │              │        │
│  5          │            │     │               │              │        │
│  6   Cost   │   Value    │     │               │              │        │
│  7  <1.00   │            │     │               │              │        │
│  8          │            │     │               │              │        │
│  9          │            │     │               │              │        │
│ 10   Cost   │   Value    │     │  Description  │    Value     │        │
│ 11  $330.21 │  $1,981.26 │     │               │              │        │
│ 12   $45.50 │   $546.00  │     │               │              │        │
│ 13    $0.96 │   $138.24  │     │               │              │        │
│ 14    $0.96 │    $68.16  │     │               │              │▼       │
│ Ready                                                                  │
└──────────────────────────────────────────────────────────────────────┘
```

14. Select column H; then select **Number** from the Format menu. Specify dollars and cents format as shown.

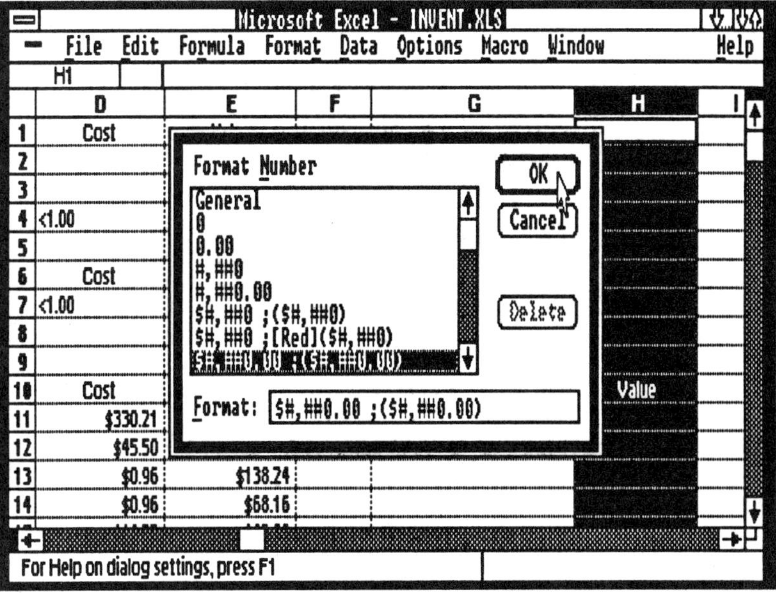

15. Pick **OK**.

16. Select cells G10 and H10, then select **Extract** from the Data menu. Pick **OK** to extract all the matching records.

All the clothing items and their values are extracted.

This extraction illustrates several important concepts. First, the selection criteria does not have to contain all fields. Second, the extracted database does not have to contain all fields. Third, the fields that make up the selection criteria do not have to be the same as, or included in, the extracted database. Finally, formulas, for example the *Value* field, are not extracted; the current numerical value is extracted.

17. Select cell H11 and examine the value on the worksheet edit line. Notice that the field contains the value $546, not a formula.

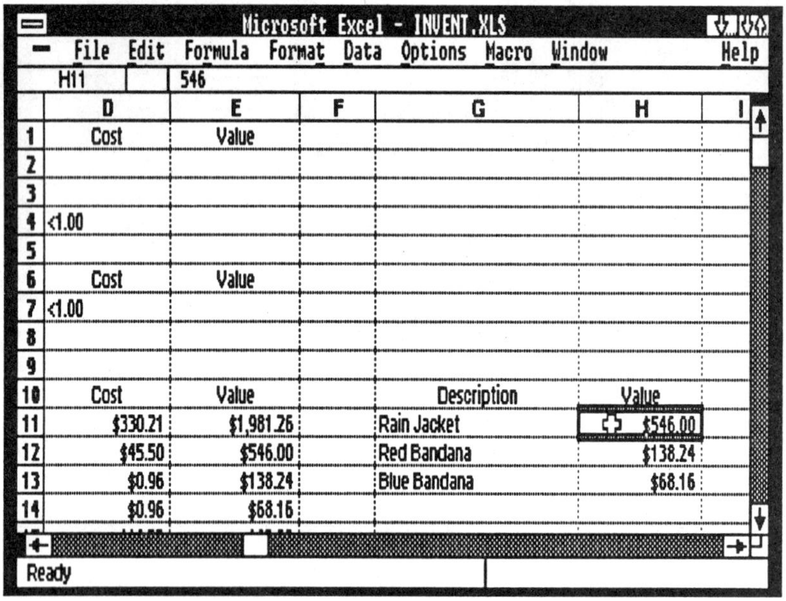

	Microsoft Excel - INVENT.XLS					
—	File Edit Formula Format Data Options Macro Window					Help
H11	546					
	D	**E**	**F**	**G**	**H**	**I**
1	Cost	Value				
2						
3						
4	<1.00					
5						
6	Cost	Value				
7	<1.00					
8						
9						
10	Cost	Value		Description	Value	
11	$330.21	$1,981.26		Rain Jacket	$546.00	
12	$45.50	$546.00		Red Bandana	$138.24	
13	$0.96	$138.24		Blue Bandana	$68.16	
14	$0.96	$68.16				
Ready						

18. Close and save the INVENT.XLS worksheet.

19. Exit Excel, or continue your work session without an active worksheet on the screen.

20. Turn to Module 60 to continue the learning sequence.

Module 23

FILL RIGHT, FILL DOWN

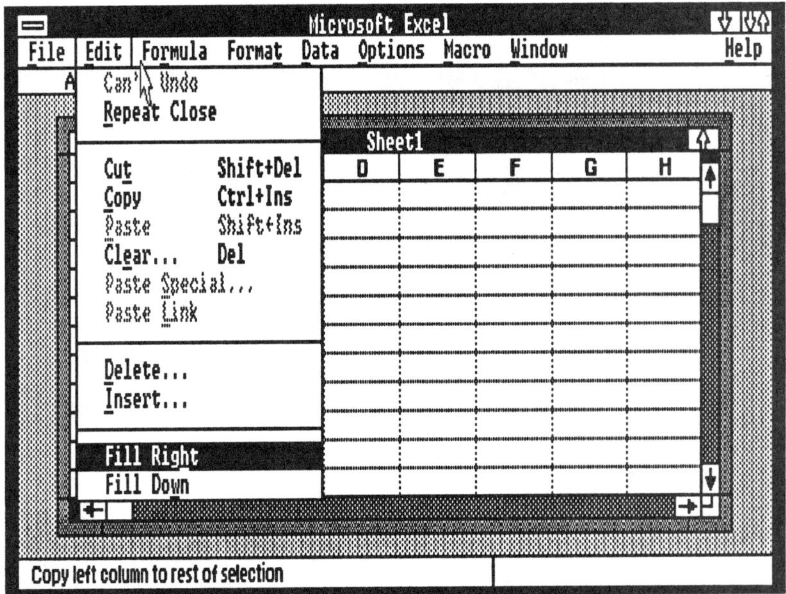

DESCRIPTION

The commands Fill Right and Fill Down are accessed through the Edit menu with the keystrokes Alt-E H and Alt-E W, respectively. The commands are used to copy text, values, and formulas from one set of cells to another set. The first command will copy original data from one set of cells to those immediately to the right and the second will copy original data from one set of cells to those immediately below. The area to receive the data must be equal to or larger than the size of the area sending the data.

APPLICATIONS

Whenever a document calls for existing data to be copied next to the existing data, the Fill commands should be considered. Although the data could be copied by hand, this is often a tedious and time consuming process. An example would be to expand a monthly budget to a projected yearly budget. In this example, the information for each month would remain the same and could therefore be duplicated exactly in a new area.

TYPICAL OPERATION

In this operation you use the Fill commands to copy budget data from one set of cells to another set. In order to have an entire year on one sheet of paper, it would require that you juggle the width and length of the document. This module illustrates the use of these commands to create a three-month budget.

1. Start Excel and open Budget1, or continue your work session from the previous module.

2. Type **Utilities** in cell D11 and **$175** in cell E11.

3. Change cell E6 to **$300** and cell E8 to **$250**.

4. Make all formulas absolute by changing the formula in cell E9 to **= $B$4-(E4 + E5 + E6 + E7 + E8 + E10 + E11)** and the formula in cell E10 to **$B$4*0.2**. (Don't forget to press **Enter**.)

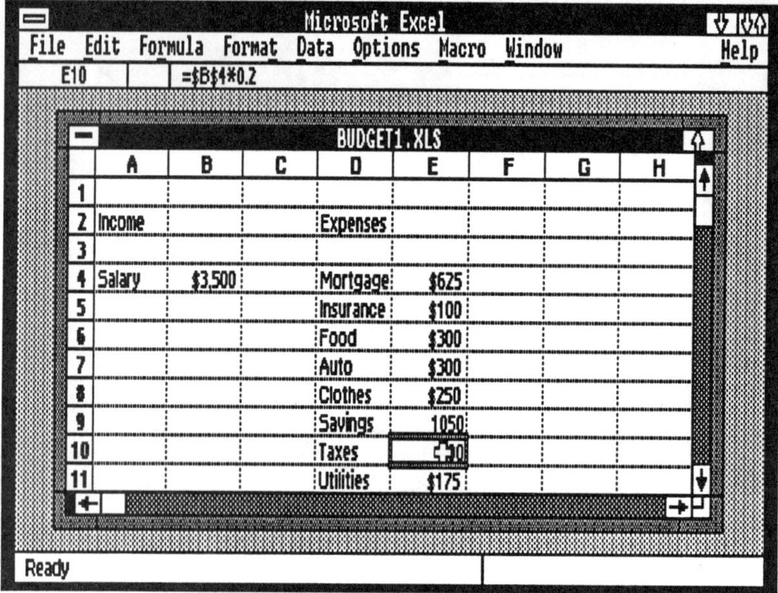

5. Create a range of the cells in columns E, F, and G through rows 4 through 11.

6. Choose **Fill Right** from the Edit menu.

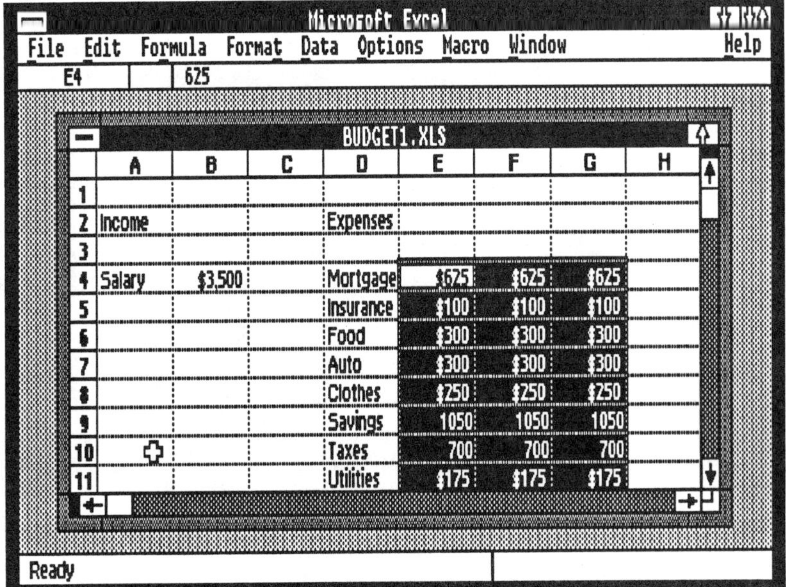

7. Type **Jan**, **Feb**, **Mar** in cells E3, F3 and G3 respectively.

8. Type **Rent** in cell A5 and **$450** in cell B5 and press **Enter**. This is for one of three houses you were able to rent.

9. Mark cells **5, 6, 7** in columns **A** and **B**.

10. Select **Fill Down** from the Edit menu.

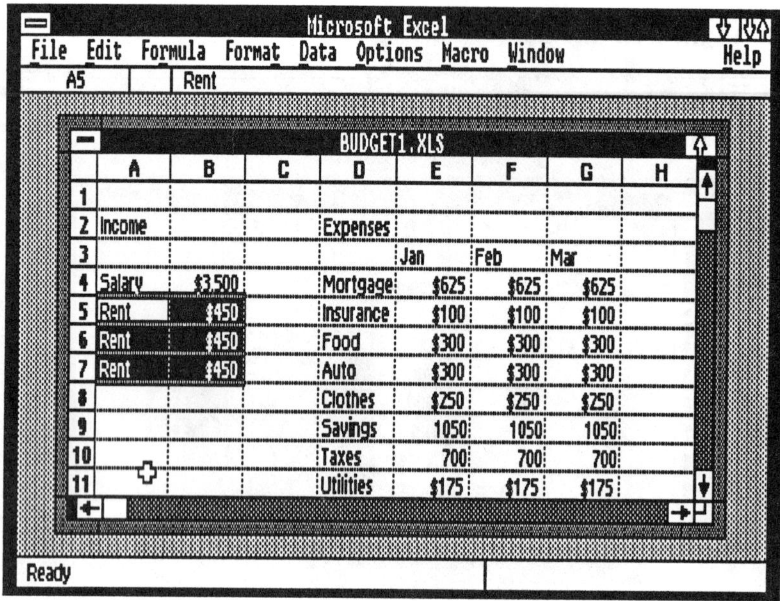

	A	B	C	D	E	F	G	H
1								
2	Income			Expenses				
3					Jan	Feb	Mar	
4	Salary	$3,500		Mortgage	$625	$625	$625	
5	Rent	$450		Insurance	$100	$100	$100	
6	Rent	$450		Food	$300	$300	$300	
7	Rent	$450		Auto	$300	$300	$300	
8				Clothes	$250	$250	$250	
9				Savings	1050	1050	1050	
10				Taxes	700	700	700	
11				Utilities	$175	$175	$175	

11. Insert a new column between column D and column E.

12. Type **Expected** in cell E3.

13. Copy and paste the information in cells F4 through F11 to E4 through E11.

14. Save the worksheet.

15. Exit Excel, or continue your work session with the active worksheet on the screen.

16. Turn to Module 51 to continue the learning sequence.

Module 24
FIND (DATABASE)

DESCRIPTION

Use the Find command on the Data menu to locate specific records in an Excel database. Before you use the Find command you must first define the database with the Set Database command, then establish the search criteria with the Set Criteria command. Finally, use the Find command to locate the first matching record in the database. Select the command with the mouse or press Alt-D F on the keyboard. Repeatedly using the Find command finds each successive record matching the search criteria. You can also use the Up Arrow and Down Arrow keys to move between records matching the search criteria. To cancel the Find command, press Esc.

APPLICATIONS

Once you establish the criteria for the information you want to examine, the Find command uses the criteria to actually locate the information in the database. The Set Criteria command provides greater flexibility in establishing selection criteria than the Criteria option of the Form command. Use the Criteria option of the Form command for locating records with simple criteria. Use the Set Criteria command and the Find command to perform more sophisticated Find operations.

TYPICAL OPERATION

In this session you use the Find command to locate specific records in the camping equipment inventory. Recall that the worksheet was created in the Set Database module, and you defined the selection criteria in the Set Criteria module.

1. Start Excel and open the worksheet INVENT.XLS, or continue your work session from the previous module.

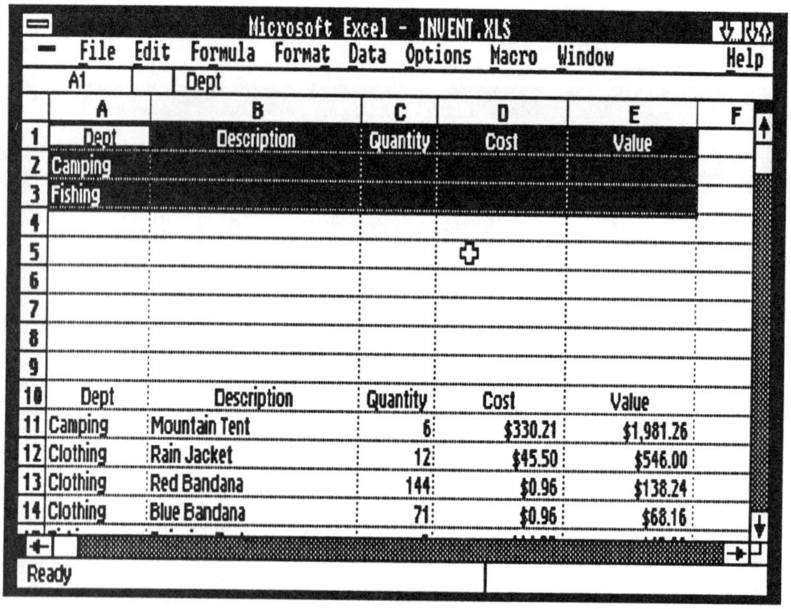

The database and the selection criteria remain selected from previous Typical Operations sessions. (If for some reason you have changed the database or selection criteria definitions, set the database to the range A10..E20 and set the criteria to the range A1..E3.)

The presently defined selection criteria matches all records with Dept = Camping and all records with Dept = Fishing. Remember that Excel pays no attention to case differences in determining a match.

2. Select **Find** from the Data menu.

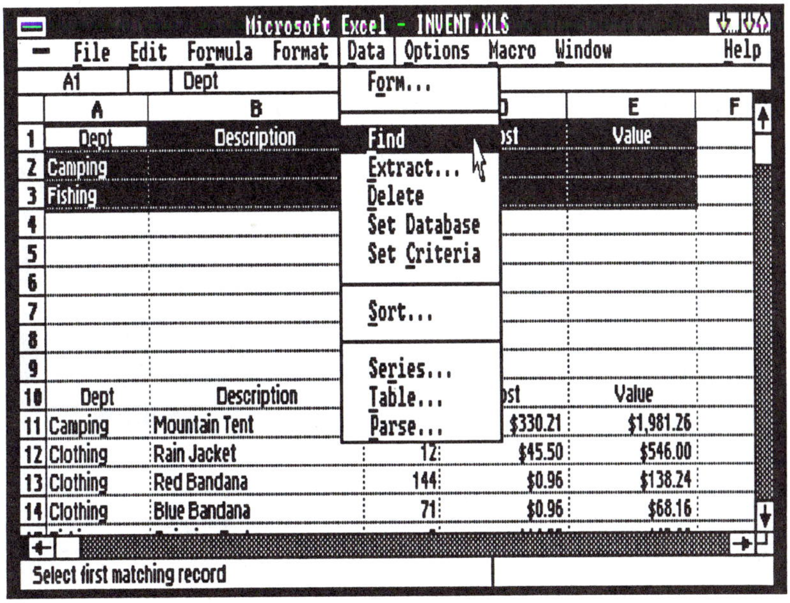

The Find command stops on the first match meeting the selection criteria, highlighting the selected record.

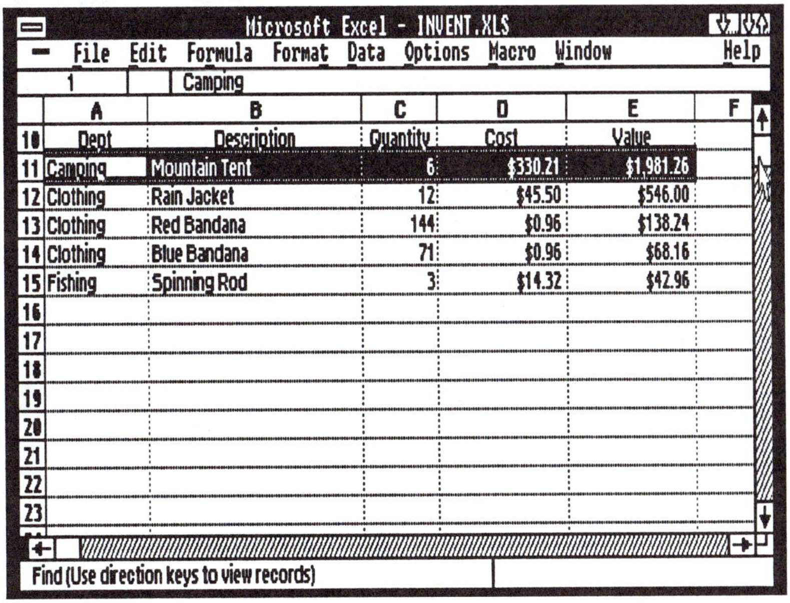

Notice that the scroll bars at the bottom and side of the worksheet change in appearance. This change shows that you are finding records in the database according to the current selection criteria. You move between matching records either by pressing the Up Arrow and Down Arrow keys on the keyboard, or by using the scroll bar to the right of the worksheet.

3. Press **Down Arrow** to view the next matching record.

	Microsoft Excel – INVENT.XLS					
—	File Edit Formula Format Data Options Macro Window					Help
5		Fishing				
	A	**B**	**C**	**D**	**E**	**F**
10	Dept	Description	Quantity	Cost	Value	
11	Camping	Mountain Tent	6	$330.21	$1,981.26	
12	Clothing	Rain Jacket	12	$45.50	$546.00	
13	Clothing	Red Bandana	144	$0.96	$138.24	
14	Clothing	Blue Bandana	71	$0.96	$68.16	
15	Fishing	Spinning Rod	3	$14.32	$42.96	
16						
17						
18						
19						
20						
21						
22						
23						

Find (Use direction keys to view records)

Notice that all the clothing records are bypassed, highlighting the Spinning Rod in the Fishing department.

4. Press **Esc** to cancel the Find command. Notice that the scroll bars revert back to their standard color and pattern.

5. Move the screen cursor to the criteria specification area of the worksheet. Add a line of criteria (row 4 of the worksheet) specifying Clothing with a unit cost less than $1.00, as shown on the following screen.

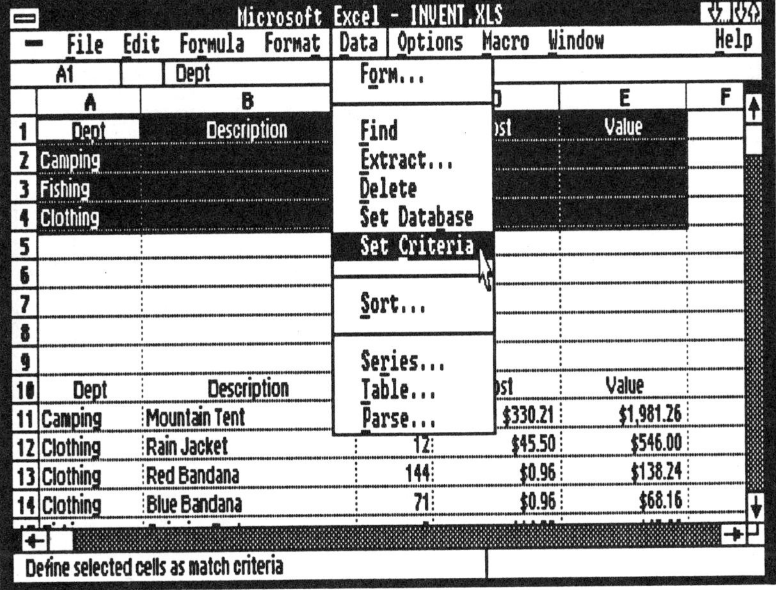

6. Select the range A1 through E4, then pick **Set Criteria** from the Data menu to redefine the selection criteria.

7. Select **Find** from the Data menu. Excel highlights the first matching record.

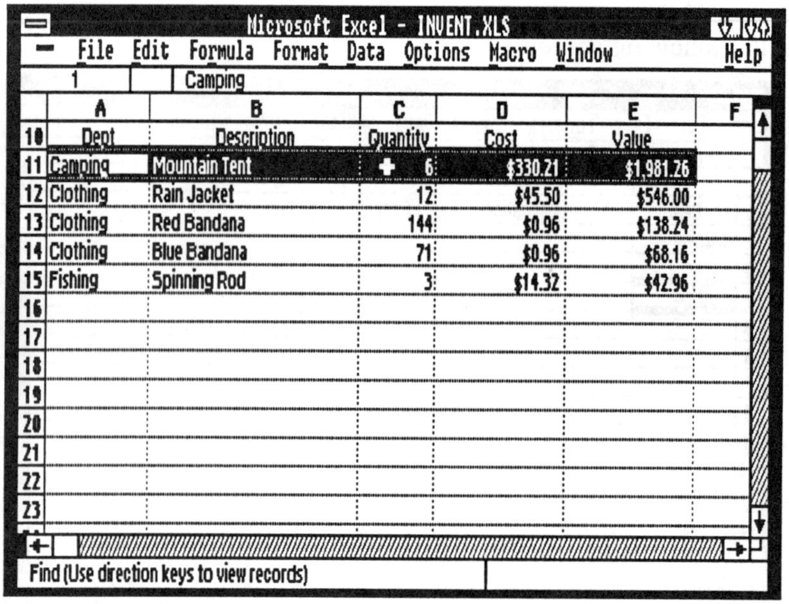

<table>
<tr><td colspan="6">Microsoft Excel - INVENT.XLS</td></tr>
<tr><td colspan="6">File   Edit   Formula   Format   Data   Options   Macro   Window   Help</td></tr>
<tr><td colspan="6">1   Camping</td></tr>
</table>

	A	B	C	D	E	F
10	Dept	Description	Quantity	Cost	Value	
11	Camping	Mountain Tent	6	$330.21	$1,981.26	
12	Clothing	Rain Jacket	12	$45.50	$546.00	
13	Clothing	Red Bandana	144	$0.96	$138.24	
14	Clothing	Blue Bandana	71	$0.96	$68.16	
15	Fishing	Spinning Rod	3	$14.32	$42.96	
16						
17						
18						
19						
20						
21						
22						
23						

Find (Use direction keys to view records)

8. Press **Down Arrow** to display the next matching record.

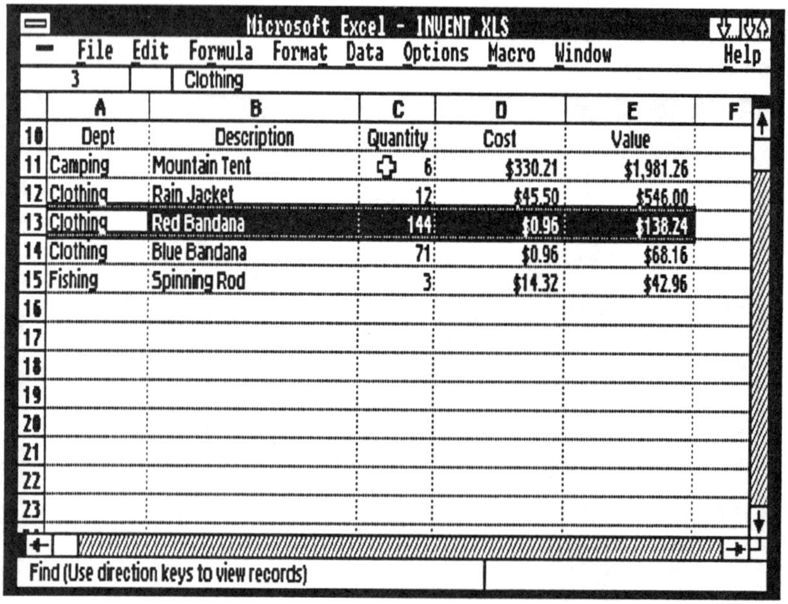

<table>
<tr><td colspan="6">Microsoft Excel - INVENT.XLS</td></tr>
<tr><td colspan="6">File   Edit   Formula   Format   Data   Options   Macro   Window   Help</td></tr>
<tr><td colspan="6">3   Clothing</td></tr>
</table>

	A	B	C	D	E	F
10	Dept	Description	Quantity	Cost	Value	
11	Camping	Mountain Tent	6	$330.21	$1,981.26	
12	Clothing	Rain Jacket	12	$45.50	$546.00	
13	Clothing	Red Bandana	144	$0.96	$138.24	
14	Clothing	Blue Bandana	71	$0.96	$68.16	
15	Fishing	Spinning Rod	3	$14.32	$42.96	
16						
17						
18						
19						
20						
21						
22						
23						

Find (Use direction keys to view records)

The Red Bandana is the next matching item. The department matches "Clothing," and the cost is less than $1.00.

9. Press **Down Arrow** to display the next matching record.

	Microsoft Excel - INVENT.XLS					
—	File Edit Formula Format Data Options Macro Window					Help
	4	Clothing				
	A	**B**	**C**	**D**	**E**	**F**
10	Dept	Description	Quantity	Cost	Value	
11	Camping	Mountain Tent	6	$330.21	$1,981.26	
12	Clothing	Rain Jacket	12	$45.50	$546.00	
13	Clothing	Red Bandana	144	$0.96	$138.74	
14	Clothing	Blue Bandana	71	$0.96	$68.16	
15	Fishing	Spinning Rod	3	$14.32	$42.96	
16						
17						
18						
19						
20						
21						
22						
23						

Find (Use direction keys to view records)

The Blue Bandanas are the next match, matching the department and meeting the required cost limit for clothing.

10. Press **Esc** to cancel the Find command.

11. Save the worksheet.

12. Exit Excel, or continue the learning sequence with the active worksheet on the screen.

13. Turn to Module 17 to continue the learning sequence.

Module 25
FIND (EDIT)

DESCRIPTION

The Find command is located in the Formula menu and is accessed by Alt-R F. The command is very simple to execute. Once you select Find you will be shown a dialog box that asks what string of letters or value you want to find and the specifications of how you want Excel to search for it. You simply answer the questions and Excel will find what you ask anywhere in the worksheet.

You can specify that you want Excel to concentrate the search in the notes, cell values, or formulas. If you specify a formula, Excel will also look at the cell values. If you want to locate a formula, you must specify that Excel look in formulas. If you only know part of the string or value you want to find, you would indicate to Excel that you are only providing part of the information. If you know the complete string or value, instruct Excel to only look for an exact match.

Finally, you can specify that Excel should look by rows or by columns.

There are two characteristics of the search pattern of which you should be aware: (1) you need to input the desired string or value exactly as it will appear in the worksheet. An extra space in front of the string or value (or in the string or value) will cause Excel to miss it; (2) if a range of cells is marked, Excel will only search there.

APPLICATIONS

The value of Find is most evident when the worksheet is large. If you are working in one portion of the worksheet and realize that you need to perform some function in another portion, but you are unable to remember where it is located, you can ask Excel to move you there if you can remember a specific letter string or value. You need to realize that Excel will search and stop at each appropriate designation in the worksheet. For example, if you ask Excel to find all of the letter strings beginning "th" it will locate and stop at every word that has those two letters in that order.

TYPICAL OPERATION

In this operation you find a string of letters and a value in the worksheet.

1. Start Excel if necessary and open BUDGET1.XLS.
2. Select cell **A1**.
3. Select **Find** from the Formula menu.

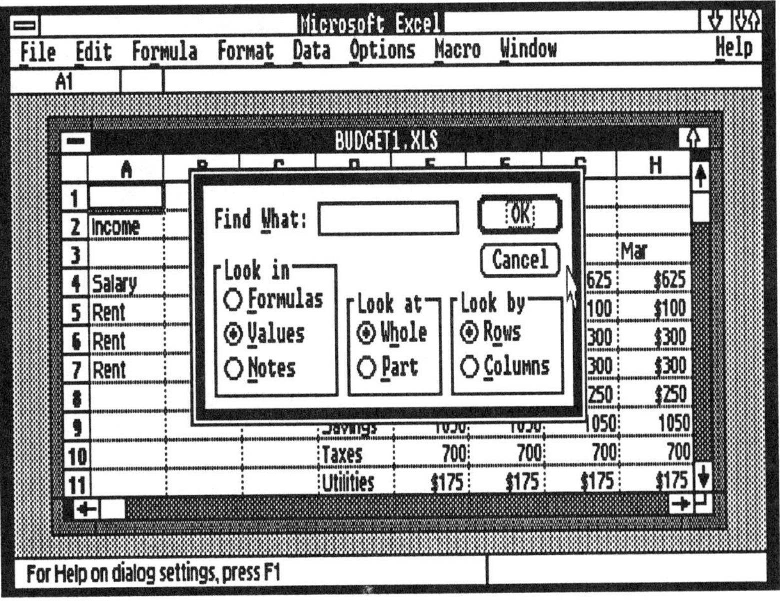

4. Type **Exp**, mark **Values**, **Whole**, and press **Enter**.

The result is no match because Excel was looking for a whole string called "exp" and none existed on the worksheet.

5. Pick **OK** and select **Find** again.

6. Pick **Part** and press **Enter**. Now Excel is able to find the desired string. It is always safer to designate Part if you are uncertain.

7. Select **Find**, pick **Formulas**, and press **Enter**. Excel still finds the string.

8. Select **Find**, type **$B**, and pick the **Values** option.

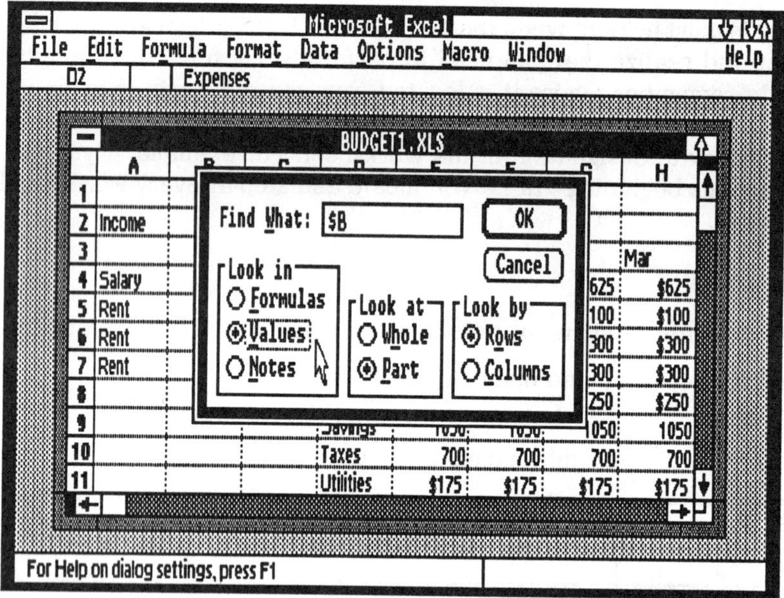

9. Press **Enter**. The result is no match. Press **Enter**.

10. Select **Find**, reactivate **Formulas**, and press **Enter**. This time Excel finds one of the formulas in the worksheet that contains the $B.

11. Exit Excel, or continue your work session with the active worksheet.

12. Turn to Module 55 to continue the learning sequence.

Module 26

FONT

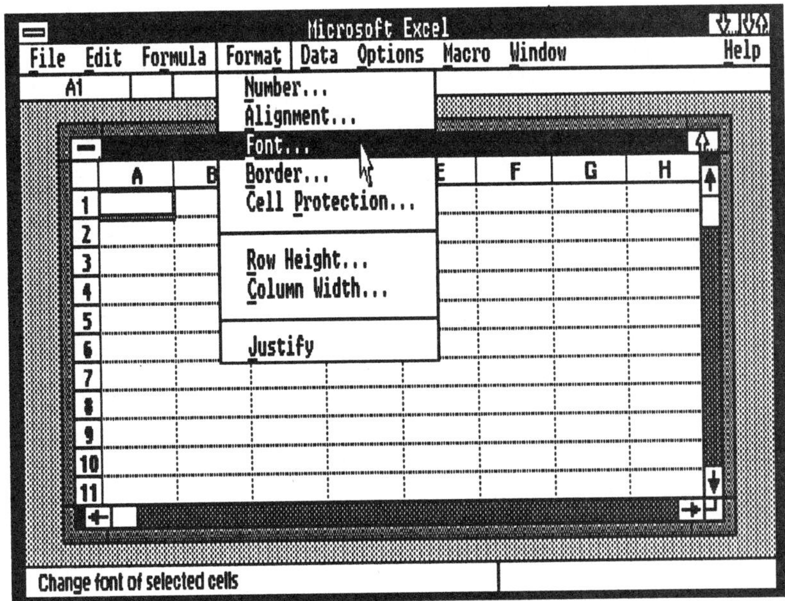

DESCRIPTION

Excel allows you to use a maximum of four fonts or type styles in a worksheet. You select the Font command from the Format menu with the mouse, or press Alt-T F. The following dialog box is displayed.

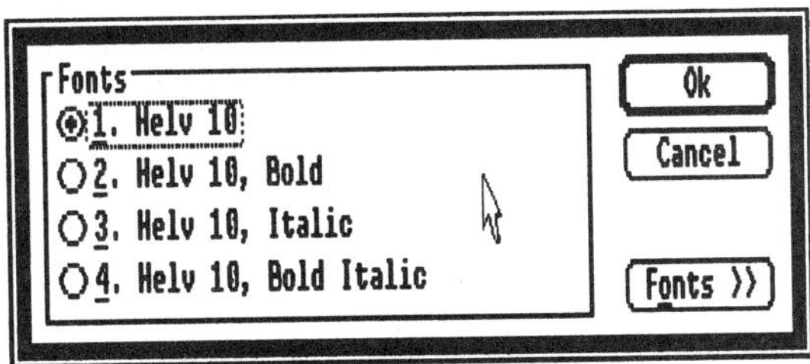

The font designated as 1 is the default font. All text in the worksheet starts as font 1. Changing font 1 changes all text in a worksheet. In this display, Excel is set to use four variations of 10 point (72 points make an inch) Helvetica type. Fonts 2, 3, and 4 are assigned to selected rows, columns, regions, or cells. Changes in their definitions modify only the selected cells.

If you want to use a different family of fonts or different sizes or styles of fonts, first pick the font you want to change, then pick the Fonts button on the dialog box to display the available options.

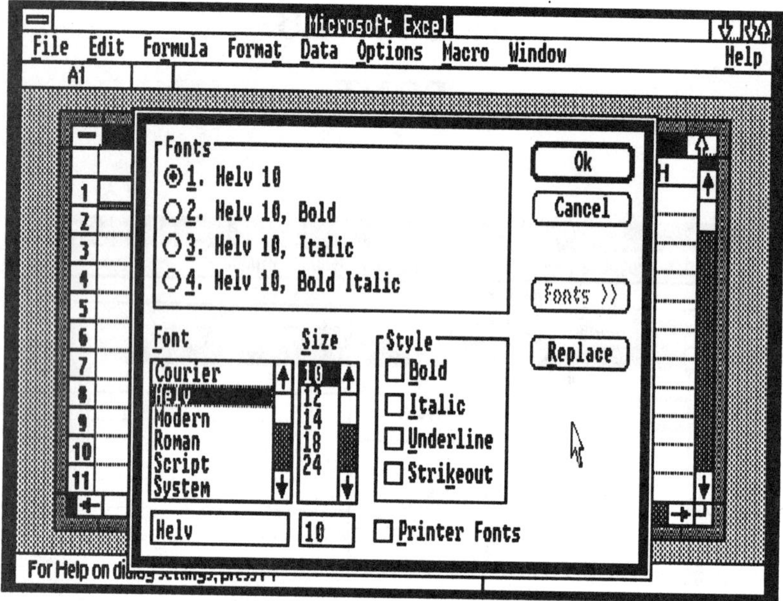

Pick the Font, the Size, and the Style in the respective check boxes. Then pick Replace to substitute that font specification for the previously selected font.

When you select the Printer Fonts check box, you then select the font groups you desire for fonts 1 through 4 for use on the printer. The fonts may or may not be the same as are available for the screen, depending on the capability of your printer, your graphics system, and any modifications you have made to the fonts through Microsoft Windows.

APPLICATIONS

The use of different fonts to convey information beyond the strict transmission of data has been common practice for centuries. The Fonts command is one of the commands that places Excel above many competing products, allowing it to produce output on the screen for large-screen presentations, or on paper for distribution that looks professionally typeset.

Font selection is both a matter of personal preference and good taste. The conservative default fonts of Excel are normally a safe bet. Changing the font to conform to one matching an official company font helps to make a statement about the unity of your company's message.

However, using difficult-to-read fonts may add confusion to your presentation. Mixing multiple fonts of different styles makes the same statement about your written communications as wearing a striped tie, a plaid shirt, and checked pants together makes about your dress.

TYPICAL OPERATION

In this session you change the screen fonts used for the INTEREST.XLS worksheet that you used most recently in the Alignment module.

1. Start Excel and open INTEREST.XLS, or continue your work session from the previous module.

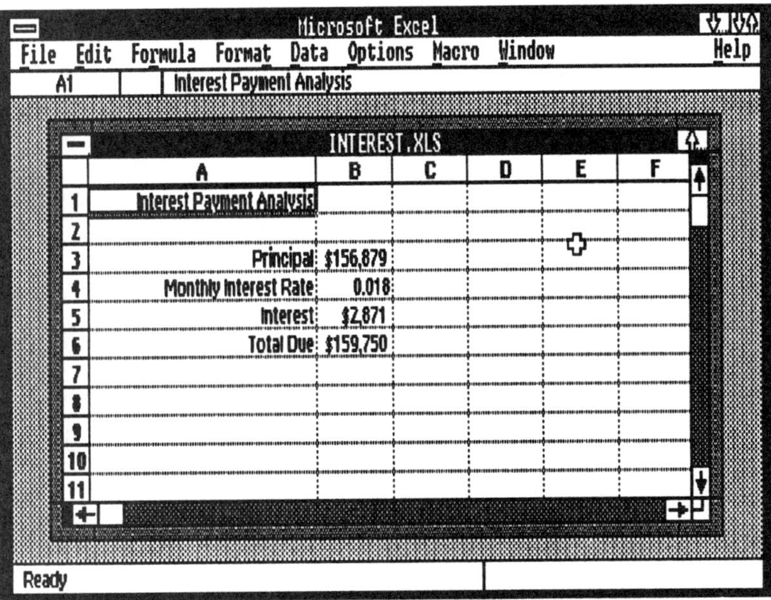

2. Select **Font** from the Format menu, then pick **Fonts** from the dialog box.

3. Pick **12** as the new font size.

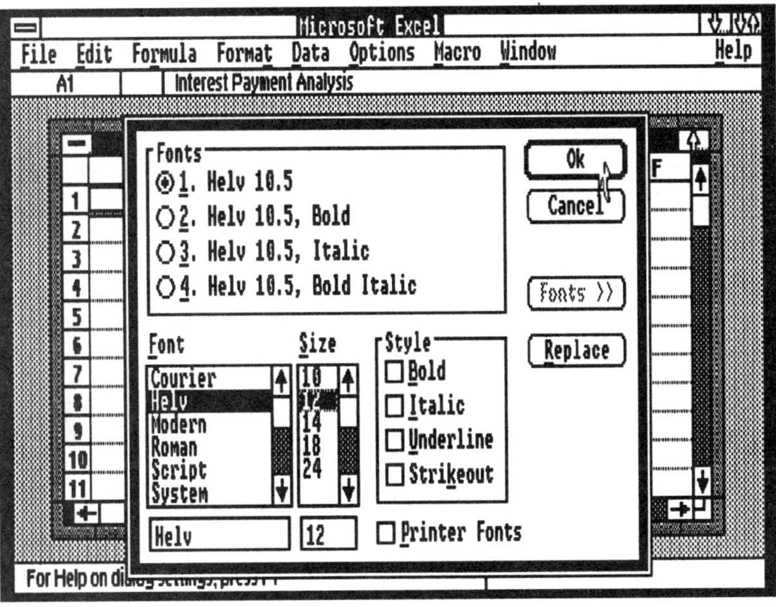

4. Pick **OK**. Notice the larger size of the text and numbers.

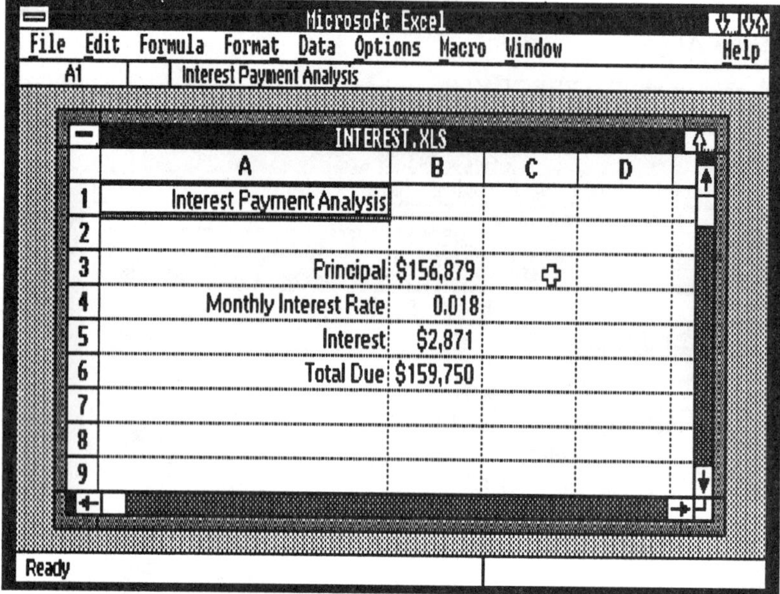

5. With cell A1 selected, pick **Font** from the Format menu.
6. Pick **2** in the dialog box, then pick **Fonts**. Specify **24** as Size.

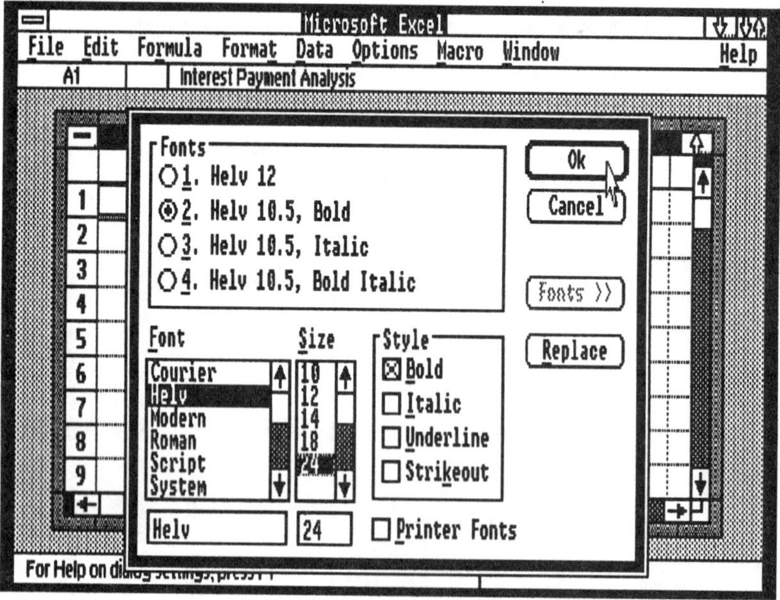

7. Pick **OK**.

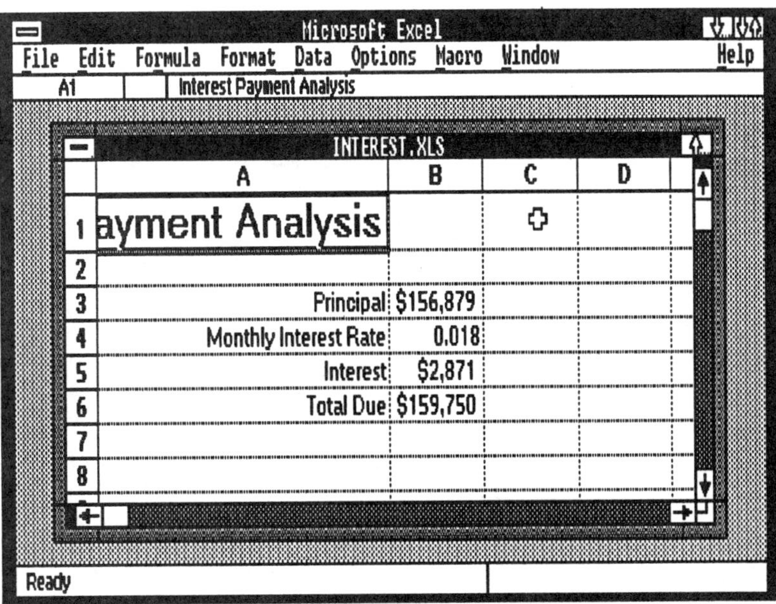

When right-aligned in cell A1, the title text does not fit on the worksheet.

8. With cell A1 selected, pick **Alignment** from the Format menu.

9. Pick **Left** on the dialog box.

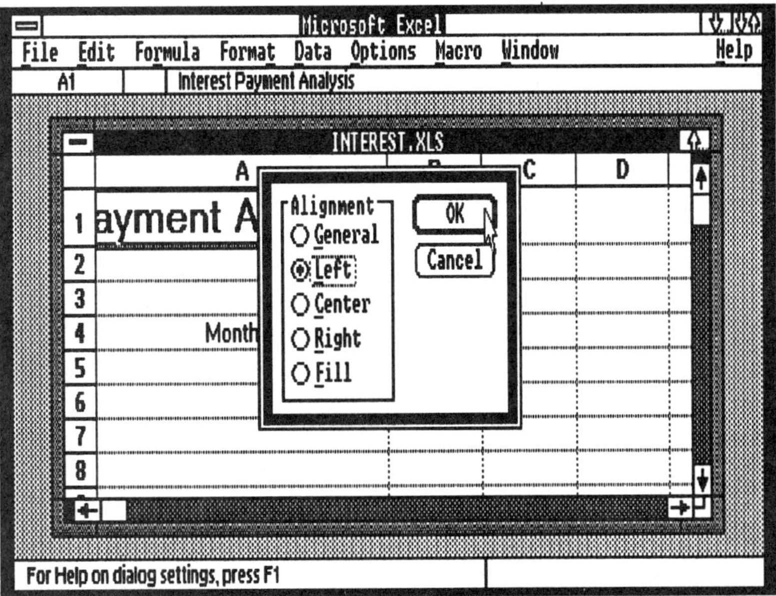

10. Pick **OK**.

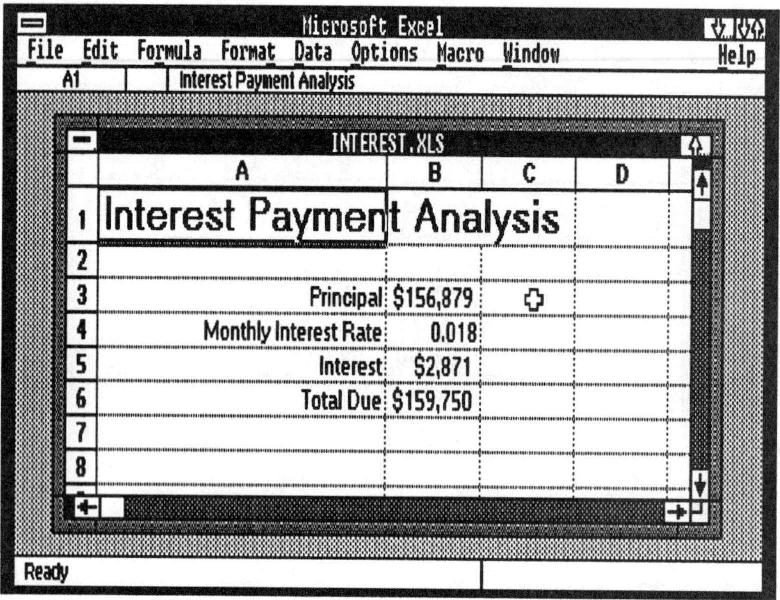

11. Save the worksheet and exit Excel, or continue the learning sequence immediately with Module 34.

Module 27

FORM

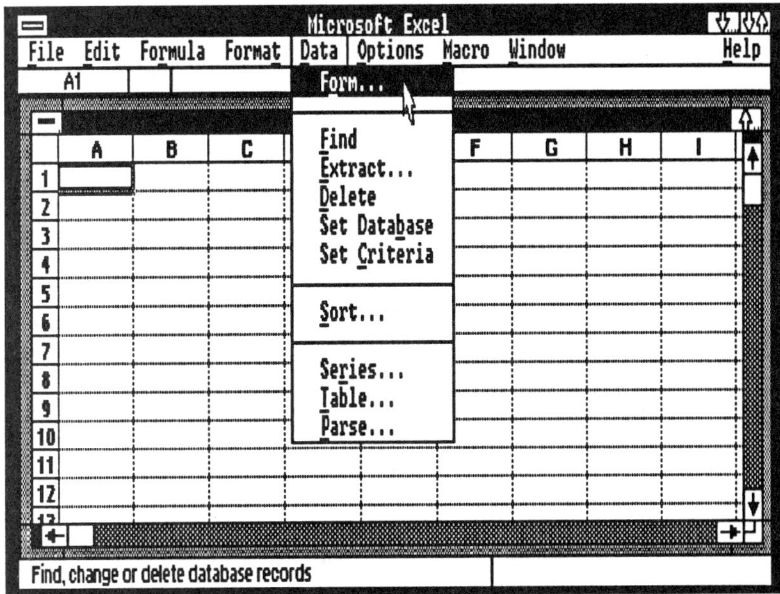

DESCRIPTION

The Form command on the Data menu creates a data input form in a window for use with an Excel database. To use the Form command you must first define the database with the Set Database command. Then you can select the Form command with the mouse or by pressing Alt-D O.

The Form command assumes that the first row of the database contains the field names and uses them for the field names in the generated input form window. The command establishes the width of each field on the form from the field width used in the worksheet. It also establishes the data type as a label, date, number, or formula by inspection of the values currently in the database.

When you use the Form command to add new records to a database, make certain that you have provided blank records within the range defined with the Set Database command. If you attempt to add records beyond the range of the Set Database definition, the results are unpredictable and potentially unpleasant.

The Form command allows you to view the records in the database one at a time. You step through the database, selecting the Find Prev and Find Next options to step forward and backward through the data. If you have used the Set Criteria command to establish selection criteria, the Form command respects the selection criteria as you step through the data. Otherwise, it moves sequentially through all the data.

A delete button is provided on the form window to allow you to delete the current database record. Once the record is gone, it's gone. There is no undo.

APPLICATIONS

There is nothing keeping you from typing data into a database with the ordinary worksheet data entry procedures. However, using a data entry form can make the process less prone to error. It is also an excellent technique when delegating data entry tasks to personnel with limited computer skills and/or spreadsheet savvy.

It is especially valuable when the database is wider than is easily displayed on the screen. The Form command allows you to organize more than a single screen-width of data on a data entry form, speeding the data entry process.

TYPICAL OPERATION

In this session you create a data entry form based on the camping equipment inventory you created in the Set Database module. If the worksheet INVENT.XLS, created in that module, is not on your disk, return to the Set Database module and create the worksheet.

1. Start Excel and open the INVENT.XLS worksheet, or continue your work session from the previous module.

2. Maximize the size of the worksheet.

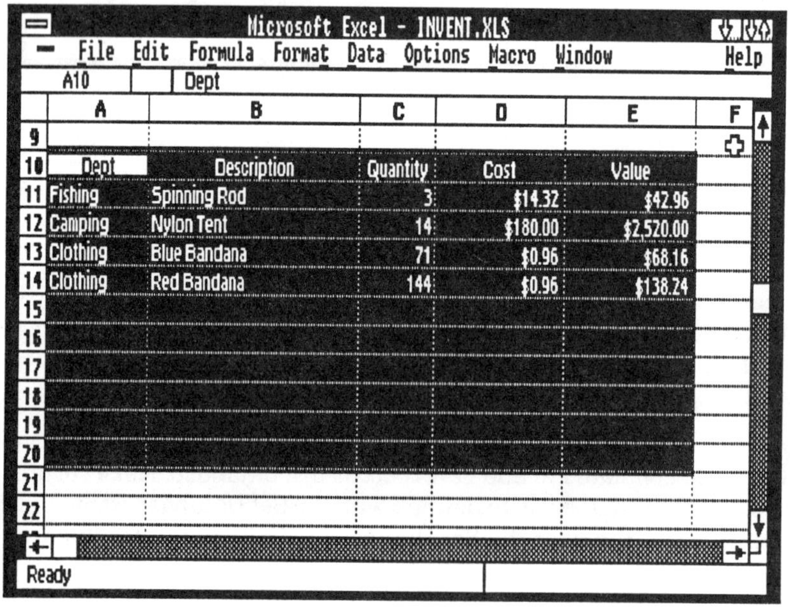

```
Microsoft Excel - INVENT.XLS
File  Edit  Formula  Format  Data  Options  Macro  Window          Help
A10          Dept
```

	Dept	Description	Quantity	Cost	Value
11	Fishing	Spinning Rod	3	$14.32	$42.96
12	Camping	Nylon Tent	14	$180.00	$2,520.00
13	Clothing	Blue Bandana	71	$0.96	$68.16
14	Clothing	Red Bandana	144	$0.96	$138.24

In the Typical Operation session for the Set Database module you defined the database as the region with cell A10 as the upper left corner and E20 as the lower right corner. When you saved the worksheet, that specification was saved with the worksheet and is still current.

3. Select **Form** from the Data menu.

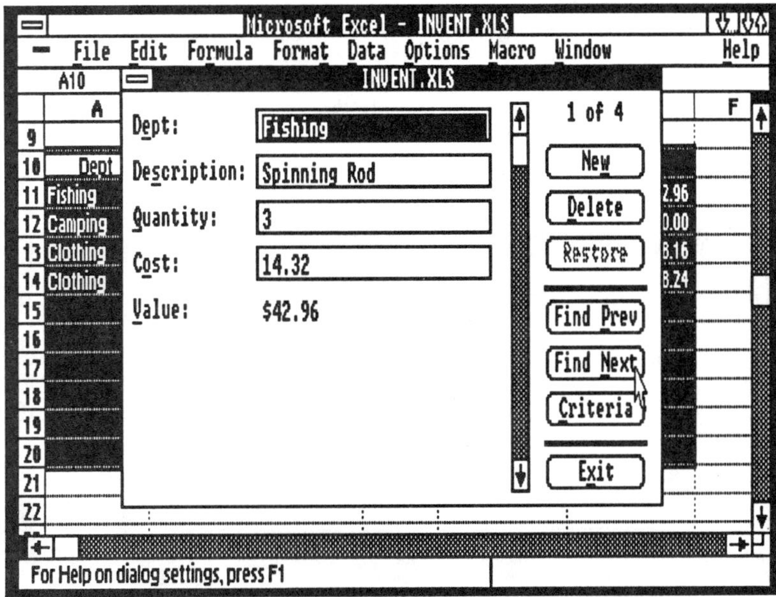

The values from the first record appear on Excel's Form window.

Notice in the upper right corner the notation "1 of 4" indicating that you are viewing the first of 4 records in the database.

4.   Select **Find Next** to view the second record of the database.

The record containing the Nylon Tents is displayed from row 12 of the worksheet, the second record of the defined database.

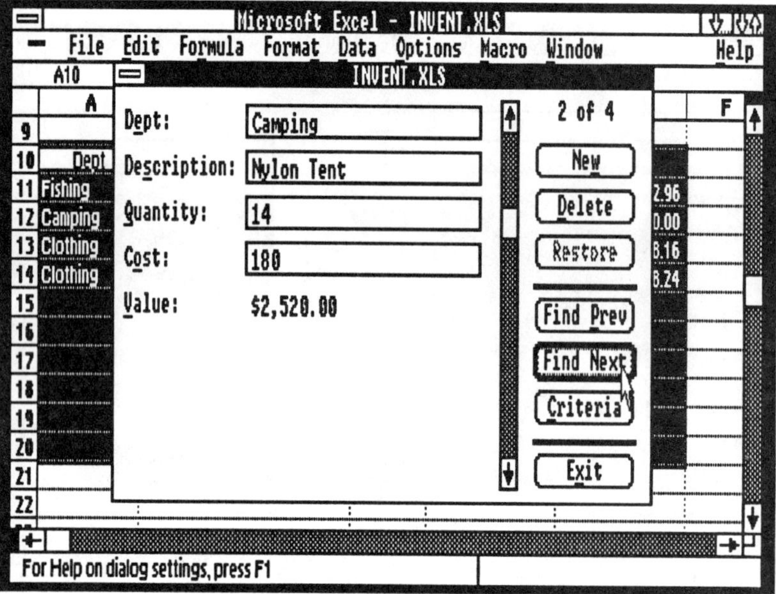

5.   Select **Delete** to delete the current (second) record from the database.

Excel warns you that the deletion is permanent.

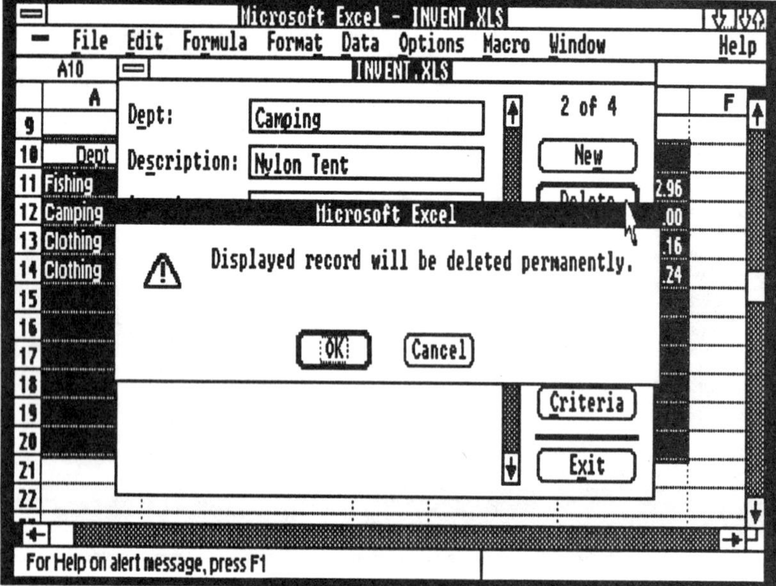

6.   Select **OK** to accept the deletion.

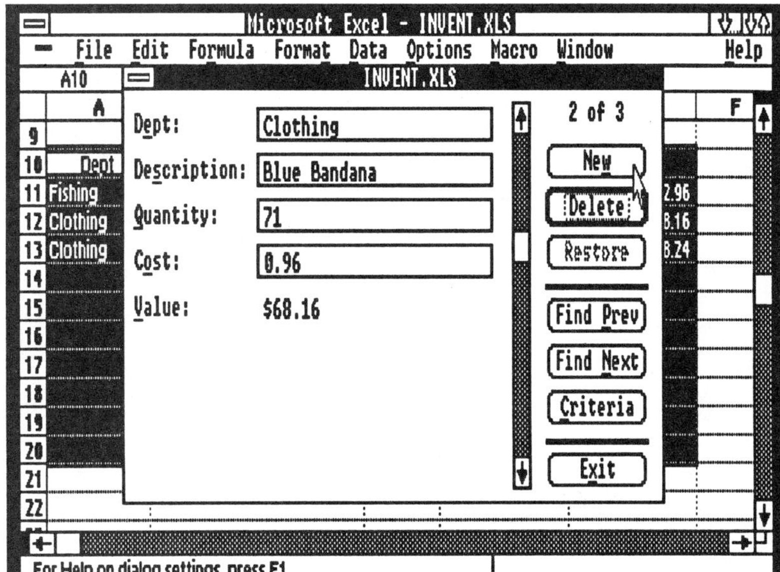

In the window behind the data form you can see that the remaining data in the database moved up to fill the space formerly occupied by the deleted record. What was record number three is moved to the number two position, appearing both in the second position in the underlying database and on the data form.

7.   Select **New** to add a record to the database.

The legend "New Record" replaces "2 of 3" in the upper right corner of the data form. This reminds you that you are ready to add data to the end of the database.

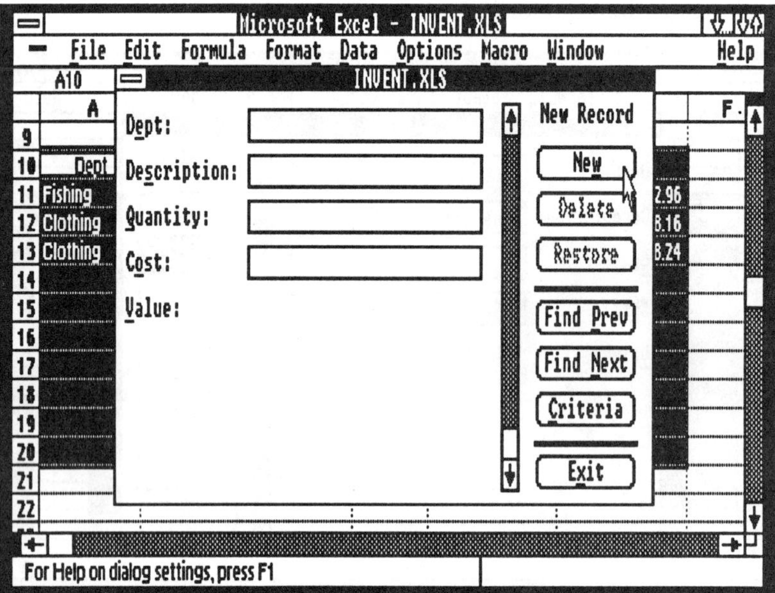

8. Add the Mountain Tent to the inventory as shown in the following screen. When moving from field to field you can either use the mouse to position the cursor or press **Tab**. (Do not press Enter to move between fields.)

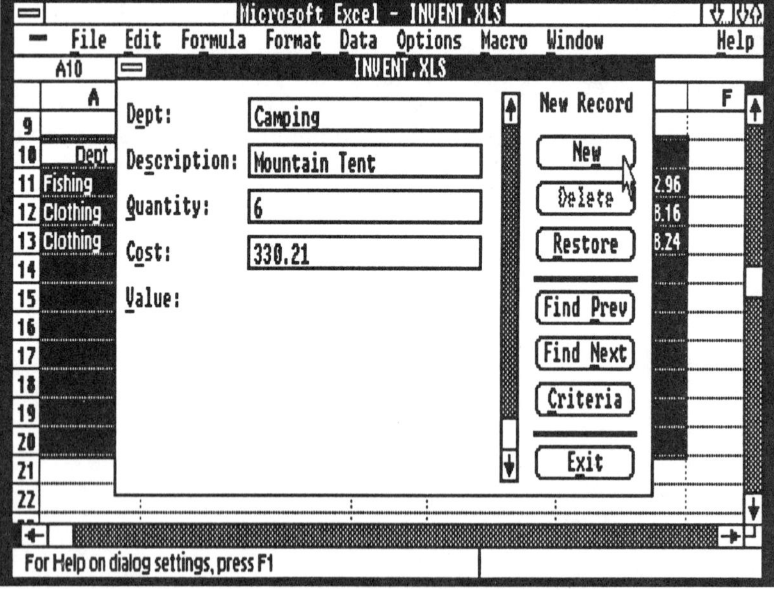

9. Press **Enter** to accept the entry. The Mountain Tent is added at the end of the database range.

10. Select **New** and add Rain Jacket as shown in the following screen.

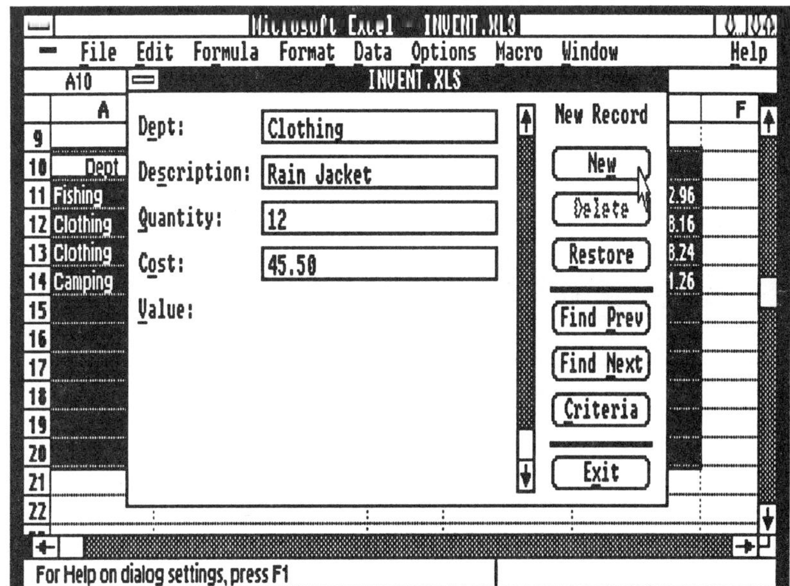

11. Select **Exit** to accept the entry and return to the worksheet.

12. Select **Save** from the File menu to save the revised camping equipment inventory. You need this worksheet next in the Sort module.

13. Exit Excel, or continue your work session with the active worksheet on the screen.

14. Turn to Module 68 to continue the learning sequence.

Module 28
FORMAT (CHART)

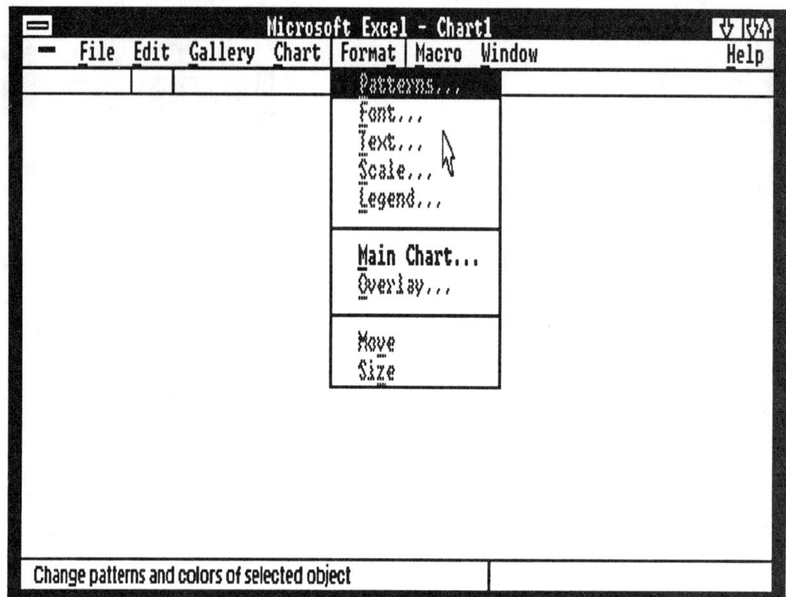

DESCRIPTION

The Format menu allows you to change patterns, fonts, and scale, and to move and size components of the chart. If more then one chart is to be created, each can be sized and moved to different locations on the screen. Sometimes you may experiment with different charts to determine which one presents the data best.

This Format menu is only available if the active worksheet is a chart. It is accessed with Alt-T. A menu is then available that permits you to change various aspects of the chart or size and move components of the chart. You can make these changes to either the Main chart or the Overlay chart. Each option in this command provides a dialog box with additional options that are available to you at that point.

APPLICATIONS

This command will permit you to create your own unique chart. You will begin with a standard chart and then make modifications until it provides exactly the information in the way you desire. This ability to customize your chart makes the use of charts as a data display format very useful.

TYPICAL OPERATION

In this operation you change the standard chart display. This operation continues the activities from Module 10, Chart. Your beginning chart should have an arrow attached as in the last screen display in Module 10.

1.   Select **Move** from the Format menu. Press **Right Arrow** forty times and press **Down Arrow** three times. Then press **Enter**.

2.   Select **Size** from the Format menu. Use the **Left, Right** and **Up Arrows** to shorten the arrow and change its direction, as illustrated in the following screen display, and press **Enter**. (Control-Arrow is a finer movement.)

If you use a mouse, you need only click on the arrow, drag it to its new location, and size it.

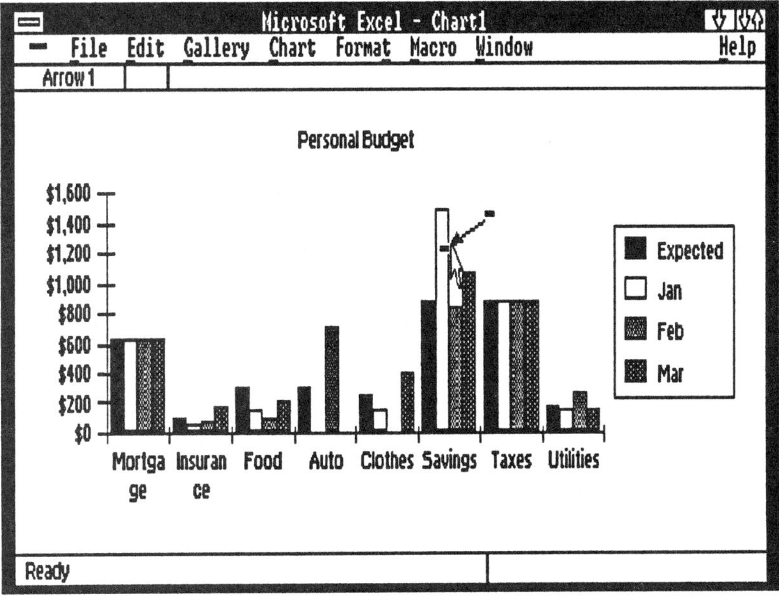

3.   Type **Good Month** and press **Enter**. This Unattached Text has been placed somewhere on the chart. Use the mouse or the **Move** command to position the text by the end of the arrow and press **Enter**.

4.   Pick **Select Chart** from the Chart menu.

5. Select **Font** from the Format menu.

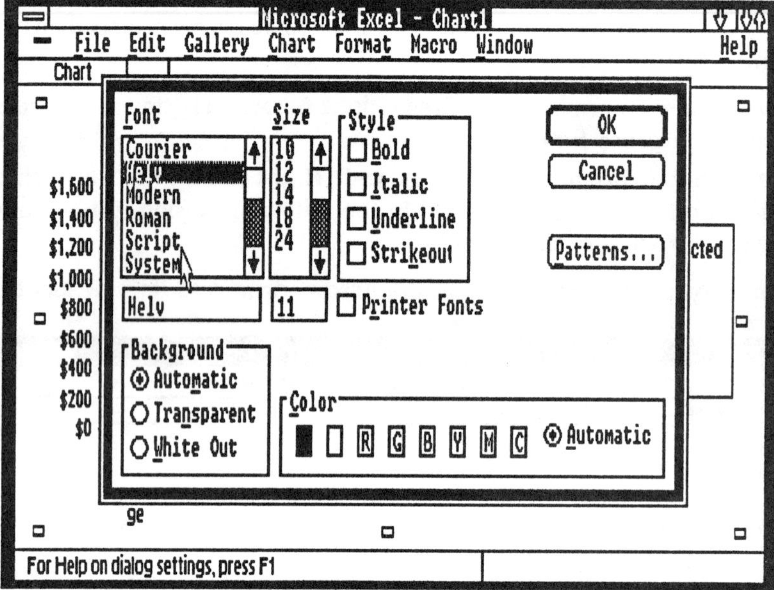

The options of the dialog box permit you to make style changes in the chart. The dialog boxes
in this menu are interrelated. Selecting some options in this dialog box will permit you to do
the same operations as selecting that option from the menu.

You can change fonts, style, and color. You can make the background white or transparent. Some
of these options may depend on the type of printer you have available. If you select Patterns
or Text, Excel will show you the dialog boxes associated with those commands from the Format
menu.

6. Select **Script** and press **Enter**.

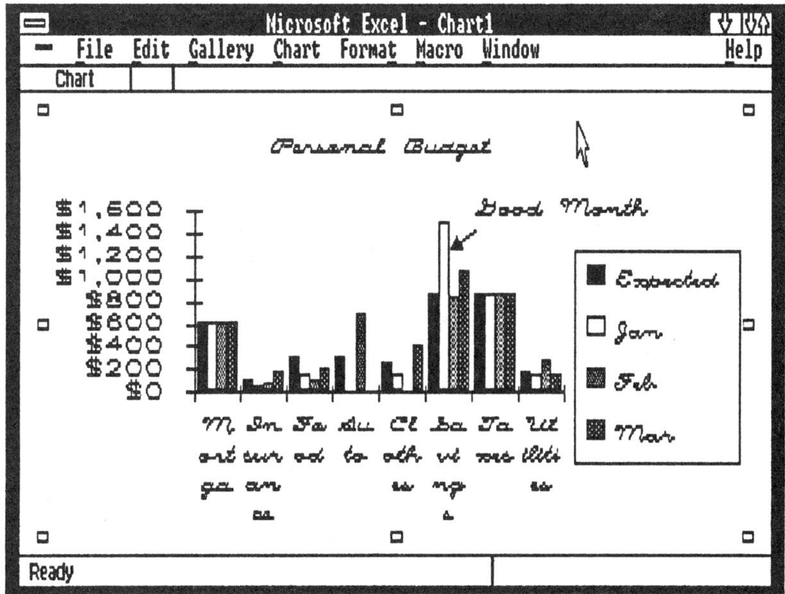

7. Return to **Helv** style by accessing **Font** from the Format menu.
8. Select **Patterns** from the Format menu.

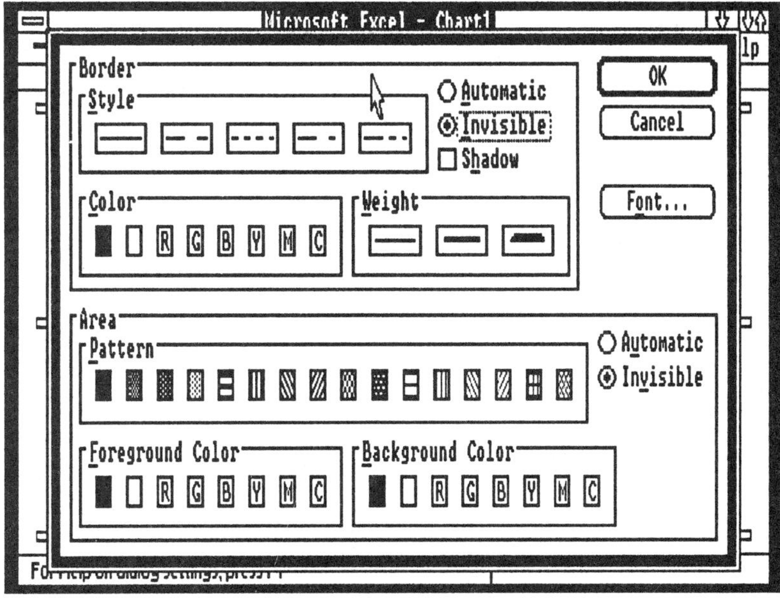

The options in this dialog box permit you to change colors of the chart and border styles and lines. The Automatic option uses the existing selections to the data points. The Invisible option removes a selected option from the chart. You can change the foreground or background colors independently. You can have the chart show negative values with inverted pattern shading. The Font option is the same as in the Format menu.

9.   Select the dotted border style and press **Enter**.

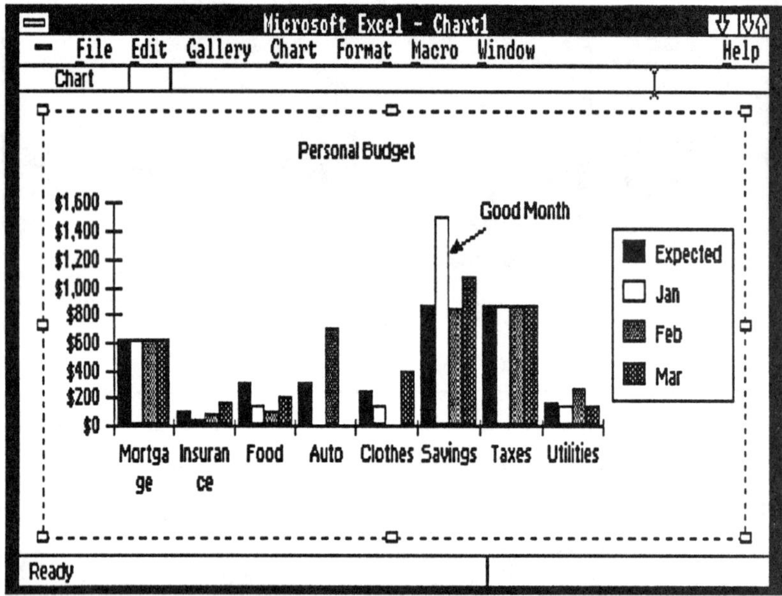

10.   Select the chart title by clicking on it with the mouse, or press **Up Arrow** repeatedly until the chart title is surrounded by six small boxes indicating its selection.

11. Select **Text** from the Format menu.

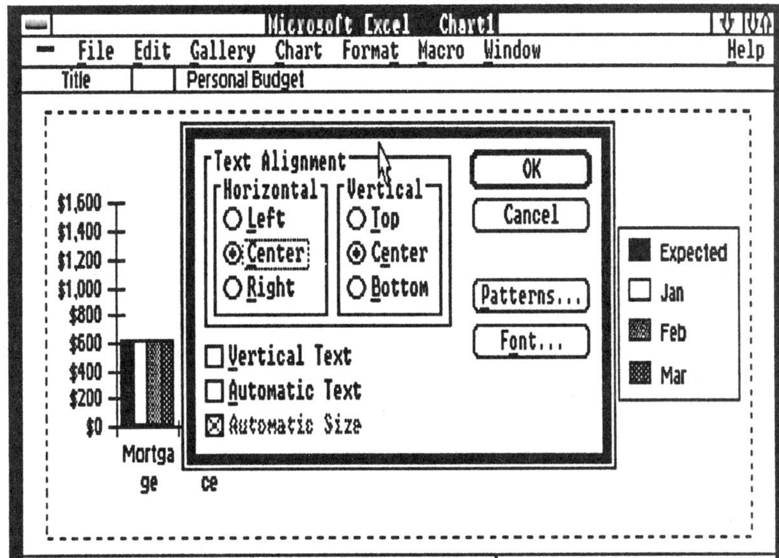

The options available to you are associated with modifying selected text. With Text Alignment, you can align text horizontally and vertically. The Vertical Text option formats the text vertically. The Automatic Text option displays the contents of worksheet cells as chart text. Automatic Size places a border around the text.

12. Select **Left** for Horizontal and **Bottom** for Vertical in the Text Alignment area. Select **Vertical Text** and press **Enter**.

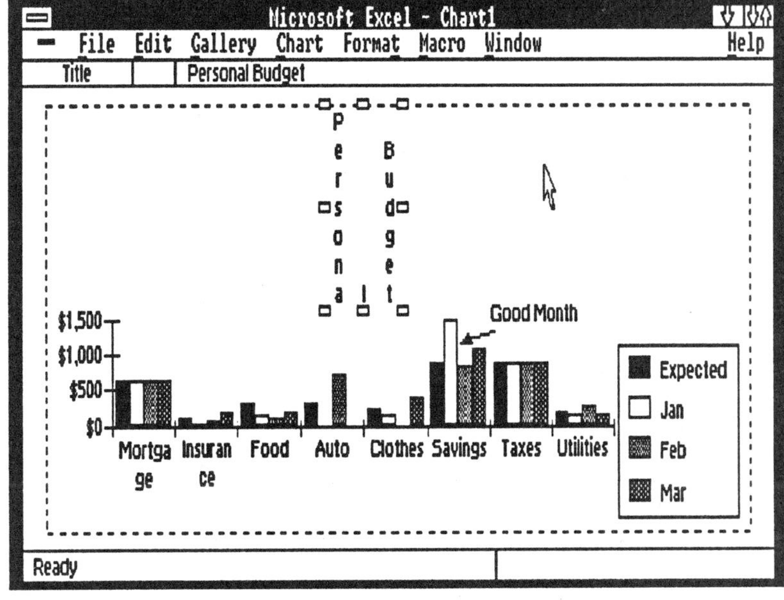

13. Since this doesn't look very good, go back to the Text option and turn off the Vertical Text and press **Enter**.

14. Pick the vertical axis with the mouse, or press **Up Arrow** several times until the Value or vertical axis is surrounded with little boxes.

15. Select **Scale** from the Format menu.

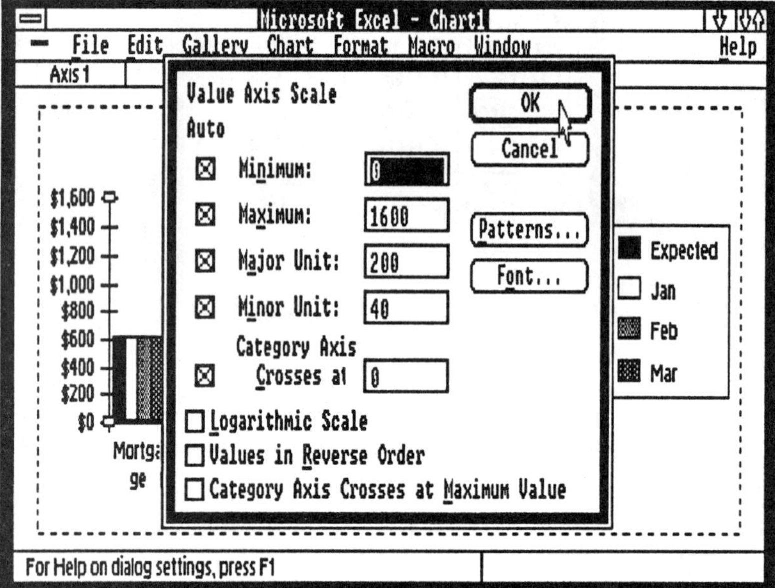

This dialog box is associated with the Value axis. A different dialog box is provided for the Category axis. These options permit you to set the beginning and ending point of the value axis. In the current setting it ranges from 0 to 1600. The values increase in units of 200 and the two axes cross at 0.

16. Activate **Values in Reverse Order** and press **Enter**.

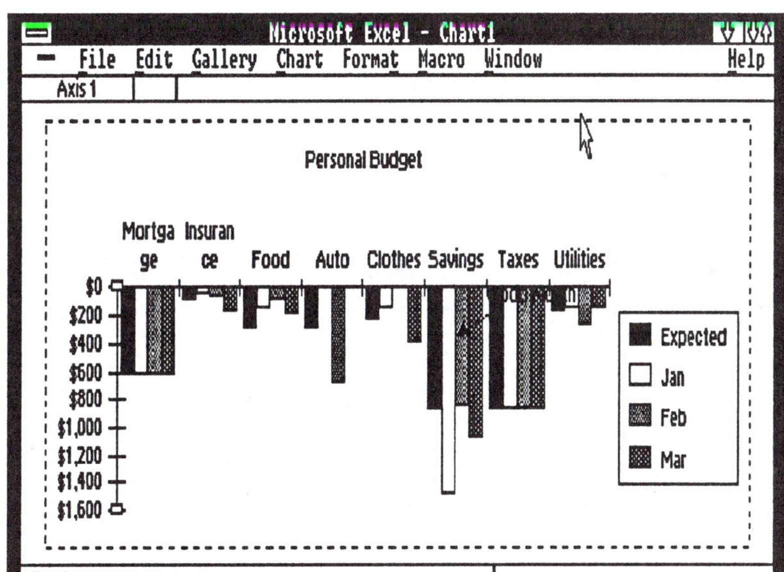

You can perform similar functions with the Category axis.

17. Return the chart to its original configuration by removing the check from **Values in Reverse Order** on the Scale dialog box from the Format menu and picking **OK**.

18. Select **Main Chart** from the Format menu.

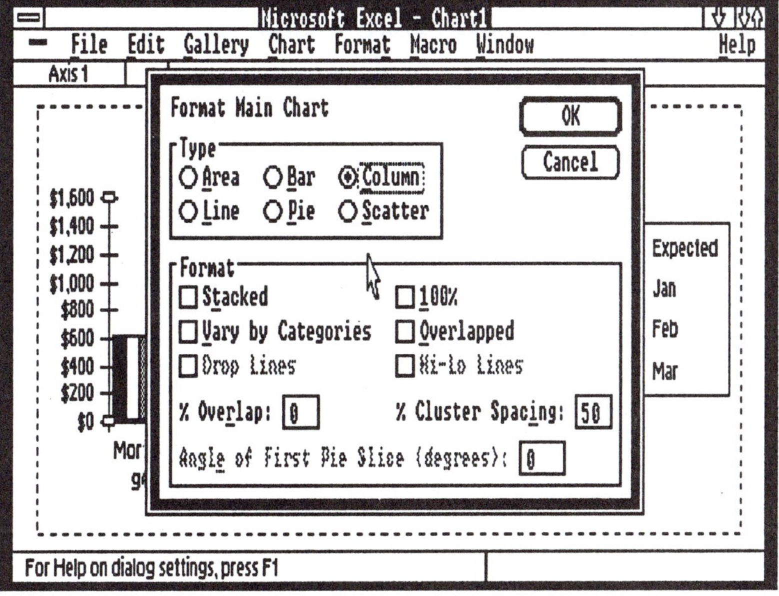

This option functions much like the Gallery menu, except that the Gallery menu provides you several standard selections, and the Main Chart option lets you customize your chart. You can change the type of chart, stack the data, or vary it by category. This last option is used when you only have one data set. The 100% option forces the values in each category to add to 100%. The Overlapped option overlaps the columns. The Drop Lines and Hi-Lo lines will produce charts like those available in the Gallery menu. You can also specify the angle of the first pie slice if you are using a Pie chart. Finally, you can specify the distance you want between clusters.

19.   Select **Stacked** and press **Enter**.

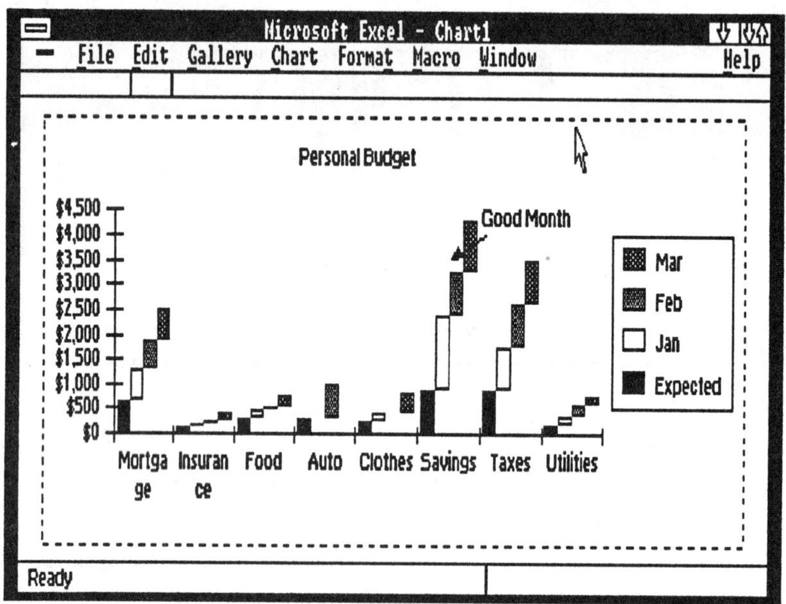

20. Select **Main Chart** from the Format menu, undo the Stacked option, select **Overlapped**, type **500** in the % Overlap box, and press **Enter**.

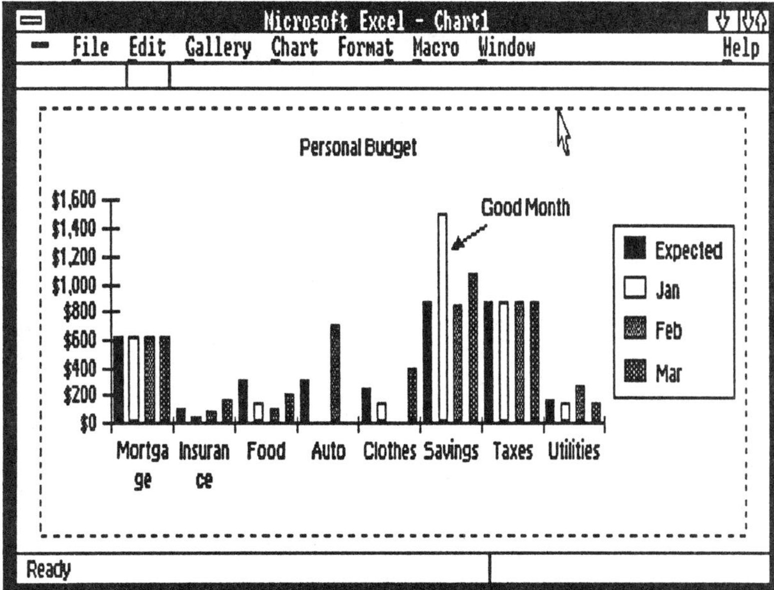

Remove the overlap from the Main Chart by clicking in the Overlapped box to remove the X.

The Overlay option in the Format menu is similar to the Main Chart option. It is only active if there is an overlay chart in use. It permits you to change parts of the overlay chart.

21. Select **Add Overlay** from the Chart menu.

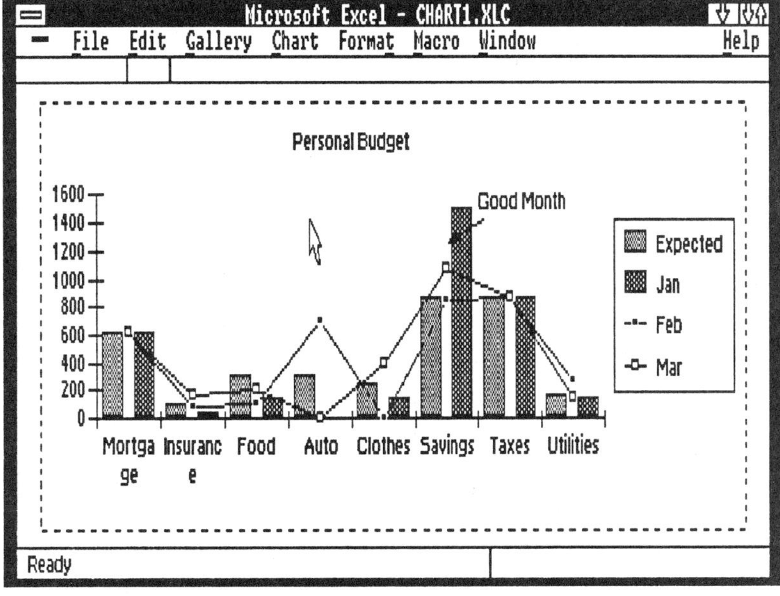

22. Select **Overlay** from the Format menu.

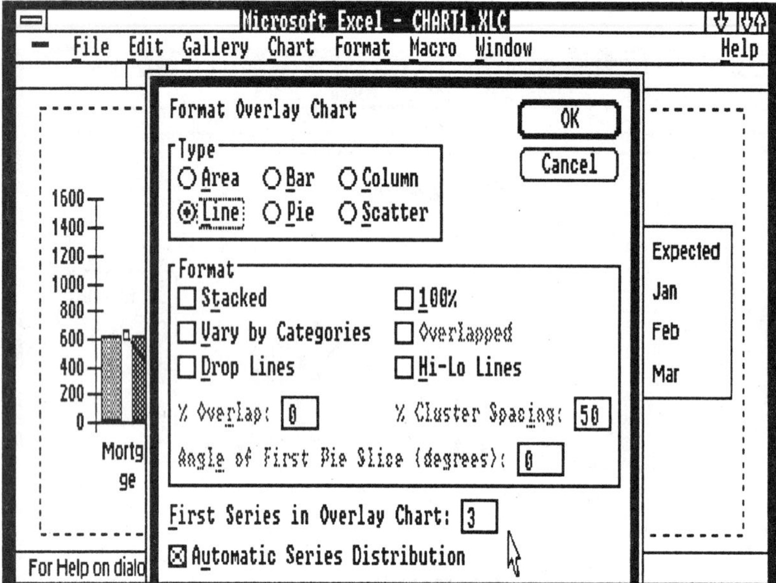

The illustrated screen is very similar to the one you have already used. Two exceptions are at the bottom. First Series in the Overlay Chart indicates at what data point the overlay chart begins. The Automatic Series Distribution equally divides the data between the overlay and main chart.

23. Type **1** to replace the 3 in the First Series in Overlay Chart and press **Enter**.

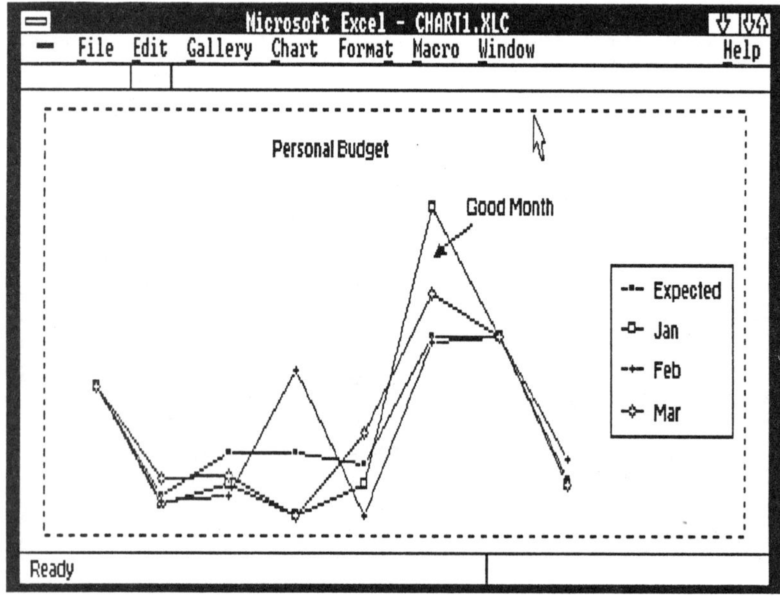

All of the data is now in the overlay chart.

The Legend command permits you to change the legend. There are four options in the dialog box. The Top and Bottom option places the legend in the those respective locations. The Corner option places the legend in the upper right corner of the chart. The Vertical option places the legend on the right of the chart.

Experiment with the various options in these menus and when you are finished, close the chart.

24. Close the chart. It is not needed again in the learning sequence. You may, however, choose to save it for future reference.

25. Save BUDGET1.XLS. Exit Excel, or continue the learning sequence with BUDGET1.XLS as the active worksheet.

26. Turn to Module 8 to continue the learning sequence.

Module 29

FREEZE PANES/UNFREEZE PANES

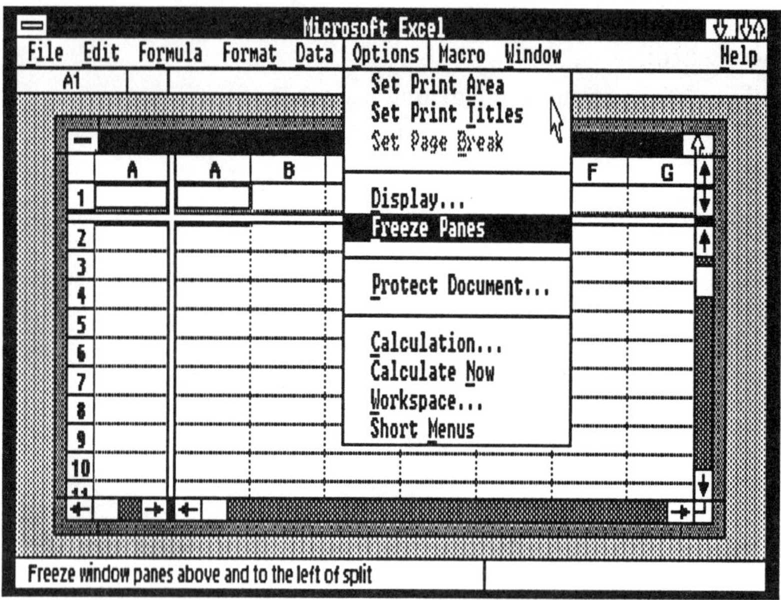

DESCRIPTION

When you use the Split command to divide the screens into two or four parts, each part is called a *pane*. When you scroll the worksheet in one of the panes, the adjacent horizontal or vertical view also scrolls. To defeat this scrolling action, first select the worksheet pane to lock into position, then select the Freeze Panes command from the Options menu using the mouse or by pressing Alt-O F. When panes are frozen, the dividing line between the regions changes, as shown in the following screen.

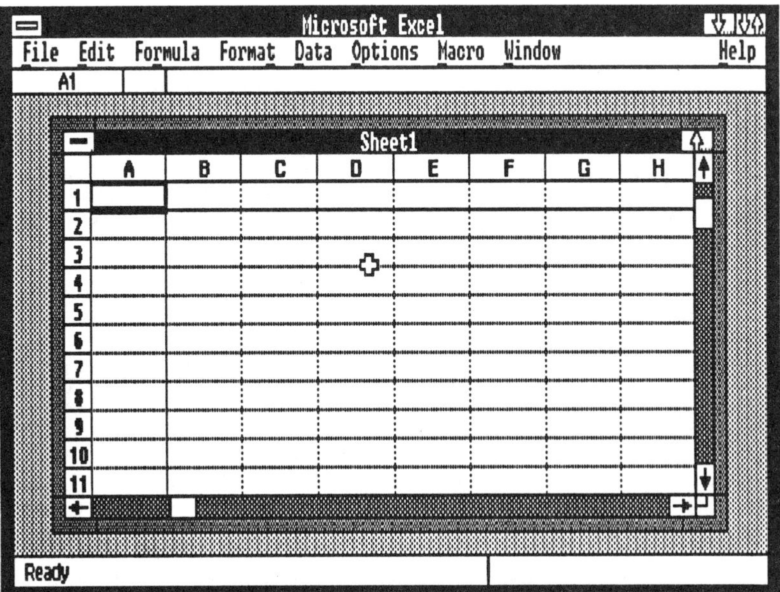

In this example, the pane containing cell A1 was frozen with the Freeze Panes command. This forces row 1 and column A to remain on the screen when the display scrolls. For example, moving the cell selector to X44 produces the following display.

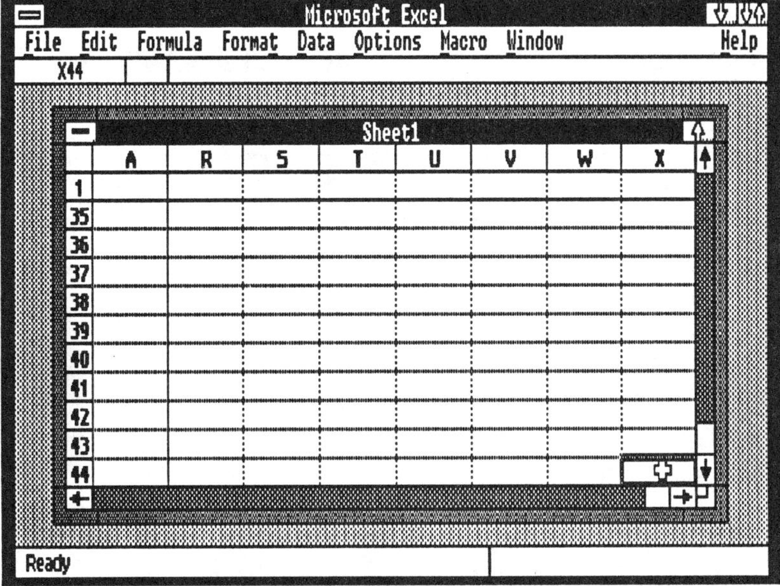

Notice that row 1 and column A remain visible on the screen.

When you select Freeze Panes from the Option menu, the Freeze Panes command is replaced by the Unfreeze Panes command, as shown in the following display.

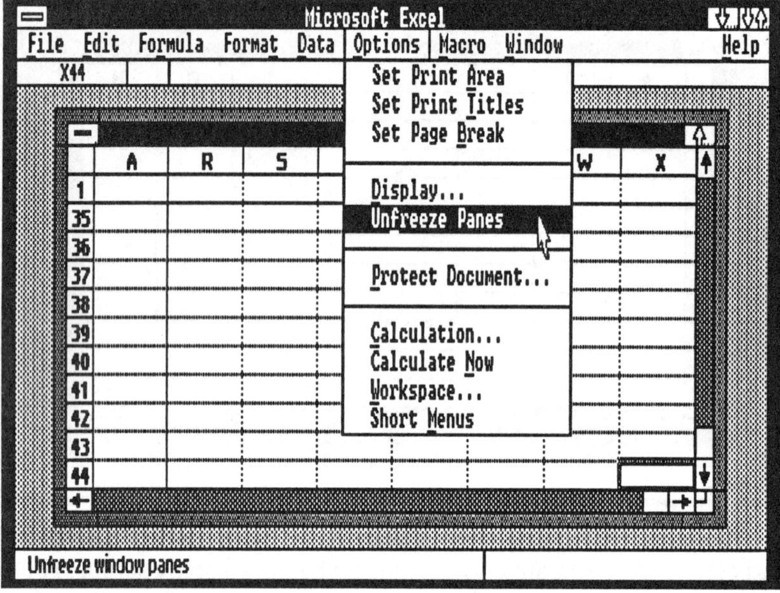

Select Unfreeze Panes from the Option menu to return the worksheet to its split configuration, as shown in the following screen.

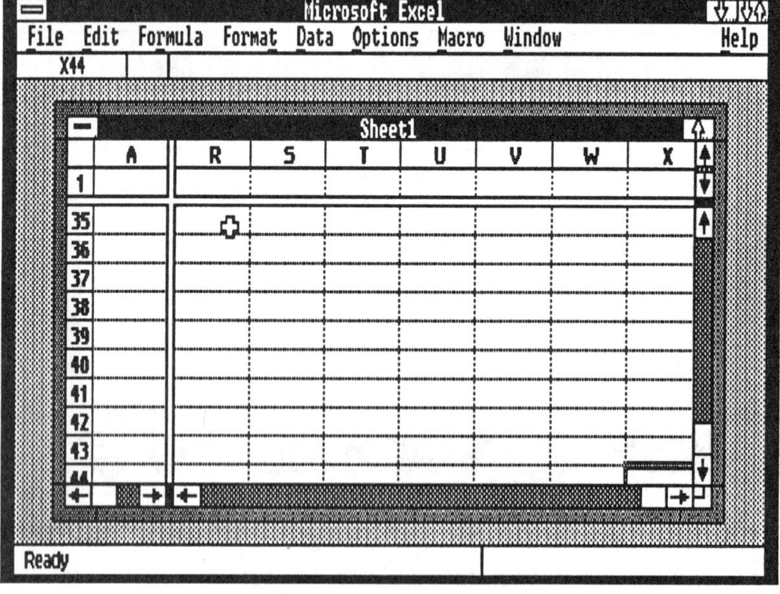

APPLICATIONS

The Freeze Panes command is excellent for "permanently" locking titles on the screen. Split the screen immediately below, above, or to the side of the title area, select the title pane, then select Freeze Panes from the Options menu.

To create both horizontal and vertical titles: 1. Split the worksheet into four panes, where the row and column of titles each occupy a pane. 2. Select the cell where the row and column of titles meet. 3. Select Freeze Panes from the Options menu.

To create titles in the horizontal or vertical direction only: 1. Split the worksheet into two panes, where the row or column of titles occupy a pane. 2. Select the row or column containing the titles. 3. Select Freeze Panes from the Options menu.

TYPICAL OPERATION

In this session you use the Freeze Panes operation to lock titles in place.

1. Start Excel, or continue your work session from the previous module.
2. Open GASOLINE.XLS, created in the Table module, and expand the worksheet to fill the screen.
3. Scroll the worksheet to place cell B3 in the upper left corner of the screen.

	Microsoft Excel − GASOLINE.XLS								
File	Edit	Formula	Format	Data	Options	Macro	Window		Help

B3		=1000/B2*B1							
	B	C	D	E	F	G	H	I	J
3	40.00	14	16	18	20	22	24	26	28
4	0.70	$50	$44	$39	$35	$32	$29	$27	$25
5	0.75	$54	$47	$42	$38	$34	$31	$29	$27
6	0.80	$57	$50	$44	$40	$36	$33	$31	$29
7	0.85	$61	$53	$47	$43	$39	$35	$33	$30
8	0.90	$64	$56	$50	$45	$41	$38	$35	$32
9	0.95	$68	$59	$53	$48	$43	$40	$37	$34
10	1.00	$71	$63	$56	$50	$45	$42	$38	$36
11	1.05	$75	$66	$58	$53	$48	$44	$40	$38
12	1.10	$79	$69	$61	$55	$50	$46	$42	$39
13	1.15	$82	$72	$64	$58	$52	$48	$44	$41
14	1.20	$86	$75	$67	$60	$55	$50	$46	$43
15	1.25	$89	$78	$69	$63	$57	$52	$48	$45
16	1.30	$93	$81	$72	$65	$59	$54	$50	$46

Ready

Notice that the GASOLINE.XLS worksheet Control menu icon is located in the upper left corner of the worksheet. It is just to the left of the File menu selector and just below the Excel Control menu icon.

4. Click on the GASOLINE.XLS worksheet Control menu icon, or press **Alt-Hyphen**.

```
 Microsoft Excel - GASOLINE.XLS
 File  Edit  Formula  Format  Data  Options  Macro  Window          Help

  Restore   Ctrl+F5  /B2*B1
  Move      Ctrl+F7   D      E      F      G      H      I      J
  Size      Ctrl+F8
  Maximize  Ctrl+F10
  Close     Ctrl+F4
  Split

 Split window into two or four panes
```

	D	E	F	G	H	I	J
	16	18	20	22	24	26	28
	$44	$39	$35	$32	$29	$27	$25
	$47	$42	$38	$34	$31	$29	$27
	$50	$44	$40	$36	$33	$31	$29
	$53	$47	$43	$39	$35	$33	$30
	$56	$50	$45	$41	$38	$35	$32
9 0.95 $68	$59	$53	$48	$43	$40	$37	$34
10 1.00 $71	$63	$56	$50	$45	$42	$38	$36
11 1.05 $75	$66	$58	$53	$48	$44	$40	$38
12 1.10 $79	$69	$61	$55	$50	$46	$42	$39
13 1.15 $82	$72	$64	$58	$52	$48	$44	$41
14 1.20 $86	$75	$67	$60	$55	$50	$46	$43
15 1.25 $89	$78	$69	$63	$57	$52	$48	$45
16 1.30 $93	$81	$72	$65	$59	$54	$50	$46

5. Select **Split**, or type **T**.

6. Place the split bars between columns B and C and between rows 3 and 4, as shown in the following screen.

```
 Microsoft Excel - GASOLINE.XLS
 File  Edit  Formula  Format  Data  Options  Macro  Window          Help
 B3            =1000/B2*B1

 Split (Use direction keys to split)
```

	B	C	D	E	F	G	H	I	J
3	40.00	14	16	18	20	22	24	26	28
4	0.70	$50	$44	$39	$35	$32	$29	$27	$25
5	0.75	$54	$47	$42	$38	$34	$31	$29	$27
6	0.80	$57	$50	$44	$40	$36	$33	$31	$29
7	0.85	$61	$53	$47	$43	$39	$35	$33	$30
8	0.90	$64	$56	$50	$45	$41	$38	$35	$32
9	0.95	$68	$59	$53	$48	$43	$40	$37	$34
10	1.00	$71	$63	$56	$50	$45	$42	$38	$36
11	1.05	$75	$66	$58	$53	$48	$44	$40	$38
12	1.10	$79	$69	$61	$55	$50	$46	$42	$39
13	1.15	$82	$72	$64	$58	$52	$48	$44	$41
14	1.20	$86	$75	$67	$60	$55	$50	$46	$43
15	1.25	$89	$78	$69	$63	$57	$52	$48	$45
16	1.30	$93	$81	$72	$65	$59	$54	$50	$46

7. Click the mouse button or press **Enter**.

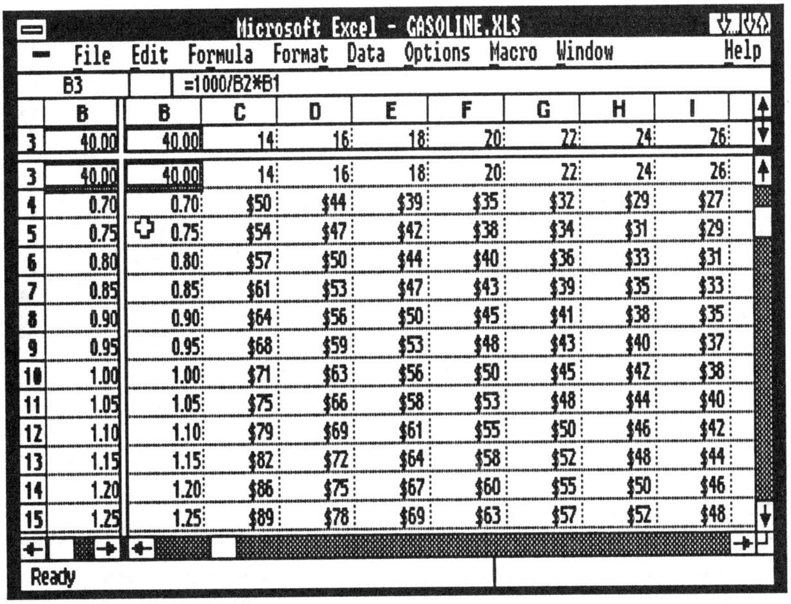

Microsoft Excel - GASOLINE.XLS

File   Edit   Formula   Format   Data   Options   Macro   Window   Help

B3   =1000/B2*B1

	B	B	C	D	E	F	G	H	I
3	40.00	40.00	14	16	18	20	22	24	26
3	40.00	40.00	14	16	18	20	22	24	26
4	0.70	0.70	$50	$44	$39	$35	$32	$29	$27
5	0.75	0.75	$54	$47	$42	$38	$34	$31	$29
6	0.80	0.80	$57	$50	$44	$40	$36	$33	$31
7	0.85	0.85	$61	$53	$47	$43	$39	$35	$33
8	0.90	0.90	$64	$56	$50	$45	$41	$38	$35
9	0.95	0.95	$68	$59	$53	$48	$43	$40	$37
10	1.00	1.00	$71	$63	$56	$50	$45	$42	$38
11	1.05	1.05	$75	$66	$58	$53	$48	$44	$40
12	1.10	1.10	$79	$69	$61	$55	$50	$46	$42
13	1.15	1.15	$82	$72	$64	$58	$52	$48	$44
14	1.20	1.20	$86	$75	$67	$60	$55	$50	$46
15	1.25	1.25	$89	$78	$69	$63	$57	$52	$48

Ready

8. Press **Right Arrow** to scroll the worksheet to the right. Notice that the titles move with the sheet.

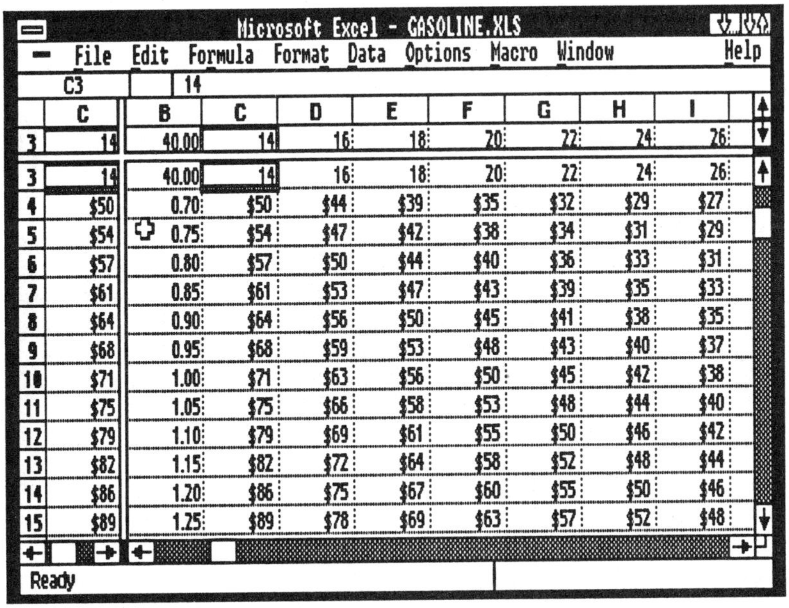

Microsoft Excel - GASOLINE.XLS

File   Edit   Formula   Format   Data   Options   Macro   Window   Help

C3   14

	C	B	C	D	E	F	G	H	I
3	14	40.00	14	16	18	20	22	24	26
3	14	40.00	14	16	18	20	22	24	26
4	$50	0.70	$50	$44	$39	$35	$32	$29	$27
5	$54	0.75	$54	$47	$42	$38	$34	$31	$29
6	$57	0.80	$57	$50	$44	$40	$36	$33	$31
7	$61	0.85	$61	$53	$47	$43	$39	$35	$33
8	$64	0.90	$64	$56	$50	$45	$41	$38	$35
9	$68	0.95	$68	$59	$53	$48	$43	$40	$37
10	$71	1.00	$71	$63	$56	$50	$45	$42	$38
11	$75	1.05	$75	$66	$58	$53	$48	$44	$40
12	$79	1.10	$79	$69	$61	$55	$50	$46	$42
13	$82	1.15	$82	$72	$64	$58	$52	$48	$44
14	$86	1.20	$86	$75	$67	$60	$55	$50	$46
15	$89	1.25	$89	$78	$69	$63	$57	$52	$48

Ready

9. Press **Left Arrow**, selecting cell B3. Then select **Freeze Panes** from the Options menu.

	B	C	D	E	F	G	H	I	J
	B3		=1000/B2*B1						
3	40.00	14	16	18	20	22	24	26	28
4	0.70	$50	$44	$39	$35	$32	$29	$27	$25
5	0.75	$54	$47	$42	$38	$34	$31	$29	$27
6	0.80	$57	$50	$44	$40	$36	$33	$31	$29
7	0.85	$61	$53	$47	$43	$39	$35	$33	$30
8	0.90	$64	$56	$50	$45	$41	$38	$35	$32
9	0.95	$68	$59	$53	$48	$43	$40	$37	$34
10	1.00	$71	$63	$56	$50	$45	$42	$38	$36
11	1.05	$75	$66	$58	$53	$48	$44	$40	$38
12	1.10	$79	$69	$61	$55	$50	$46	$42	$39
13	1.15	$82	$72	$64	$58	$52	$48	$44	$41
14	1.20	$86	$75	$67	$60	$55	$50	$46	$43
15	1.25	$89	$78	$69	$63	$57	$52	$48	$45
16	1.30	$93	$81	$72	$65	$59	$54	$50	$46

Microsoft Excel – GASOLINE.XLS — File Edit Formula Format Data Options Macro Window Help — Ready

10. Press **F5** (Goto) and type **K30** as the Reference. Select **OK** on the Goto dialog box or press **Enter**. Notice that row 3 and column B remain frozen on the screen as shown in the following display.

	B	D	E	F	G	H	I	J	K
	K30		{=TABLE(B2,B1)}						
3	40.00	16	18	20	22	24	26	28	30
18	1.40	$88	$78	$70	$64	$58	$54	$50	$47
19	1.45	$91	$81	$73	$66	$60	$56	$52	$48
20	1.50	$94	$83	$75	$68	$63	$58	$54	$50
21	1.55	$97	$86	$78	$70	$65	$60	$55	$52
22	1.60	$100	$89	$80	$73	$67	$62	$57	$53
23	1.65	$103	$92	$83	$75	$69	$63	$59	$55
24	1.70	$106	$94	$85	$77	$71	$65	$61	$57
25	1.75	$109	$97	$88	$80	$73	$67	$63	$58
26	1.80	$113	$100	$90	$82	$75	$69	$64	$60
27	1.85	$116	$103	$93	$84	$77	$71	$66	$62
28	1.90	$119	$106	$95	$86	$79	$73	$68	$63
29	1.95	$122	$108	$98	$89	$81	$75	$70	$65
30	2.00	$125	$111	$100	$91	$83	$77	$71	$67

Microsoft Excel – GASOLINE.XLS — File Edit Formula Format Data Options Macro Window Help — Ready

11. Close the worksheet (It is not necessary to save the changes.) and exit Excel.

12. Turn to Module 46 to continue the learning sequence.

Module 30

GALLERY (CHART)

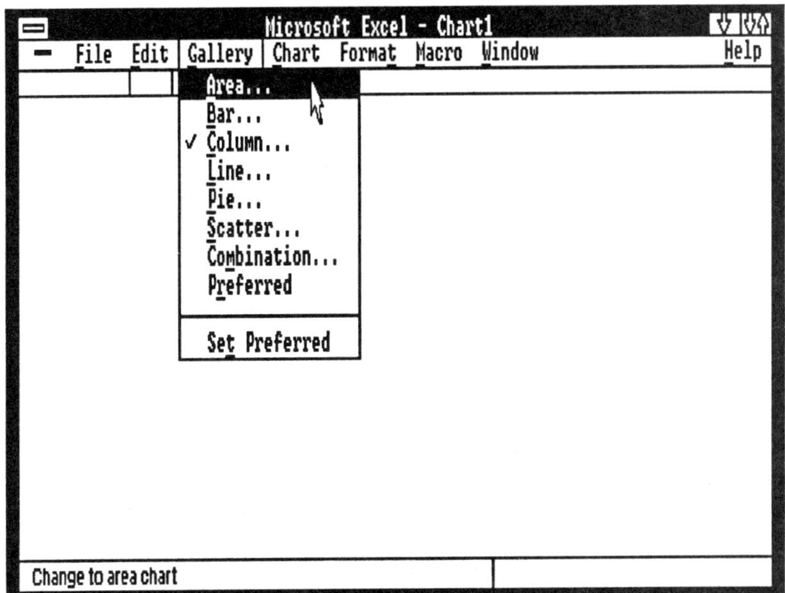

DESCRIPTION

Charts are created from the New command in the File menu with Alt-F N and by selecting the Chart option. To create a chart you need only define the area of the worksheet you want to chart (or use the entire worksheet), select the New command, and choose the Chart option. (Data that is to be charted is normally based on two or more categories that vary over time.)

When working with charts, you have three menus that will modify your chart; Gallery, Chart, and Format. These menus are only active when a chart is the active window. The Gallery menu (Alt-G) offers a variety of available charts or the option of designing your own.

The Gallery menu permits you to create or change a chart by selecting from 42 standard formats that are built into Excel. This menu is different from the Chart menu in that you are limited to the choices of chart type from which to select. It doesn't permit you to completely customize your chart. However, if one of the standard charts will work in your particular application, it is a simple matter to select one.

The first option in the Gallery menu is the default choice. You can provide Excel with a different preferred chart with the Set Preferred command that will automatically designate a particular chart option as the preferred style for your charts. All you need to do is select the desired format for an active chart and use the Set Preferred command. In practice this format will become the default format as long as you leave it in operation. To return to the original default option, set the first choice in the menu as the preferred option with the Set Preferred command.

With this menu you can select a combination of formats by choosing the Combination option.

APPLICATIONS

Some data can be easily illustrated with the standard chart formats that are available from Excel. This avoids the necessity of designing your own chart.

TYPICAL OPERATION

In this operation you use the Gallery menu to change a chart.

1. Start Excel and open BUDGET1.XLS.

If your BUDGET1 doesn't look exactly like the one illustrated, it is ok, since you will be changing this information to make it more visual for the chart.

2. Clear the numerical data in columns E, F, G and H.
3. Type **$625** in cells E4, F4, G4 and H4.
4. Type **$100, $50, $75** and **$175** in cells E5, F5, G5 and H5.
5. Type **$300, $150, $100** and **$200** in cells E6, F6, G6 and H6.
6. Type **$300, $0, $700** and **$0** in cells E7, F7, G7 and H7.
7. Type **$250, $150, $0** and **$400** in cells E8, F8, G8 and H8.
8. Type **875, 1500, 850** and **1075** in cells E9, F9, G9 and H9.
9. Type **875** in cells E10, F10, G10 and H10.
10. Type **$175, $150, $275** and **$150** in cells E11, F11, G11 and H11.

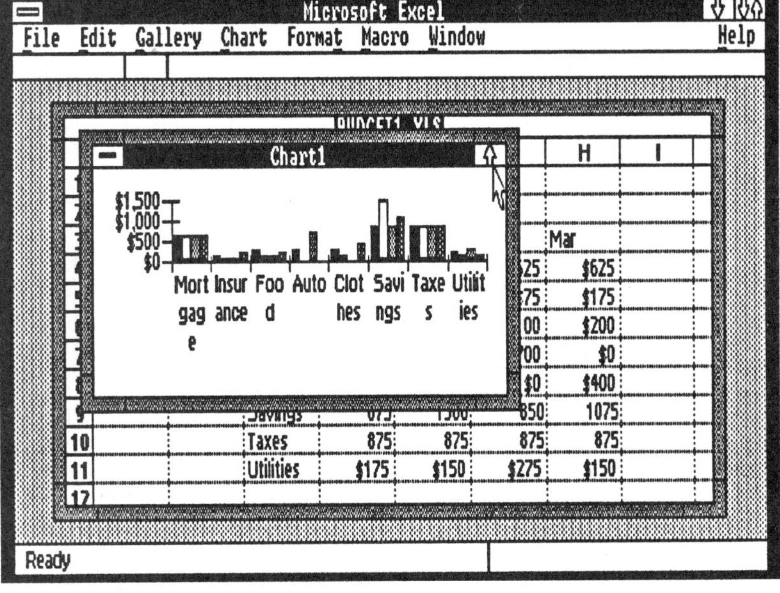

11. Mark as a block the cells D3 through H11.

12. Select **New** from the File menu.

13. Select the **Chart** option from the New command on the File menu and press **Enter**.

14. Maximize the Chart. (Use the Maximize Arrow icon in the upper right corner of the chart.)

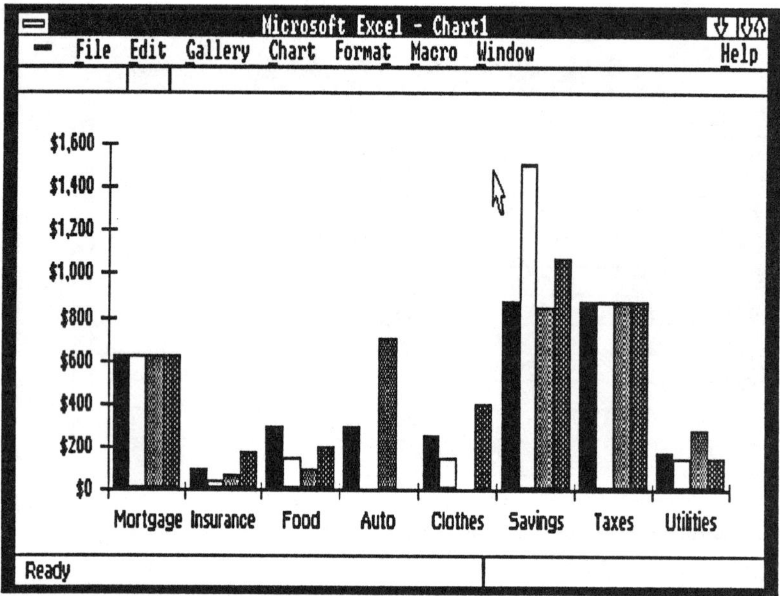

15. Select **Line** from the Gallery menu.

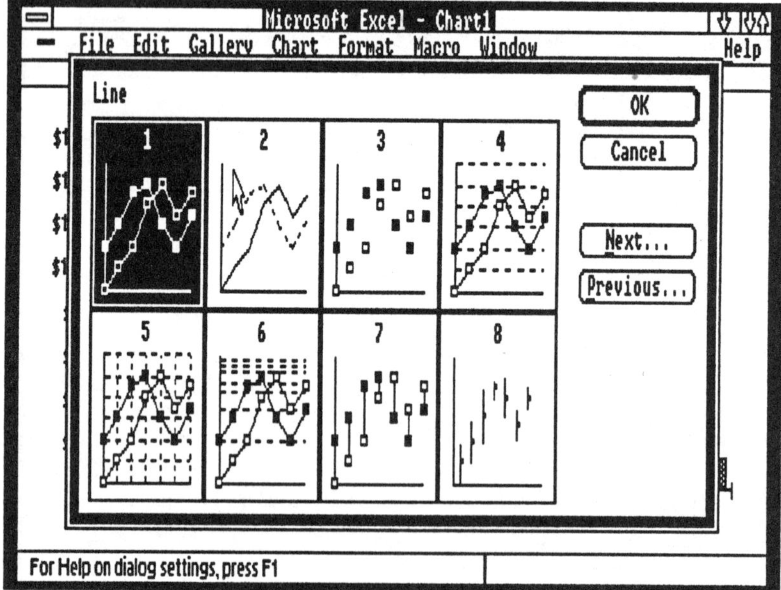

These are the different Line chart options.

16. Select **Next**.

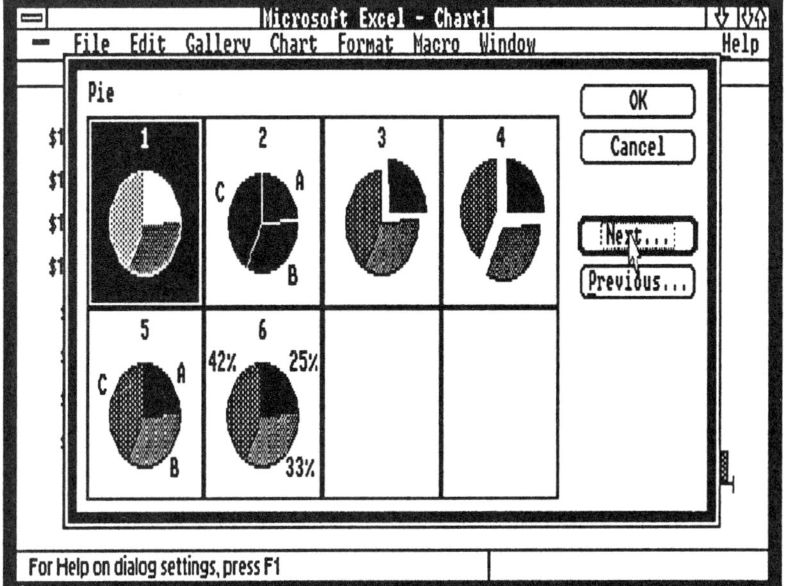

17. Select option **4** and press **Enter**.

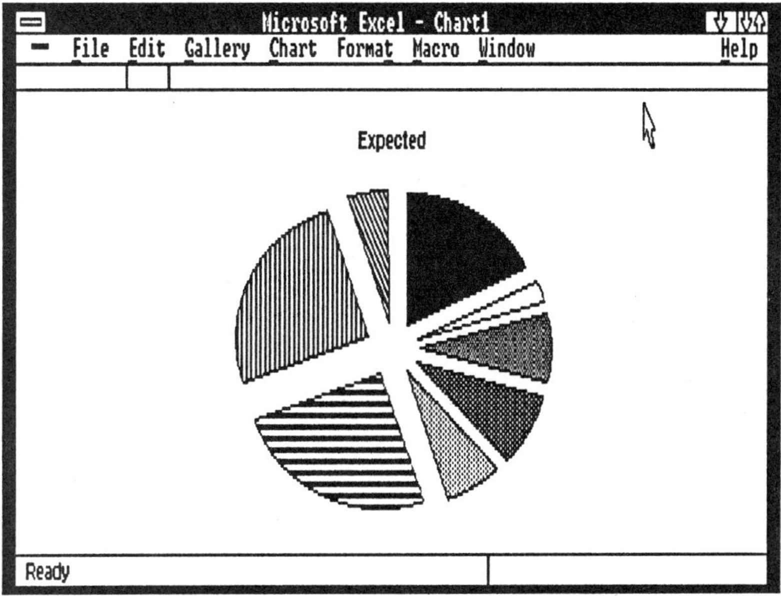

18.   From the Gallery menu select **Column** and then select **1** and press **Enter**.

Explore the other options in this menu until you understand how they affect your chart. Clear all changes until you have the standard bar chart on the screen, as illustrated in the fourth screen display.

19.   Turn to Module 10 to continue the learning sequence.

Module 31
GOTO

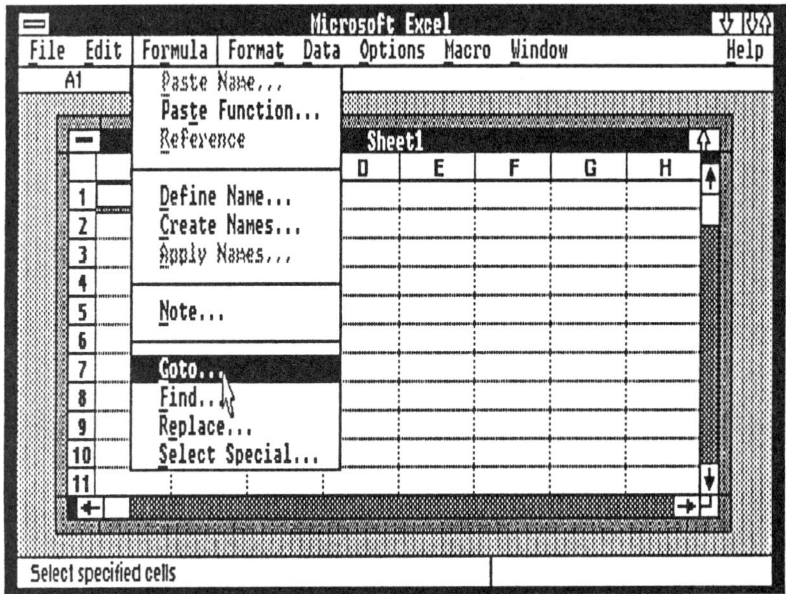

DESCRIPTION

The Goto command permits you to move rapidly to designated areas of the workspace. It is accessed from the Formula menu with Alt-R G.

APPLICATIONS

When working in a worksheet, it is often useful to be able to move to a different location to enter related data or to move to already existing data and then return to the starting point. The Goto command permits you to enter the cell address you want to access and move immediately to that location.

TYPICAL OPERATION

In this operation you use the Goto command to move to specified locations in the worksheet.

1. Start Excel, or continue your work session by opening a new worksheet.

2. Select **Goto** from the Formula menu.

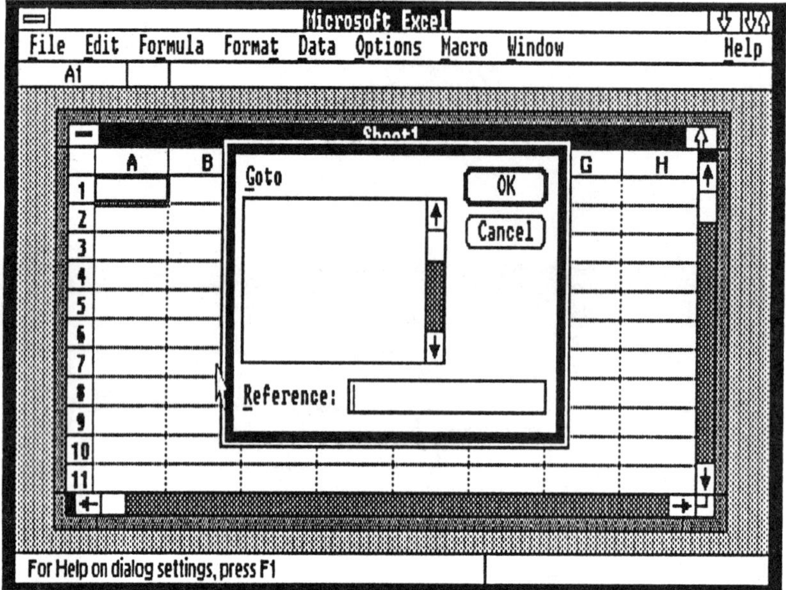

If you have created some Names that you use as references (see Module 15, Create Names) they would appear in this listing and you could select one and move to that location. You could also type the name of a Named Reference.

3. Type **T95** as a cell reference and press **Enter**.

The cursor has moved to the new location.

4. Select **Goto** from the Formula menu. Notice that Excel has entered the point of origin to facilitate returning to that location.
5. Press **Enter**. Cell A1 is selected on the worksheet.
6. Exit Excel, or close the worksheet and continue your work session.
7. Turn to Module 41 to continue the learning sequence.

Module 32

HIDE/UNHIDE

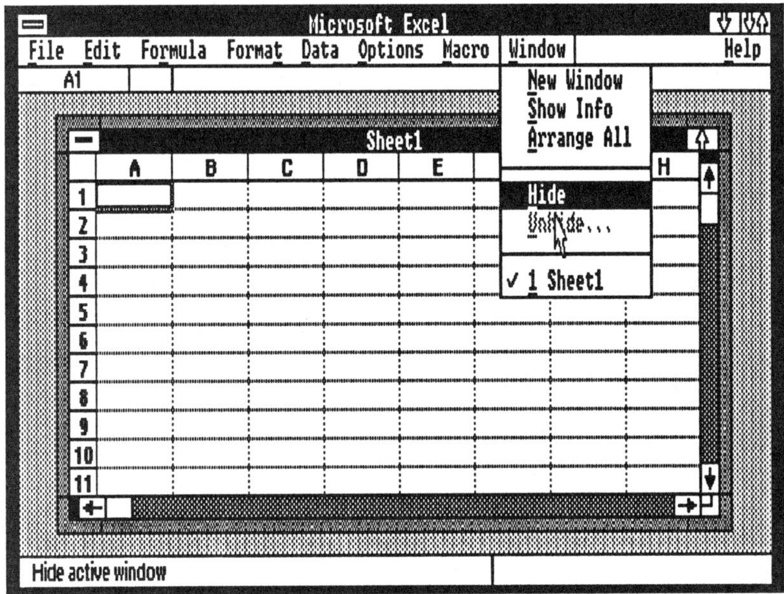

DESCRIPTION

Excel permits you to remove a worksheet from the screen without closing it. The Hide command is located in the Window menu and is accessed with Alt-W H. You can use the Hide command to remove one or more worksheets from the screen. Once you use the Hide command the Unhide command becomes active to allow you to reverse the Hide command. The Unhide command lists the windows that you have hidden and you select the window or windows that you want to make visible.

If you only want to hide from view certain portions of data in a worksheet and you want the rest of the worksheet to remain visible, you would simply collapse the row or column that contains the sensitive information.

APPLICATIONS

Many users of data management systems will find that being able to hide sensitive information from unauthorized individuals is a valuable tool. If you are planning to use Excel in your work, such sensitive information as salaries, bids, or special projects may be common. For personal use, you may decide to hide information relating to budgets, income taxes, etc.

Since Excel permits an unlimited number of documents to be opened at the same time, these commands are useful in helping you work with the documents. You can temporarily remove (hide) a document while you work on another and then easily retrieve it.

Sometimes there isn't enough space on the screen to accommodate all of the screens that were organized with the Arrange All command. The Hide command will allow you to temporarily remove one or more worksheets from the screen and retrieve them later.

TYPICAL OPERATION

In this module you use the Hide and Unhide commands to remove worksheets from the screen and retrieve them and you hide a row or column.

1. Start Excel, or continue your work session from the previous module.
2. Open BUDGET.XLW and select **Arrange All** from the Window menu to organize the worksheets on the screen.

Your screen may not look exactly like the one illustrated because the Arrange All command may have organized your workspace differently. If you are missing any of the illustrated worksheets, locate them in your library file, add them to the screen, and arrange them as illustrated.

3. Type **Clothes** in cell B1 of Sheet1.

4. Type **Shoes** in cell B3.

5. Type **Slacks** in cell B4.

6. Type **Shirt** in cell B5.

7. Type **$75** in cell C3.

8. Type **$45** in cell C4.

9. Type **$30** in cell C5.

10. Type **Total** in cell B7.

11. Type **=C3+C4+C5** in cell C7 and press **Enter**.

Since the total in cell C7 is $150, we need to see how this compares with the amount budgeted for clothes.

12. Select **Hide** from the Window menu.

Sheet1 has been removed. You may need to make BUDGET1 the active worksheet.

13. Arrange the worksheets once more.

14. Size BUDGET1 by moving the right side until you can see the amounts assigned to each category of the budget.

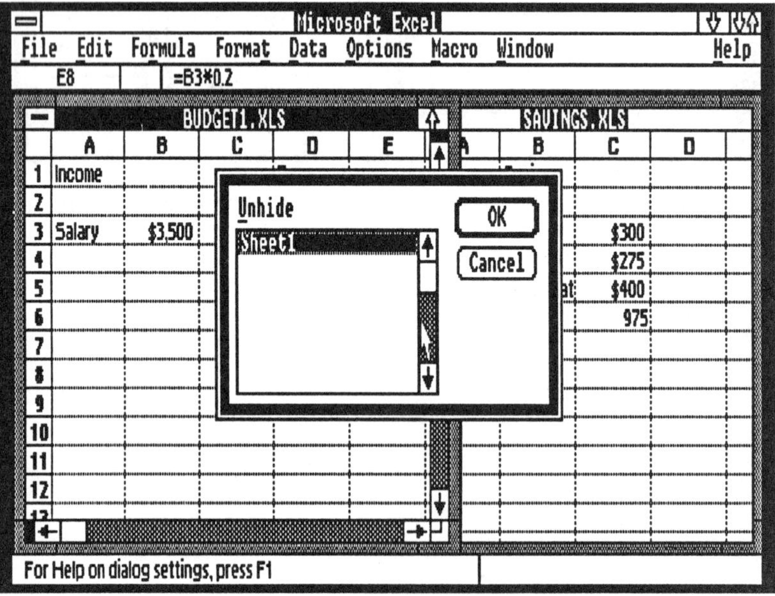

You budgeted $200 dollars for clothes.

15. Select **Unhide** from the Window menu.

The dialog box indicates that only one worksheet has been hidden. If you had hidden more than one, you would now select the one you want to return to the screen.

16. Press **Enter**.
17. Type **$75** in cell C4 and **$50** in cell C5.

> **NOTE**
> The following information is presented here as a technique used to hide information. A more detailed description of the procedure can be found in Module 13 and Module 57.

Assume that you want to hide the amount you are paying for shoes. There are two ways you can hide the information in a row or column.

> **CAUTION**
> When hiding a row or column by reducing its size to zero, it becomes difficult to access it when you want to reverse the operation. It can more easily be recovered by using the Format menu. First, define the two rows or columns surrounding the hidden one as a block. Second, open the Format menu and select the Row Height command or the Column Width command. Third, at the dialog box, select the Standard option and press Enter.

MOUSE: Move the cursor to the line that separates two rows or columns and when the cursor changes to a narrow "cross," press and hold the left button and drag one of the rows or columns across the row or column you wish to hide.

KEYBOARD: Activate any cell in the row or column you wish to hide. Access either Row Height or Column Width from the Format menu, change the height or width to zero, and press Enter.

18. Return Sheet1 to its original configuration.
19. Select **Save As** from the File menu.
20. Type **Clothes** as the name under which to save Sheet1 and press **Enter**.
21. Exit Excel, or close the worksheet and continue your work session.
22. Turn to Module 14 to continue the learning sequence.

Module 33
INSERT

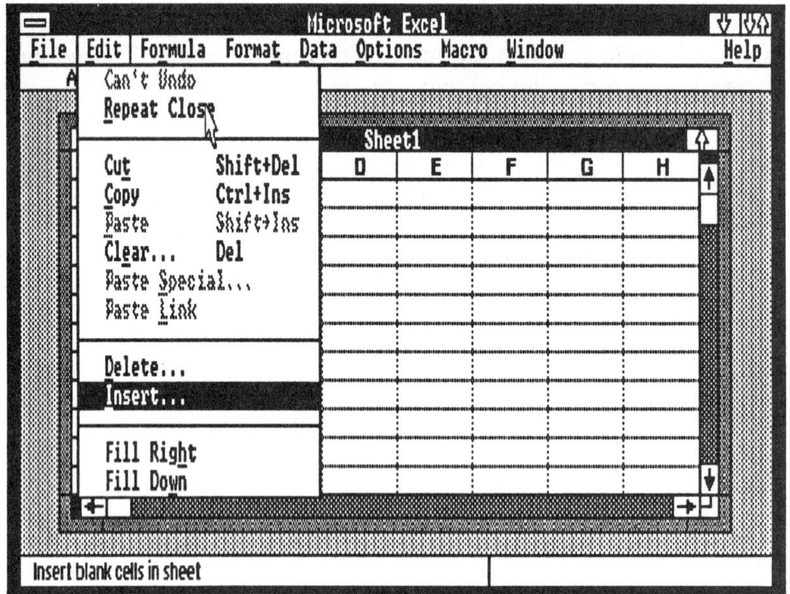

DESCRIPTION

Excel allows the user the flexibility of inserting spaces within existing worksheets. The Insert command is in the Edit menu and is accessed with Alt-E I. The user can insert blank cells or entire rows and columns. The Insert command can be done so that only a portion of the worksheet is affected, or it can be accomplished so that the entire worksheet is adjusted to accommodate the new spaces.

APPLICATIONS

Occasionally, despite careful planning, you will forget to include some information in your worksheet or some new information will become available to you that needs to be included, and you will want to include it in an already existing portion of the worksheet.

Excel permits this to happen without interfering with the existing information.

TYPICAL OPERATION

In this operation you insert new space in an existing file to allow new data to be entered.

1. Start Excel, or continue your work session from the previous module.

2. Open BUDGET1.

3. Click on the row number 4 or activate any cell in that row and press **Shift-Space**.

4. Select **Insert** from the Edit menu and press **Enter**. A new row has been inserted between mortgage and food for the entire worksheet.

5. Select **Undo Insert** from the Edit menu to return the worksheet to its original status.

6. Mark cell D4 and E4 as a range (block).

7. Select **Insert** from the Edit menu.

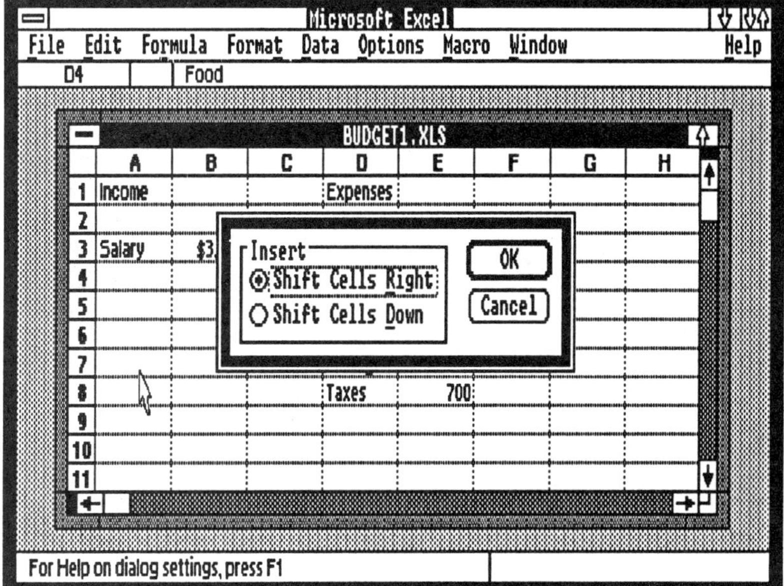

8. Select **Shift Cells Down** and press **Enter**.

9. Type **Insurance** in cell D4, **$100** in cell E4, and press **Enter**.

10. Mark E3 through E9 as a range.

11. Select **Insert** from the Edit menu.

12. Select **Shift Cells Right** and press **Enter**.

13. Select **Undo Insert** from the Edit menu.

14. Insert a new row where row 1 is located so that Income is in cell A2 and Expenses is in cell D2.

15. Save the worksheet.

16. Exit Excel, or continue your work session.

17. Turn to Module 23 to continue the learning sequence.

Module 34

JUSTIFY

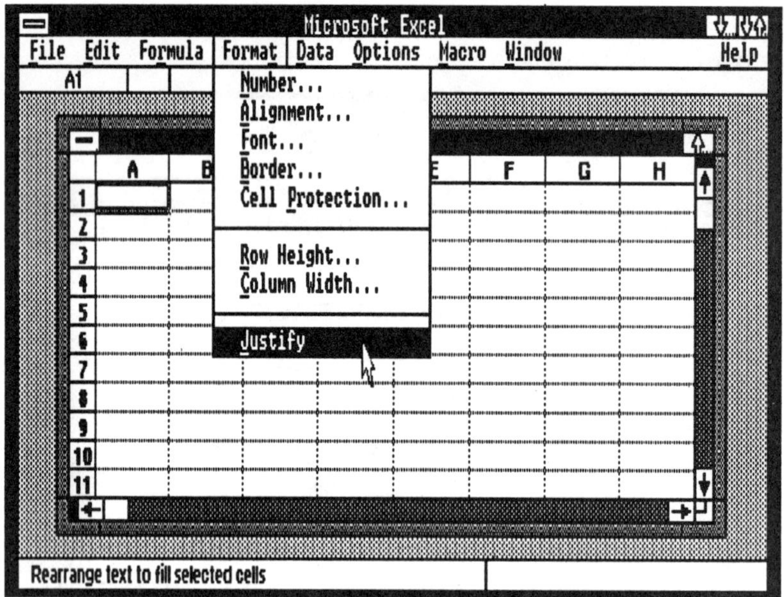

DESCRIPTION

Select Justify from the Format menu or press Alt-T J to rearrange text to fit an area of a worksheet. When placing text into Excel, it is often difficult to obtain visually pleasing spacing. Using this command, you first type the text in the desired cells, highlight the cell range the text should occupy, and select Justify from the Format menu.

APPLICATIONS

The most common use for the Justify command is to place descriptive text in a column of the worksheet. When you want the text on your worksheet to be invisible, use the Note command to attach a note to a cell. When you want the worksheet text visible on the screen or the printout, type the text into a worksheet column, select the range of cells for the text to occupy, and finally, select Justify from the Format menu.

TYPICAL OPERATION

In this session you continue to add information and formatting to the INTEREST.XLS worksheet you last used in the Font module.

1. Start Excel and open INTEREST.XLS, or continue your work from the previous session.

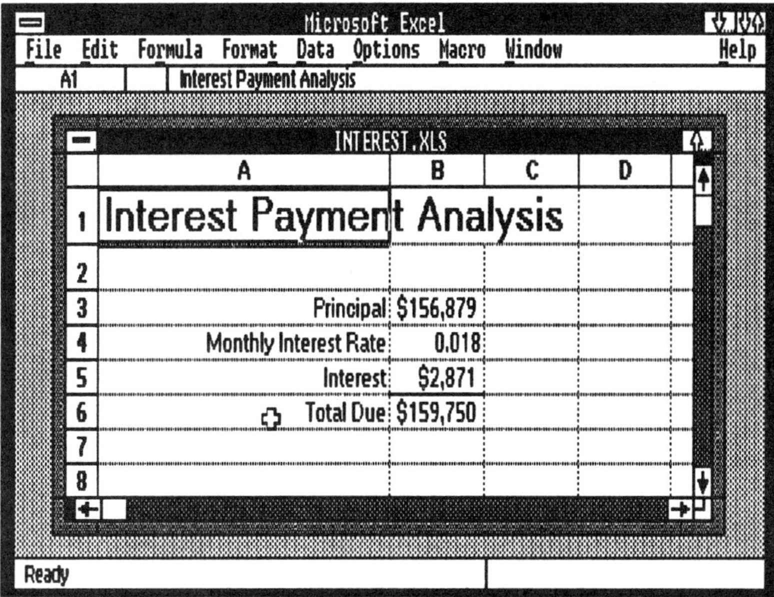

2. Pick the hollow arrow in the upper right corner of the worksheet to expand the worksheet to fill the screen.

3. Type **This worksheet shows a principal amount and a total** in cell A8.

4. Type **amount owed based on a given monthly interest rate.** in cell A9.

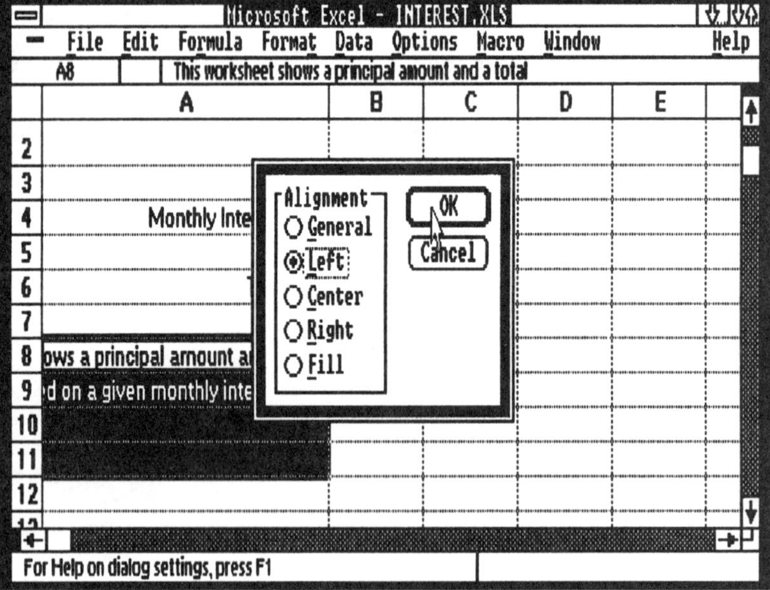

5. Select cells A8 through A11, then select **Alignment** from the Format menu. Select **Left** on the dialog box.

6. Pick **OK**.

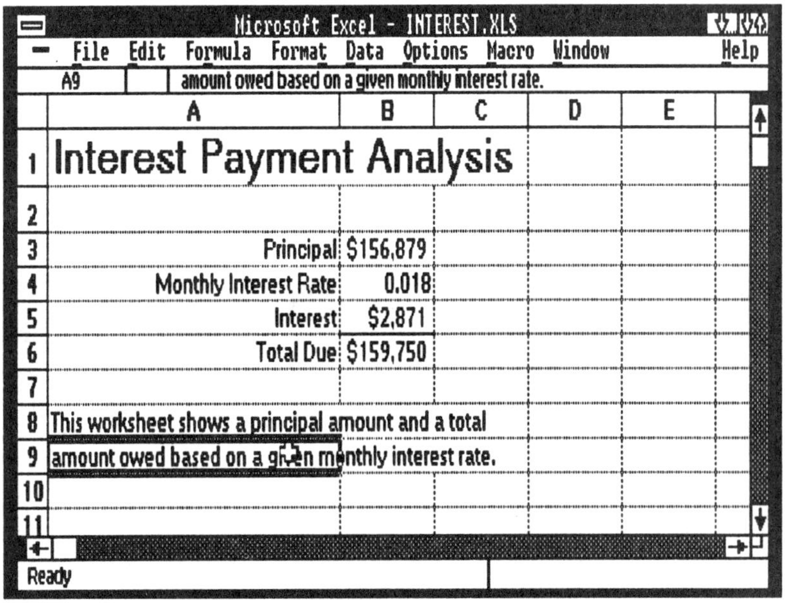

7. Select the region A8 through B11, then select **Justify** from the Format menu.

8. Pick cell A11.

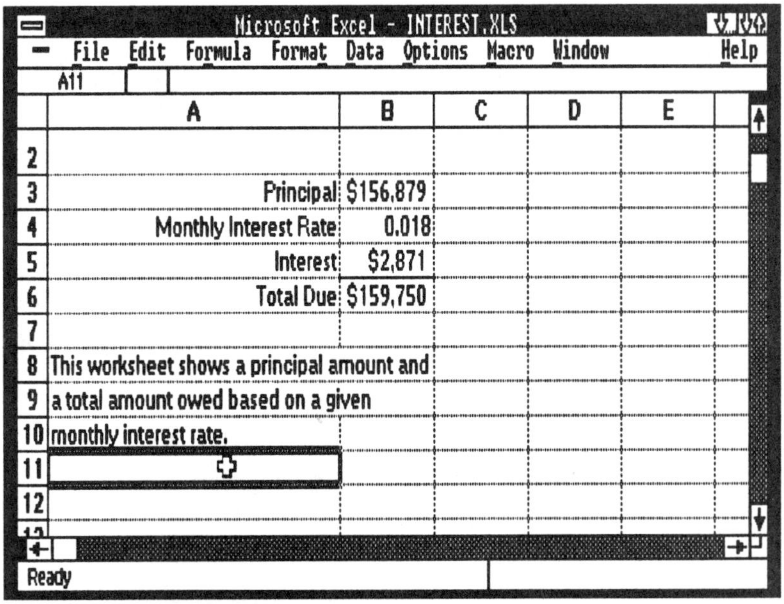

9. Save the worksheet and exit Excel, or continue the learning sequence directly by turning to Module 56.

Module 35

LINKS

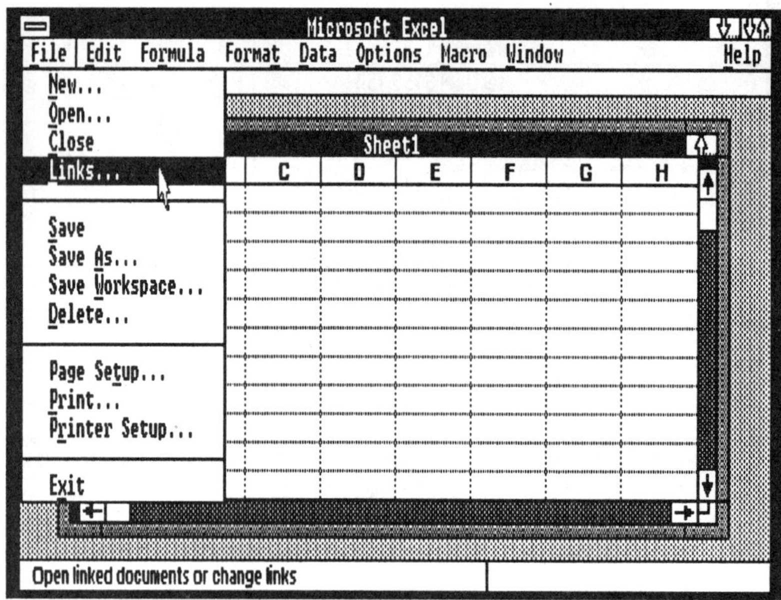

DESCRIPTION

The Links command on the File menu allows you to view, open, and change the links and filenames for the worksheets (or other documents when using the full version of Windows) supporting the active worksheet. When you pick the Links command with the mouse or by pressing Alt-F L, a dialog box similar to the following appears.

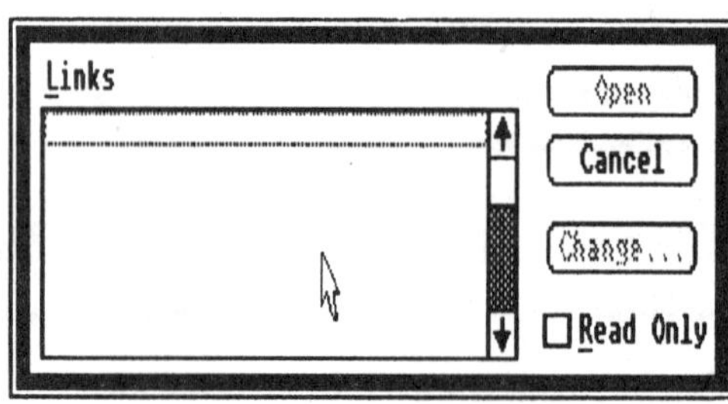

To open supporting linked documents, select the ones you want to open from the list, then pick "Open." The Read Only check box is especially useful when using supporting documents across a network. When you open a worksheet as read only, another network user can update the document at the same time as you view it.

To change the linked documents, select the document you want to change, then pick the Change button. A dialog box similar to the following appears.

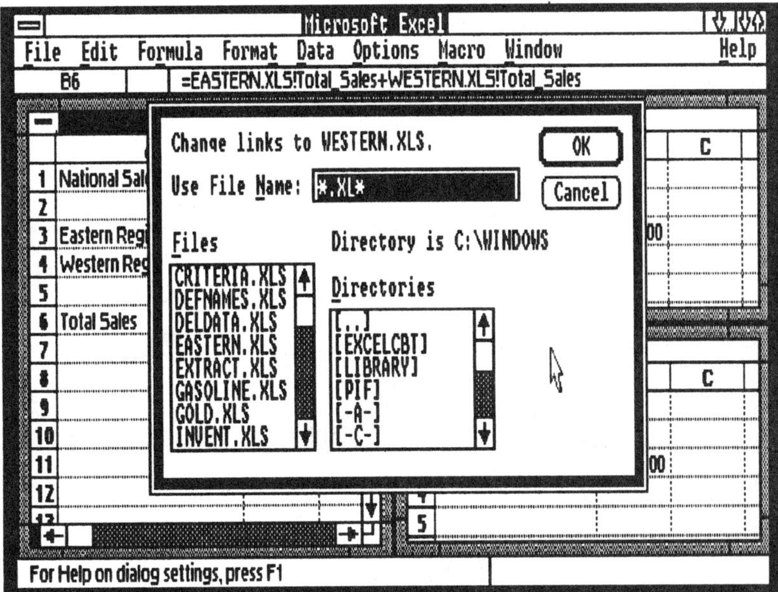

This dialog box initially lists the file extension in the Use File Name field. The files matching the extension in the current directory are listed in the Files selector box, and the available disk drives and directories are listed in the Directories selector box. To change the reference of the supporting worksheet, first select the new directory if different from the current directory, then select the filename from the Files listing. Select OK to record your new external reference link.

APPLICATIONS

A link can refer either to an absolute cell reference or a name. When the link is established to an absolute cell, inserting or deleting rows or columns that change the position of the cell in the supporting worksheet do *not* change the external link. This is an excellent way to get yourself in trouble. When the link is established to a named cell or range, the link automatically follows any change of position of the named cell on the supporting worksheet through row and column insertions, deletions, moves, etc. A named reference is much safer than an absolute reference.

If you find yourself opening the same set of linked worksheets over and over again, consider using the Save Workspace command on the File menu to save your entire Excel workspace instead of saving and opening single files.

External reference formulas in an Excel worksheet contain the complete drive and directory path name of the supporting worksheet. If you move the supporting worksheet (foolish you) to another drive or directory, you need to fix the links, which are not updated automatically. The Change option allows you to manually update the links to reflect the changes you make to your disk file organization.

TYPICAL OPERATION

In this session you use the Link command to open supporting worksheets and view the supporting worksheets you created in the Paste Link module.

1. Start Excel and close the default sheet, Sheet1, or continue your work session from the previous module.

2. Open the NATIONAL.XLS worksheet.

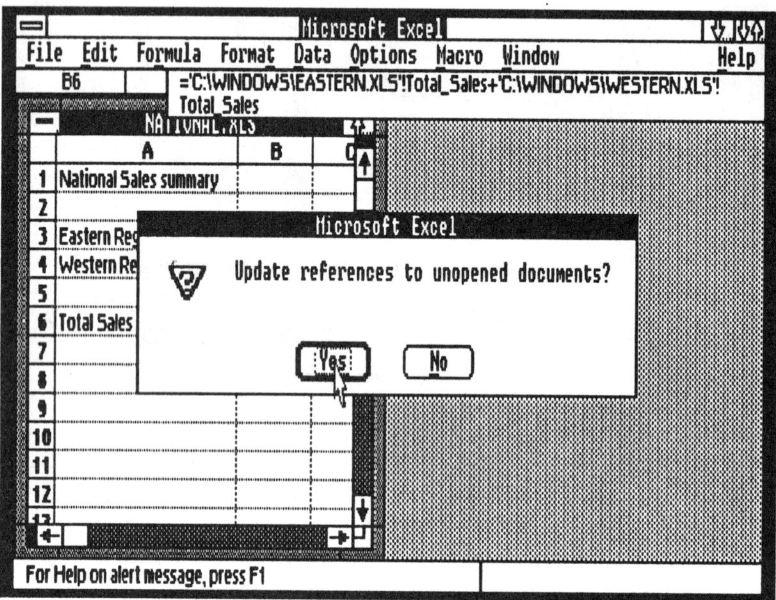

3. Pick **Yes** in the dialog box.

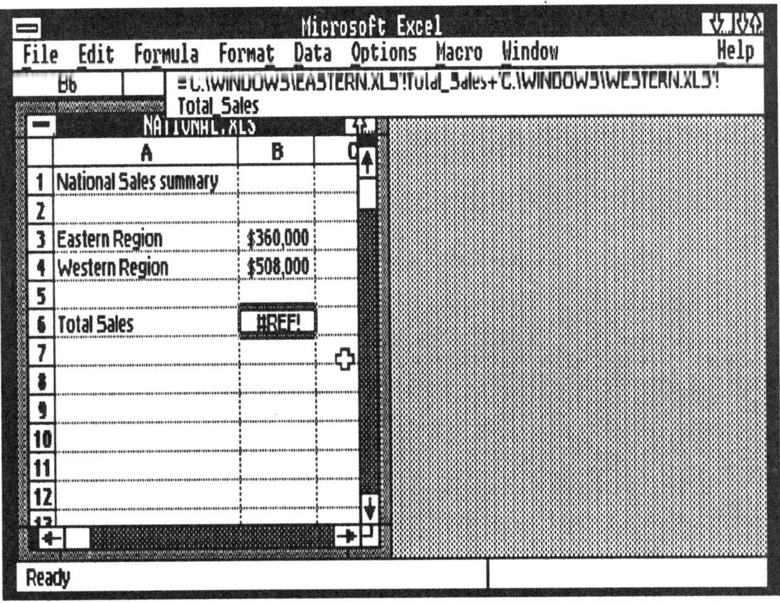

Notice that there are two major changes in the worksheet. First, examine the formula bar at the top of the screen. The reference to cell B6 in NATIONAL.XLS is changed to reflect a full disk drive and path description. Second, notice that cell B6 contains the #REF! error. Cell B6 is a complex reference. Because EASTERN.XLS and WESTERN.XLS are not open, Excel cannot properly evaluate the complex reference. Notice, however, that Excel has no problem with simple references to the same data, as seen in cells B3 and B4.

4. Pick **Links** on the File menu.

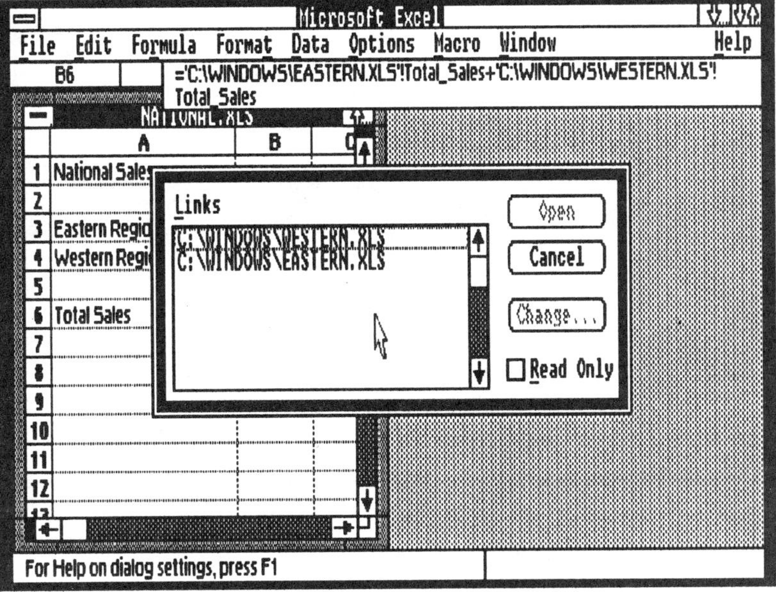

5. Highlight both supporting worksheets. (Hold the **Shift** key down while picking the names with the mouse or moving the selection box with the cursor control keys.)

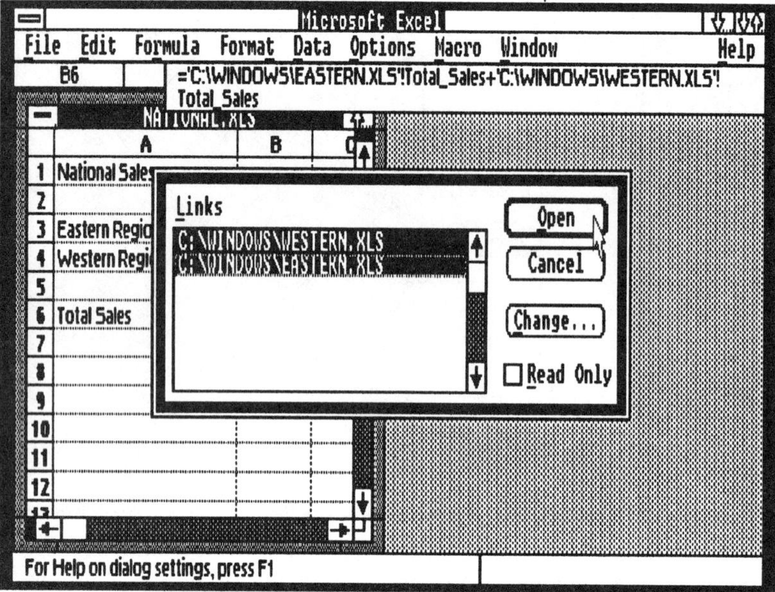

6. Pick **Open**. Both supporting worksheets are opened on the screen. Notice that the complex reference in cell B6 of NATIONAL.XLS is updated.

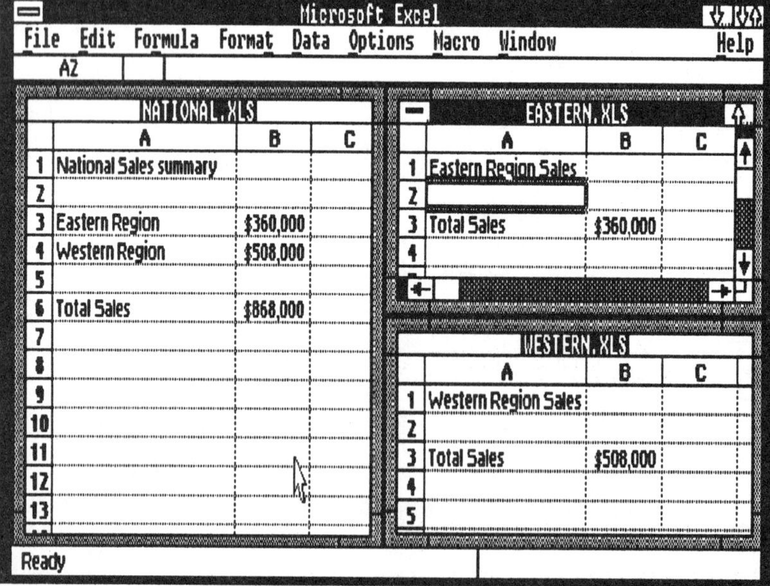

7. Exit Excel. It is not necessary to save the worksheets.

8. Turn to Module 48 to continue the learning sequence.

Module 36

MENUS

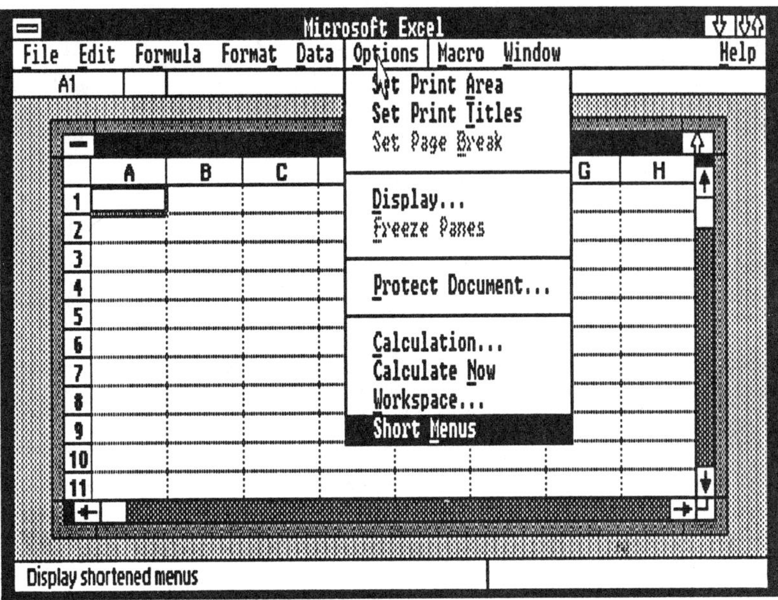

DESCRIPTION

Excel uses a system of drop-down menus that permits you to designate what you want the software to do. The name of each menu is listed at the top of the screen in the *menu bar*. The menus are not specific to any single document worksheet, but are associated with the application window in Excel. That is why you find them on the menu bar for Microsoft Excel. The menu system Excel uses is built in layers so that opening any menu gives you access to several commands, which in turn might provide access to various options for the command. The menus can be accessed with the keyboard or with a mouse. If you use a keyboard, you need to learn the basic keystrokes that will access each menu. Accessing menus in Excel normally will require two or more keystrokes. In some instances the keys must be pressed simultaneously. The conventional method of designating this type of action is to connect the keystrokes with a hyphen. In other instances the keys may be pressed successively or simultaneously. In this book we will use the convention of identifying the keystrokes as if they are to be pressed simultaneously, even if it is not necessary. You will discover, with use, the keystrokes that need not be pressed simultaneously.

The operation is simpler if you use a mouse. You need only click on the desired menu name.

Another feature of Excel is that it provides two types of menus. The *short* menu version lists only the most commonly used commands of each menu. The *full* menu version allows you to select from a larger range of commands contained in each menu. The Options menu illustrated at the beginning of this module is a full menu. Compare that illustration with the following illustration showing the short version of the same menu.

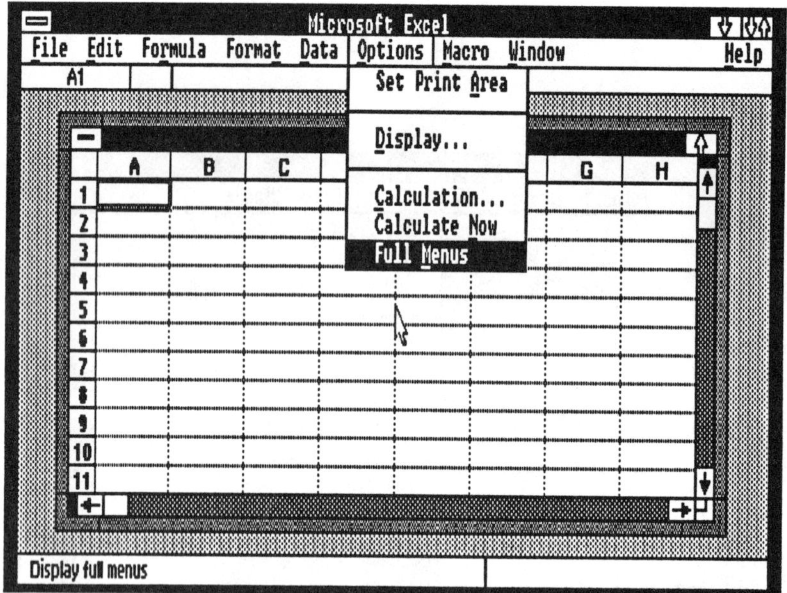

You use the Options menu to select the menu version for all of the menus. If the menus are currently short, the Full Menus option is available to switch to that version; if the menus are currently full, the Short Menus option is available. You can do all the most common and basic activities using the short menu but there is an advantage to having the full menu option since it will help you become familiar with the commands that you can access in each menu.

You will notice that some commands in the various menus are followed by a keystroke sequence. These keystrokes comprise an additional method of accomplishing an action. If a particular action becomes commonplace in the work you do, you can use these designated keystrokes to perform the action, rather than opening the menu and selecting the command. You cannot use these keystrokes after the menu has been opened.

Excel has another feature which is very helpful in the menus. Examine the full menu illustrated previously and you will see that two of the options "Set Page Break" and "Freeze Panes" are considerably lighter then the other options. These options are not available for you to use. Excel keeps track of the work you are currently doing and if one of more options do not apply, then you will not be able to access them. This helps you to not make a mistake.

SELECTING MENUS AND COMMANDS

To access the menu bar using the keyboard, either press the Alt key or the forward Slash key. The menu names and subsequently the commands change color on a color monitor, or shades on a monochrome monitor, to indicate the default menu. Once the default menu is accessed, you can move to any desired menu using the arrow keys. Alternatively, you can select any menu or command by typing the *underlined* letter in its name. When using a mouse, simply point the arrow at the desired menu and click the left button once. (Be sure to click only once since one click will open the menu and a second click will select one of the commands in the menu.)

If you are using the keyboard, Excel's menus are designed to help select the correct option or command. The menus and the options change color on a color monitor or are shaded on monochrome monitors. This indicates the selection that is in the default mode. One letter in the name of each menu or option is always underlined. You can open a menu or select an option by typing the underlined letter. Finally, you can leave any menu by pressing Esc. If you use a mouse, you can also leave any opened menu by moving the mouse pointer outside the menu and clicking once.

TYPICAL OPERATION

In this operation you access, leave, and move through menus.

1. Start Excel.
2. Press **Alt-O** to access the Options menu from the menu bar. (Mouse users click on Options from the menu bar.) The Options menu drops down. For this activity, you use the Full Menu option. If you need to, set Excel to show short menus.
3. Click on Full Menus or type **M** which is the underlined letter for that option.
4. Open the File menu by pressing **Alt-F** or clicking on the name with the mouse.

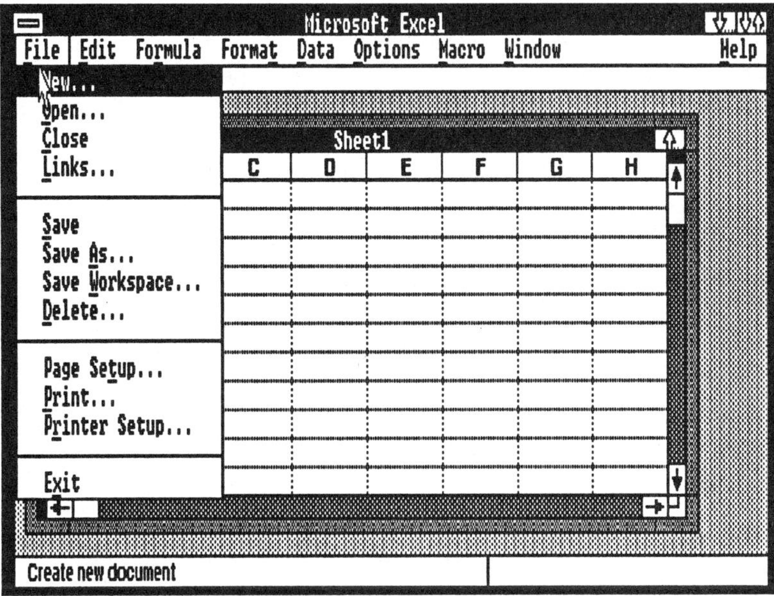

5. Press the **Right Arrow** twice to move to the Formula menu. Notice that the name of the menu opened is bracketed with vertical lines. Notice also that some of the commands in the menu are in light print because they are not available to use at this time.

6. Press the **Down Arrow** eight times to highlight the Find command and press **Enter**.

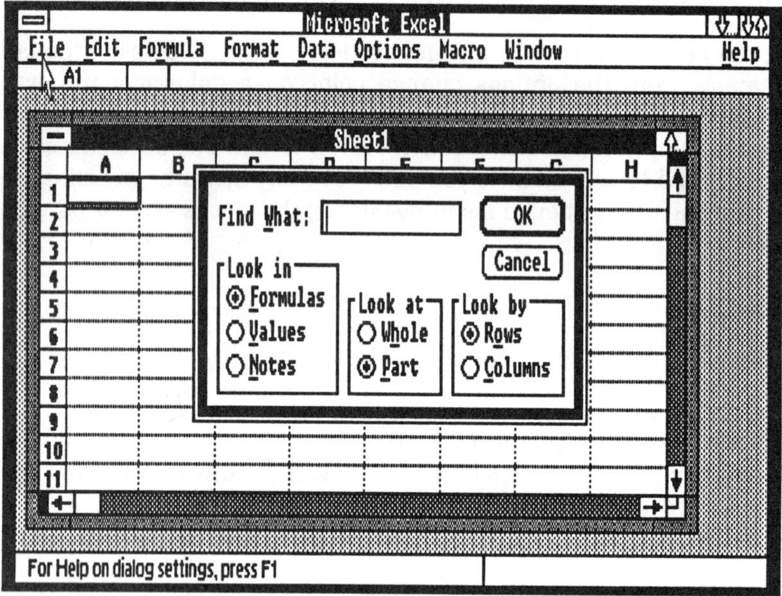

What you see on your screen is called a *dialog box*. There are two types of dialog boxes which you will become familiar with in the course of learning how to use Excel. This type of dialog box requires you to not only make selections but to also type a character string in the vacant cell. To make selections you can simply click with the mouse on any option and finish with "OK" or you can press Enter to accept all of the default options which have the dark dot in front of them. If you want to change a particular option, use the mouse to click on the desired option or use the keyboard Tab to move around the dialog box and the arrow keys to select new options within the dialog box.

7. Use the **Tab** key and the **arrow** keys to move around the dialog box.

Each dialog box also has a Help screen to provide you with additional information.

8. Press **F1** to access Help.

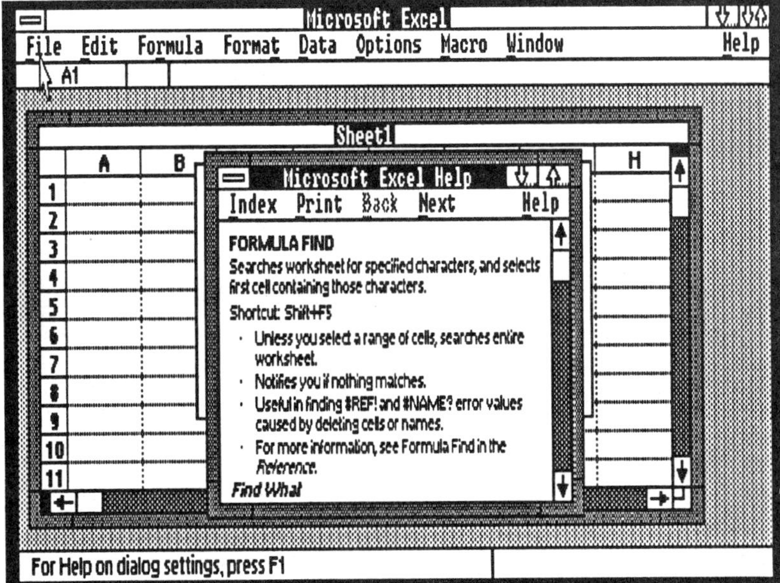

This illustrates the second type of dialog box. It is essentially a new window. It has a Control menu icon, Minimize and Maximize arrows, and a menu bar with menus that are accessed in exactly the same way as the menus in the application window. You can exit any menu or dialog box by pressing Esc.

9. Press **Esc** to return to the earlier dialog box.

NOTE

You could have also opened the Control menu
with the Control menu icon and then "Closed"
the dialog box.

10. Press **Esc** to leave this dialog box or use the Cancel option.

11. Turn to Module 71 to continue the learning sequence.

Module 37

MOVE

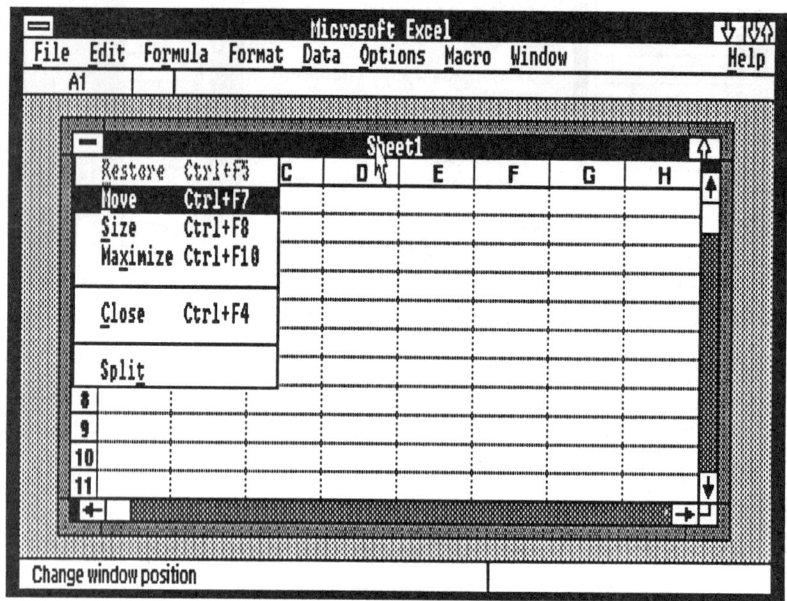

DESCRIPTION

The Move command is located on the Control menu for each active window. Accessing this command permits you to move a window to another location on the screen. This command is used in conjunction with Size command. The keystrokes Ctrl-F7 will also permit you to move a worksheet.

APPLICATIONS

The Move command allows you to organize your worksheets on the screen in any manner you want. This allows you to see all of the worksheets you have available at any time.

TYPICAL OPERATION

In this operation you reorganize your available worksheets on the screen. You should begin this operation with the worksheets you had on the screen at the end of the Size module. If you have done this, then BUDGET1.XLS:1 is the active worksheet on the screen. If you did not come directly from the Size module, you can simply place three different worksheets on the screen and size them so that they are all visible.

1. Continue your work session from the previous module, or start Excel and open the workspace you saved at the end of the Size module.

2. Press **Ctrl-F7** or select **Move** from the Control menu.

3. Press **Right Arrow** once.

4. Press **Up Arrow** 12 times, then press **Enter**.

5. Press **Ctrl-F6** to move to BUDGET1.XLS:2. Mouse users can click on this worksheet to activate it.

6. Press **Ctrl-F7** and press **Left Arrow** once.

7. Press **Right Arrow** 32 times and press **Enter**.

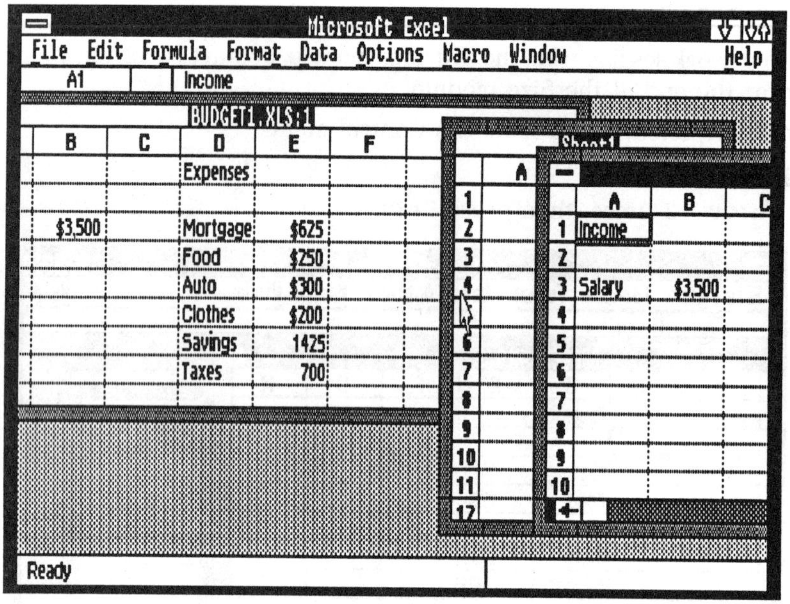

Continue to experiment with these commands until you have rearranged the worksheets to your satisfaction.

8. Save the workspace and exit Excel, or continue the work session directly with the next module.

9. Turn to Module 6 to continue the learning sequence.

Module 38

NEW

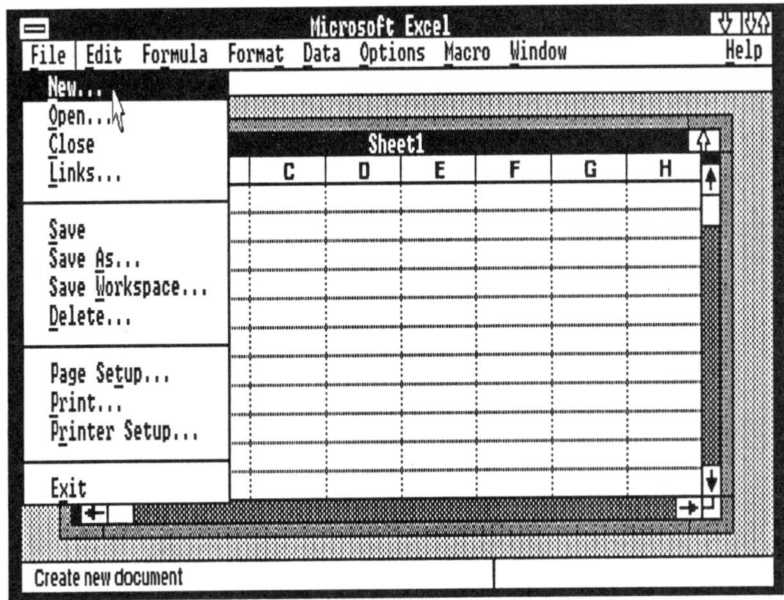

DESCRIPTION

The New command is located on the File menu. To access this command use the mouse to click on the File menu and select the New command. When using the keyboard press Alt-F N.

When you select the New command, a dialog box appears and you can designate whether you want to create a worksheet, a chart, or a macro sheet. The worksheet is used to develop a spreadsheet application, the chart is used to illustrate the worksheet data in a chart format, and the macro permits you to develop a series of fixed commands. A macro can also be opened from the Macro menu and will be presented in Module 52, Record.

Each new worksheet you create is given a default name by Excel. The first name used is Sheet1, the second is Sheet2, then Sheet3, Sheet4, etc. You can rename the worksheet by selecting Save As from the File menu. Do this any time you feel that you are concurrently working with too many worksheets to keep track of what information is in each of them. Once you save a worksheet, you can reopen it by using the Open command in the File menu.

APPLICATIONS

Many times, when working on one worksheet, you will find it useful to be able to create another worksheet, even temporarily. Generally, the new worksheet is created to perform some related function that is associated with the currently active window. In many cases, it is useful to reduce the active worksheet in size and add the new worksheet so that both are visible at the same time. In Module 6, Arrange All, you learn to organize the various open worksheets in order to work with several of them at one time.

It is often more advantageous to create several smaller worksheets than to try and put too much information in one large worksheet.

TYPICAL OPERATION

In this operation you create new worksheets and close them.

1. Start Excel.
2. Select **New** from the File menu.

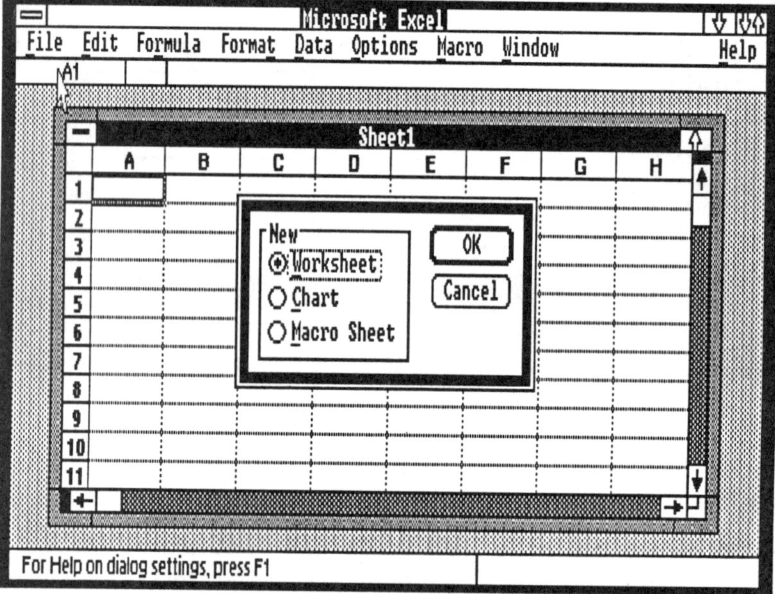

From this dialog box you can use the arrow keys to highlight one of the three available options.

3. Select Worksheet and click on **OK** or press **Enter**. Notice that the new worksheet is called Sheet2. This is the default name provided by Excel.

4. Open another worksheet by repeating the process you just completed.

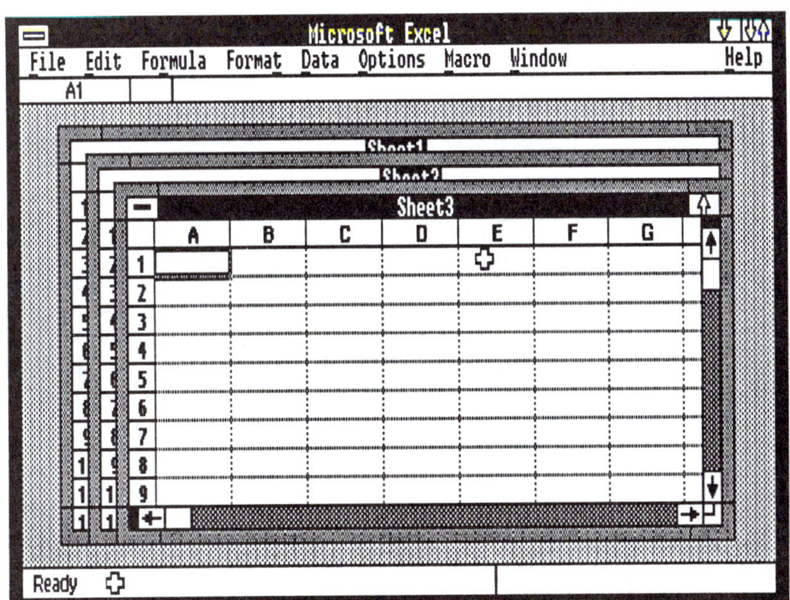

The new worksheet called Sheet3 is now in front of the two earlier sheets. As you finish with each worksheet you can close it.

5. Open the Control menu by pressing **Alt-Hyphen** or clicking on the Control icon in the upper left corner of Sheet3.

6. Select Close from the options in the menu. Sheet3 is removed and Sheet2 becomes the active worksheet. Even if you maximize Sheet2 to fill the entire screen, you need to remember that any worksheet created earlier, and not closed, still exists behind the active worksheet.

7. Maximize the worksheet so that it fills the entire screen. There are several methods of maximizing the worksheet:

   a. you can open the Control menu for the worksheet and select Maximize,
   b. you can open the Control menu and use the Size command,
   c. you can use the Maximize arrow in the upper right corner of the worksheet,
   d. you can use the mouse arrows to drag the sides out, or
   e. you can use the Size icon in the bottom right corner of the worksheet.

8. Open the Control menu for Sheet2 and select **Close**. Sheet1 now is the active worksheet.

9. Type **Savings** in cell B1.

10. Type **Bank** in cell B3.

11. Type **Stocks** in cell B4.

12. Type **Real Estate** in cell B5.

13. Type **Total** in cell B6.

14. Type **$300** in C3.

15. Type **$275** in C4.

16. Type **$400** in C5.

17. Type **= C3 + C4 + C5** in C6 and press **Enter**.

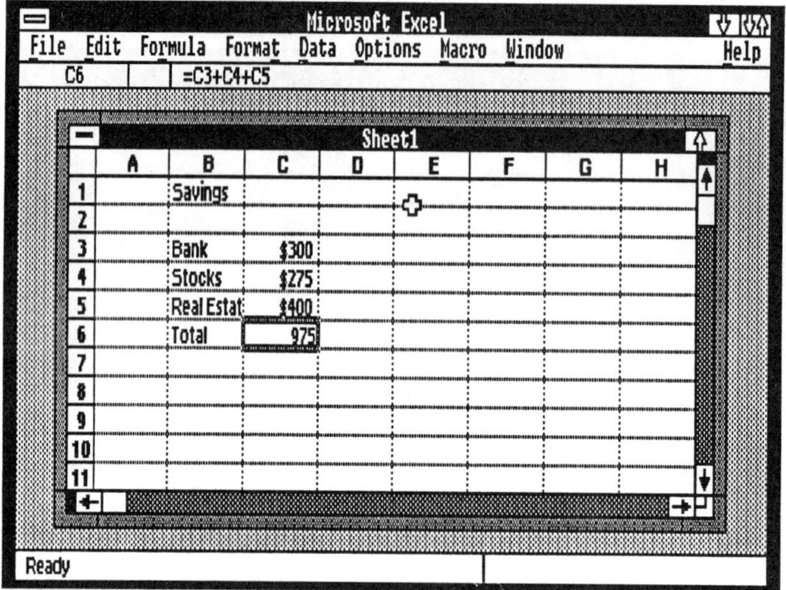

18. Continue the learning sequence by turning to Module 58.

Module 39

NEW WINDOW

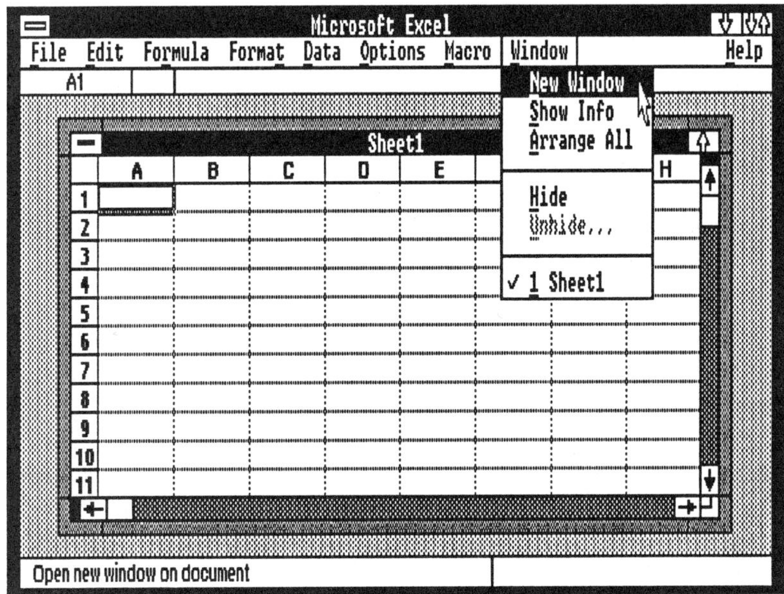

DESCRIPTION

Excel provides two different methods for creating a new worksheet. One of these methods, using the New command, is available through the File menu. This method is discussed in Module 38, New. The second method is the New Window command, accessed through the Window menu. Using the keyboard to access this command involves pressing Alt-W N. When the New command is used, Excel creates a completely unique worksheet. When the New Window command is used, the new worksheet is associated with the currently open window. The new worksheet will have the same title as the currently active worksheet, with an additional extension to provide a discrimination.

APPLICATIONS

The advantage of using the New Window command is that it permits you to interrupt your activity with a worksheet and try a particular operation on the data without changing the original data. The New Window command allows you to create a duplicate document with which to experiment.

You can also use this command to open a new window for the same document, which will permit you to view different portions of the same document on the screen.

Moving between windows that are opened with the New Window command is easily done by accessing the Window menu and clicking on the desired window, since all the available windows are listed at the bottom of the menu.

Another practical method of moving between multiple windows is by pressing Control-F6. Each time you press Ctrl-F6, Excel displays the next open worksheet as displayed in the Window menu.

TYPICAL OPERATION

In this operation you open a new window that is associated with a currently active window.

1. Start Excel.
2. Access the File menu and open the document BUDGET1.
3. Access the Window menu.

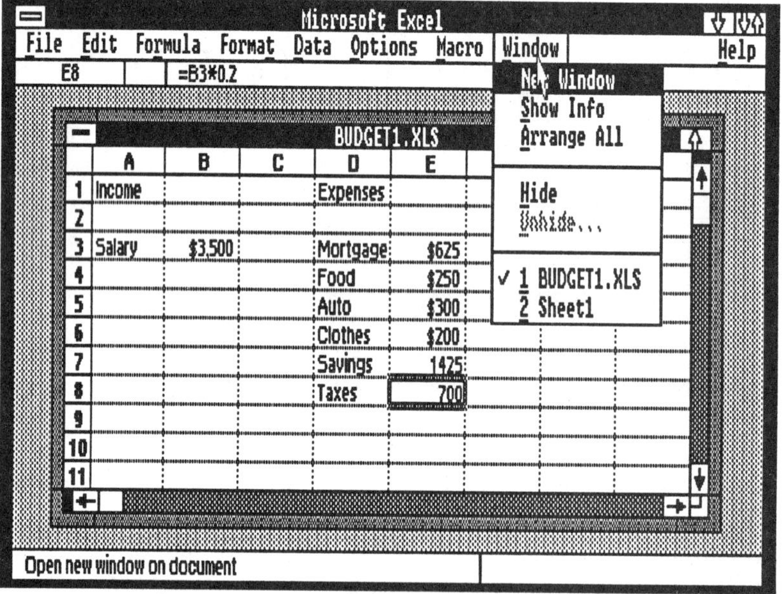

The Window menu indicates that there are two worksheets available at this time, BUDGET1 and Sheet1.

4. Type **N** or click on **New Window**.

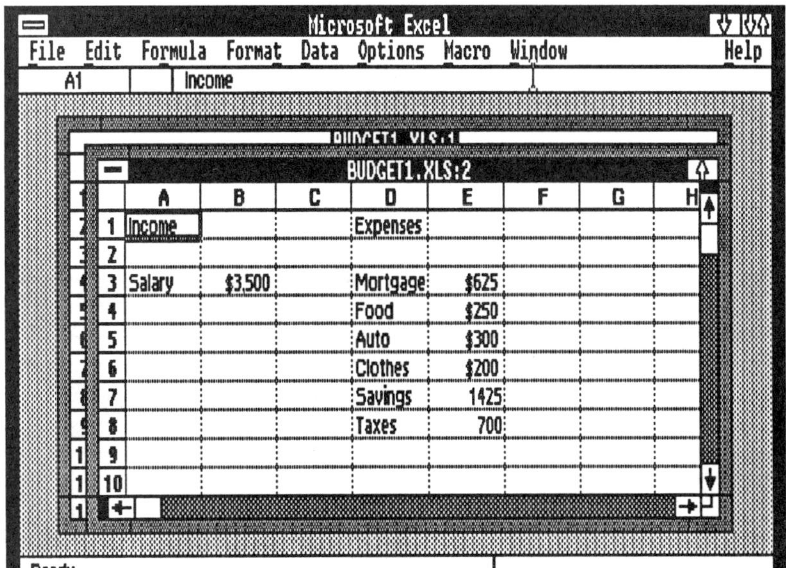

A new window, associated with BUDGET1, has been created. If your document was large and you wanted to see another portion of the worksheet, you could now scroll this new worksheet to the portion you wished to view. This would not change the position of the original BUDGET1 worksheet.

5. Open the Window menu. The three windows that are now available to you are displayed.

6. Click on **BUDGET1.XLS:1** or press **Down Arrow** to move to its location and press **Enter**. The original worksheet becomes the active worksheet. Both the second budget worksheet and Sheet1 are still available to you.

7. Press **Ctrl-F6**. The second budget worksheet is now the active window.

8. Press **Ctrl-F6**. Sheet1 is now the active window.

9. Continue the learning sequence with Module 67.

Module 40

NOTE

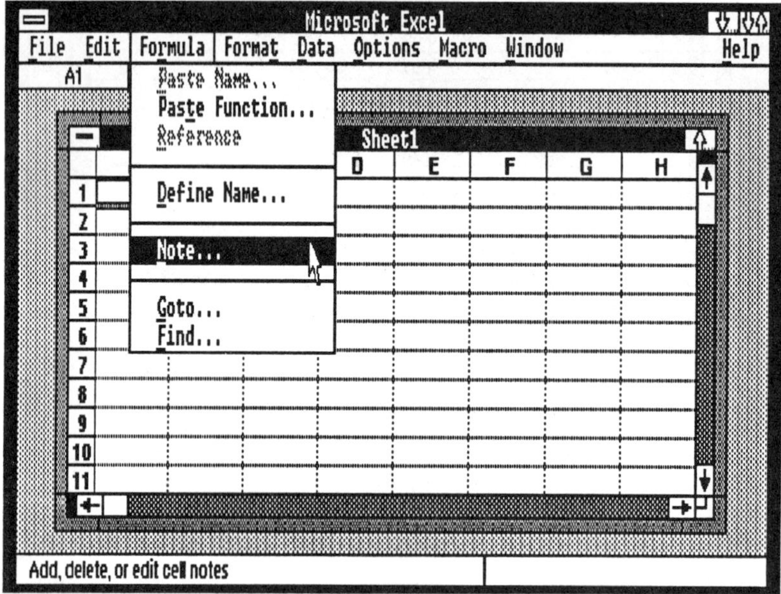

DESCRIPTION

The Note command is located on the Formula menu. Notes are comments about the worksheet that are not normally visible when you view the worksheet. However, you can choose to display or edit them at any time. When you execute the Notes command, either by selecting it from the Formula menu, or by pressing Shift-F2, the Notes shortcut command key, the following dialog box appears.

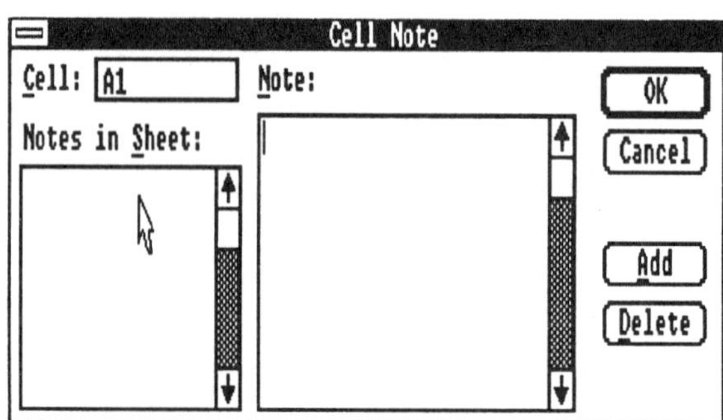

The Note box contains the text of the note corresponding to the cell referenced in the Cell box. Use the scroll bar to the right of the Note box to read long cell notes. The Notes in Sheet selection box allows you to view the cell reference and the first portion of each worksheet note. If a cell is selected prior to executing the Notes command, its reference is placed in the Cell box. You may view another cell note by typing its cell reference in the Cell box or by picking it from the Notes in Sheet box. Move the cursor (with the mouse or the Tab key) to the Note box to create a new note for a cell or to edit an existing note.

The Cell Note dialog box is a movable window. Move the mouse pointer to the dialog box title bar, depress the left mouse button, drag the dialog box to the desired location, then release the mouse button.

APPLICATIONS

Notes are useful for adding comments or explanations to formulas and tables. They are especially valuable for communicating your problem solving strategy to a colleague, or reminding yourself of the techniques you used to develop a worksheet when you have been away from it for a while.

When you create a note, try to begin the text of the note with something distinctive so that you can later recall the identity of the note when you view only the first portion in the Notes in Sheet dialog box.

TYPICAL OPERATION

In this session you add notes to the worksheet you created in Module 16 (Define Name). The notes provide additional information about the data and the formulas.

1. Start Excel and open the GOLD.XLS worksheet, or continue your work session from the previous module. Expand the worksheet to fill the screen if necessary, as shown in the following display.

	A	B	C	D	E	F	G	H	I
1		Gold Prices							
2	Hong Kong	$403.85							
3	New York	$405.24							
4	London	$403.05							
5	Paris	$401.47							
6	Frankfurt	$404.24							
7	Zurich	$404.25							
8									
9	Average	$403.68							
10	Future	$413.80							
11	Cost	$415.29							
12									
13									
14									

Microsoft Excel – GOLD.XLS
File Edit Formula Format Data Options Macro Window Help
B11 =(1+(Prime+0.015)/4)*Average
Ready

2. Select cell B3, the price of New York gold. Pick **Note** from the Formula menu. Notice that B3 appears in the Cell reference box of the dialog box.

3. Type **Comex spot market** in the Note box to designate which New York price is used in this calculation.

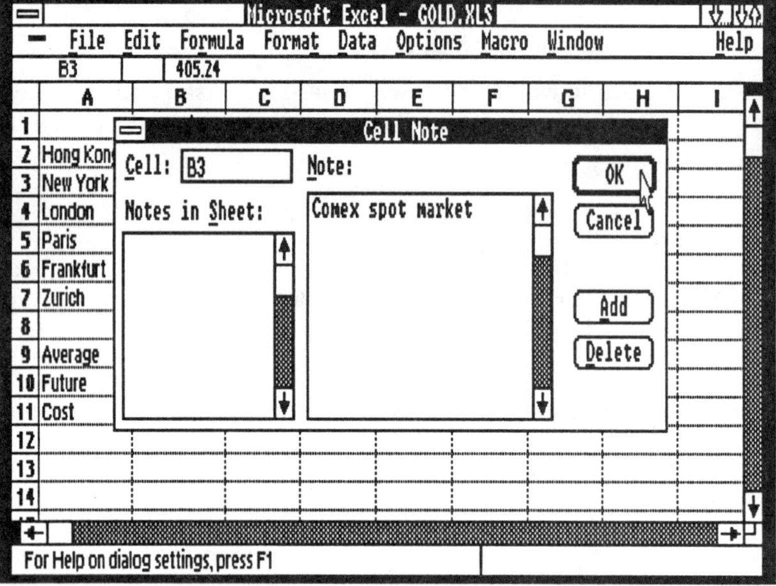

4. Select **OK**.

5. Select cell B11; then pick **Note** from the Formula menu.

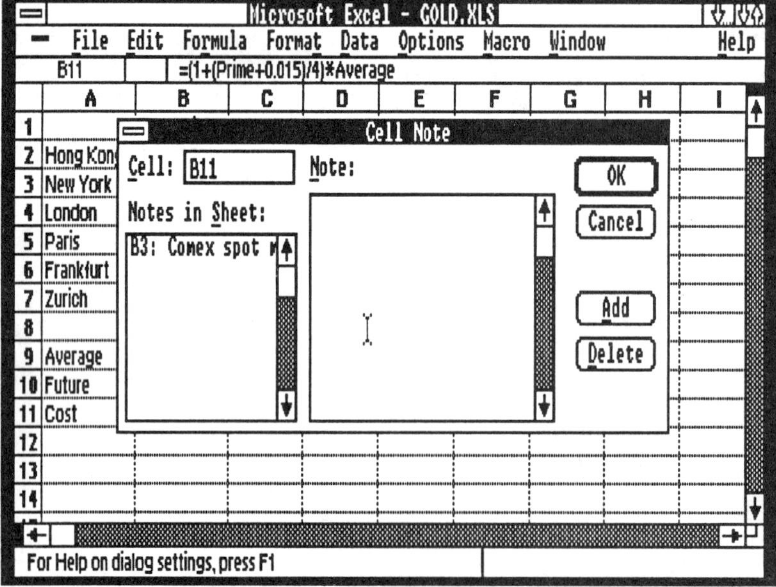

Notice that part of the previous note appears in the Notes in Sheet selection box.

6. Type the note **Interest computed at the prime rate plus 1.5% for 90 days.**

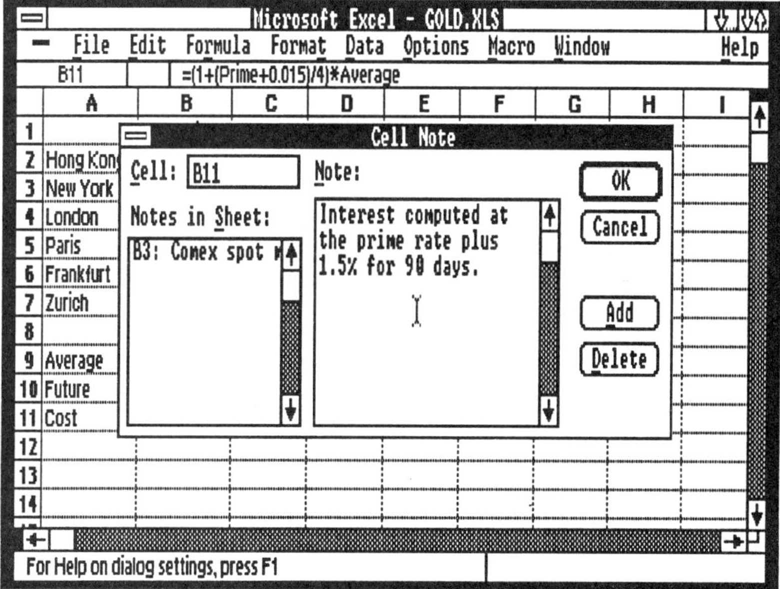

7. Select **OK**.
8. Save the worksheet.
9. Exit Excel, or continue your work session with the active worksheet on the **screen.**
10. Turn to Module 15 to continue the learning sequence.

Module 41

NUMBER

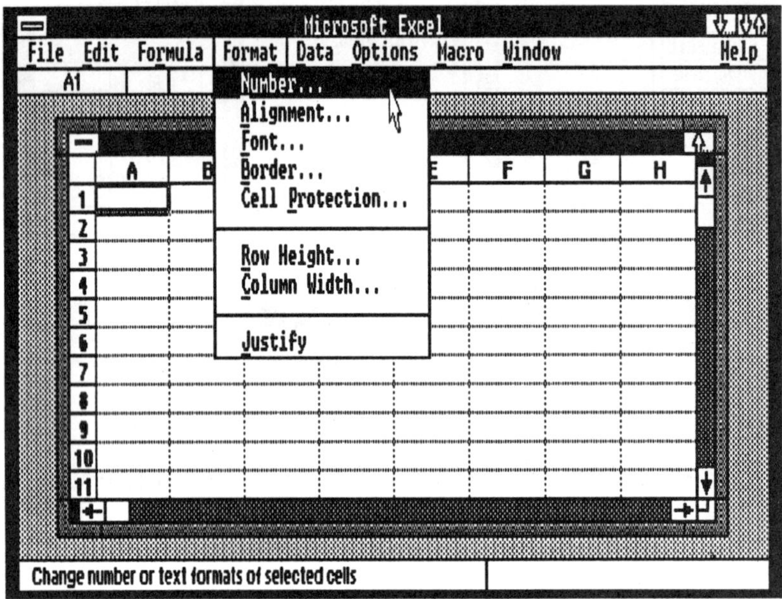

DESCRIPTION

Use the Number command on the Format menu to control the display style for numbers and dates. You may assign numeric formats to individual cells, a range of cells, a row, a column, or the entire worksheet. When you assign a particular numeric format to a row, it overrides the global format specifications for the worksheet. When you assign a particular format to a single cell, the selected format overrides the format for the row and the format of the worksheet in general.

When you pick Number from the Format menu with the mouse, or press Alt-T N, the Format Number dialog box appears, providing choices about the display of numbers and dates.

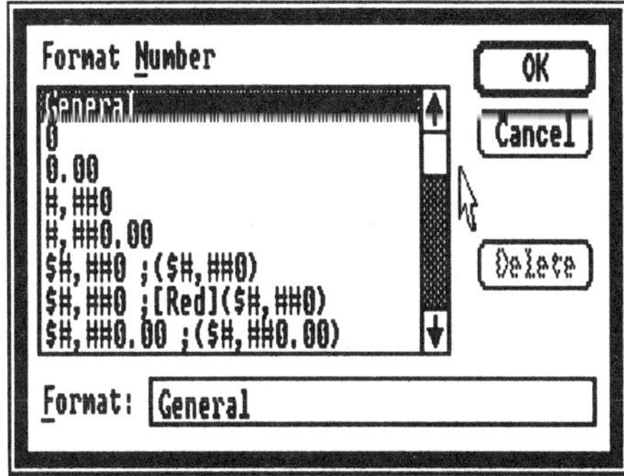

The selection box provides a variety of options for displaying numbers. The patterns use the digit 0 to specify a required 0 in the display format. For example, the format 0.00 specifies that two decimal places are always provided. The character # is used to represent an optional digit position. Format patterns with commas provide comma delimited output. You may also select the display format for negative values, choosing between minus signs, parentheses, and red text display.

This selection box also provides the options for displaying times and dates, by scrolling down in the scroll bar, as shown in the following display.

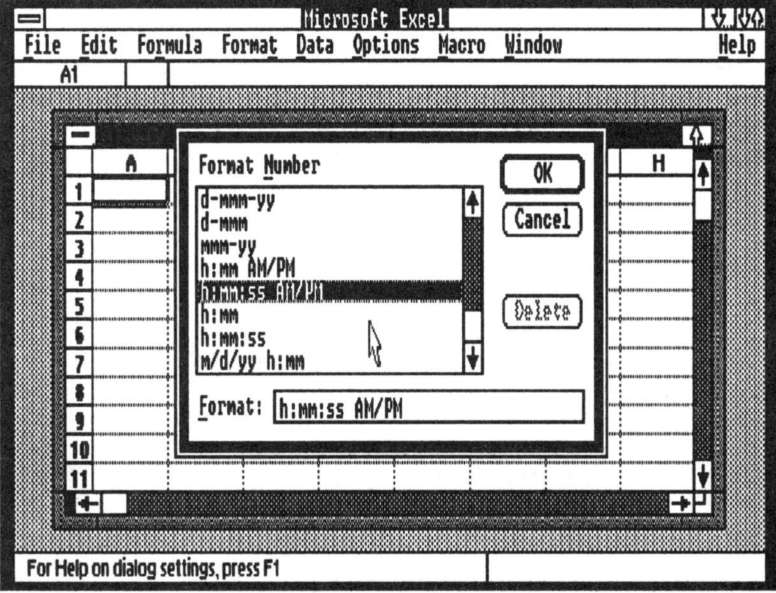

The patterns provide a variety of date and time formats and the optional inclusion of AM or PM designations for 12-hour time display.

If none of the predefined number formats meets your needs, you may use Excel's pattern characters to type your own custom format specifications into the Format field of the dialog box.

APPLICATIONS

Excel's powerful formatting options allow you to create visually pleasing output. Anytime you perform calculations, the inherent error of the way computers store numbers creates small error factors that quickly create numbers with many decimal digits. Use Excel's formatting options to suppress excess numeric digits.

Dollar amounts are typically expressed with two decimal digits, where Excel's default General format suppresses unneeded decimal places.

Normally, the displayed precision of a number has nothing to do with the internal precision Excel uses to retain numbers. Excel maintains the accuracy of all numbers to the limits of the computer hardware. However, you may check the Precision as Displayed Sheet Options check box, accessed from the Calculate command on the Options menu, to force Excel to perform calculations using the displayed resolution of the values. This is especially useful in financial applications where subtotals are frequently rounded to the nearest cent, or for preparing a federal income tax worksheet, rounded to the nearest whole dollar.

TYPICAL OPERATION

In this session you use Excel's formatting options to add formatting specifications to numeric data. In this session you compute the monthly interest charge to borrow money.

1. Start Excel. Use the default worksheet, Sheet1, to perform your work.
2. Type the borrowed amount **156879** in cell B3.
3. Type the monthly interest rate **0.0183** in cell B4.
4. Type the formula for the interest amount **=B3*B4** in cell B5.
5. Type the formula for the total amount due **=B3+B5** in cell B6 and press **Enter**.

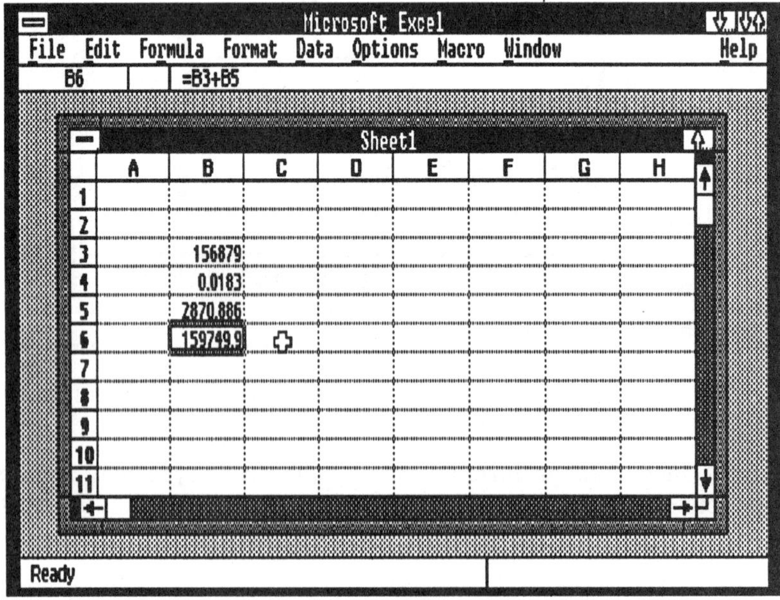

6. Select column B, (Pick the B with the mouse, or select a cell in column B and press Ctrl-Spacebar.) then select **Number** from the Format menu.

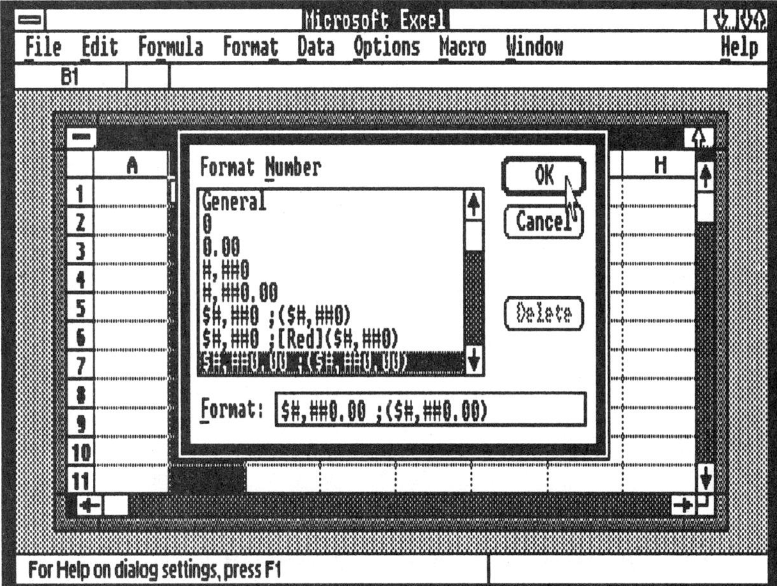

7. Select **$#,##0 ;($#,##0)**, a whole-dollars format that places negative values in parentheses, then select **OK**.

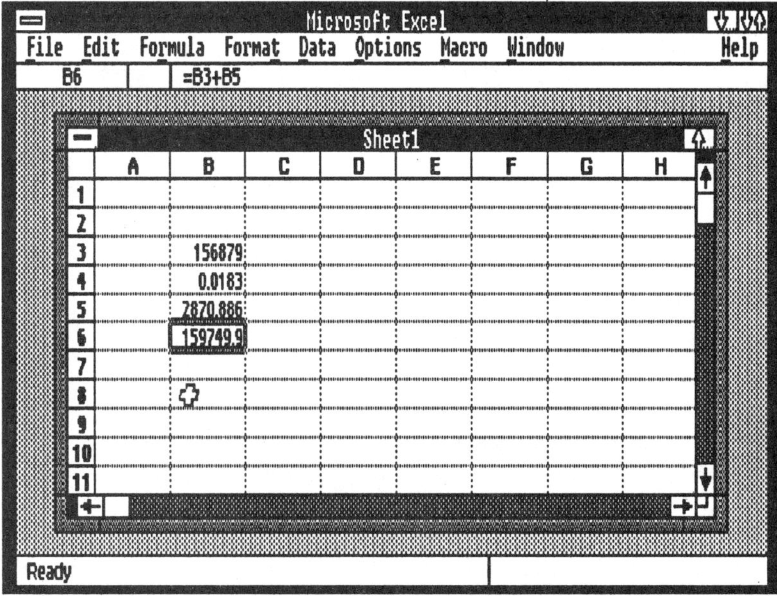

8. Select cell B4, then select **Number** from the Format menu.

There is no predefined format that shows three fixed decimal places. Therefore you create a custom format to show the interest rate.

9. Press **Tab** or pick in the Format box with the mouse. Type **0.000**.

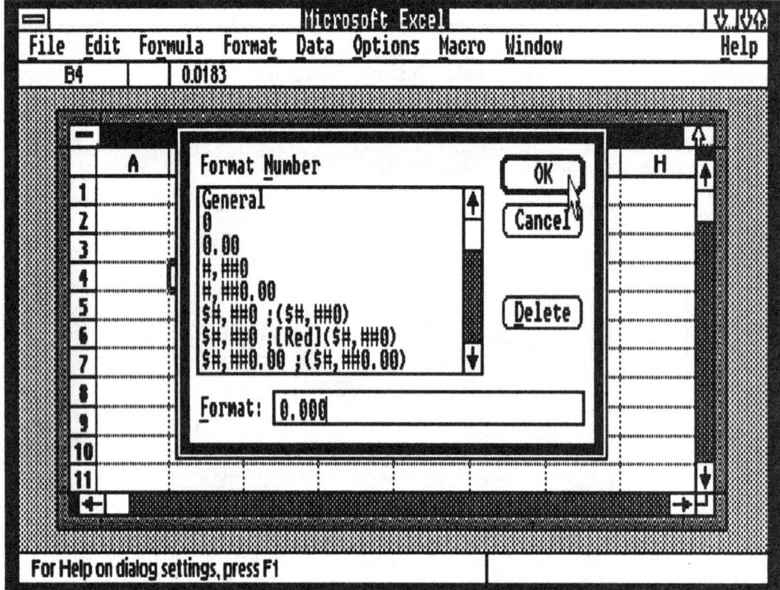

10. Pick **OK** or press **Enter**. The number is reformatted to your custom specifications.

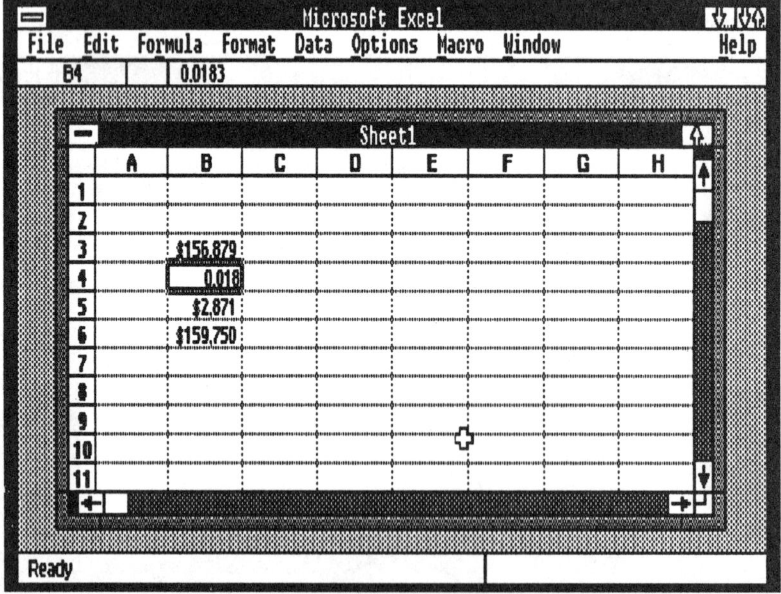

11. Select **Save As** from the File menu and type **INTEREST.XLS** as the filename. Then select **OK**.

12. Exit Excel or continue your work session with the current worksheet.

13. Turn to Module 13 to continue the learning sequence.

Module 42

OPEN

DESCRIPTION

The Open command from the File menu allows you to open any document that you previously saved. It is a command that you will use with increasing frequency as you explore the capabilities of Excel. To use the Open command, click on the File menu with the mouse cursor and then click on Open. From the keyboard, press Alt-F O. When you select this command you will be presented a dialog box.

The dialog box shows lists of files that are in your library, the directory you are currently in, and the subdirectories you can access. When you load Excel it will create some subdirectories. You can open a file from this dialog box by typing the name of the file you want to open or by clicking on the name with the mouse. If your library is large, you can scroll through the files by using the mouse on the scroll bars or by using the arrow keys. (See Module 3, Sample Session, for information on how to move within a dialog box.)

NOTE

It is important that you assign each document a name that you will be able to recognize. The alternative is to open each document until you find the one you want, a time consuming process if your library is large.

APPLICATIONS

The Open command provides an easy method of recalling a worksheet that you wish to modify. A good example of this type of worksheet is a budget or home inventory. By recalling the existing document, you can make changes and thus avoid creating a new worksheet each time.

This same process can be used effectively with documents that are seldom used but are, nevertheless, important. For example, once you have used Excel to calculate your income taxes for one year, you can recall that document each year and replace the old information with new information, adding any new categories or deleting any old categories. In all of these cases you use the Open command to access the existing document.

TYPICAL OPERATION

In this operation you open a file that has already been saved on the disk.

1. Start Excel.
2. Access the File menu and select the **Open** command.

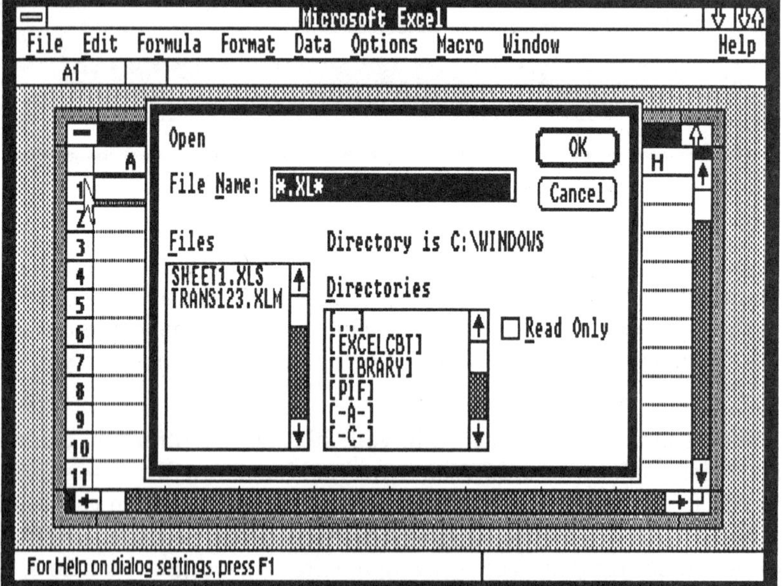

The dialog box lists the files that are in your library. Unless you have been creating and saving files, you will only have two files on your screen: SHEET1.XLS and TRANS123.XLM.

SHEET1.XLS is the same file you saved in the Sample Session module.

The TRANS123.XLM is a system file that is used to create compatibility between a Lotus 1-2-3 file and Excel.

3. Type **SHEET1.XLS** or click on **SHEET1.XLS** with the mouse.

4. Press **Enter** or click on **OK**.

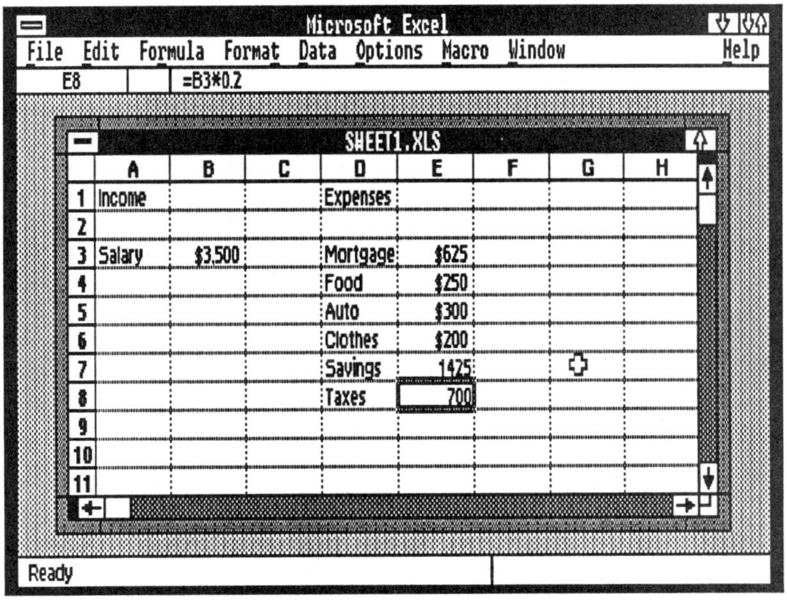

The budget document you saved on disk as SHEET1.XLS is placed over Sheet1 and is now designated as the active document window by the scroll bars on the bottom and side.

NOTE
Remember if you want to expand the worksheet
SHEET1.XLS to fill the entire screen, you can
open the Control icon to access Size or Maximize,
or you can use the mouse to click on the Up
Arrow in the upper right corner.

You can open additional files in the same manner.

5. Select **Exit** from the File menu. There is no need to save the worksheet.

6. Turn to Module 38 to continue the learning sequence.

Module 43

PAGE SETUP

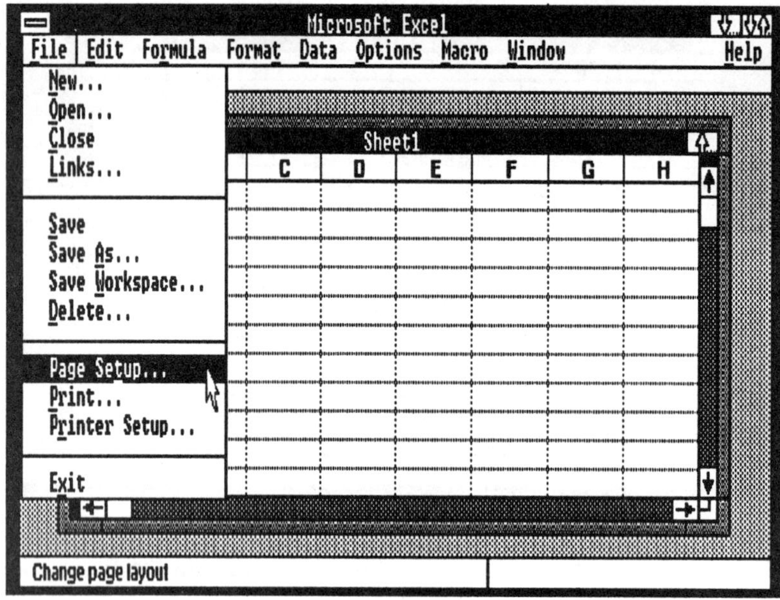

DESCRIPTION

Use the Page Setup command on the File menu to control print formatting features such as margins, row and column headings, headers, footers, and gridlines. When you select the command, either with the mouse or by pressing Alt-F T, the following dialog box appears.

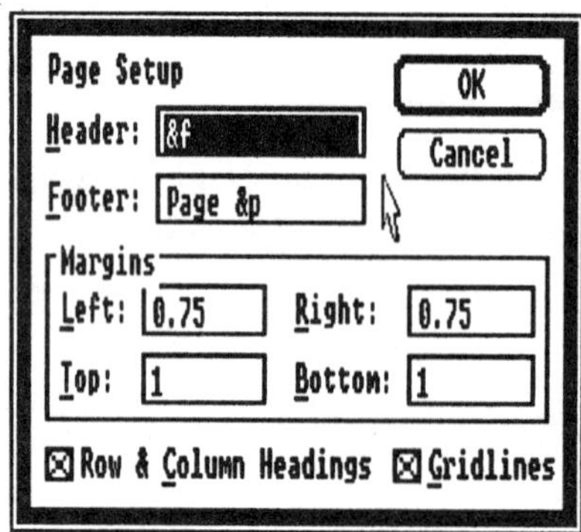

The Header field has the default value *&f*, which, when printed, prints the worksheet's filename.

Tho Footor fiold hao tho dofault valuo *Page &p*, which prints the word "Page" followed by the current printout page number.

The margin specifications are in decimal inches.

The check boxes for Row & Column Headings and for Gridlines are normally checked, meaning that row headings, column headings, and gridlines are printed on the printout.

Change the values and pick OK or pick Cancel.

When you save the worksheet, the Page Setup options become part of its definition, allowing you to have different Page Setup options for each worksheet.

APPLICATIONS

One of the great strengths of Excel is the extensive control of the way your worksheet appears on the screen and on paper. You can adjust the margins to place the printout in the most appropriate location on the paper. Turning off the row and column headings allows your printout to look less like a "spreadsheet" and more like a "report." Depending on the nature of the data you present, including the gridlines may either clarify or confuse information. Try printing a copy both ways to see which is better for your application.

TYPICAL OPERATION

In this session you use the Page Setup command to alter the appearance of the budget printout you created in the Print module.

1. Start Excel and open the worksheet BUDGET1.XLS, or continue your work session from the previous module.

2. Select **Page Setup** from the File menu.

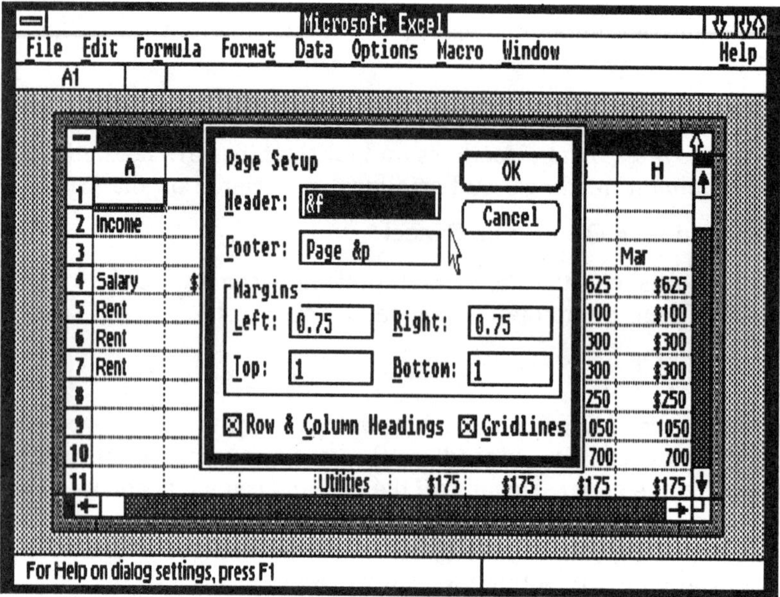

3. Pick the **Row & Column Headings** check box, removing the X from the box.
4. Pick the **Gridlines** check box, removing the X from the box.

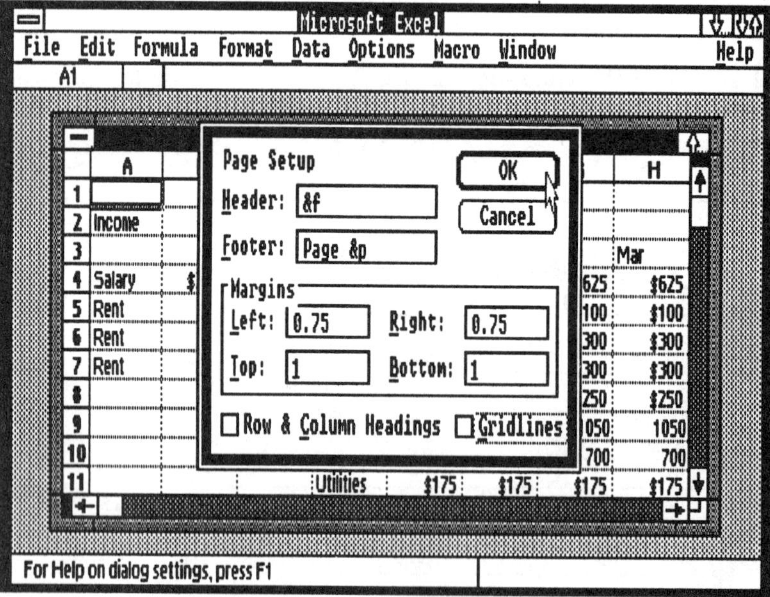

5. Pick **OK**.
6. Select **Print** from the File menu.

7. Pick **Preview** on the Print dialog box, then pick **OK**.

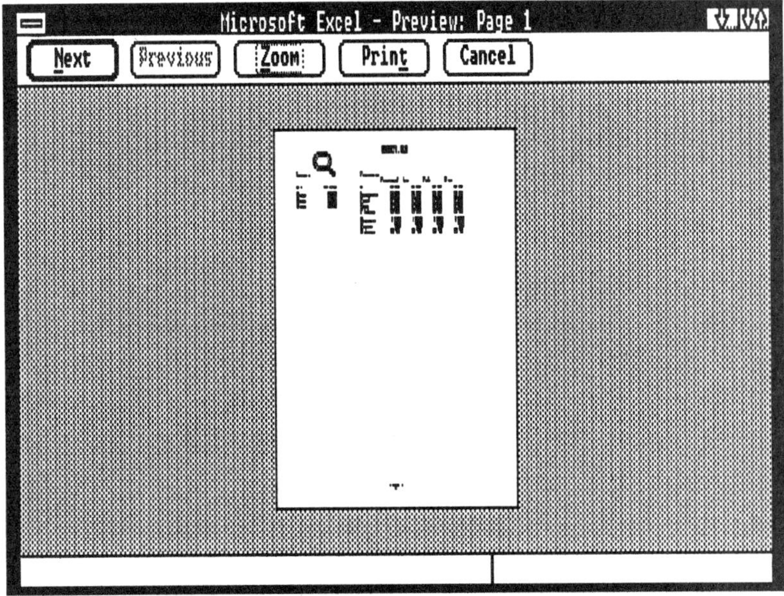

8. Pick on the upper left portion of the page image, then move the scroll bars to view the preview as shown in the following screen. Notice that the row headings, column headings, and gridlines are missing.

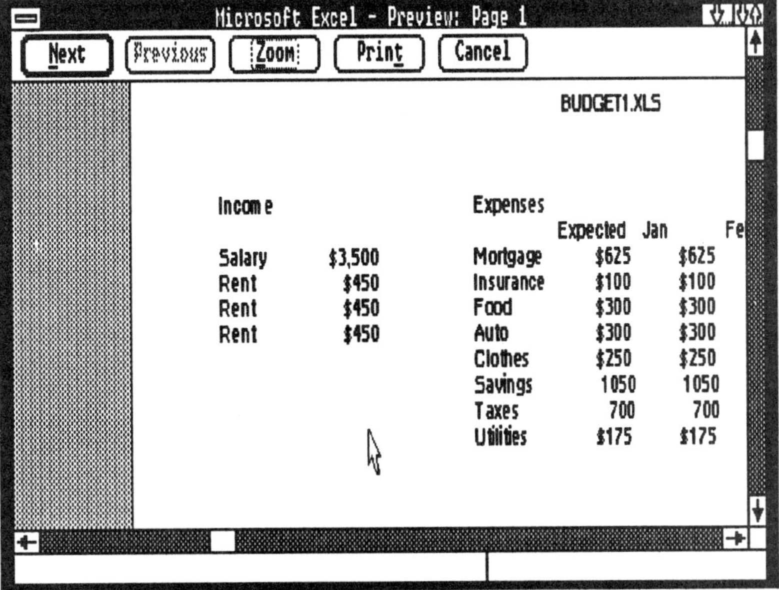

9. Pick **Cancel** to leave the page preview operation.

10. Save the worksheet to retain the Page Setup options for use in subsequent modules in the learning sequence.

11. Exit Excel, or continue your work session with the active worksheet on the screen.

12. Turn to Module 63 to continue the learning sequence.

Module 44

PARSE

DESCRIPTION

Use the Parse command on the Data menu to split text strings (long labels) into multiple cells for analysis in Excel.

When Excel opens an ASCII text file as a worksheet, each line of text appears as one long label. The numbers and dates embedded in the line cannot be manipulated, summarized, graphed, or otherwise analyzed as long as they are part of a long label. The Parse command transforms these unusable text strings into meaningful numbers, dates, and data that can then be manipulated with Excel's analysis features.

First, open an ASCII text file as a worksheet. (Although not required, text files often use the file extension .TXT to distinguish them from other files.) The data appears as a single column of labels on the worksheet. Next, highlight the single column containing the text data; then pick the Parse command from the Data menu with the mouse or by pressing Alt-D P. The following dialog box appears.

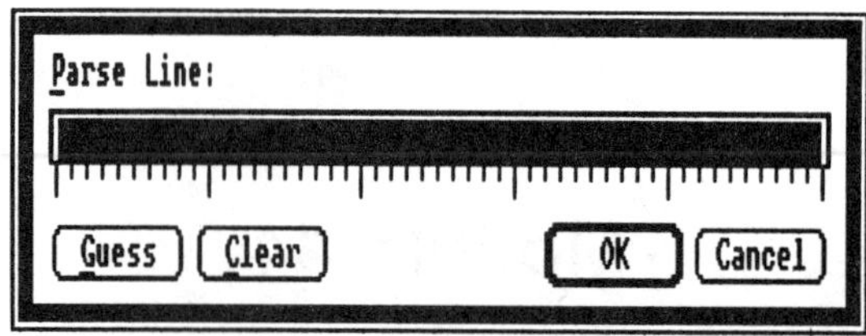

The dialog box has the contents of the first cell of the line of data in the Parse Line. Excel uses the square brackets [] to enclose prospective elements for splitting up the data. You may either enter the brackets manually, or pick Guess to allow Excel to take its best shot at how the data should be parsed. After allowing Excel to guess at how the data should be divided into cells, you have the opportunity to fine-tune the process manually before selecting OK or pressing Enter to execute the parse operation.

APPLICATIONS

Excel's Open command on the File menu is capable of automatically reading and manipulating a number of file formats used by leading software publishers. However, there are cases when you need to import data into Excel from a program that Excel does not fully support. Typical examples inlude data downloaded from a public information utility such as Compuserve, from your company's mainframe, or from a PC application with its own "better" way of maintaining data. Information captured from a remote mainframe or information service with a communications program usually ends up as an ASCII text file on your disk. Even PC applications with "better," yet obscure, undocumented, and unsupported file formats are usually capable of printing a "report" to disk that contains all the information in the file as ASCII text. The Parse command allows you to transform this text data into a form that Excel can manipulate.

TYPICAL OPERATION

In this session you type several lines of ASCII text into a column in a worksheet, simulating the result of loading an ASCII file into Excel. Then you use the Parse command to divide your text into separate cells.

1. Start Excel. Use Sheet1, the default sheet, for your work.
2. Type **189.34 43.19 11/01/87** in cell A1.
3. Type **203.12 66.98 10/12/88** in cell A2.

4. Type **144.87 51.41 12/12/88** into cell A3 and press **Return**.

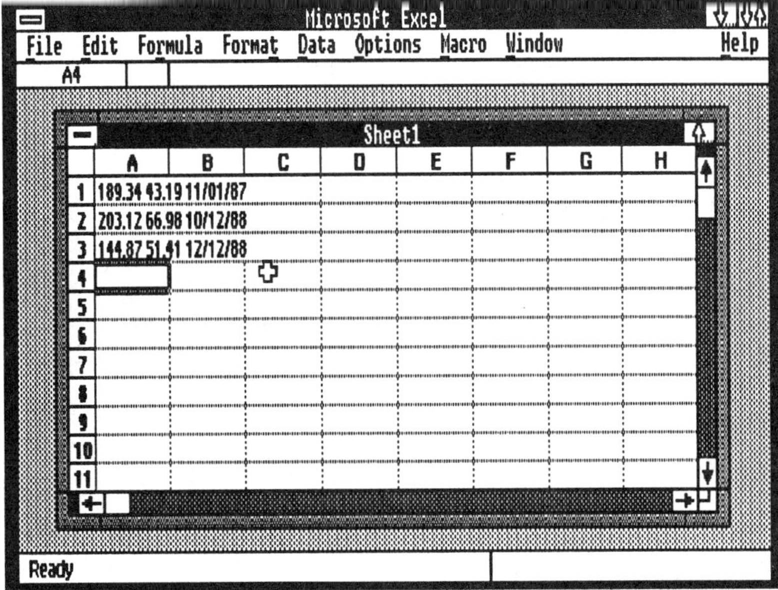

5. Select the cell range A1 through A3, then select **Parse** from the Data menu. Notice that the data from cell A1 appears on the Parse Line.

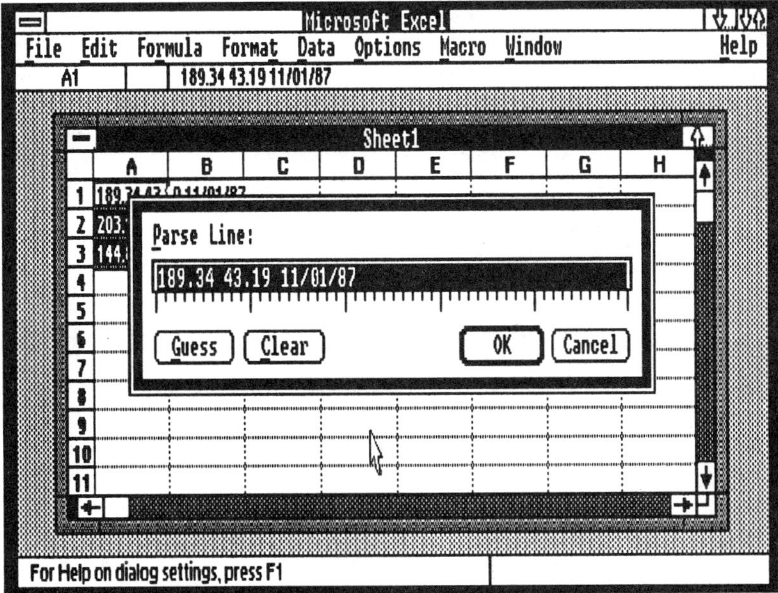

6. Pick **Guess** on the Parse dialog box to allow Excel to attempt to decode the data.

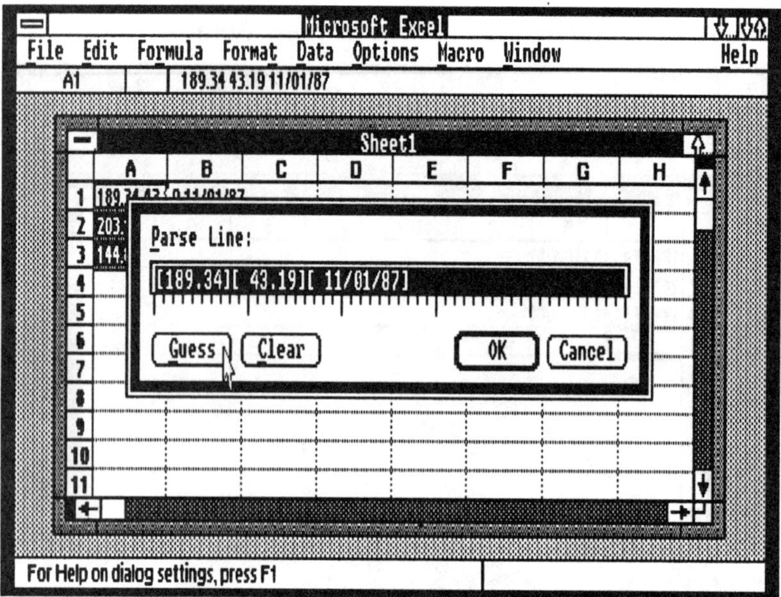

The Parse Line is divided with square brackets to determine the division points that Excel proposes to use to divide the data. In most cases, Excel makes very good guesses about data formats.

7. Pick **OK** to accept the proposed division. The data now occupies columns A through C in a form suitable for further analysis with Excel.

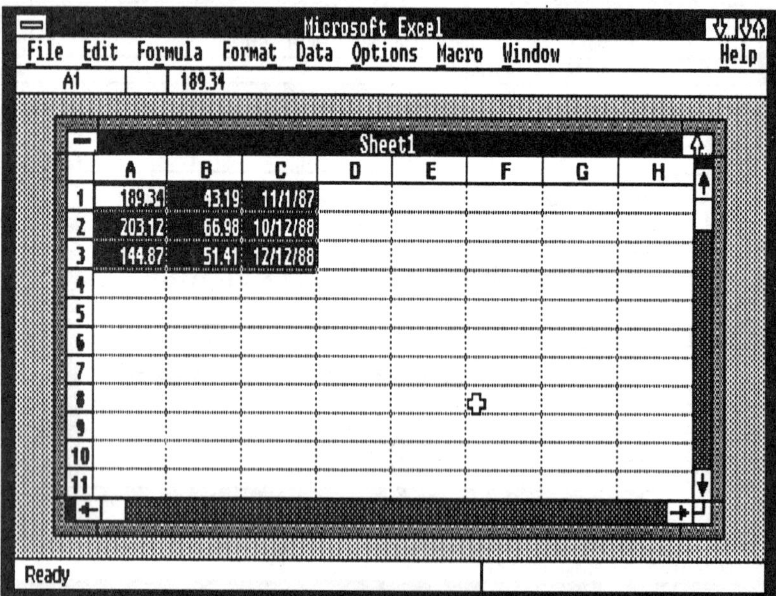

8. Close the worksheet without saving.

9. Exit Excel, or continue your work session without an active worksheet on the screen.

10. Turn to Module 69 to continue the learning sequence.

Module 45

PASTE FUNCTION

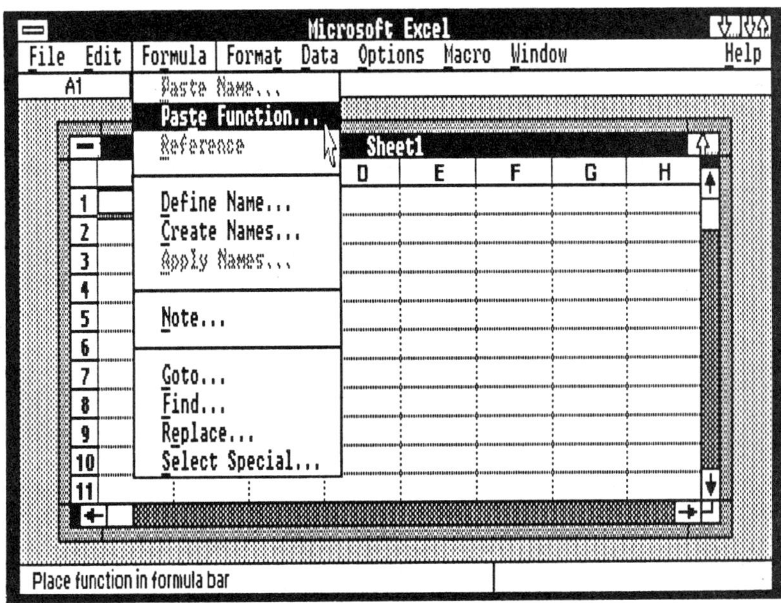

DESCRIPTION

Excel provides many built-in functions to make constructing your worksheets faster and easier. Use the Paste Function command on the Formula menu to paste the function you require, either at the formula bar or a selected insertion point. Optionally, the command inserts placeholders for the arguments to the function.

PASTE FUNCTION DIALOG BOX   When you select the Paste Function command with the mouse or by pressing Alt-R T, the following dialog box opens on the screen.

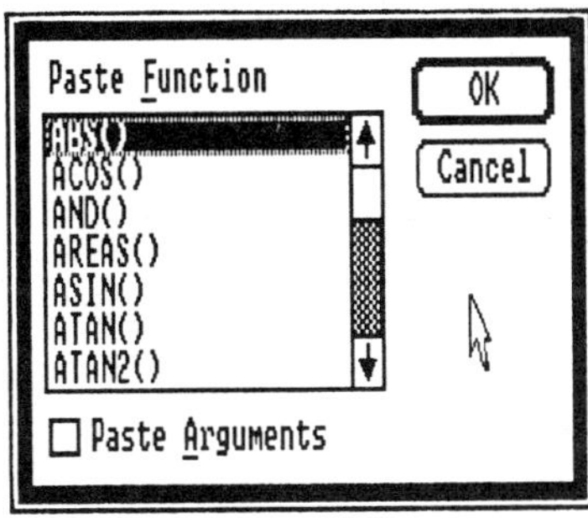

The function selection box in the dialog box presents the available functions in alphabetical order.

FUNCTION GROUPS   In the following sections, the functions available in Excel are grouped by function category. These categories include database, date and time, financial, information, logical, lookup, mathematical, matrix, statistical, text, and trigonometric functions. Within each group the functions are arranged in alphabetical order. The arguments (parameters) of each function are listed in parentheses after the function name. Required parameters are printed in normal type. Optional parameters are printed in italics.

Database Functions

DAVERAGE(database, field, criteria)

Returns the average of numbers specified in *field* of records in the *database* meeting the *criteria*.

DCOUNT(database, field, criteria)

Returns the number of numbers specified in *field* of records in the *database* meeting the *criteria*.

DCOUNTA(database, field, criteria)

Returns the number of non-empty cells in the specified *field* of records in the *database* meeting the *criteria*.

DMAX(database, field, criteria)

Returns the maximum value of numbers in the *field* of records in the *database* meeting the *criteria*.

DMIN(database, field, criteria)

Returns the minimum value of numbers in the *field* of records in the *database* meeting the *criteria*.

DPRODUCT(database, field, criteria)

Returns the product of numbers in the specified *field* of records in the *database* meeting the *criteria*.

DSTDEV(database, field, criteria)

Uses the sample formula for computation of the standard deviation of the numbers in the specified *field* of records in the database meeting the *criteria*.

DSTDEVP(database, field, criteria)

Uses the population formula for computation of the standard deviation of the numbers in the specified *field* of records in the *database* meeting the *criteria*.

DSUM(database, field, criteria)

Computes the sum of all numbers in the *field* in each record of the *database* meeting the *criteria*.

DVAR(database, field, criteria)

Computes the sample variance of all numbers in the *field* in each record of the *database* meeting the *criteria*.

DVARP(database, field, criteria)

Computes the population variance of all numbers in the *field* in each record of the *database* meeting the *criteria*.

Date and Time Functions

DATE(year, month, day)

Returns the Excel serial number of the date specified.

DATEVALUE(date_text)

Returns the Excel serial number of the data specified.

DAY(serial_number)

Converts *serial_number* to a day of the month.

HOUR(serial_number)

Converts *serial_number* to an hour of the day.

MINUTE(serial_number)

Converts *serial_number* to a minute of an hour.

MONTH(serial_number)

Converts *serial_number* to a month of a year.

NOW()

Accesses the current date stored in the operating system and converts it to an Excel date serial number. Even though there are no arguments, the parentheses are important to identify NOW as a function.

SECOND(serial_number)

Converts *serial_number* to a second of a minute.

TIME(hour, minute, second)

Returns the serial number of the specified time.

TIMEVALUE(time_text)

Returns the serial number of the specified time.

WEEKDAY(serial_number)

Converts *serial_number* to a day of the week.

YEAR(serial_number)

Converts *serial_number* to a year.

Financial Functions

DDB(cost, salvage, life, period)

Computes the depreciation of an asset using the double-declining balance method.

    FV(rate, nper, pmt, *pv*, *type*)

Computes the future value of an investment.

    IPMT(rate, per, nper, pv, *fv*, *type*)

Computes the required interest payment for an investment.

    IRR(values, *guess*)

Computes the internal rate of return for *values*.

    MIRR(values, finance_rate, reinvest_rate)

Computes the modified internal rate of return for *values*.

    NPER(rate, pmt, pv, *fv*, *type*)

Computes the number of payments of investment.

    NPV(rate, *value1*, *value2*, ...)

Computes the net present value of the *value1* and optional values *value2*, etc.

    PMT(rate, nper, pv, *fv*, *type*)

Computes the required periodic payment on the principal of an investment.

    PPMT(rate, per, nper, pv, *fv*, *type*)

Returns the payment on the principal for an investment.

    PV(rate, nper, pmt, *fv*, *type*)

Computes the present value of an investment.

    RATE(nper, pmt, pv, *fv*, *type*, *guess*)

Computes the rate returned on an investment.

    SLN(cost, salvage, life)

Computes the depreciation of an asset using the straight-line method.

    SYD(cost, salvage, life, per)

Computes the depreciation of an asset using the sum-of-the-years-digits method.

Information Functions

    AREAS(reference)

Returns the number of areas in *reference*.

    CELL(type_of_info, *reference*)

Returns information about location, formatting, or contents of *reference*.

COLUMN(reference)

Returns the column numbers in *reference*.

COLUMNS(array)

Counts the number of columns in *array*.

INDIRECT(ref_text, type_of_ref)

Returns the contents of the cell from its *ref*.

ISBLANK(value)

Returns True if *value* is blank.

ISERR(value)

Returns True if *value* is an error value other than #N/A.

ISERROR(value)

Returns True if *value* is any error value, including #N/A.

ISLOGICAL(value)

Returns True if *value* is a logical value.

ISNA(value)

Returns True if *value* is the error value #N/A.

ISNONTEXT(value)

Returns True if *value* is not text.

ISNUMBER(value)

Returns True if *value* is a number.

ISREF(value)

Returns True if *value* is a reference.

ISTEXT(value)

Returns True if *value* is text.

N(value)

Translates *value* into a number.

NA()

Returns the error value #N/A.

ROW(reference)

Returns the row numbers in *reference*.

ROWS(array)

Counts the number of rows in *array*.

T(value)

Translates *value* into text.

TYPE(value)

Returns the type of *value*.

Logical Functions

AND(logical1, *logical2*, ...)

Returns True if all arguments are true. Only *logical1* is required. Additional arguments are optional.

FALSE()

Returns the logical value False. Although there are no arguments, the parentheses are important to identify FALSE as an Excel function.

IF(logical_test, value_if_true, *value_if_false*)

If *logical_test* is true, returns *value_if_true*. If *logical_test* is false, returns *value_if_false*.

NOT(logical)

Returns the logical negative of *logical*. If *logical* is True, the function returns False. If *logical* is False, the function returns True.

OR(logical1, *logical1*, ...)

Returns the value True if any of the arguments are true.

TRUE()

Returns the logical value True. Although there are no arguments, the parentheses are important to identify TRUE as an Excel function.

Lookup Functions

CHOOSE(index_number, value1, *value2*, ...)

Index_number is a numeric value used as an index to a range specified by *value1*, or a list of values specified by *value1*, *value2*, etc. The function returns the value corresponding to the position of *index_number*.

HLOOKUP(lookup_value, table_array, row_index_num)

A table-lookup function operating by rows (compare with VLOOKUP).

INDEX(ref, row_num, column_num, *area_num*)

INDEX(array, row_num, column_num)

There are two forms of the INDEX function. The function returns either the reference in *ref* or the value in *array* as determined by the *row_num* and *column_num* index values.

LOOKUP(lookup_value, lookup_vector, result_vector)

This is the preferred form of the LOOKUP function, which searches *lookup_vector* for the largest value less than or equal to *lookup_value*. The values in *lookup_vector*, which can be numbers, text, or logical values must be in ascending order. If *lookup_value* is smaller than the smallest value in *lookup_vector*, the result is the #NA error. *lookup_vector* and *result_vector* do not need to have the same direction, but must be the same size.

LOOKUP(lookup_value, array)

Looks up *lookup_value* in the array and returns its value. This form of the LOOKUP function is provided for compatibility with Microsoft's Multiplan. Because the search direction of *array* depends on whether the array has more rows or columns, it is easily misused. The alternate version of the LOOKUP function is the preferred form.

MATCH(lookup_value, lookup_array, *type_of_match*)

Returns the number of *lookup_value* in *lookup_array* where the optional argument *type_of_match* determines the matching criteria.

VLOOKUP(lookup_value, table_array, col_index)

A table-lookup function operating by columns (compare with HLOOKUP).

Mathematical Functions

ABS(number)

Computes the absolute value of *number*.

EXP(number)

Raises *e* to the power *number*.

FACT(number)

Computes the factorial of *number*.

INT(number)

A truncation function that returns the integer portion of a decimal *number*. Identical to TRUNC.

LN(number)

Computes the natural logarithm (base *e*) of *number*.

LOG(number, *base*)

Computes a base *base* logarithm of *number*.

    LOG10(number)

Computes the base 10 logarithm of *number*.

    MOD(number, divisor_number)

The modulus or remainder function, returns the remainder resulting from the division of *number* by *divisor_number*.

    PI()

Returns the value of pi.

    PRODUCT(number1, *number2*, ...)

Multiplies the series of numbers specified, returning the product.

    RAND()

Returns a random number between zero and one. Every time the worksheet is recalculated, RAND generates a new random number.

    ROUND(number, number_of_digits)

Rounds *number* to a decimal number with *number_of_digits* specifying the number of digits to the right of the decimal point.

    SIGN(number)

Returns the sign of *number*.

    SQRT(number)

Computes the square root of *number*.

    TRUNC(number)

Returns the integer part of *number*. Identical in operation to INT.

Matrix Functions

    MDETERM(array)

Computes the determinant of the *array*.

    MINVERSE(array)

Computes the matrix inverse of *array*.

    MMULT(array1, array2)

Performs matrix multiplication on the two arrays.

    TRANSPOSE(array)

Computes the matrix transpose of *array*.

Statistical Functions

AVERAGE(number1, number2, ...)

Computes the arithmetic mean of the numbers or range specified.

COUNT(value1, *value2*, ...)

Counts the number of values in the cells or ranges specified. Each *value* (to a maximum of 14) may be a single cell reference, such as A1, or a cell range, such as A1:A5.

COUNTA(value1, value2, ...)

Counts the number of values in the list of arguments.

GROWTH(known_y's, *Knownx's*, *new_x's*)

Computes values on an exponential trend.

LINEST(known_y's, known_x's)

Computes parameters of a linear trend.

LOGEST(known_y's, known_x's)

Computes parameters of an exponential trend.

MAX(number1, *number2*, ...)

Returns the maximum numeric value of the arguments. The arguments may be either individual cells, named cells, named values, or ranges.

MIN(number1, *number2*, ...)

Returns the minimum numeric value of the arguments. The arguments may be either individual cells, named cells, named values, or ranges.

STDEV(number1, *number2*, ...)

Standard deviation using the sample formula.

STDEVP(number1, number2, ...)

Standard deviation using the population formula.

SUM(number1, *number2*, ...)

Computes the sum of the arguments. The arguments may be either individual cells, named cells, named values, or ranges.

TREND(number1, *number2*, ...)

Computes values in a linear trend.

VAR(number1, *number2*, ...)

Variance of a population based on a sample.

VARP(number1, *number2*, ...)

Variance of a population based on the population.

Text Functions

CHAR(number)

ASCII character corresponding to number.

CLEAN(text)

Strips control characters from *text*.

CODE(text)

ASCII code of the first character in text.

DOLLAR(number, decimals)

Rounds number and returns text in currency format.

EXACT(text1, text2)

Exact matching function.

FIND(find_text, within_text, *start_at_num*)

Locates *find_text* in *within_text* starting the search at the first position in *within_text*, or at *start_at_num* if specified.

FIXED(number, *decimals*)

Rounds *number* to the number of places in *decimal* and returns the text value.

LEFT(text, *number_of_characters*)

Copies the first *number_of_characters* from *text*, or one character if *number_of_characters* is omitted.

LEN(text)

Computes the length of a text string.

LOWER(text)

Converts a text string to lowercase.

MID(text, start_number, number_of_characters)

Extracts *number_of_characters* from *text*.

PROPER(text)

Converts text to initial caps.

REPLACE(old_text, start_num, num_chars, new_text)

Replaces num_chars characters in old_text with new_text.

REPT(text, number_times)

Repeats text for the specified number_times.

  RIGHT(text, number_of_chars)

Returns the rightmost *number_of_chars* from text.

  SEARCH(find_text, within_text, start_at_num)

Searches for *find_text* in the text *within_text*, starting at *start_at_num*.

  SUBSTITUTE(text, old_text, new_text, *instance_number*)

Substitutes *new_text* for *old_text* in *text*, performing the substitution *instance_number* of times.

  TEXT(value, format_text)

Converts *value* to text using the format specified in *format_text*.

  TRIM(text)

Removes spaces from *text*.

  UPPER(text)

Converts *text* to uppercase.

  VALUE(text)

Converts *text* to a number.

Trigonometric Functions

  ACOS(number)

Returns the arccosine of *number*.

  ASIN(number)

Returns the arcsine of *number*.

  ATAN(number)

Returns the arctangent of *number*.

  COS(radians)

Returns the cosine of *radians*.

  SIN(radians)

Returns the sine of *radians*.

  TAN(radians)

Returns the tangent of *radians*.

APPLICATIONS

Excel's functions provide a shortcut method for performing sometimes complex calculations without having to develop complex formulas yourself. Use the Paste Function command to avoid having to memorize the correct spelling and format for each of Excel's functions.

There is a small "gotcha" when working with dates if you plan to interchange data between the MS-DOS version of Excel and the Macintosh version. The dates in the two systems are kept internally as serial numbers. The dates in the MS-DOS version of Excel are based on assigning January 1, 1900 the serial number 1. This maintains date compatibility with dates generated by Lotus 1-2-3. The Apple Macintosh computer assigns a serial number of 1 to January 2, 1904. Excel for the PC automatically converts these dates when it reads Macintosh Excel worksheets. However, the reverse is not necessarily true. If you create a worksheet for eventual use with the Macintosh, turn on the 1904 Date System check box in the Calculations dialog box on the Options drop-down menu to create your worksheets with the Macintosh date system.

TYPICAL OPERATION

In this session you generate a list of random numbers, compute their sum and average, and select the largest and smallest value using Excel's built-in functions.

1. Start Excel. Expand Sheet1 to fill the screen.

2. With cell A1 selected, pick **Paste Function** from the Formula menu.

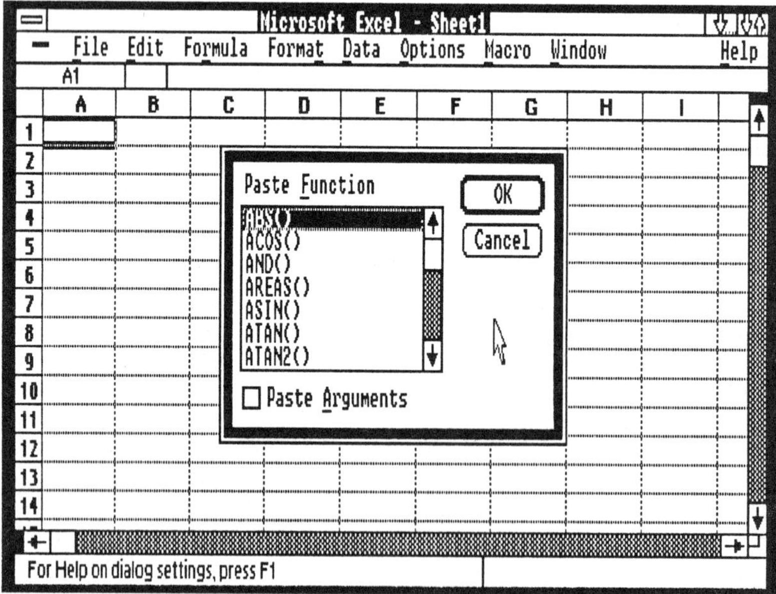

3. Scroll the selection box to display the RAND() function. The selection box can be sensitive to small mouse movements. You may want to click the mouse just above and just below the scroll box or on the up and down scroll arrows for more selection box control. Pick the **RAND()** function, which generates a new random number with each recalculation.

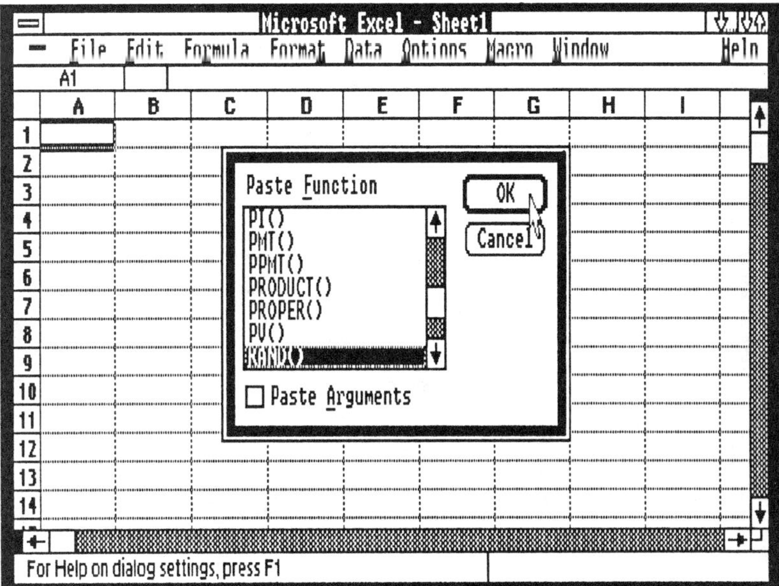

4. Pick **OK**.

5. Highlight the column range A1:A5; then select **Fill Down** from the Edit menu.

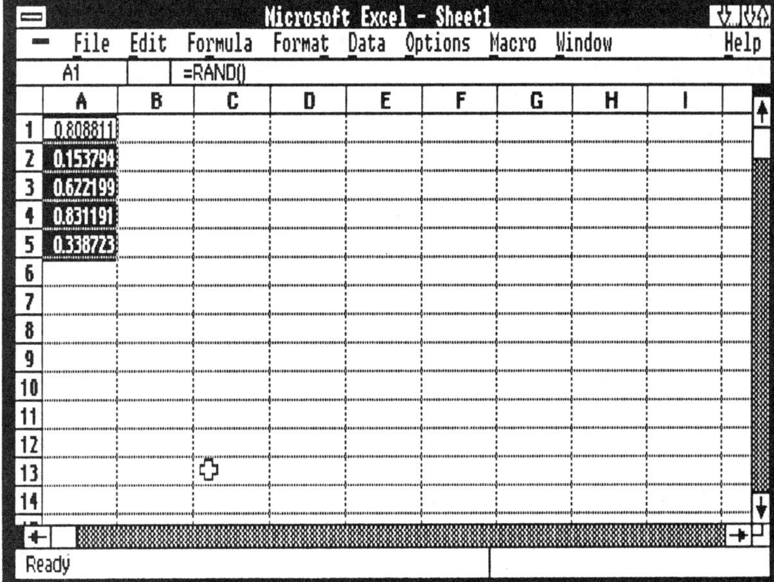

6. Type **Sum** in cell B6.

7. Type **Average** in cell B7.

8. Type **Maximum** in cell B8.

9. Type **Minimum** in cell B9.

10. Select cell C6, then select **Paste Function** from the Formula menu. Select the **SUM** function and pick **Paste Arguments**.

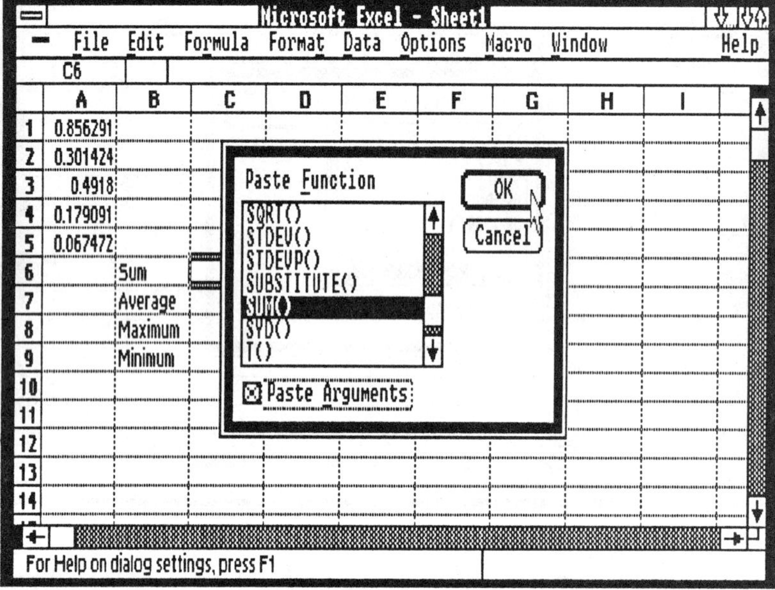

11. Select **OK**.

12. Edit the function arguments in the formula bar to specify A1:A5.

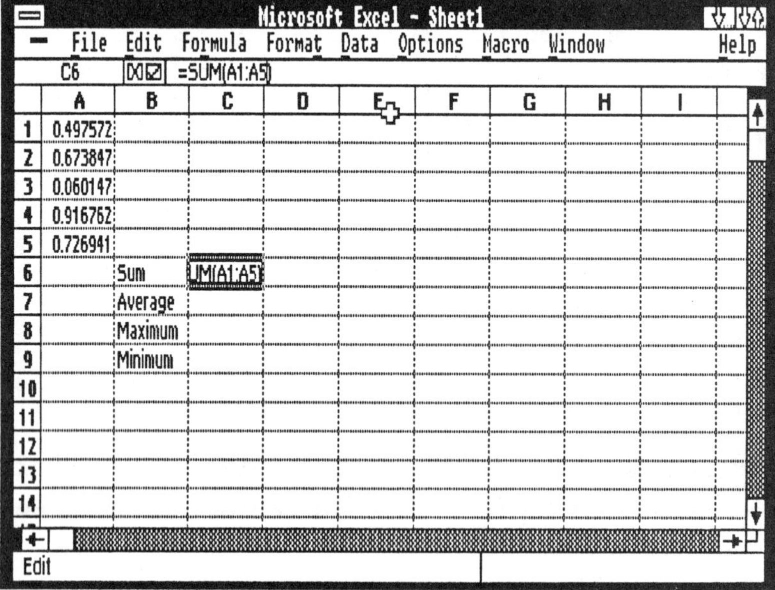

13. Press **Enter**.

14. Select cell C7, then select **Paste Function** from the Formula menu. Select the **AVERAGE** function and select **OK**.

15. Edit the function arguments in the formula bar to specify A1:A5 and press **Enter**.

<table>
<tr><td colspan="10">Microsoft Excel - Sheet1</td></tr>
<tr><td>File</td><td>Edit</td><td>Formula</td><td>Format</td><td>Data</td><td>Options</td><td>Macro</td><td>Window</td><td colspan="2">Help</td></tr>
<tr><td colspan="2">C7</td><td colspan="8">=AVERAGE(A1:A5)</td></tr>
<tr><td>A</td><td>B</td><td>C</td><td>D</td><td>E</td><td>F</td><td>G</td><td>H</td><td>I</td><td></td></tr>
<tr><td>1</td><td>0.066549</td><td></td><td></td><td></td><td></td><td></td><td></td><td></td><td></td></tr>
<tr><td>2</td><td>0.218617</td><td></td><td></td><td></td><td></td><td></td><td></td><td></td><td></td></tr>
<tr><td>3</td><td>0.250494</td><td></td><td></td><td></td><td></td><td></td><td></td><td></td><td></td></tr>
<tr><td>4</td><td>0.308401</td><td></td><td></td><td></td><td></td><td></td><td></td><td></td><td></td></tr>
<tr><td>5</td><td>0.017601</td><td></td><td></td><td></td><td></td><td></td><td></td><td></td><td></td></tr>
<tr><td>6</td><td></td><td>Sum</td><td>0.861661</td><td></td><td></td><td></td><td></td><td></td><td></td></tr>
<tr><td>7</td><td></td><td>Average</td><td>0.172332</td><td></td><td></td><td></td><td></td><td></td><td></td></tr>
<tr><td>8</td><td></td><td>Maximum</td><td></td><td></td><td></td><td></td><td></td><td></td><td></td></tr>
<tr><td>9</td><td></td><td>Minimum</td><td></td><td></td><td></td><td></td><td></td><td></td><td></td></tr>
<tr><td>10</td><td></td><td></td><td></td><td></td><td></td><td></td><td></td><td></td><td></td></tr>
<tr><td>11</td><td></td><td></td><td></td><td></td><td></td><td></td><td></td><td></td><td></td></tr>
<tr><td>12</td><td></td><td></td><td></td><td></td><td></td><td></td><td></td><td></td><td></td></tr>
<tr><td>13</td><td></td><td></td><td></td><td></td><td></td><td></td><td></td><td></td><td></td></tr>
<tr><td>14</td><td></td><td></td><td></td><td></td><td></td><td></td><td></td><td></td><td></td></tr>
<tr><td colspan="10">Ready</td></tr>
</table>

16. Select cell C8, then select **Paste Function** from the Formula drop-down menu. Select the **MAX** function and select **OK**.

17. Edit the function arguments in the formula bar to specify A1:A5 and press **Enter**.

18. Select cell C9, then select **Paste Function** from the Formula menu. Select the **MIN** function and select **OK**.

19. Edit the function arguments in the formula bar to specify A1:A5 and press **Enter**.

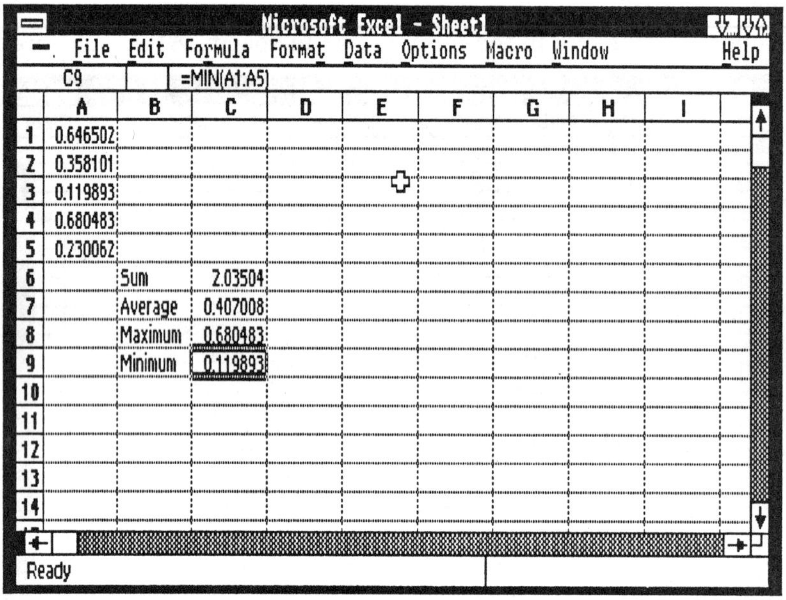

20. Select **Save As**, name the worksheet **Random**, and press **Enter**.

21. Close the worksheet, and optionally, exit Excel.

22. Turn to Module 16 to continue the learning sequence.

Module 46

PASTE LINK

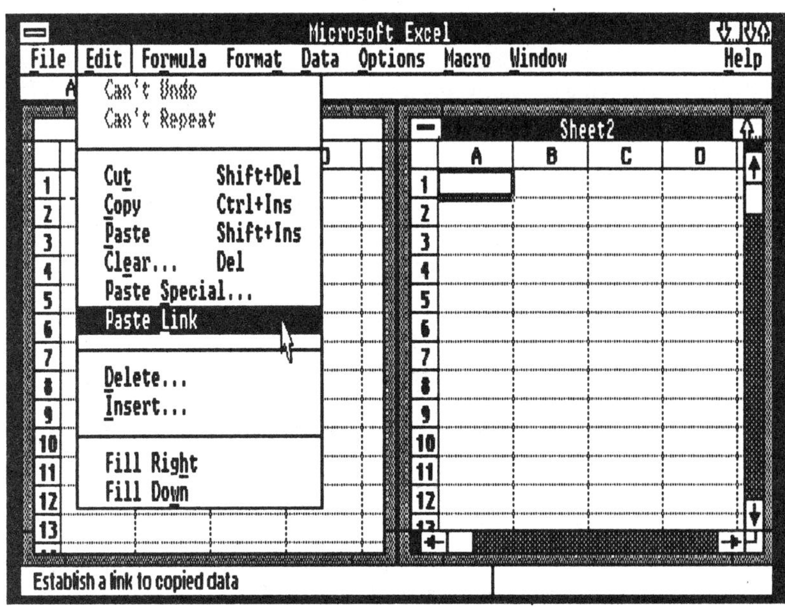

DESCRIPTION

Use the Paste Link command on the Edit menu to establish links between multiple spreadsheets. You can consolidate the results of several spreadsheets using links. Any change in the linked value in the supporting worksheet is automatically carried forward to the dependent worksheet.

Links can be either simple or complex. A *simple link* is a reference to an absolute cell or cell range, or a named cell or cell range. A *complex link* is anything else. When you use a simple link, it is not necessary for the supporting worksheets to be open at the same time as the dependent worksheet. With a complex link, references to a closed supporting worksheet produce the message "#REF" in the dependent worksheet. Additionally, the more complex the link, the greater the opportunity for operator error.

To establish a link with the Paste Link command:

1. Select the cell or cell range containing the information in the supporting worksheet.
2. Select Copy from the Edit menu, or press Ctrl-Ins to copy the information into memory.
3. Select the cell or same-size cell range in the dependent worksheet.
4. Select the Paste Link command from the Edit menu.

An external reference, or link, looks much like an ordinary Excel formula. The first element is an equals sign. The second is the name of the dependent worksheet, followed by an exclamation point. The remainder is a cell or cell range reference. For example:

    = Sheet1!$A$1

refers to cell $A$1 in worksheet Sheet1.

It is not necessary to explicitly use the Paste Link command to create links to other worksheets. You may choose to treat the links as an additional specification and type them as part of a formula.

If the dependent worksheet is open when the link is created, only the sheet name is required. If the dependent worksheet is closed when the link is created, the sheet name must contain a full MS-DOS file specification including the disk drive, directory, and filename. The name of the worksheet is followed by an exclamation point and the reference to the cell or range in the supporting worksheet. For example:

    = Sheet1!$F$29

refers to cell F29 in "Sheet1." If Sheet1 were closed, the reference would need to be similar to the following:

    = C: \ Windows \ Sheet1.XLS!$F$29

Of course, the best technique is to use the Define Name command in Sheet1 to to give cell F29 a name. If you define the name to be "Receivables" then the external reference can be written as

    = Sheet1!Receivables

or

    = C \ Windows \ Sheet1.XLS!Receivables

When you make a reference to a sheet that is not open, Excel opens a dialog box to allow you to select the required worksheet from the current directory.

APPLICATIONS

When projects grow past a certain size, they are often cumbersome to treat as single worksheets. Splitting the project into supporting worksheets and bringing the summary data forward onto a dependent consolidation worksheet makes many tasks more manageable and less prone to error. It also allows you to work on larger models than would otherwise be possible without adding memory to your computer.

There are other reasons for linking together small worksheets instead of working on one single sheet. Individual managers can create worksheets containing their operations and performance data, which can then be linked together in a consolidated statement, resulting in an excellent division of labor. Data security can also be enhanced through the use of multiple worksheets that are eventually consolidated. There is little reason for the temporary employee hired to enter telephone charges into a worksheet to have access to other confidential financial data that may be part of a consolidated income statement. Breaking a large data gathering project down into component parts allows greater use of source point data capture — data is entered into the computer at the point closest to its origination; but the low-level employees performing the data entry have no access to confidential or proprietary information that may eventually be combined with that data in the preparation of consolidated reports.

TYPICAL OPERATION

In this session you link information from an Eastern Region worksheet and a Western Region worksheet into a national summary worksheet.

CREATE A SIMPLE LINK   In the first portion of this session you create the worksheets and use the Paste Link command to establish two *simple* links.

1. Start Excel. Select the **New** command on the File menu twice to create two additional worksheets.
2. Select **Arrange All** on the Window menu.

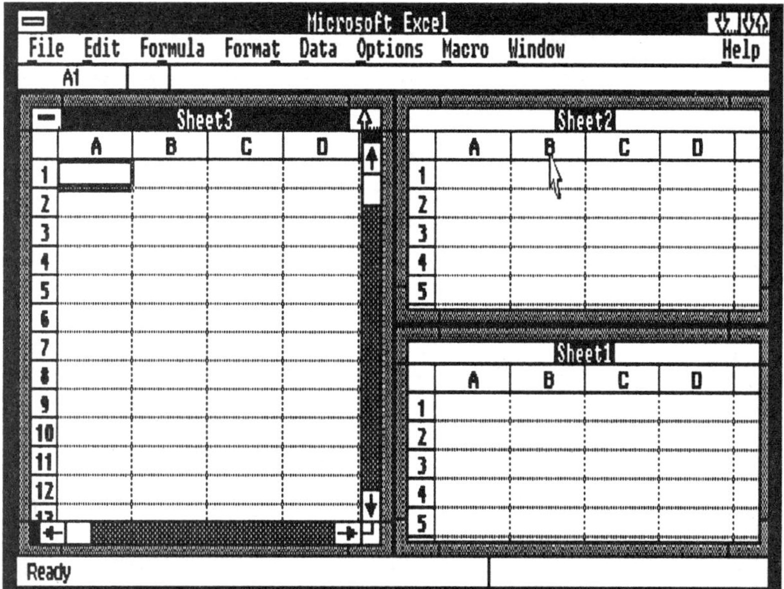

3. Type **National Sales Summary** in cell A1 of Sheet3 and press **Enter**.
4. Increase the width of column A in Sheet3 to accomodate the title.
5. Type **Eastern Region** in cell A3 of Sheet3.
6. Type **Western Region** in cell A4 of Sheet3 and press **Enter**.

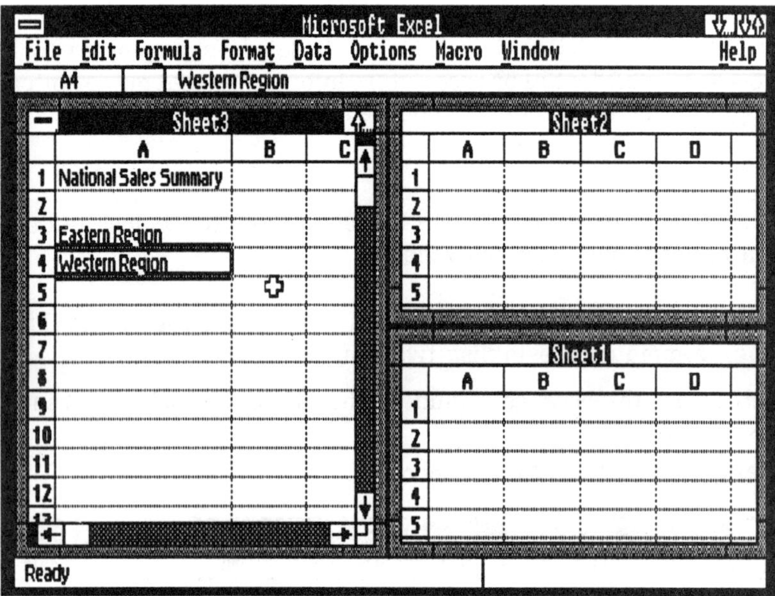

7. Click on Sheet2, making it the current worksheet.

8. Type **Eastern Region Sales** in cell A1 of Sheet2 and press **Enter**.

9. Increase the width of column A in Sheet2 to accomodate the title.

10. Type **Total Sales** in cell A3 of Sheet2.

11. Type **360000** in cell B3 of Sheet2.

12. Select column B in Sheet2. Then select dollars without cents formatting.

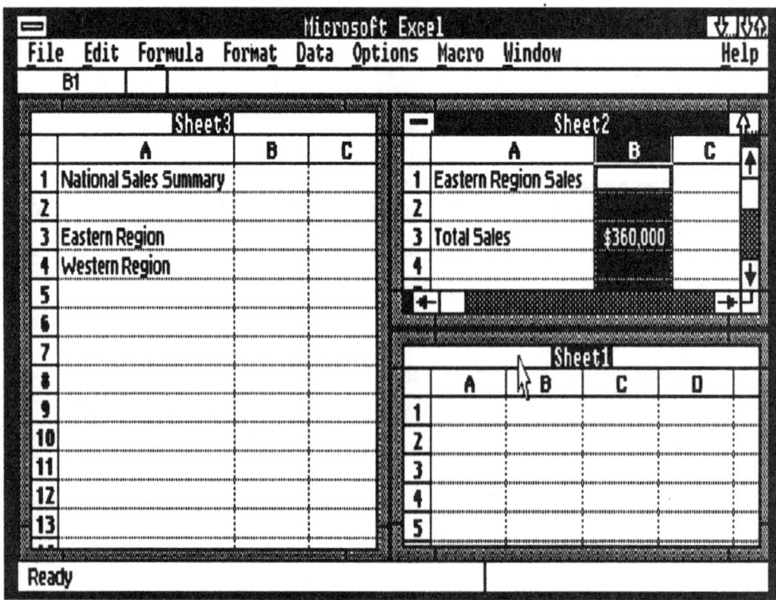

13. Click on Sheet1, making it the current worksheet.

14. Type **Western Region Sales** in cell A1 of Sheet1 and press **Enter**.

15. Increase the width of column A in Sheet1 to accomodate the title.

16. Type **Total Sales** in cell A3 of Sheet1.

17. Type **508000** in cell B3 of Sheet 1.

18. Select column B in Sheet1. Then select dollars without cents formatting.

19. Select cell B3 in Sheet1.

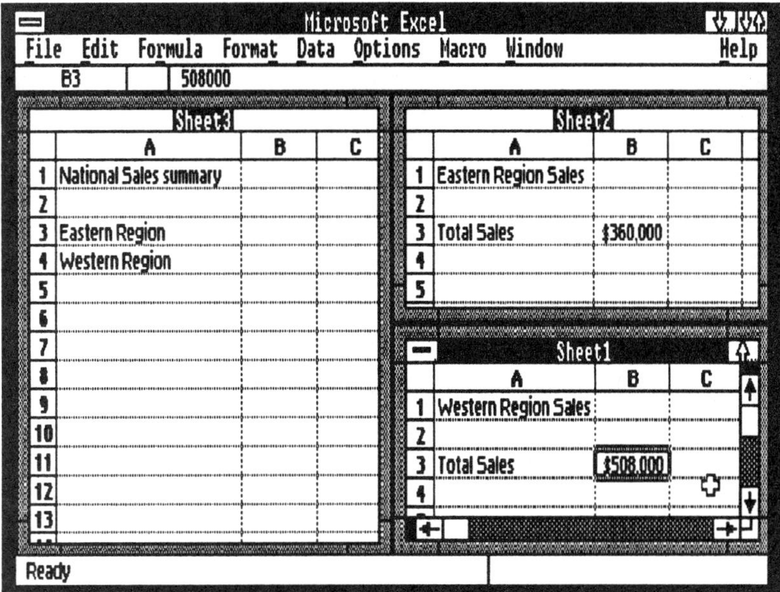

20. Select **Copy** from the Edit menu, or press **Ctrl-Ins**.

21. Move the mouse to Sheet3 and click the left button, making Sheet3 current.

22. Select cell B4 in Sheet3, the national sales summary sheet.

23. Select **Paste Link** from the Edit menu.

24. Notice that the formula bar contains a reference to Sheet1 as shown in the following screen.

25. Make Sheet2 the current worksheet and select cell B3 in Sheet2.

26. Select **Copy** from the Edit menu, or press **Ctrl-Ins**.

27. Select Sheet3, then select cell B3 in Sheet3.

28. Select **Paste Link** from the Edit menu.

29. Select column B in Sheet3. Then select dollars without cents formatting.

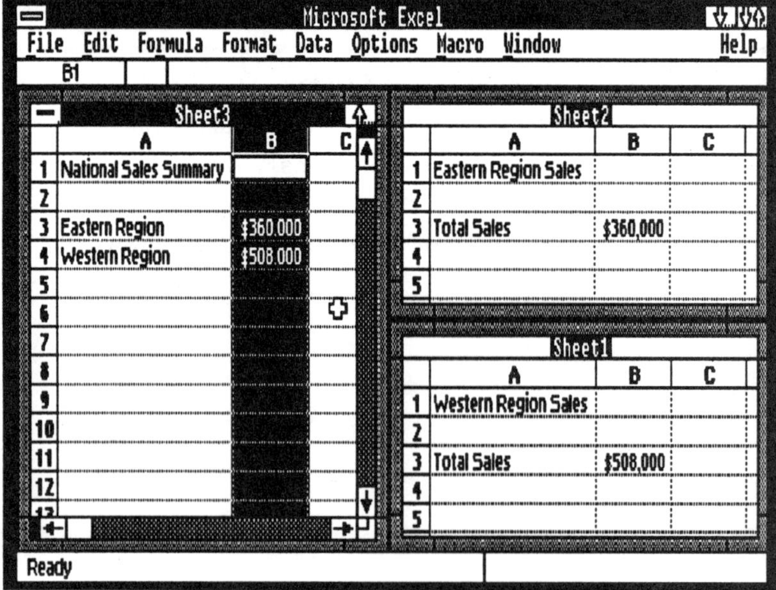

It is good practice to first save dependent worksheets, then to save the supporting worksheets.

30. Select Sheet1, then pick **Save As** from the File menu.

31. Type **WESTERN.XLS** as the worksheet name and pick **OK**.

32. Select Sheet2, then pick **Save As** from the File menu.

33. Type **EASTERN.XLS** as the worksheet name and pick **OK**.

34. Select Sheet3, then pick **Save As** from the File menu.

35. Type **NATIONAL.XLS** as the worksheet name and pick **OK**.

36. Pick cell B3 of NATIONAL.XLS. Notice that the external reference now refers to EASTERN.XLS instead of Sheet2.

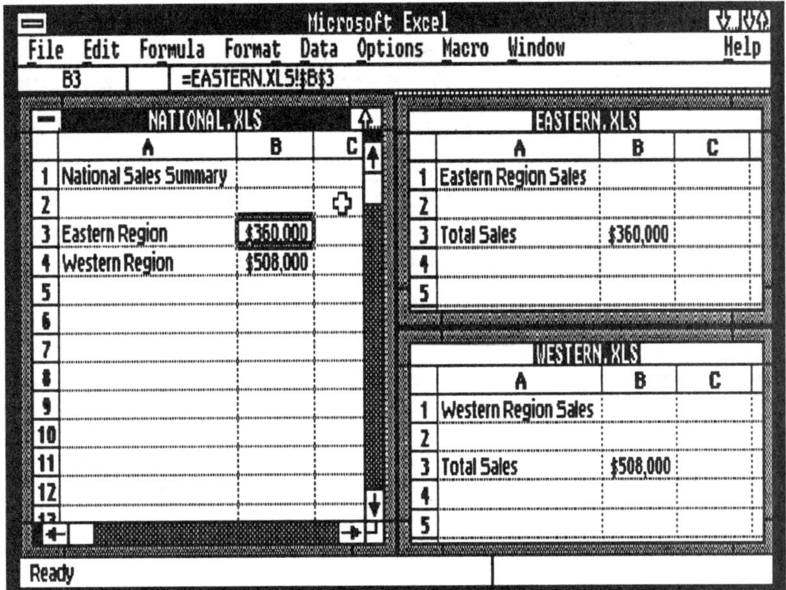

CREATING COMPLEX LINKS   Although the preferred method for calculating total sales in the NATIONAL.XLS worksheet is to add the values in B3 and B4, in this session you bring them forward separately, using a *complex* link formed from named references.

1.   Select cell B3 in EASTERN.XLS. Pick **Define Name** from the Formula menu.

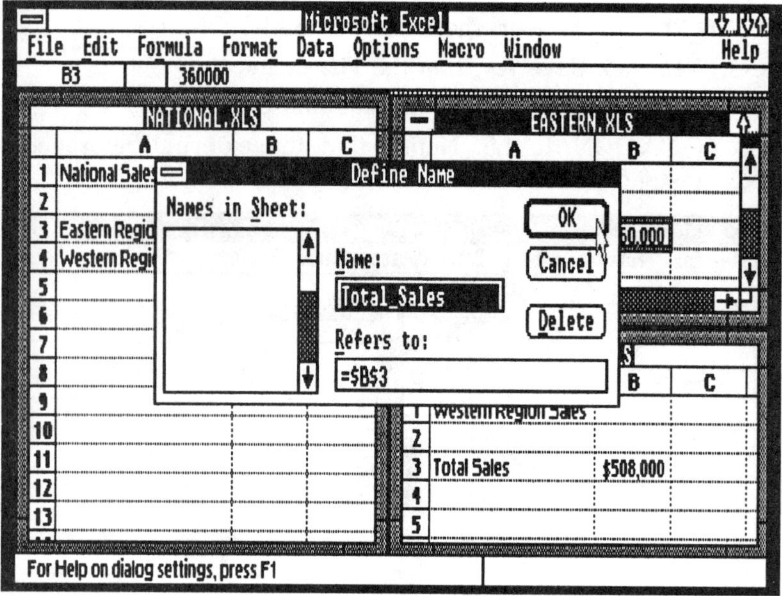

2.   Pick **OK** to confirm Total_Sales as the cell name.

3.   Pick cell B3 in worksheet WESTERN.XLS. Pick **Define Name** from the Formula menu, then pick **OK** in the dialog box to confirm Total_Sales as the cell name.

4.   Type **Total Sales** in cell A6 of worksheet NATIONAL.XLS.

5. Type **=EASTERN.XLS!Total_Sales+WESTERN.XLS!Total_Sales** in cell B6 of worksheet NATIONAL.XLS.

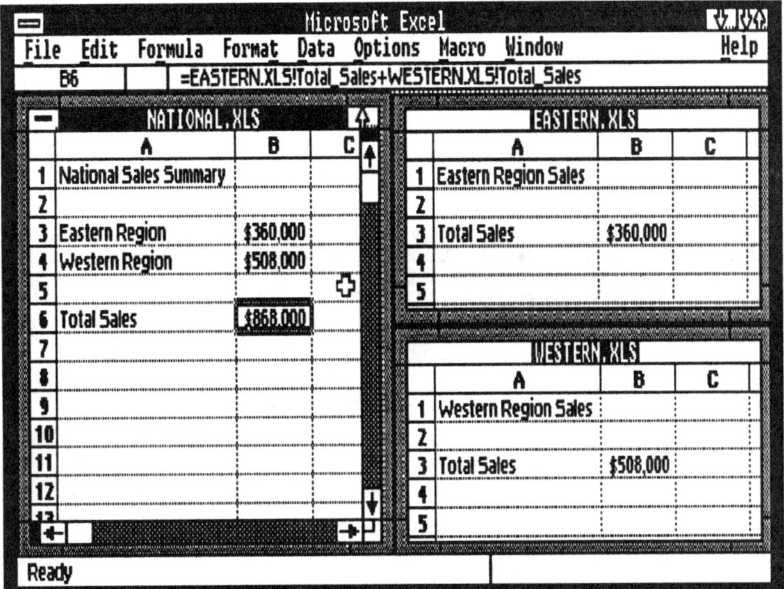

6. Close and save the three worksheets.
7. Exit Excel, or continue your work session without an active worksheet on your screen.
8. Turn to Module 35 to continue the learning sequence.

Module 47

PASTE NAME

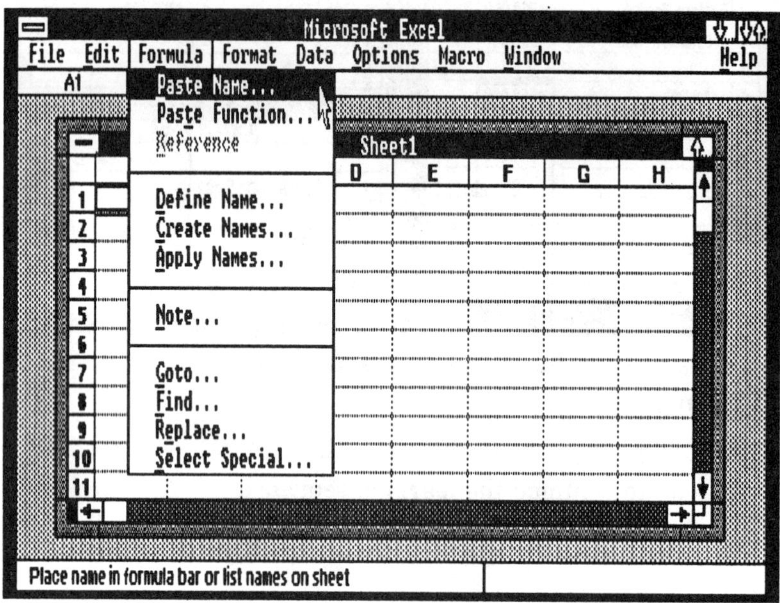

DESCRIPTION

Use the Paste Name command on the Formula menu to place the value or the definition of a name into a selected position on the worksheet. The Paste Name command is not available until you first establish names in the worksheet with the Define Name or the Create Names command. After you select the worksheet position, you select the Paste Name command with the mouse or by pressing Alt-R P. A dialog box similar to the following appears.

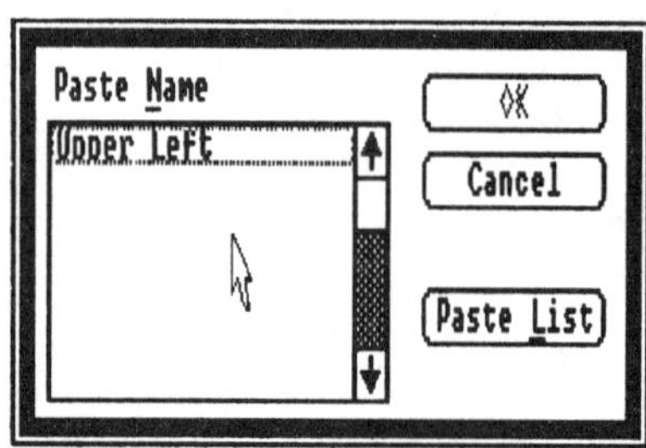

The selection box at the left lists the defined names for the worksheet. (The name "Upper Left" appears for illustration only.) To paste the value of a name, select the name you wish to paste from the list and pick OK. If you want to paste the definition of a name, pick the name and select Paste List. If you want to list the definitions of all names in the worksheet, select Paste List without selecting any names.

APPLICATIONS

It is easy to forget the exact spelling of a name you have used in creating a worksheet. The Paste Name command makes it easy to select the name from a list rather than type the name from memory.

In examining a worksheet, you may want to review one or all of the name definitions — possibly on a hunt for potential worksheet logic errors. The ability to paste a list of all name definitions is a definite asset in that task.

TYPICAL OPERATION

In this session you use the Paste Name command to paste both values and definitions on the GOLD worksheet, which was last used in the Create Names module.

1. Start Excel, or continue your work session from the previous module.
2. Open the GOLD.XLS worksheet and expand it to fill the screen. Select cell B11 to remove the region highlight from the screen.

```
 ═                  Microsoft Excel - GOLD.XLS                    ↕ ⟨X⟩
 ─    File  Edit  Formula  Format  Data  Options  Macro  Window            Help
     B11         =(1+(Prime+0.015)/4)*Average
            A         B        C          D           E      F      G      H    ↑
 1                Gold Prices
 2  Hong Kong    $403.85
 3  New York     $405.24
 4  London       $403.05
 5  Paris        $401.47
 6  Frankfurt    $404.24
 7  Zurich       $404.25
 8                              Continental High   $404.25
 9  Average      $403.68
 10 Future       $413.80
 11 Cost         $415.29      ✛
 12
 13
 14                                                                            ↓
 Ready
```

3. Type **Prime Rate** in cell A12.

4. Select cell B12, then select **Paste Name** from the Formula menu.

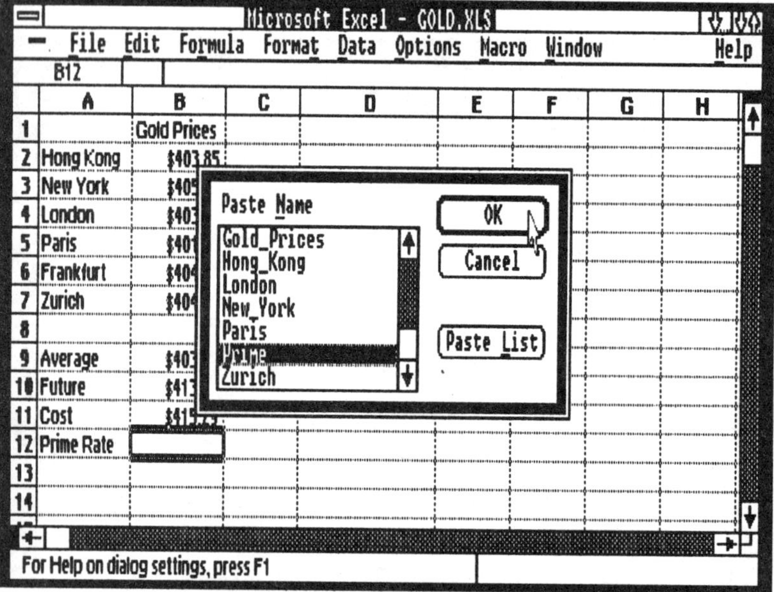

5. Scroll through the selection box and pick **Prime**.

6. Pick **OK**.

The value of Prime appears on the worksheet in cell B12.

7. Pick **Number** on the Format menu, then pick **0.00** from the Format selection box. Pick **OK**.

Microsoft Excel - GOLD.XLS
File Edit Formula Format Data Options Macro Window Help

B12 =Prime

	A	B	C	D	E	F	G	H
1		Gold Prices						
2	Hong Kong	$403.85						
3	New York	$405.24						
4	London	$403.05						
5	Paris	$401.47						
6	Frankfurt	$404.24						
7	Zurich	$404.25						
8				Continental High	$404.25			
9	Average	$403.68						
10	Future	$413.80						
11	Cost	$415.29						
12	Prime Rate	0.10						
13								
14								

Ready

8. Select cell F1, then select **Paste Name** from the Formula menu. Without selecting a name, pick **Paste List**.

Microsoft Excel - GOLD.XLS
File Edit Formula Format Data Options Macro Window Help

F1 Average

	A	B	C	D	E	F	G	H
1		Gold Prices				Average	=$B$9	
2	Hong Kong	$403.85				Frankfurt	=$B$6	
3	New York	$405.24				Gold_Pric	=$B$2:$B$7	
4	London	$403.05				Hong_Kor	=$B$2	
5	Paris	$401.47				London	=$B$4	
6	Frankfurt	$404.24				New_York	=$B$3	
7	Zurich	$404.25				Paris	=$B$5	
8				Continental High	$404.25	Prime	=0.1	
9	Average	$403.68				Zurich	=$B$7	
10	Future	$413.80						
11	Cost	$415.29						
12	Prime Rate	0.10						
13								
14								

Ready

The definitions of all defined names are pasted onto the worksheet, beginning in cell F1.

9. Close the worksheet without saving it.

10. Exit Excel, or continue your work session without an active worksheet on the screen.

11. Turn to Module 66 to continue the learning sequence.

Module 48

PASTE SPECIAL

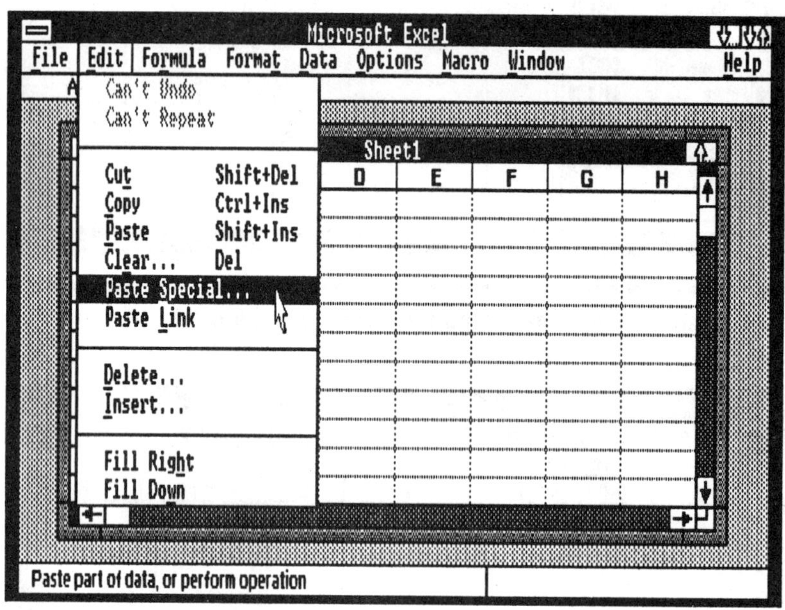

DESCRIPTION

The Paste Special command on the Edit menu allows control over the paste operation. The Paste Special command must always be used with the Copy command. It does not work with the Cut command. There are two versions of the command, depending on whether you are pasting part of a worksheet or a chart. After you copy a cell or an area with the Copy command, you must select the *paste range* (a cell, a range, or a multiple selection). Then you can use the mouse or press Alt-E S to select the Paste Special command.

When pasting part of a worksheet into the same worksheet or another worksheet, the following dialog box is displayed.

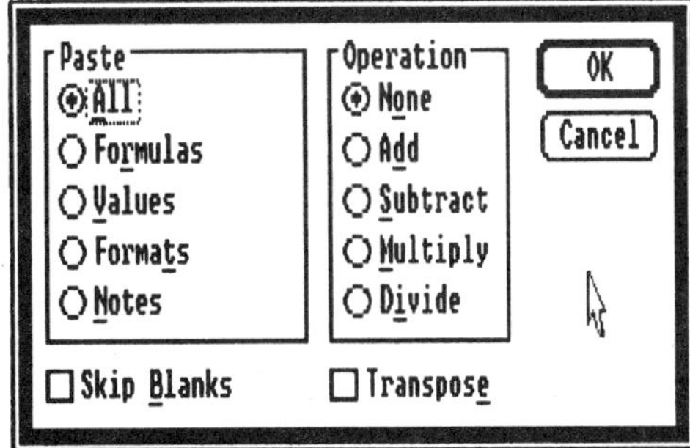

You can elect to paste only the formulas, values, formats, or notes associated with a cell or range of cells. You can also elect to use the existing contents of the paste range as part of a numerical operation by selecting either Add, Subtract, Multiply, or Divide. Checking Skip Blanks causes Excel to close up the cells in the copy range, eliminating blank rows and columns. Checking Transpose switches the row and column orientation of the data — the data in the left column becomes the data in the top row and the data in the top row is moved to the left column.

When you select Paste Special to move data from a worksheet to a chart, a different dialog box is displayed.

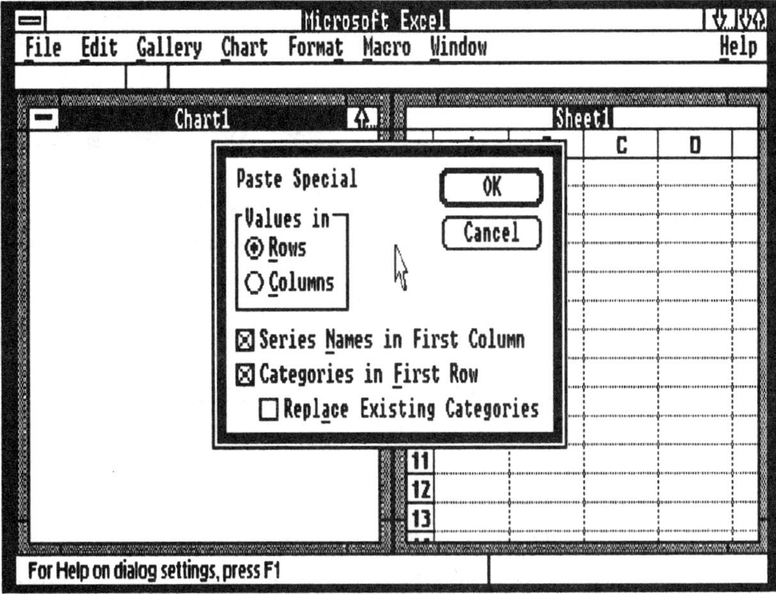

Use this dialog box to specify whether the series values are located in the worksheet rows or the columns. The check boxes for Series Names in First Column and Categories in First Row provide Excel with the information needed to interpret the data you paste. When you check these boxes, Excel interprets the left column and the top row as series and category names. Otherwise, Excel interprets the top row and left column as data points for charting. The Replace Existing Categories check box appears when the chart contains category definitions. Selecting this option deletes all existing categories, replacing them with the new categories specified in the Paste Special command.

To use the Paste Special command to transfer information and formats from one chart to another:

1. Select the chart with the Select Chart command on the Chart menu.
2. Select the Copy command from the Edit menu.
3. Activate the second chart (move the mouse to the second chart and click the left mouse button).
4. Select the Paste Special command from the Edit menu.

The following dialog box appears.

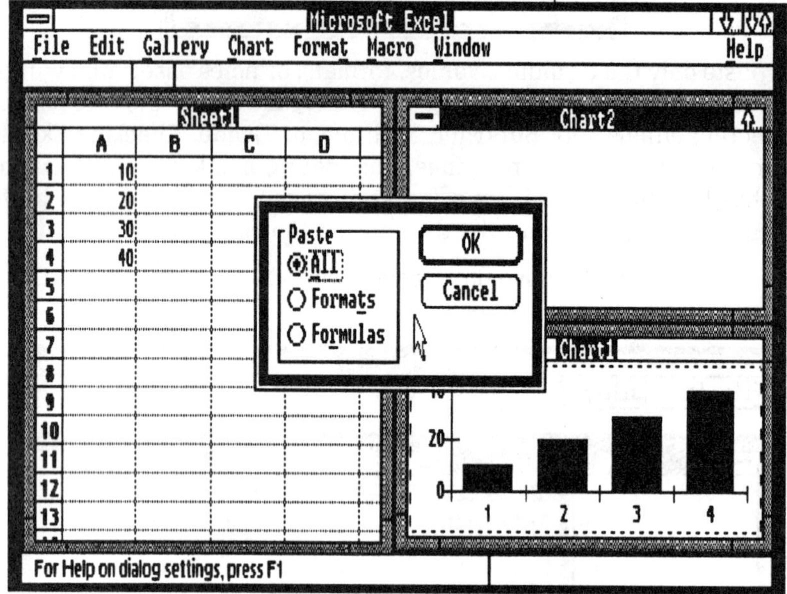

CAUTION

Selecting the All option when using the Paste Special command to paste from one chart to another completely erases any existing chart specifications.

APPLICATIONS

Use the Paste Special command when you need additional control over the paste operation.

One excellent application of the Paste Special command is in moving data between worksheets. When you copy data containing formulas from one worksheet to another, you create worksheet dependencies. Sometimes this is highly desirable as changes in one worksheet automatically update the information in the dependent worksheet. However, if the reference is a "complex reference," you receive a reference error in the dependent worksheet unless the supporting worksheet is also open. If you do not expect the data to change, use the Paste Special command to paste only the values from one worksheet to another, eliminating the worksheet dependency.

TYPICAL OPERATION

In this session you copy information between two worksheets using the Paste Special command to avoid worksheet dependencies. You then copy information from a worksheet to a chart, and then from one chart to another. You start with the RANDOM.XLS worksheet created in the Paste Function module.

PASTE SPECIAL BETWEEN WORKSHEETS

1.   Start Excel. Open the RANDOM.XLS worksheet.

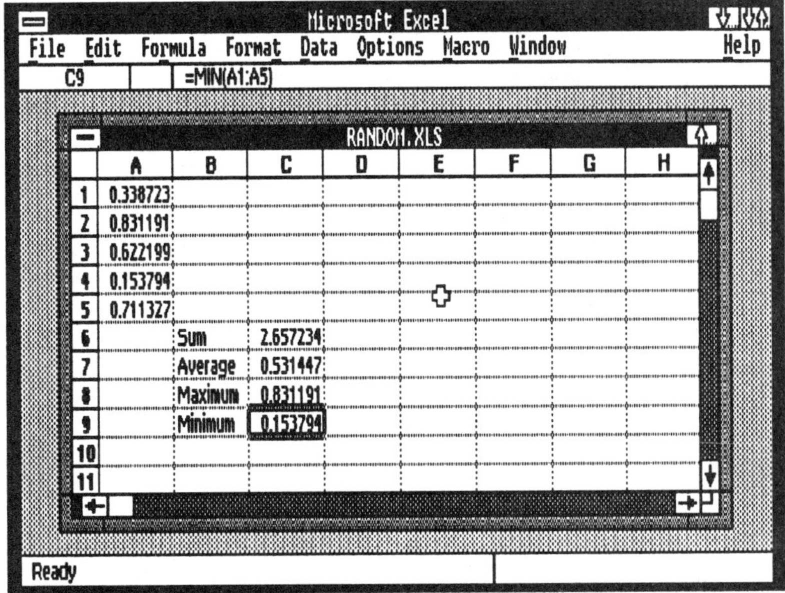

2.   Select **Arrange All** from the Window menu.

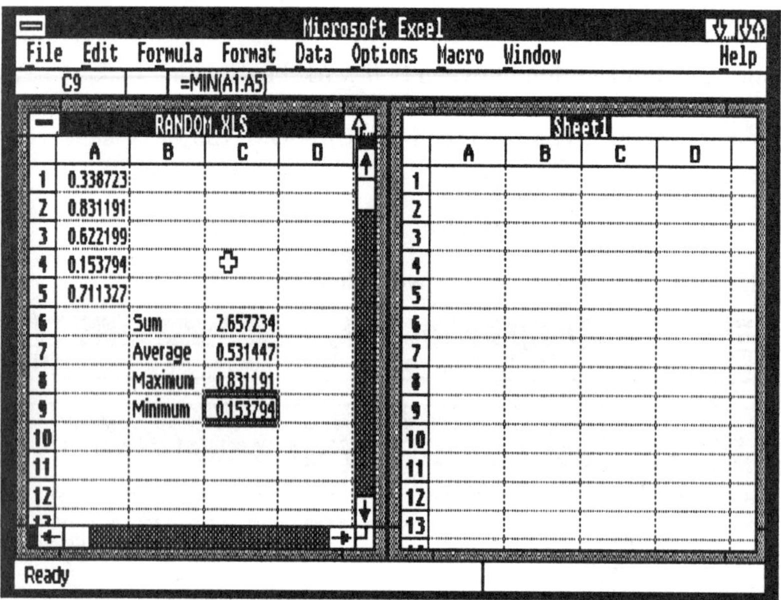

3. Select the range B6 through C9 from RANDOM, then pick **Copy** from the Edit menu or press **Ctrl-Ins**.

4. Pick the title bar of Sheet1, making it the active worksheet, then select cell A1.

5. Pick **Paste Special** from the Edit menu.

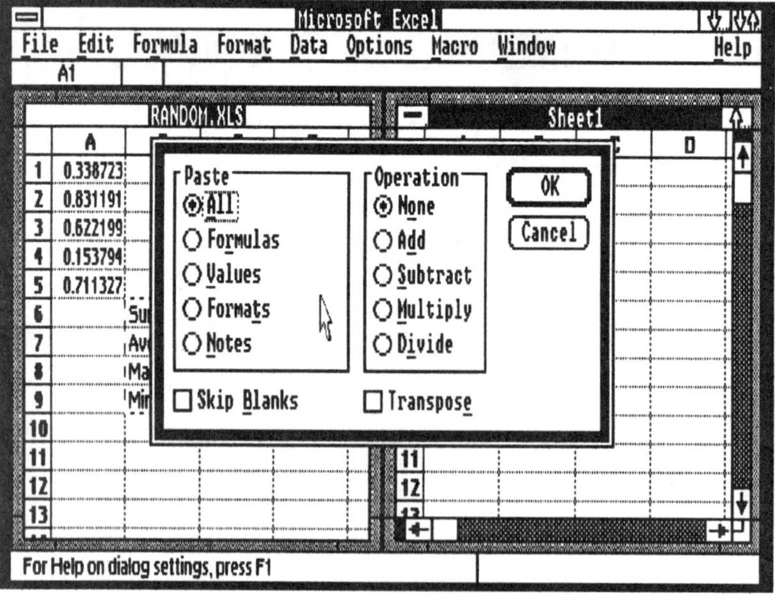

6. Pick **Values** from the dialog box.

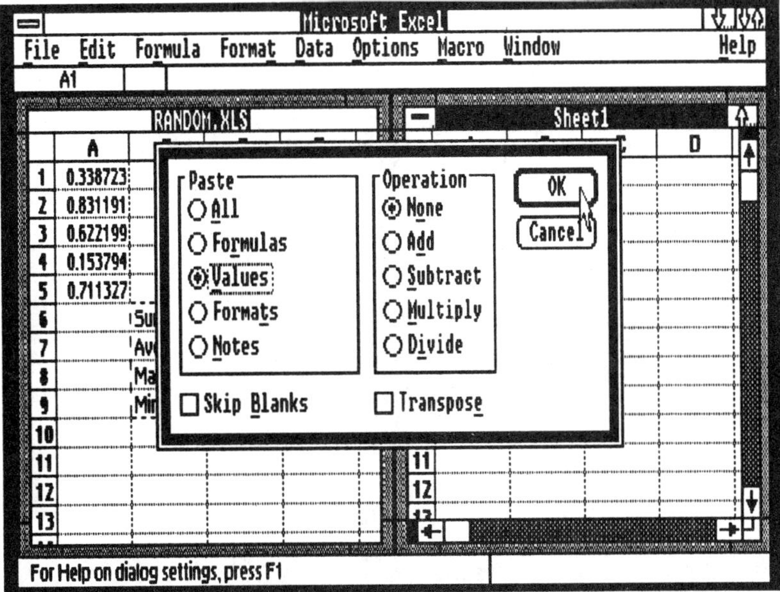

7. Pick **OK**. Notice that when RANDOM.XLS is automatically recalculated at the end of the Paste Special command that the changes only affect the cells in RANDOM. The changes do not carry forward to Sheet1 because only the values were pasted.

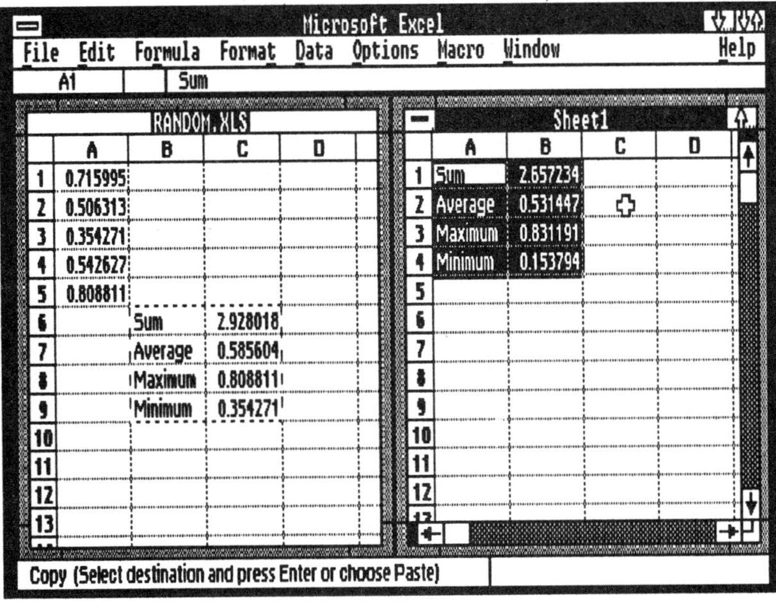

8. Select cell B1 in Sheet1. Examine the formula bar showing that the contents of the copied cells are values, not formulas.

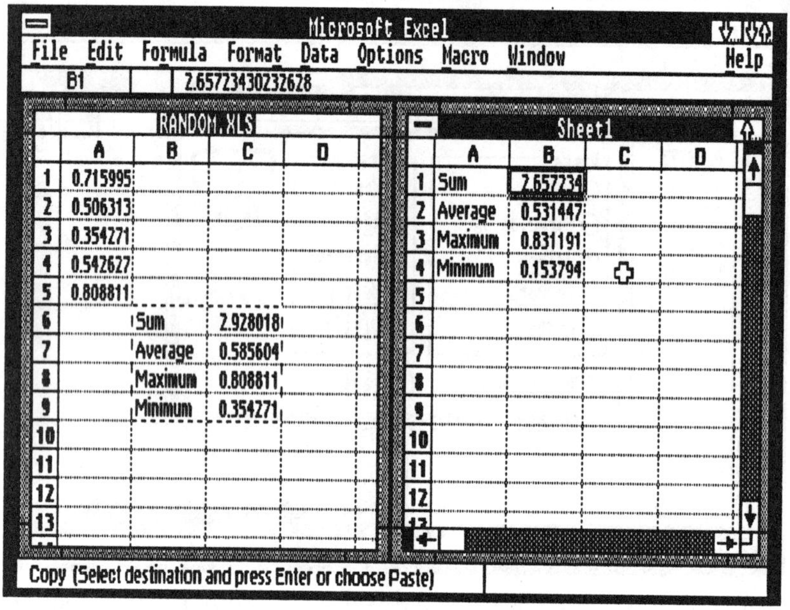

PASTE SPECIAL BETWEEN A WORKSHEET AND A CHART

1. Select cell C1 in Sheet1.
2. Select **New** from the File menu, then pick **Chart**.
3. Pick **OK**.

4. Select **Arrange All** from the Window menu.

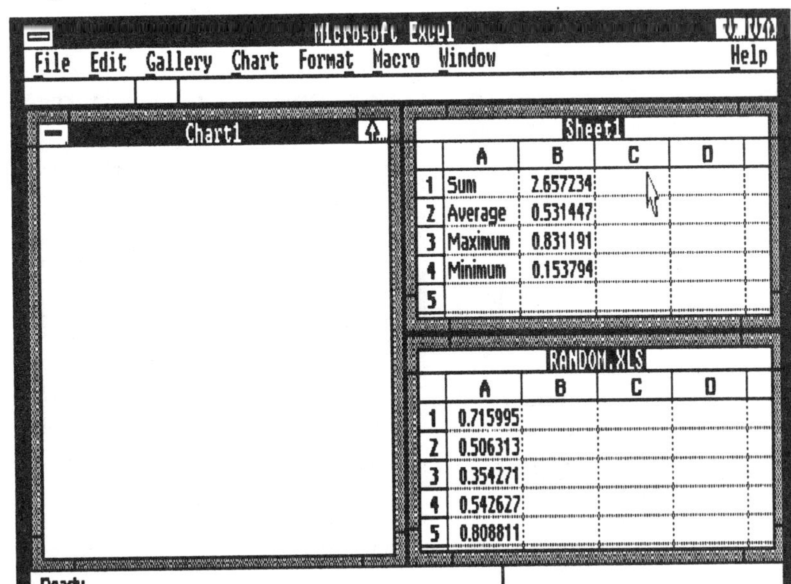

5. Activate Sheet1, highlight the region A1 through B4, then press **Ctrl-Ins** or pick **Copy** from the Edit menu.

6. Pick the title bar of Chart 1, making it the current window.

7. Pick **Paste Special** from the Edit menu. The following dialog box appears.

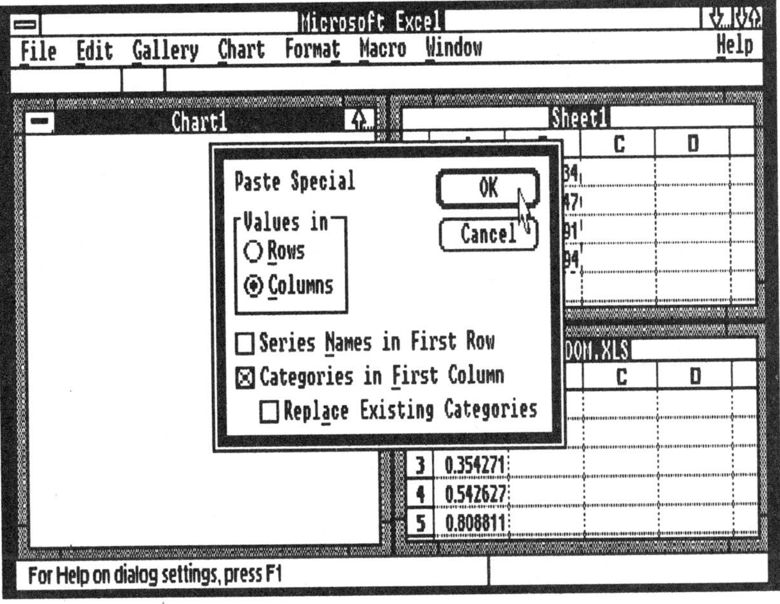

8. Pick **OK** to accept the default values.

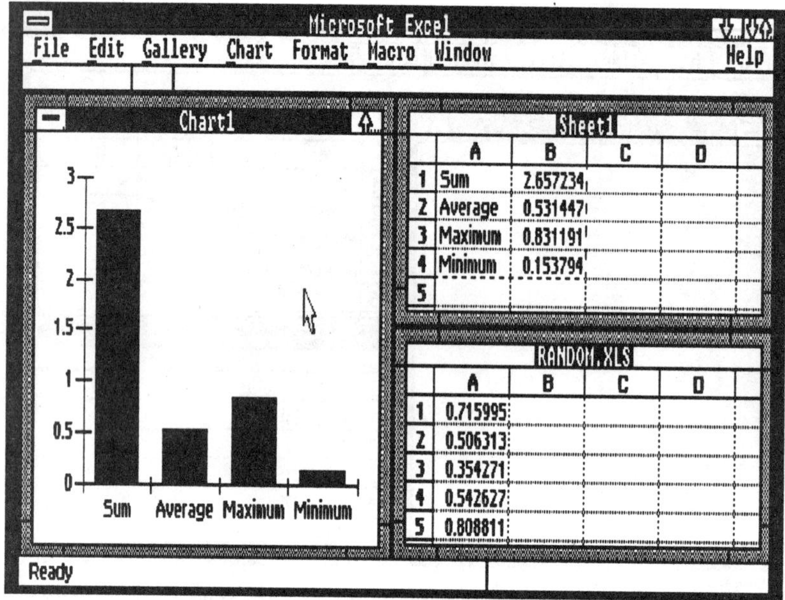

PASTE SPECIAL BETWEEN CHARTS

1. Pick in the title bar of Sheet1, making it the current worksheet. (This prevents the new chart from being a copy of Chart1.)

2. Select **New** from the File menu. Confirm **Chart** on the New dialog box, then select **OK**.

3. Select **Arrange All** from the Window menu.

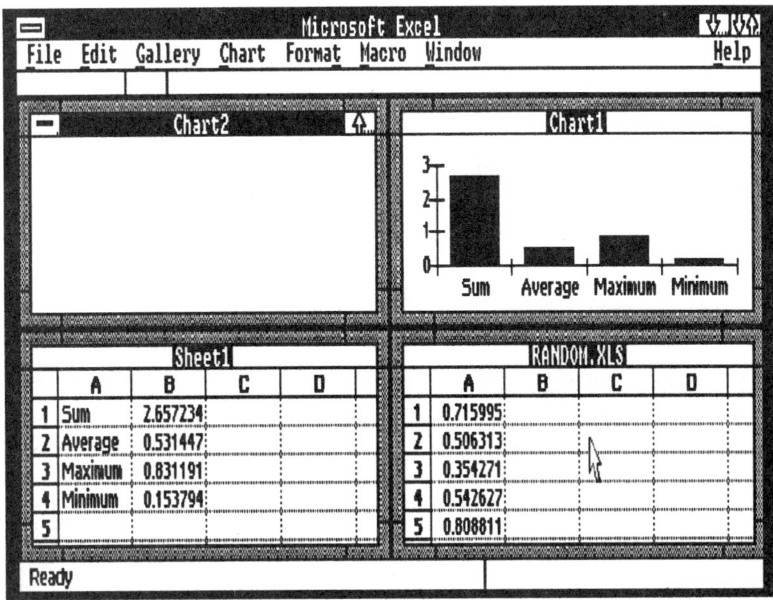

4. Select the title bar of Chart1, making it the current window.

5. Select **Select Chart** from the Chart menu.

6. Pick **Copy** from the Edit menu, or press **Ctrl-Ins**.

7. Select the title bar of Chart2, making it the current window.

8. Select **Paste Special** from the Edit menu.

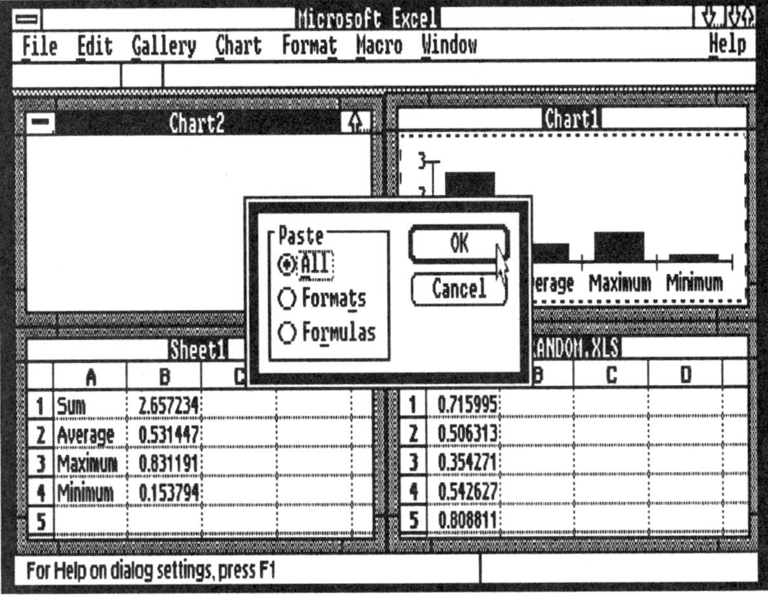

9. Confirm the default setting **All** and pick **OK**.

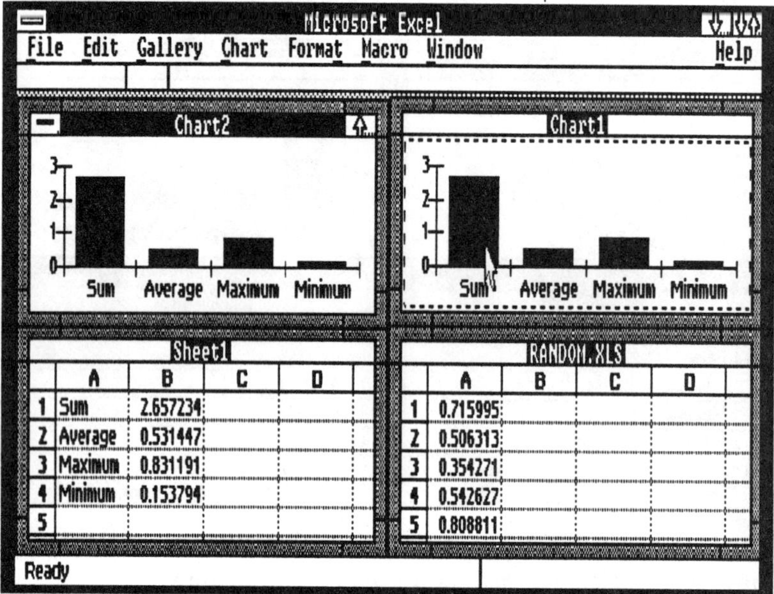

10. Close the worksheets and charts. There is no need to save them.

11. Turn to Module 19 to continue the learning sequence.

Module 49

PRINT

Microsoft Excel

File Edit Formula Format Data Options Macro Window   Help

New...
Open...
Close
Links...

Save
Save As...
Save Workspace...
Delete...

Page Setup...
Print...
Printer Setup...

Exit

Sheet1

C   D   E   F   G   H

Print or preview document

DESCRIPTION

The Print command is available through the File menu with Alt-F P. It permits you to print any document that you create in Excel, both worksheets and charts. The user of the full Windows version has the flexibility to print any file that is listed in the MS-DOS window. However, it is likely that this option will be employed by the Excel user only to print text that may have been created using the "Notepad." More than one file can be placed in line to be printed at one time, and you can continue to use the Excel application while printing.

It is generally easier to use the Print command from Excel when printing is desired since this selection is very flexible, and printing of the desired material is done immediately. When the print command is selected from Excel, you are presented a dialog box that provides you specific options. You can designate certain pages to be printed or print the entire document. You can print in a draft quality that will print faster because it excludes the special instructions, for example boldface, from the document.

In addition, you can print only the worksheet or the notes or both. One final option you will appreciate is the ability to preview how the printed document will look.

APPLICATIONS

There are numerous occasions when it is insufficient to view the work you do in Excel on the monitor screen. It is necessary to print the material for filing or sharing with another person. The Print command in Excel offers several advantages over the Print option in Windows. You can print all or part of a document. You can view the document to see what it will look like before you print it and you can print any notes you may have written to help you.

Excel also permits you to print a specific section of the worksheet, add footers and headers, or change widths and heights of printed charts.

TYPICAL OPERATION

In this operation you access the Print command in Excel and explore its options. In order to print a document from Excel the document must be made the active one. Before proceding with this operation you need to have completed the module on Printer Setup.

1. Open BUDGET1 from your library of files.
2. Select **Print** from the File menu.

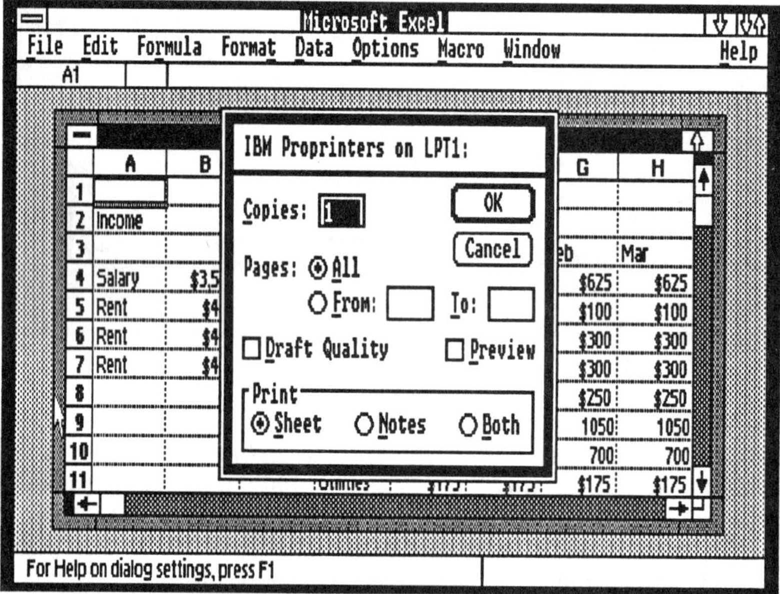

The default settings are for all of the pages in a document to be printed, better than draft quality, and worksheets only. You can change any of these settings.

All of the options will be reflected in the printed document except Preview.

3. Type **2** in the space provided for the number of copies.
4. Leave **All** active since BUDGET1.XLS is only one page.
5. Make **Draft Quality** active and press **Enter**. The document should be printed. If you have a problem, check the type of printer and its configuration in Printer Setup.

6. Print another copy but this time de-activate the **Draft Quality**. Compare the results of the two printings.

7. Activate **Preview** from the Print dialog box, and press **Enter**.

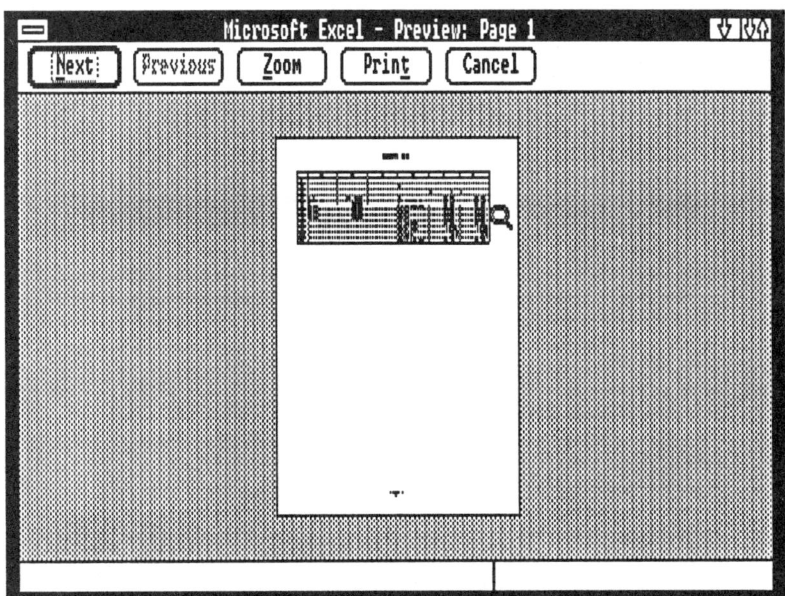

From this picture you can see what the printed document will look like.

8. Click on Zoom or type **Z**.

9. Scroll the window to view more of the data.

You can return to the original preview by typing Z or clicking on Zoom or you could go to the next page or the previous page if there were any.

10. Type **Z.**

Another method for magnifying the preview with a mouse is by placing the mouse cursor (it will change to a magnifying glass) on the portion to view and pressing the left button.

11. Move the cursor (magnifying glass) to the first column and press the **left** button.

```
 Microsoft Excel - Preview: Page 1

 [ Next ]  [ Previous ]  [ Zoom ]  [ Print ]  [ Cancel ]

        A          B         C         D          E
  1
  2   Income                          Expenses
  3                                              Expected    Jar
  4   Salary     $3,500               Mortgage     $625
  5   Rent         $450               Insurance    $100
  6   Rent         $450               Food         $300
  7   Rent         $450               Auto         $300
  8                                   Clothes      $250
  9                                   Savings      1050
 10                                   Taxes         700
 11                                   Utilities    $175
```

You can view the entire page of a document using the scroll bars, Page Up and Page Down, arrow keys, or Home and End keys. You can move through a multiple-page document by pressing Enter or picking the Next command. (Pressing Enter also returns to the original document). Finally you can print from this position.

12. Select **Cancel** (or press **Enter**) to return to the worksheet. Notice that your worksheet now has a heavy dotted line between columns F and G. This is the automatic page break Excel makes visible when you select the Preview command. It will not interfere with your work.

NOTE
Once you activate the Preview command it
remains in force until you de-activate it.

13. Exit Excel, or continue your work session with the active worksheet on the screen.
14. Turn to Module 43 to continue the learning sequence.

Module 50
PRINTER SETUP

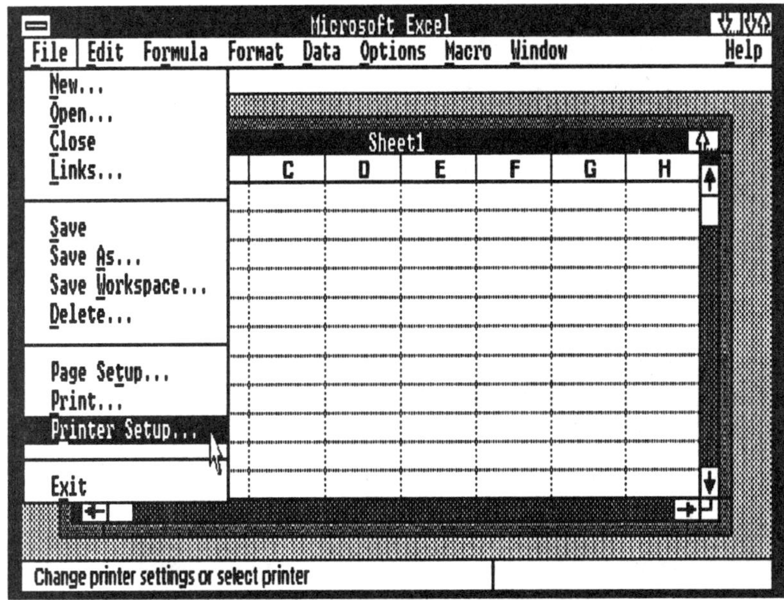

DESCRIPTION

When you installed Excel and/or Windows on your computer, you identified the names of the printers connected to your computer system and the name of the printer interface to which they were connected. However, for Excel to make proper use of your printer(s) you must provide more information about it and indicate your preferences about specific print options that are available. The Printer Setup command on the File menu lets you do this.

To select this command click on File, then Printer Setup with the mouse, or press Alt-F R. Excel displays a dialog box showing the names of the installed printers, similar to the following:

Highlight the printer you want to use, then pick Setup to specify options for that printer. If your printer is not on the list, you need to use the Windows Control Panel to copy the printer device driver onto your fixed disk. (See Adding a Printer at the end of the Typical Operation in this module.)

The exact options vary for whatever printer you choose (Excel and Windows support hundreds of variations), but the types of options remain similar. For example, with IBM Proprinters highlighted (typical of dot-matrix printers), picking Setup displays the following dialog box for further information on the particular IBM Proprinter you are using.

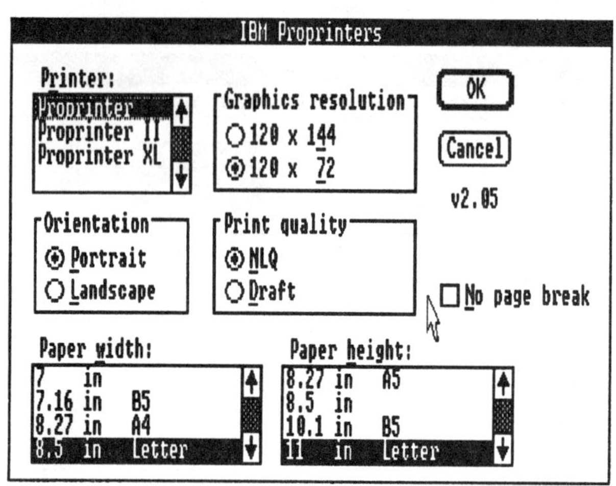

When Excel/Windows is installed, a software program called a printer driver is copied to your fixed disk. Some printer drivers work for more than one variation of a printer family. When this is the case, this dialog box allows you to choose the exact model you have. When more than one graphics resolution is available on your printer, the available resolutions are displayed. Pick the resolution that best meets your needs. Higher resolutions produce more detailed output but take longer to process and print. When making choices about paper orientation, remember that *portrait* orientation is the orientation used in most business correspondence, the narrow edge running along the top and the long edge down the sides. If your printer provides for more than one level of print quality, the options are presented for your selection. Again, the higher the print quality, the longer the print process requires. Paper width refers to the *usable* width of the paper. For example, 9.5" x 11" laser-perforated paper is a common size used in the United States. The 9.5" width includes a half inch on each side for the tractor feed perforations. The finished size is 8.5 inches in width. When using this paper, choose *8.5 in Letter* as the paper width. The B5 and A4 sizes are commonly used in Europe. If your printer has more than one input paper tray, you can choose the one you want to use. Excel allows you the choice of defeating automatically inserted page breaks. Automatic page breaks provide a top and bottom margin; defeating them causes the output to be printed on top of the perforations. Your application dictates which is most appropriate. Pick OK to record your changes and return to the first dialog box. Pick OK on the first dialog box to return to the worksheet.

Picking a PostScript printer displays a similar set of options.

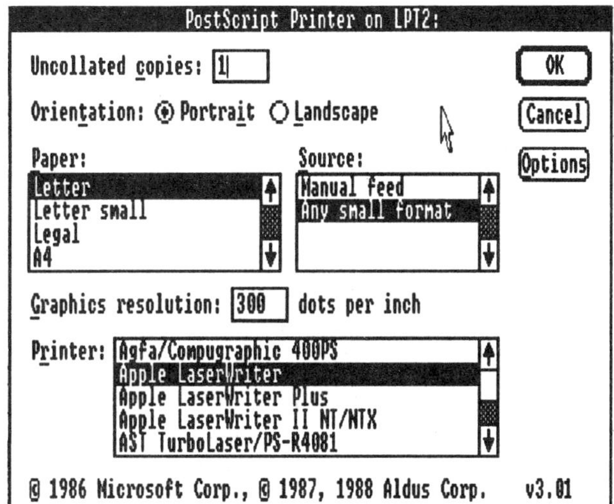

The options for the PostScript laser printers are similar to the dot-matrix options. However, notice the "Options" button directly below the "OK" and "Cancel" buttons. All the options for PostScript printers do not fit into a single dialog box. The Options button displays additional options for PostScript printers.

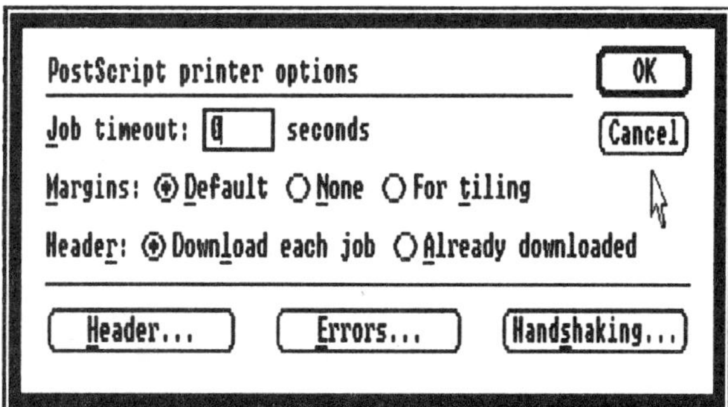

These additional options can be used to fine-tune the performance of your PostScript laser printer. When printing complex jobs, the printer may take a long time to respond, displaying a timeout error in a dialog box on your screen. You can restart the job by selecting "Retry." If this happens often, you may want to use a larger number for *Job timeout*.

Every time a job is sent to a PostScript printer, a header file is first sent to initialize a number of printer parameters. This process takes about 30 seconds. If you have exclusive use of your printer, you can elect to download this header file only once when you turn on your printer, and select "Already downloaded" to save yourself about 30 seconds each time you print. When connected across a network, other network users may reset parameters required for your printing. You should select Automatic Downloading Each Job when printing across a network.

Another possible source of network printing errors can be addressed through the Handshaking option. If you have problems printing to your Postscript laser printer across a network, use this option to set Handshaking to "Hardware."

Pick OK in each dialog box to record your changes and return to the worksheet.

APPLICATIONS

You must use the Printer Setup command before you print for the first time. You can also use it anytime you want to switch between printers or change the options on a printer.

When developing a project, you use a low graphics resolution and the draft mode of your printer for rapid draft output, then reset your output device to use the higher resolution for final output. If you have both a laser printer and a color printer, you may want to produce the text on the laser printer and your charts on the color printer. Use the Printer Setup command to switch between then.

Excel remembers the most recently set selections for printers and uses the most recently selected printer for all its output.

TYPICAL OPERATION

In this operation you select a printer for use in subsequent modules. Because Excel allows you to customize your system for hundreds of printers, the following steps are only a general guideline.

1. Start Excel and select **Printer Setup** from the File menu.

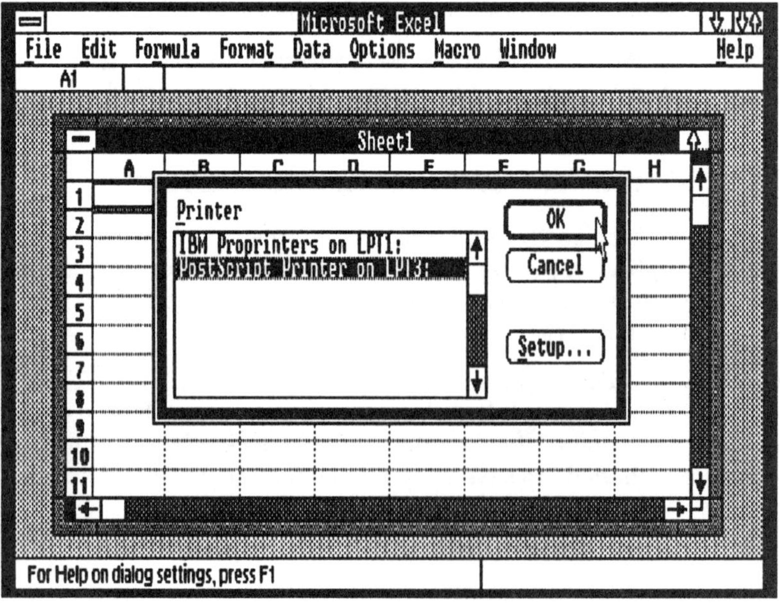

2. Pick the desired printer from the list of installed printers. Pick **OK**.

NOTE
If your printer isn't on the list, pick Cancel and
go to the section *ADDING A PRINTER*.

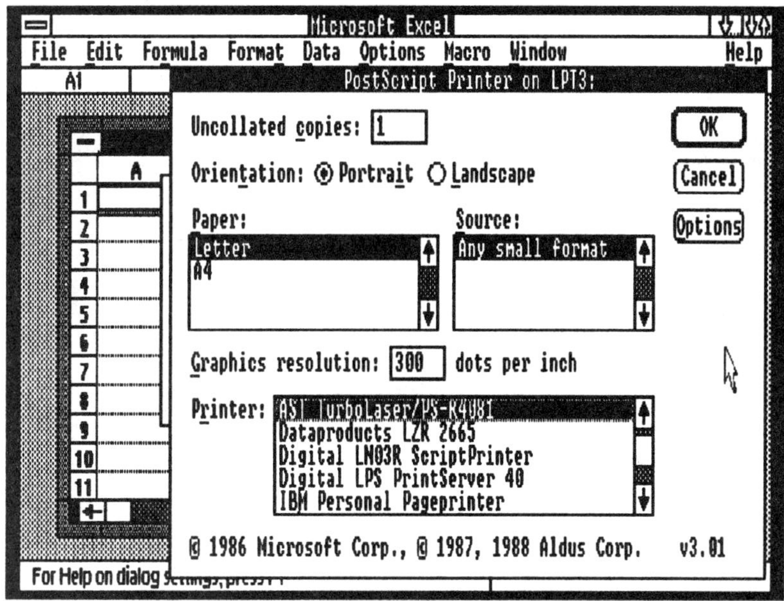

3. Pick the desired options from the dialog box that appears for your selected printer, then pick **OK**.

4. Pick **OK** in the original dialog box. Your printer selection preferences are saved on disk for use in this and future sessions of Excel. The choices remain effective until you change them.

5. Turn to Module 49 to continue the learning sequence.

ADDING A PRINTER

If the name of your printer does not appear on the Printer dialog box, its driver was not properly installed when you installed Windows or Excel. To add a printer driver file follow these steps.

If you are using the full version of Windows, you will need the original copies of the Windows disks, otherwise you will need the original copies of your Excel disks.

1. Click on the Microsoft Excel **Control menu icon,** or press **Alt-Spacebar.**

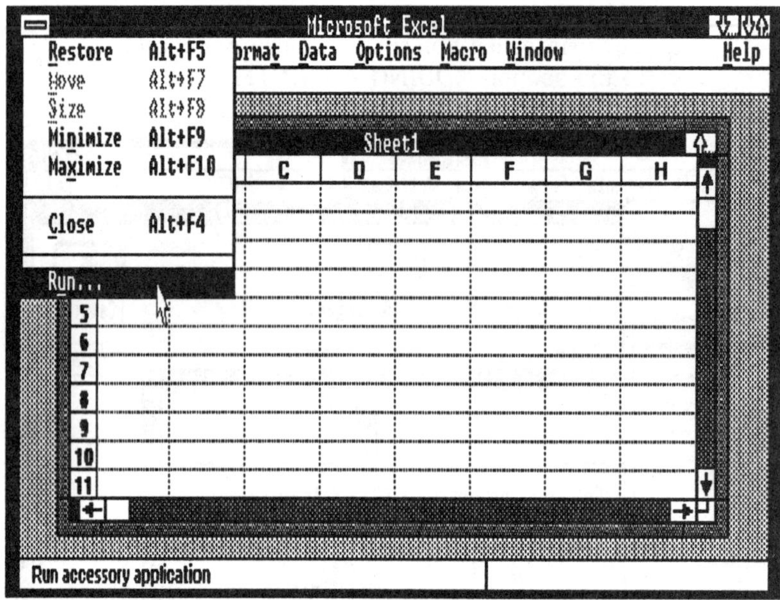

2. Select **Run** or type **U.**

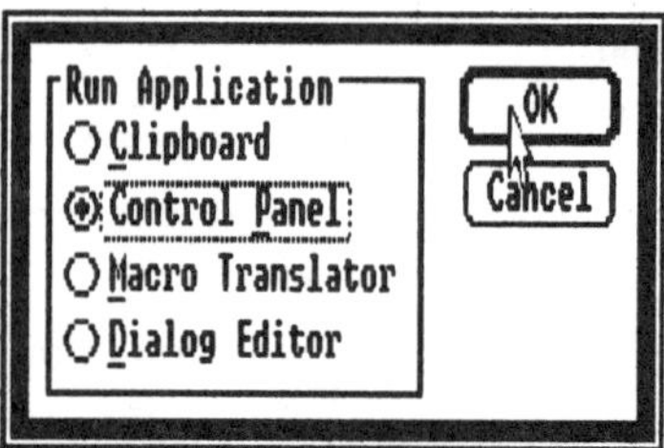

3. Select **Control Panel** and then **OK.**
4. Select **Installation** from the Control Panel dialog box menu bar.

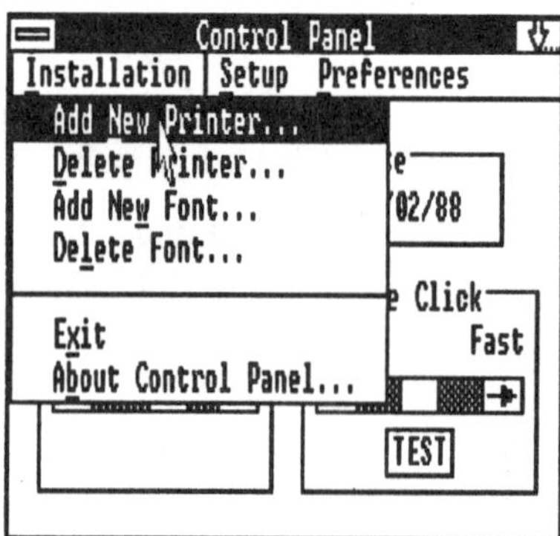

5. Select **Add New Printer**.

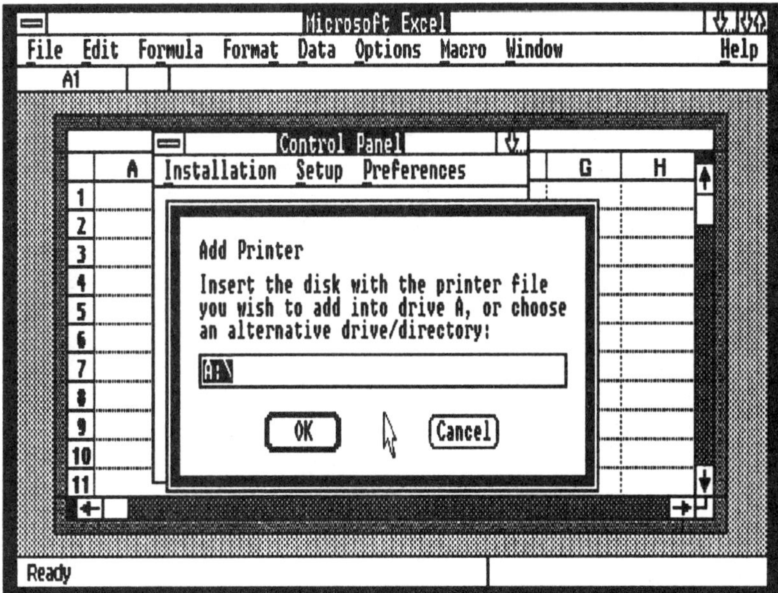

6. The printer drivers are located on one or more diskettes labeled "Utility" or "Utility 1" and "Utility 2" depending on the distribution disk format of your particular copy. Insert one of the disks into a disk drive, make sure the drive letter in the dialog box matches your choice, and press **OK**. If the required printer driver isn't on the first disk you try, select **Cancel** and try the other Utility disk.

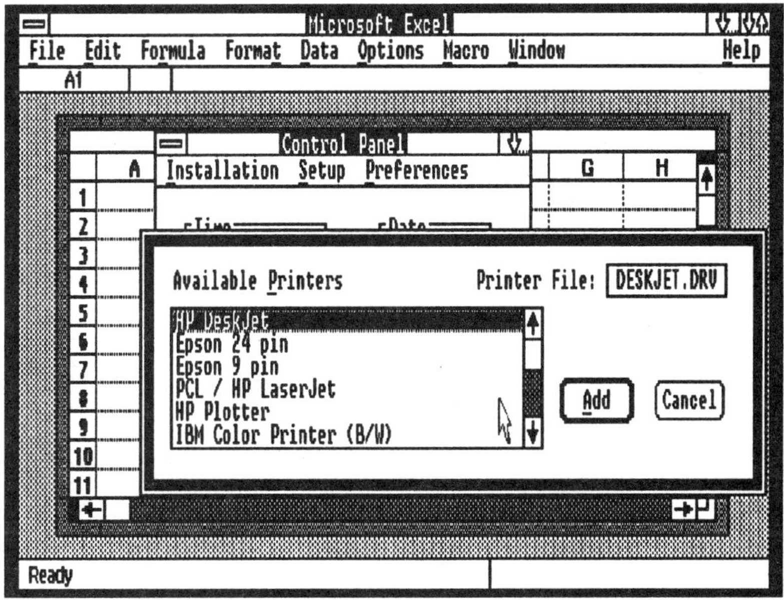

7. Select your printer from the list and select Add. If it isn't there, select Cancel and try another disk. If you still can't find it, it may not be supported by Excel or Windows. If your printer isn't supported, it may be "compatible" with a printer that is supported. Check your printer manual for details. If it isn't supported and isn't compatible with any of the supported printers, you may still be able to use it by selecting the Generic Printer (text only) printer driver. In this example, the Hewlett Packard Laserjet printer is chosen.

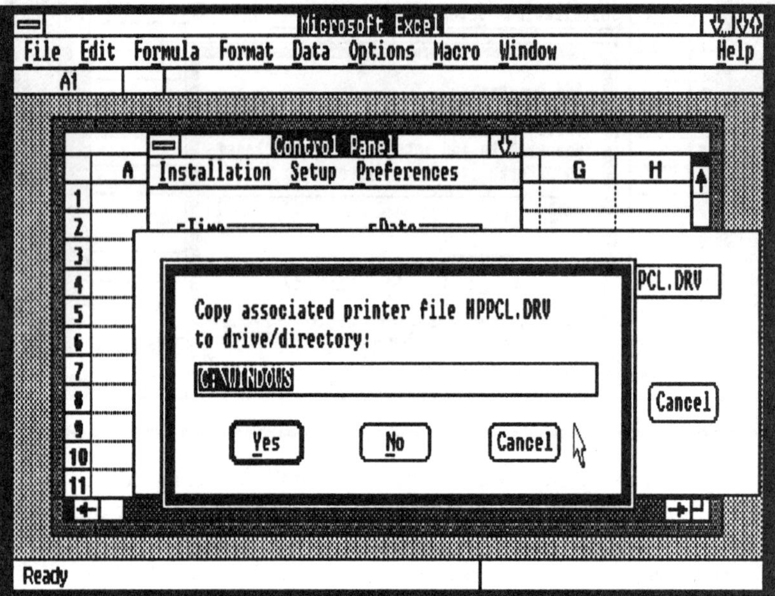

8. The installation program needs to know the location of Windows on your computer. By default, Excel, Windows, and Windows/286 are installed in a subdirectory named \ WINDOWS. Windows/386 is installed in a subdirectory named \ WIN386. If in doubt, the default is probably correct. Correct the drive and directory if necessary and select **Yes**.

9. Pick the **Control menu icon** of the Control Panel (press **Alt-Spacebar**).

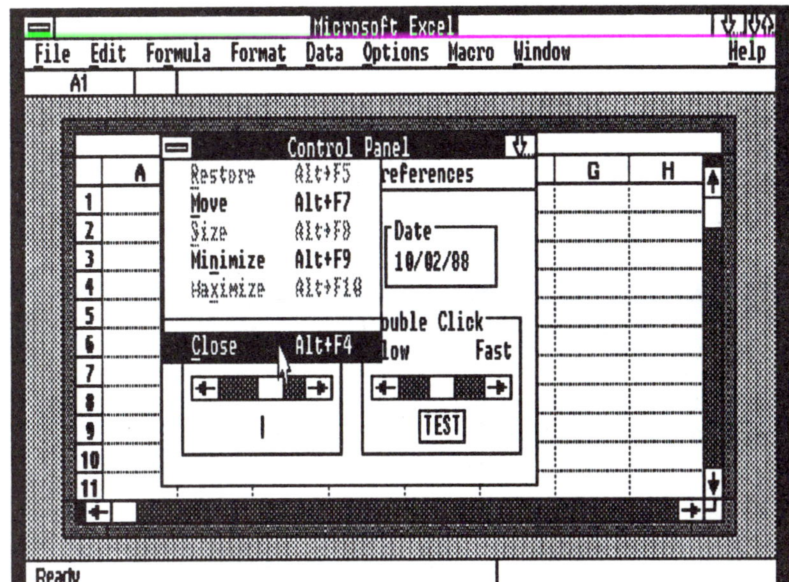

10. Select **Close** to return to the Excel worksheet.

11. Perform the Typical Operation section of this module to set your preferences for your newly installed printer.

Module 51
PROTECT DOCUMENT

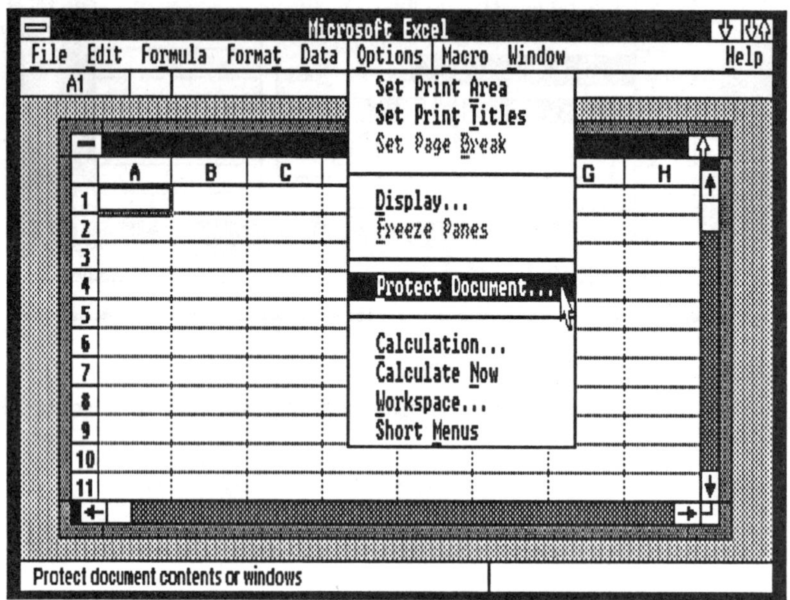

DESCRIPTION

The Protect Document command is accessed from the Options menu using Alt-O P. This command permits you to protect all or part of a document from being accidentally changed. The command also permits you to hide certain portions from unauthorized viewing. The Protect Document allows you to protect a document with or without a password.

CAUTION

If you use a password to protect your document,
be sure to keep the password in a safe place
because there is no way to unprotect a document
without it.

(A companion command to the Protect Document command is the Cell Protection command in the Format menu.)

APPLICATIONS

There are various times when documents need to be protected. Sometimes protection is necessary to avoid accidental changes to documents. Sometimes protection is necessary to avoid the deliberate changing of document data. Sometimes it is simply a prudent activity to protect document information from unauthorized viewing.

TIP: The simplest way to protect one or more rows or columns from being viewed is to designate those rows or columns as having zero width. This action will not affect the information that is contained in the rows and columns but will make it unavailable until the dimensions are increased. This procedure was presented in Module 13, Column Width, Module 56, Row Height and Module 32, Hide/Unhide.

TYPICAL OPERATION

In this operation you protect a document, the data in the document, and the shape of the document. You also protect from view or hide information in the document. You will need a document that you can practice on without risking the original data.

1. Start Excel and open BUDGET1.XLS.
2. Select **New Window** from the Window menu.
3. Select **Protect Document** from the Options menu.

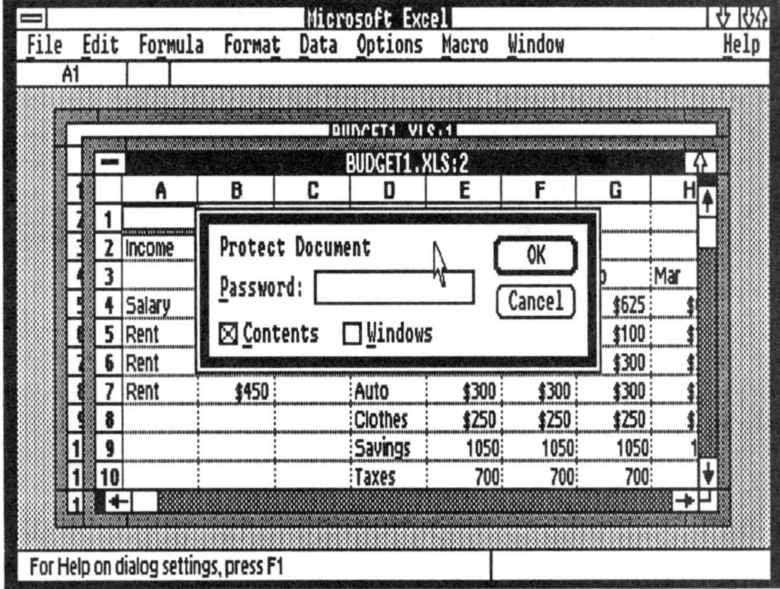

The default setting is to protect the contents.

4. Type **money** as the password and press **Enter**.

5. Attempt to change the data in this worksheet.

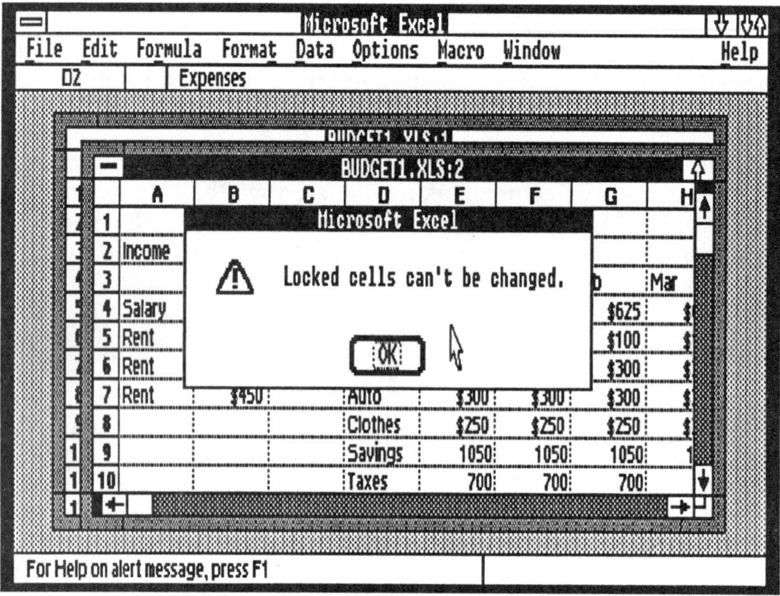

6. Press **Enter**.

7. Select **Unprotect Document** from the Options menu.

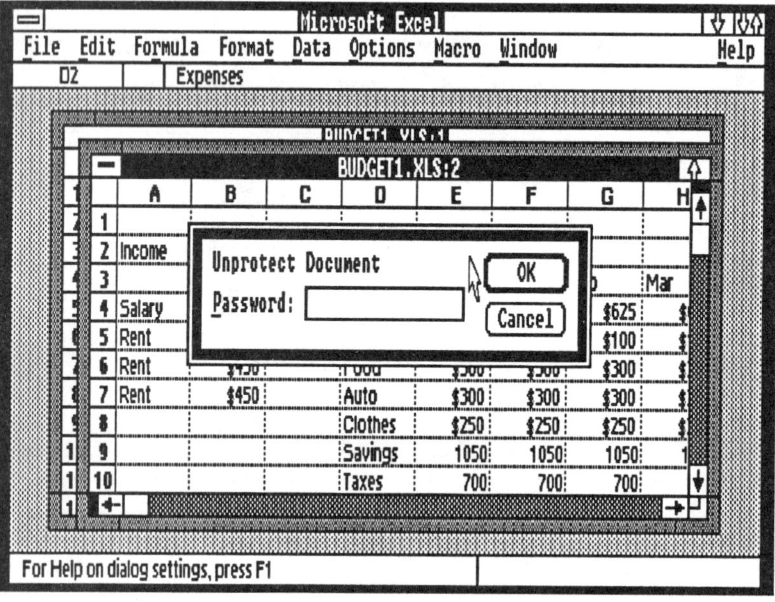

8. Type **Nothing** and press **Enter**.

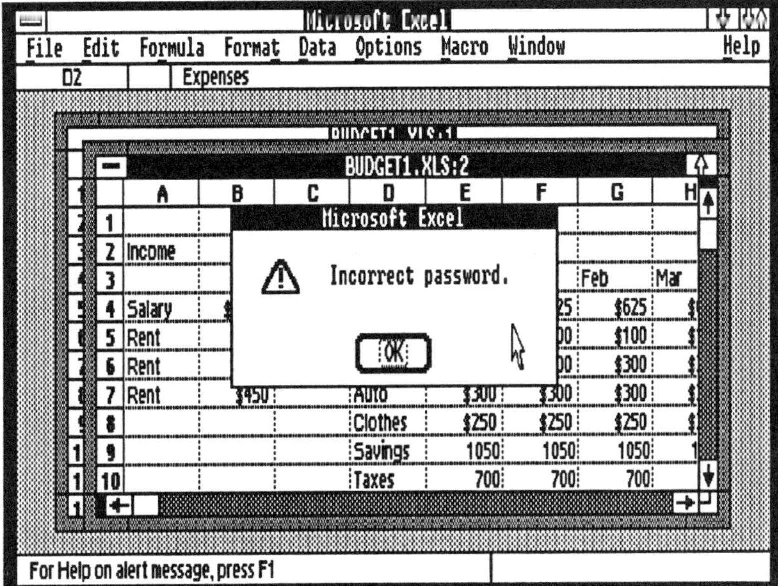

9. Press **Enter**.
10. Select **Unprotect Document**, type **money**, and press **Enter**.
11. Change the shape of BUDGET1.XLS:2.

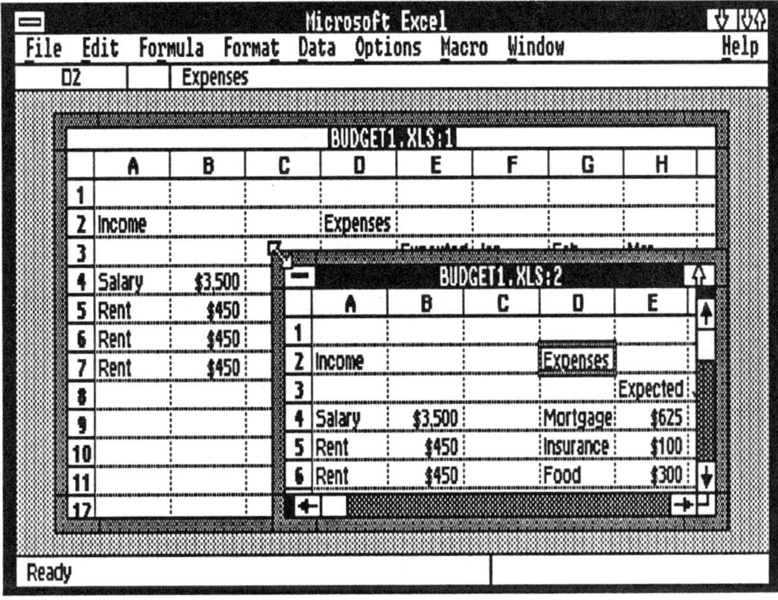

12. Select **Protect Document** from the Options menu, activate the **Windows** option, and press **Enter**.

The Control menu icon is gone from this worksheet, preventing access to the Size and Move commands.

13. Select **Arrange All** from the Window menu. The shape of the protected window will remain in effect until it is unprotected.

14. Select **Unprotect Document**.

15. Turn to Module 9 to continue the learning sequence.

Module 52
RECORD

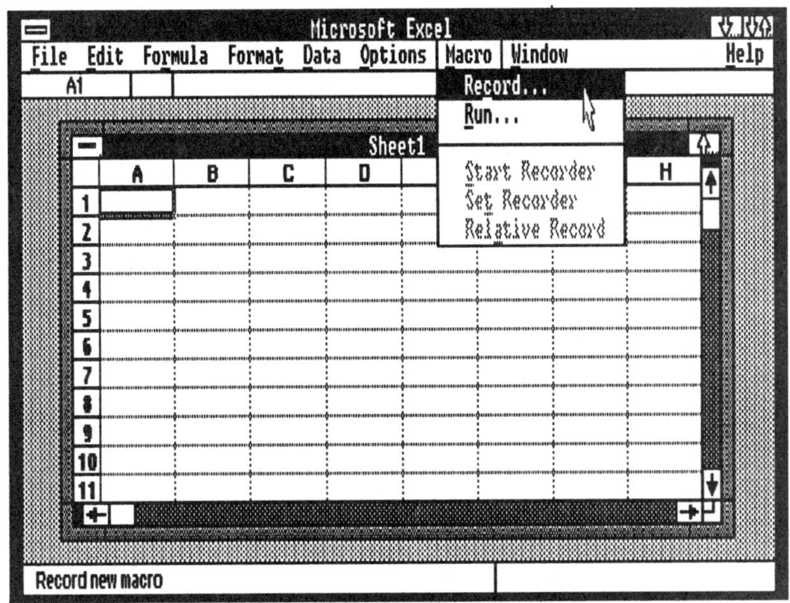

DESCRIPTION

Excel has a powerful macro language that allows you to automate worksheet tasks. A macro is a series of Excel commands that performs an operation. Macros are stored on macro sheets. The full description of the macro language is beyond the scope of this book. However, the Record command allows you to record sequences of keystrokes and mouse clicks interactively to create a macro that can be replayed with the Run command — without having to learn the intricacies of the Excel macro language.

When you create a macro, you specify a control key combination that you can use later as a shortcut key to activate the macro. Shortcut keys are case sensitive. Select the key with the case you desire.

When Excel records macro commands it interprets your actions as absolute references. You can change this interpretation to relative by selecting Relative Record from the Macro menu. You can later change back to absolute references by selecting Absolute Record from the Macro menu.

APPLICATIONS

If you plan on performing a task in Excel a number of times, for example consolidating monthly production or sales figures into a summary and producing a report, constructing a macro can save work and prevent you from having to remember the exact sequence of commands required every time you perform the task. A macro is also an excellent tool to use when delegating worksheet tasks to subordinates. The use of a well constructed macro, or series of macros, can help reduce the amount of training required to allow them to perform tasks that you have designed.

When selecting control key combinations, attempt to use a scheme that is easy to remember, such as a mnemonic scheme, to make your macros easy to use.

Use the Repeat command to repetitively perform a single command. Use the Record command to repetitively perform a sequence of commands.

TYPICAL OPERATION

In this session you perform the steps necessary to create a macro to produce a summary sales report where sales figures are sorted in decending order.

1. Start Excel.
2. Pick **Record** from the Macro menu.
3. Type **Summary** as the Name, press **Tab**, and type **s** as the Key.

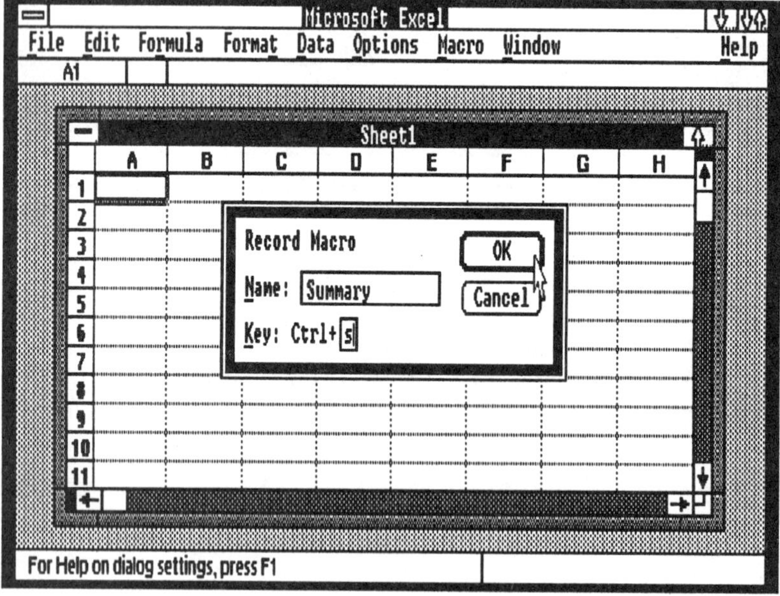

4. Pick **OK**.

The macro recorder is now on, and every command that you issue Excel is recorded as part of the macro. As you perform following operations, notice that the use of the mouse and the keyboard are intermixed indescriminately. The macro recorder allows you complete freedom in the method you use to specify commands.

5. Pick **Open** from the File menu.

6. Pick **EASTERN.XLS** from the Files selector box. Pick **OK**.

7. Press **Alt-F** and type **O** to open an additional file.

8. Type **WESTERN.XLS** and press **Enter**.

9. Pick **Open** from the File menu.

10. Scroll the File selector until the file NATIONAL.XLS appears in the selector window. Pick **NATIONAL.XLS**, then pick **OK**.

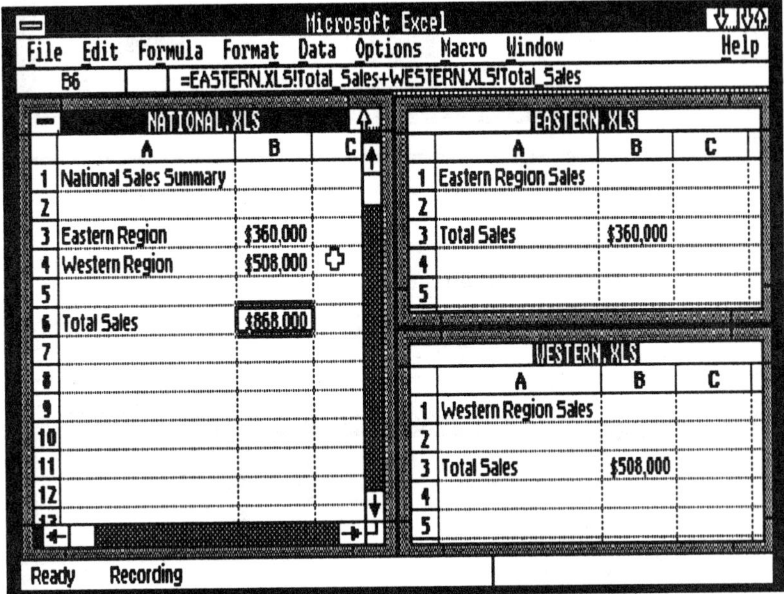

11. Highlight the region A3 through B4 in the National worksheet.

12. Pick **Sort** from the Data menu.

13. Type **$B$3** as the 1st Key and pick **Descending** as the order.

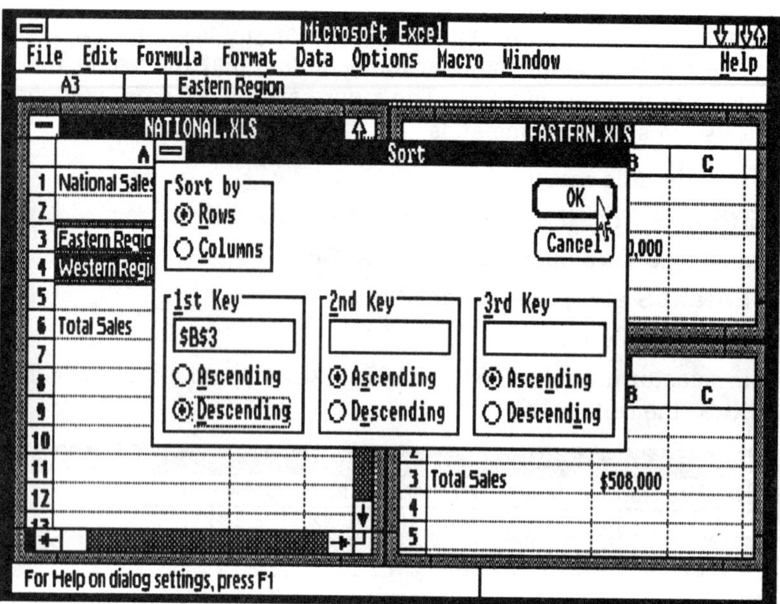

14. Pick **OK**.

15. Pick **Print** from the File menu.

16. Select **Preview** on the Print dialog box.

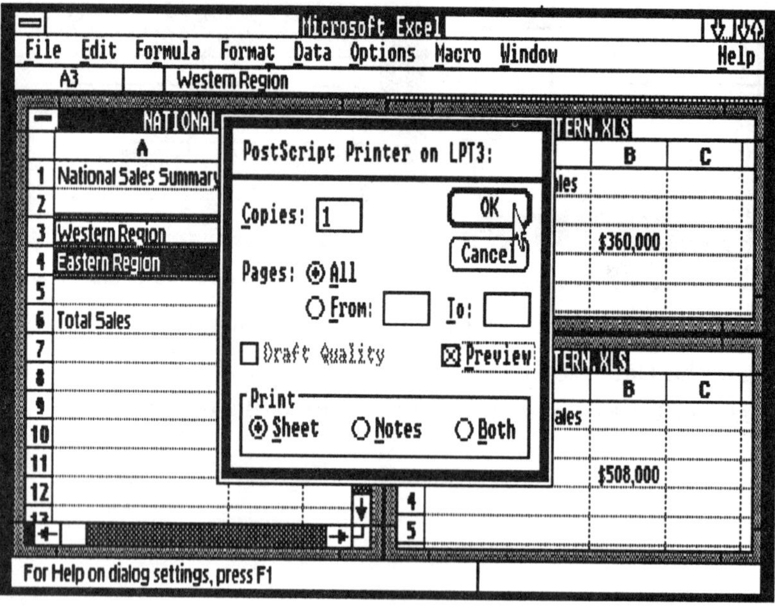

17. Pick **OK**.

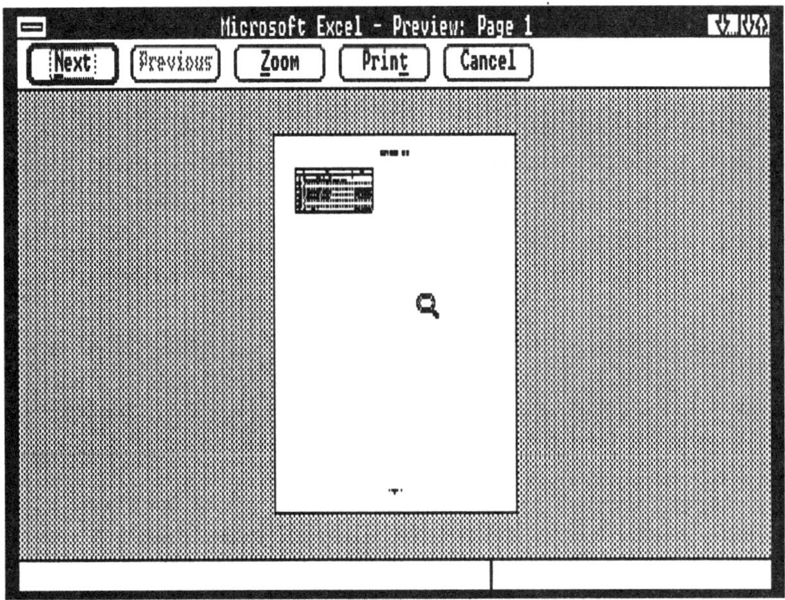

18. Pick **Cancel**.

19. Pick **Stop Recorder** from the Macro menu.

20. Pick **Macro1** from the Window menu to view the macro you created.

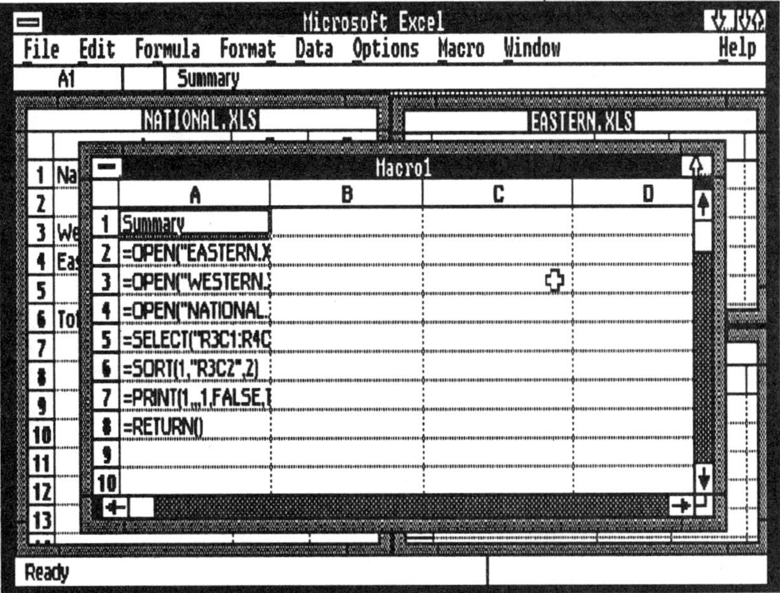

Now that the macro is created, you can modify it if you want using standard Excel editing techniques.

21. Save the macro as **SUMMARY.XLM**. (By convention, Excel macros are saved with the file extension XLM.)

22. Close each open worksheet but do not save any changes!

23. Quit Excel.

24. Turn to Module 57 to continue the learning sequence.

Module 53

REFERENCE

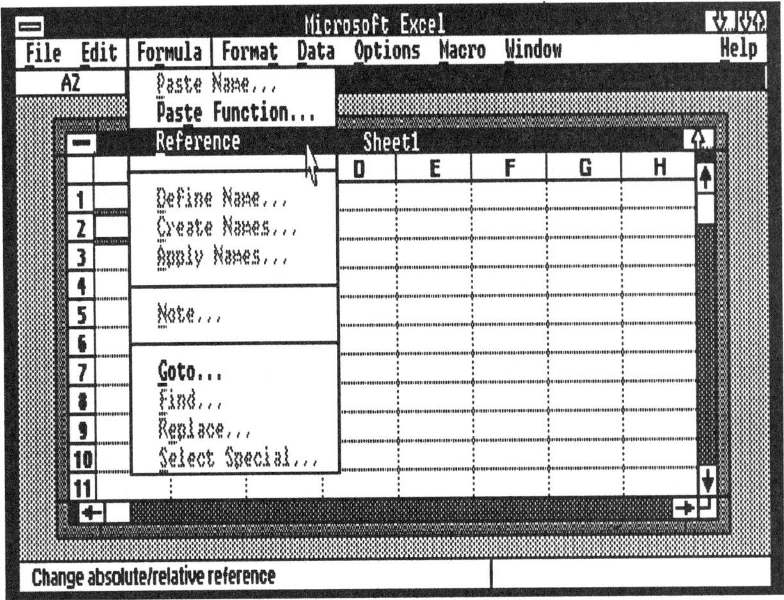

DESCRIPTION

Use the Reference command on the Formula menu to change cell references in order:

- from relative to absolute,
- from absolute to mixed with a relative row and absolute column,
- to mixed with an absolute row and relative column,
- to relative.

First, select the cell containing the reference. Second, move the mouse cursor to the formula bar at the top of the window and highlight the reference or group of reference that you want changed by dragging the mouse cursor over the references with the mouse button pressed. Third, select Reference from the Formula menu, or press F4 or Alt-R R. The type of cell reference toggles to the next type.

APPLICATIONS

When you create an Excel formula, you do not always think about using it in multiple locations on a worksheet. When you copy a formula from one worksheet location to another, Excel respects your designation of relative, absolute, and mixed cell references. The dollar sign is used to designate an absolute row or column specification. The lack of a dollar sign designates a relative reference. For example, A1 is a relative reference. $A$1 is an absolute reference. The reference $A1 is a mixed reference where the column is absolute and the row is relative. The reference A$1 is a mixed reference where the row is absolute and the column is relative.

The Reference command is an editing technique to make it easier for you to modify formulas prior to copying them.

TYPICAL OPERATION

In this session you use the Reference command to change the reference types in a formula.

1. Start Excel. Use Sheet1 for your work.

2. Type **10** in cell A1, **20** in A2, and **30** in A3.

3. Type the formula **=A1+A2+A3** in cell A4 and press **Enter**. Notice that the formula is formed entirely from relative references.

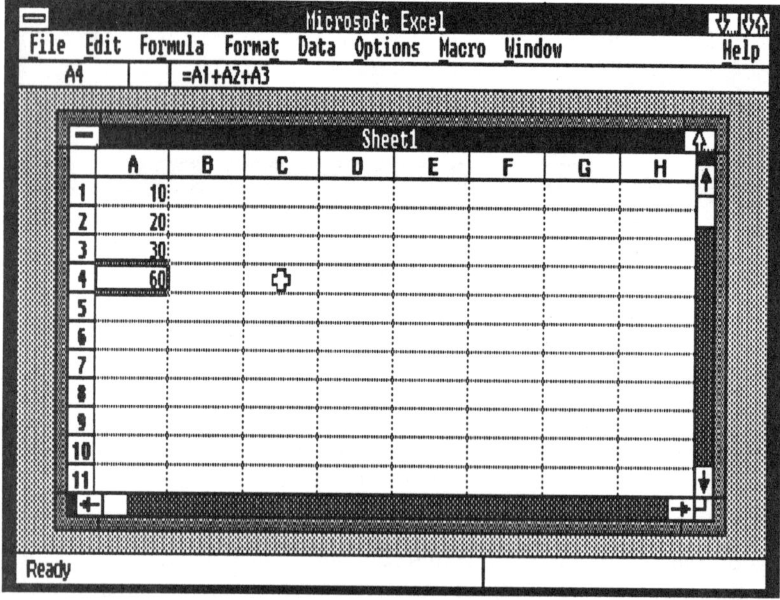

4. With cell A4 selected, select **Copy** from the Edit menu, select cell B4, and press **Enter**.

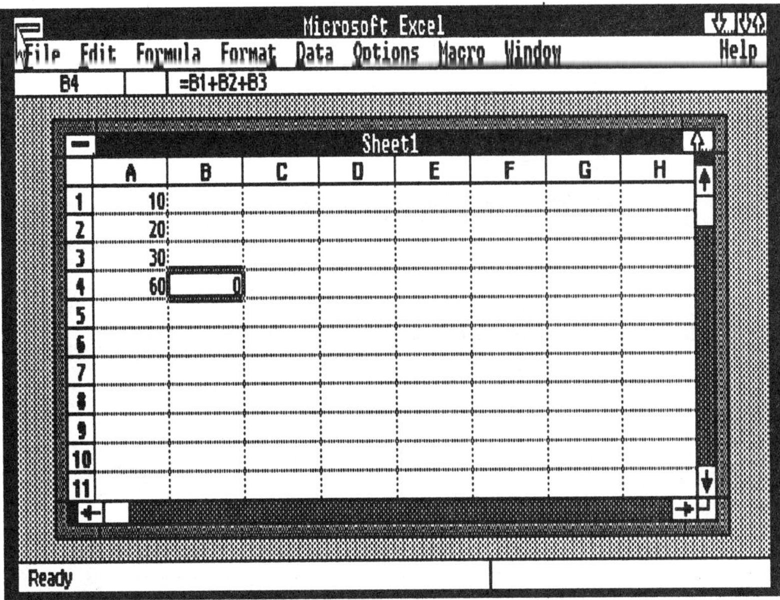

The formula copies as = B1 + B2 + B3. Because all of the references in the formula are relative references, they are adjusted.

5. Select cell A4. Press the mouse button and drag the mouse cursor across the entire formula bar, highlighting it as shown in the following screen. Then release the mouse button.

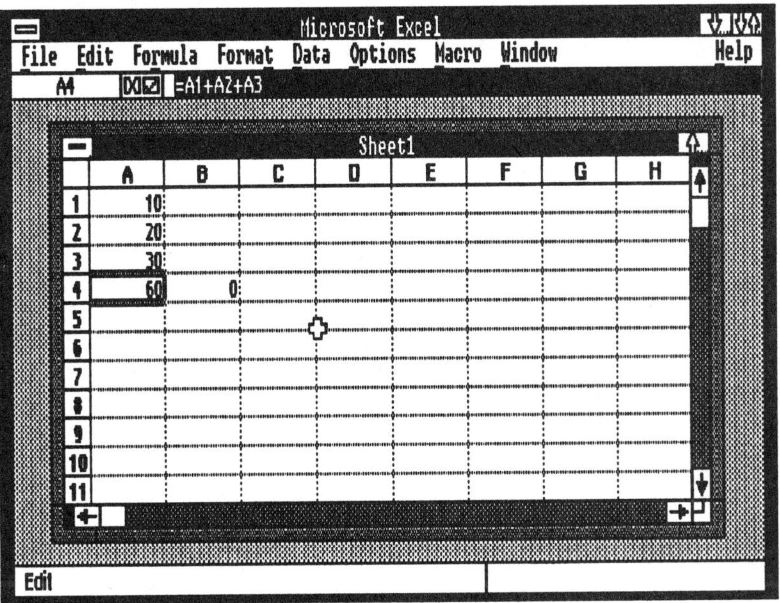

6. Select **Reference** from the Formula menu, then press **Enter**. Notice that all cell references are changed to absolute references.

7. Select **Copy** from the Edit menu.

8. Select cell B4 and press **Enter**. Notice that the value 60 appears in the cell, and that the formula bar shows $= \$A\$1 + \$A\$2 + \$A\$3$ as the formula for cell B4.

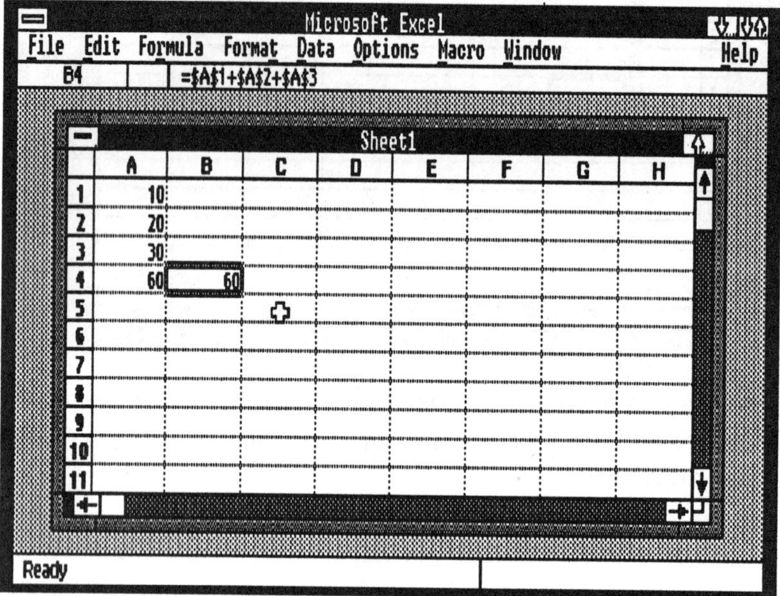

9. Close the worksheet. There is no need to save it.

10. Turn to Module 31 to continue the learning sequence.

Module 54

REPEAT

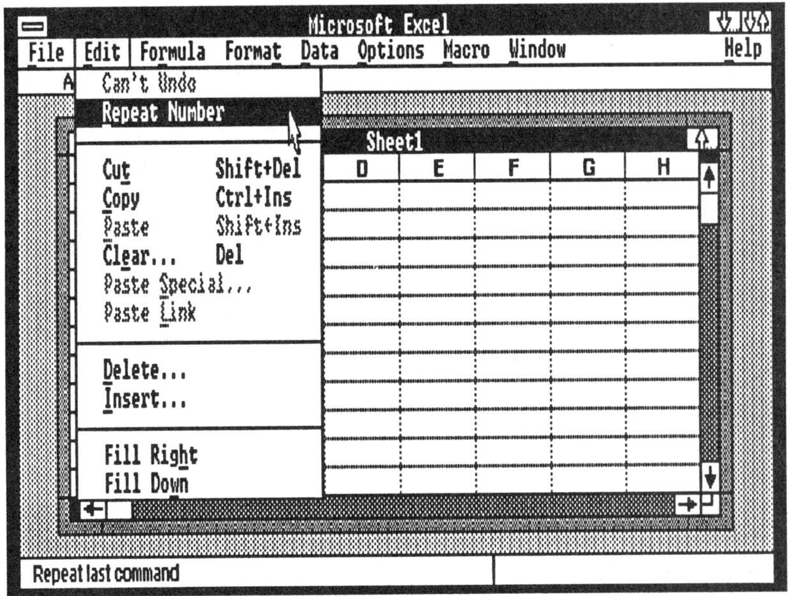

DESCRIPTION

The Repeat command, located on the Edit menu allows you to repeat the most recently used command. The Repeat command only allows repetition of commands that can reasonably be repeated. When the command is unavailable, it is gray on the Edit menu. When a command is repeated, the repetition includes all the options selected from the dialog box associated with the command.

APPLICATIONS

When using simple commands, like Fill Down, that have no options, the use of the Repeat command is helpful, but does not increase productivity. Where the repeat command shines, however, is when repeating commands that have several options. For example, to format several areas of the worksheet for dollars and cents numeric display, first apply the format to one cell or region, then select each additional cell or region in turn and issue the Repeat command. The Format command is then repeated with its options.

TYPICAL OPERATION

In this session you use the Repeat command to repotitively apply a format to numbers in the worksheet.

1. Start Excel. Expand Sheet1 to fill the screen.
2. Type **123.45** in cell A1.
3. Type **89.2** in cell C4.
4. Select cell A1; then select **Number** from the Format menu. Specify dollars and cents format and pick **OK**.

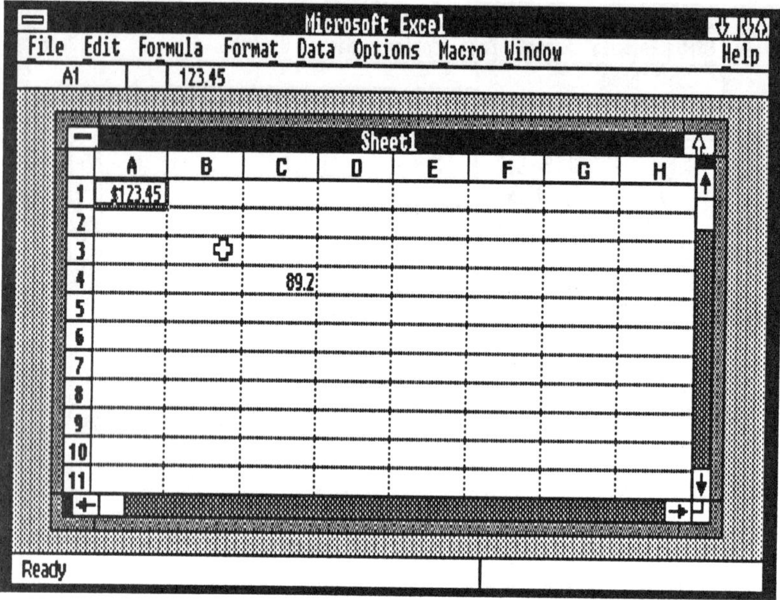

5. Select cell C4; then select **Repeat** from the Edit menu.

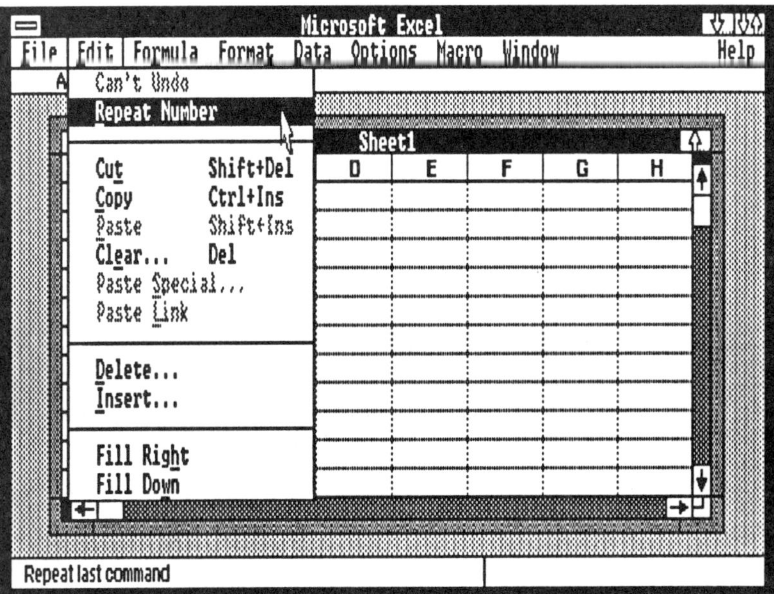

The format is applied to the new cell.

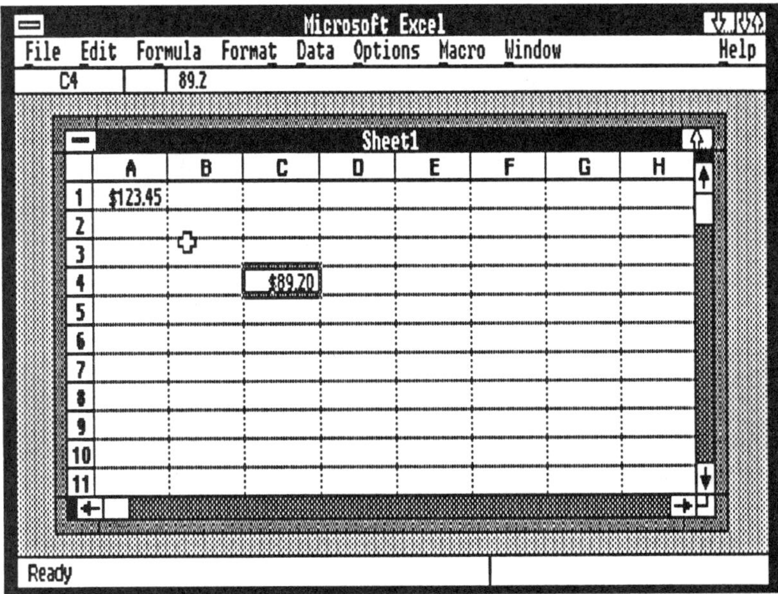

If you had many cells or regions, you could continue to repeat the Format commands.

6. Close the worksheet, there is no need to save it.

7. Continue the learning sequence with Module 52.

Module 55

REPLACE

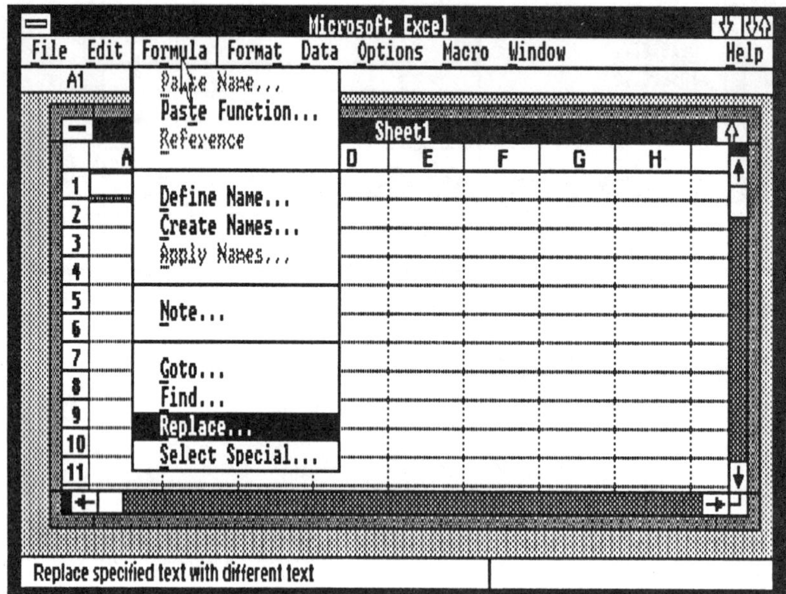

DESCRIPTION

The Replace command is located in the Formula menu under the Find command. It is accessed with Alt-R E and is used to find a string or value and then replace it with a new string or value.

Once you access the Replace command, Excel provides you a dialog box in which you will enter the string or value you want located and the string or value you want to substitute. Excel will replace all of the located strings of values throughout the worksheet, or you can elect to make each change one at a time.

The same conditions apply to this command as to the Find command. You must enter the string or value exactly as it appears in the worksheet, including spaces, and if you have designated a range, Excel will only look there.

APPLICATIONS

Using the Replace command is an accurate and quick method of correcting information in a worksheet or of updating information. It will cause Excel to change any type of data that is entered in the worksheet.

TYPICAL OPERATION

In this operation you locate a specific bit of information in a document and replace it with new information using the Replace command.

1. Start Excel and open BUDGET1.XLS, or continue your work session from the previous module.

2. Select cell A1, then select **Replace** from the Formula menu.

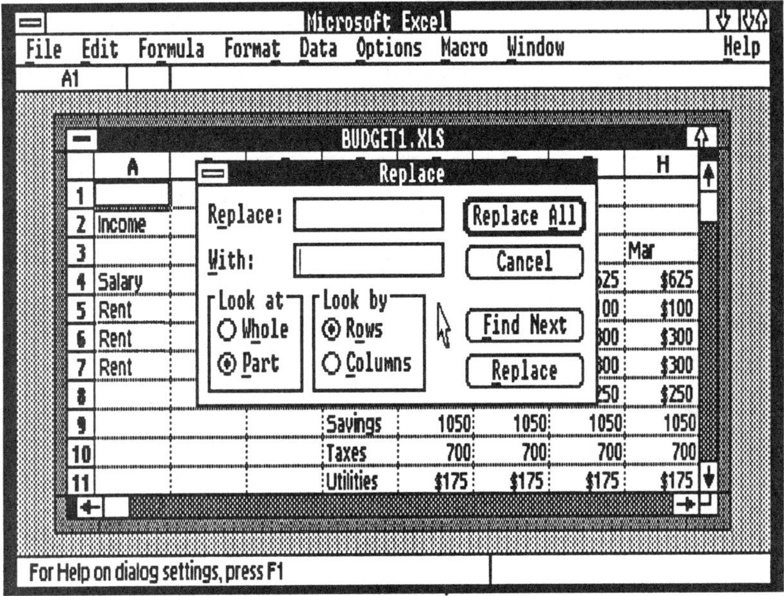

3. Type **Savings** in the Replace box.

4. Use the mouse or press **Tab** to move to the With box.

5. Type **Excess** in the With box.

6. Press **Enter**. The replacement has been made.

7. Access **Replace** from the Formula menu.

8. Change Savings to **Rent**, and change Excess to **Surplus**.

9. Activate **Find Next**. Use the mouse or the Tab key.

10. Press **Enter**.

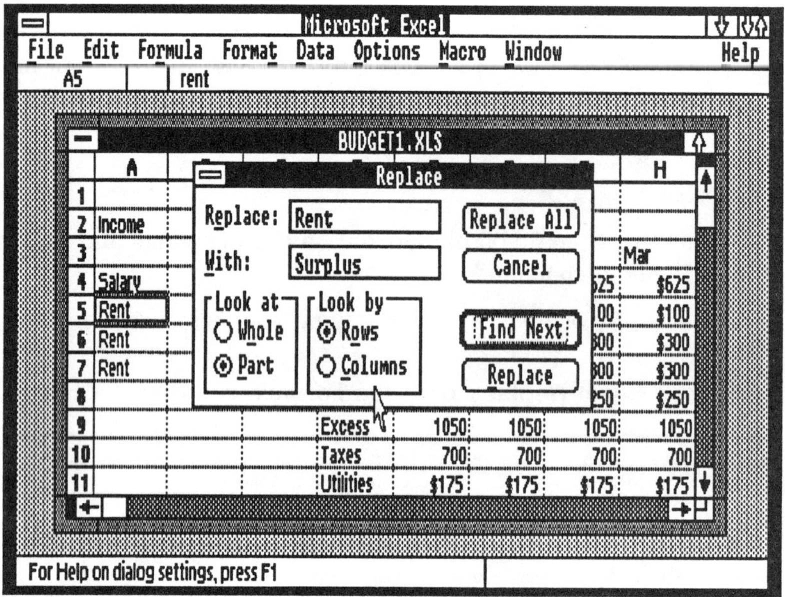

The first string is found.

11. Press **Tab** to move to **Replace** and press **Enter**. Continue the process until all of the strings are replaced.

12. Click on **Cancel**, or press **Tab** twice and press **Enter**.

13. Close the worksheet without saving the changes.

14. Exit Excel, or continue your work session with the next module.

15. Turn to Module 72 to continue the learning sequence.

Module 56

ROW HEIGHT

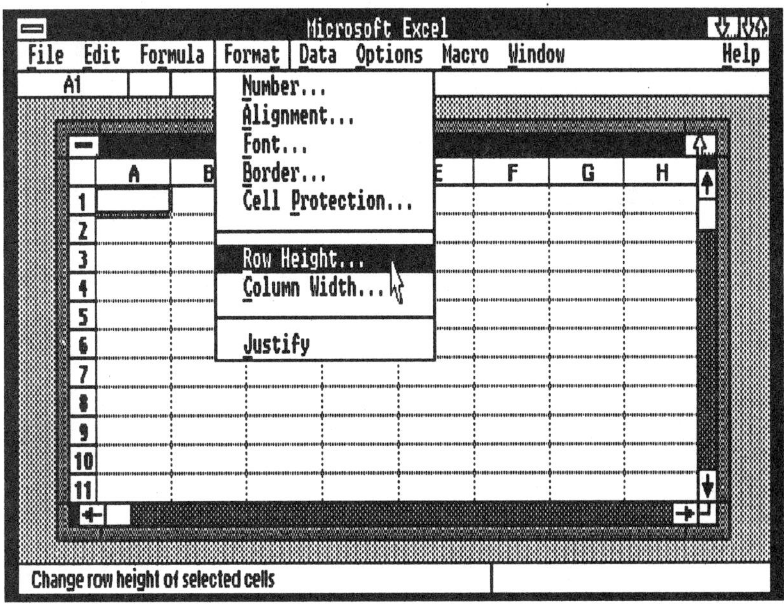

DESCRIPTION

The Row Height command on the Format menu allows you to vary the height of worksheet rows. Pick Row Height with the mouse, or press Alt-T R to display the Row Height dialog box.

The height of each row is measured in points. (There are 72 points per inch.) You can type a new value in the Row Height box and press OK. You can also elect to return a previously changed row height to its standard height by checking the Standard Height check box.

You may also change the height of a row visually with the mouse. Move the mouse to the area between the row numbers so that the cursor becomes a cross, as shown between rows three and four in the following screen.

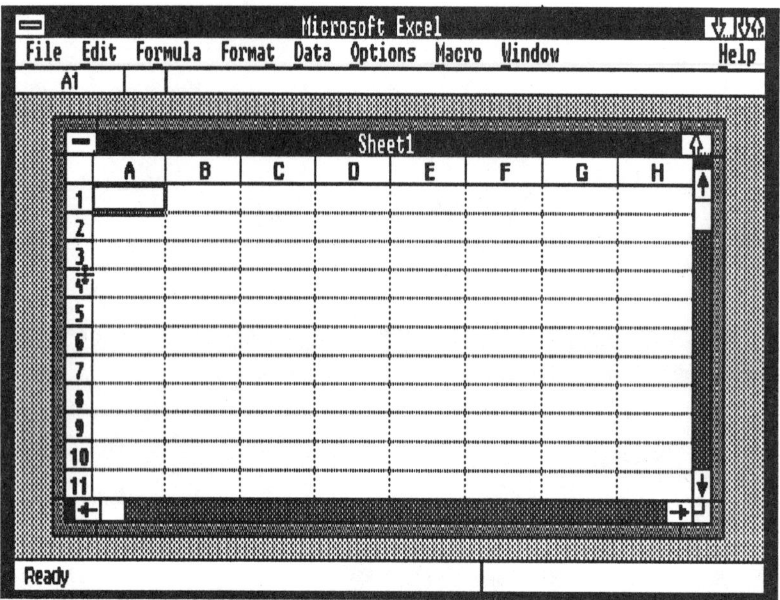

Press and hold the left mouse button and drag the cell border to the desired height. Release the mouse button when the height is correct. The worksheet format is revised as shown in the following screen.

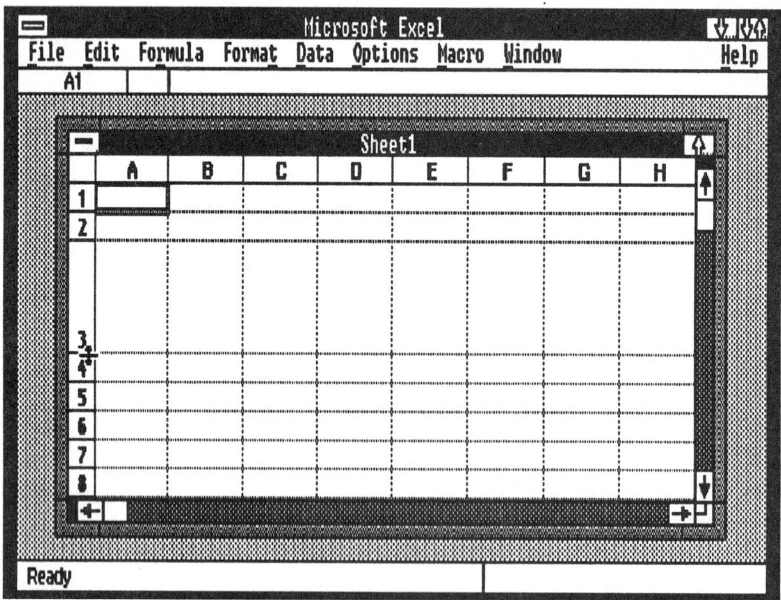

Careful adjustment of the row height can be used to hide an entire row or group of worksheet rows. First place the cursor between two row numbers until the cursor becomes a cross, as shown between rows 4 and 5 in the following screen.

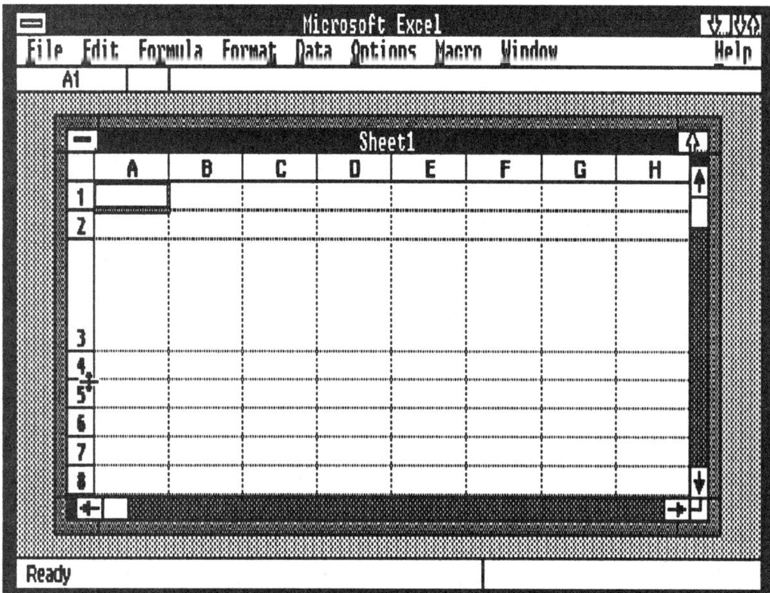

Press and hold the left button while moving the top of cell 5 into perfect alignment with the bottom of cell 2. Release the mouse button to confirm the change. The result is similar to the following screen. Notice that rows 3 and 4 are not shown.

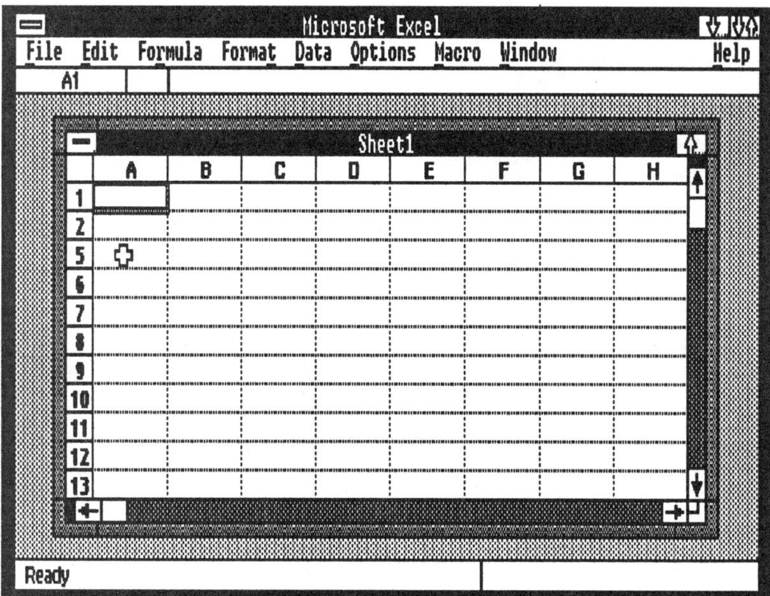

To restore rows 3 and 4, select a range of rows including the hidden rows. In this case, highlight rows 2 and 5 as shown in the following screen.

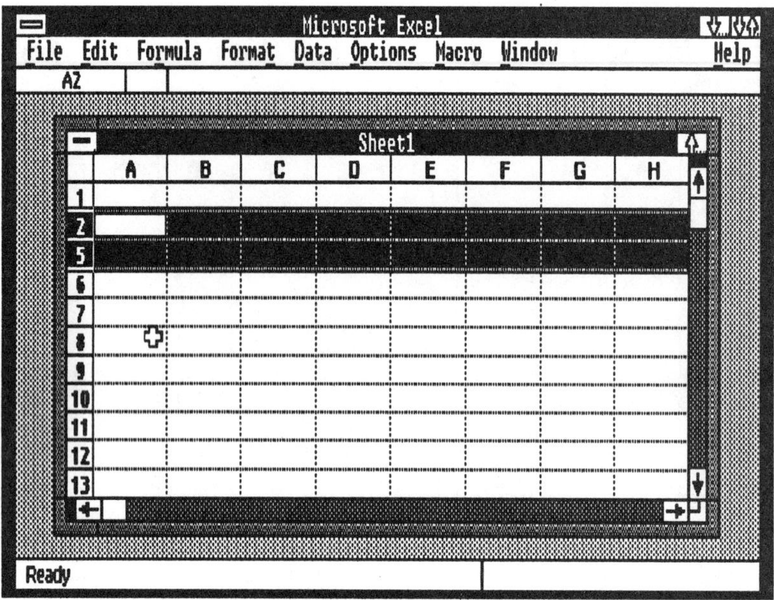

Select Row Height from the Format menu, then check the Standard Height check box.

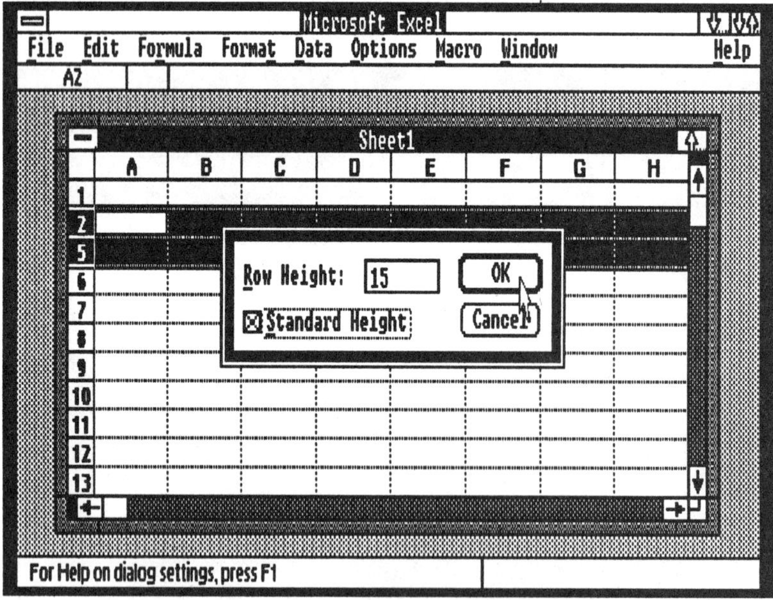

Pick OK, and the range of rows appears at the standard height.

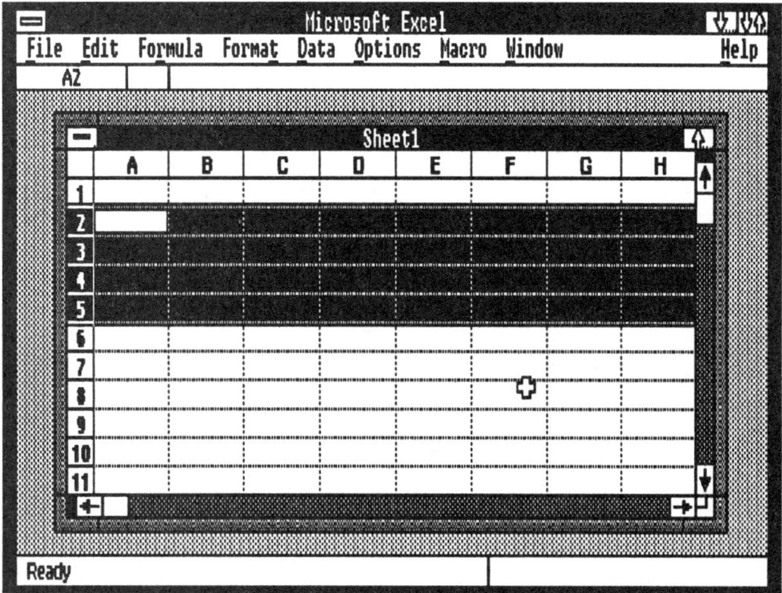

The ability to hide rows of data is an excellent feature for using a worksheet in a presentation environment. You may have rows of intermediate data that obscure the impact of the final results you want to communicate. You may also have confidential information. Excel's ability to hide rows can help you hide this data, while providing you with the flexibility to work with numbers derived from the hidden data.

The height of a worksheet row is independent of the font size used in the row. Increasing the font size automatically increases the row height, but increasing the row height has no effect on the font size.

TYPICAL OPERATION

In this session you adjust the row height of the INTEREST.XLS worksheet that you used in the Justify module.

1. Start Excel, open the INTEREST.XLS worksheet, and expand it to fill the screen, or continue your work session from the previous module.

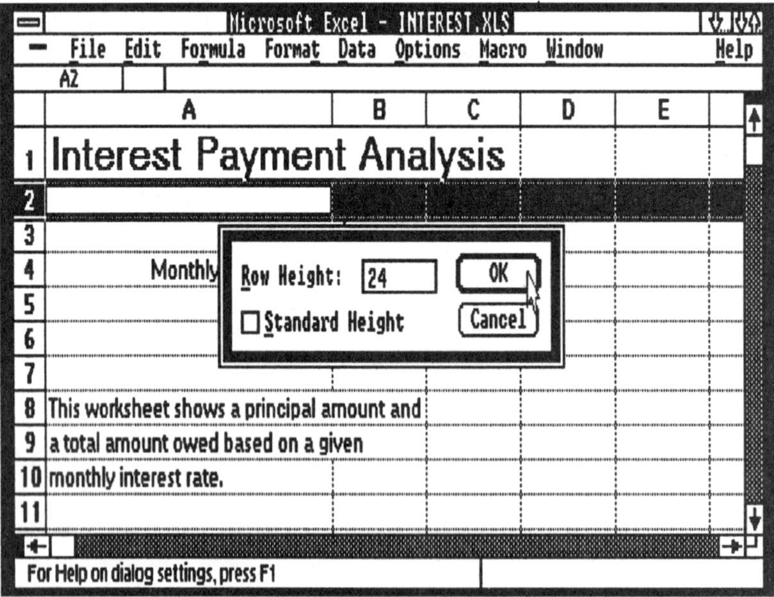

2. Select row 2, then select **Row Height** from the Format menu.

3. Type **24** as the Row Height.

4. Pick **OK**.

Microsoft Excel - INTEREST.XLS

File   Edit   Formula   Format   Data   Options   Macro   Window   Help

A2

	A	B	C	D	E
1	Interest Payment Analysis				
2					
3	Principal	$156,879			
4	Monthly Interest Rate	0.018			
5	Interest	$2,871			
6	Total Due	$159,750			
7					
8	This worksheet shows a principal amount and				
9	a total amount owed based on a given				
10	monthly interest rate.				
11					

Ready

5. Save the worksheet and exit Excel, or continue the learning sequence directly by turning to Module 7.

Module 57

RUN

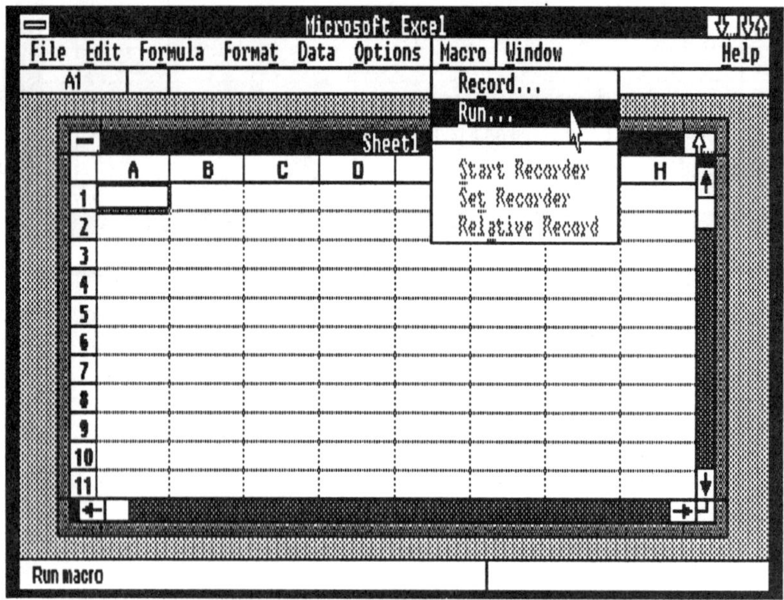

DESCRIPTION

The Run command on the Macro menu activates a previously recorded or written macro. You may also activate a macro by pressing its shortcut key combination. First, open the macro sheet (or sheets) containing the desired macro(s). Then pick Run from the Macro menu. The following dialog box appears.

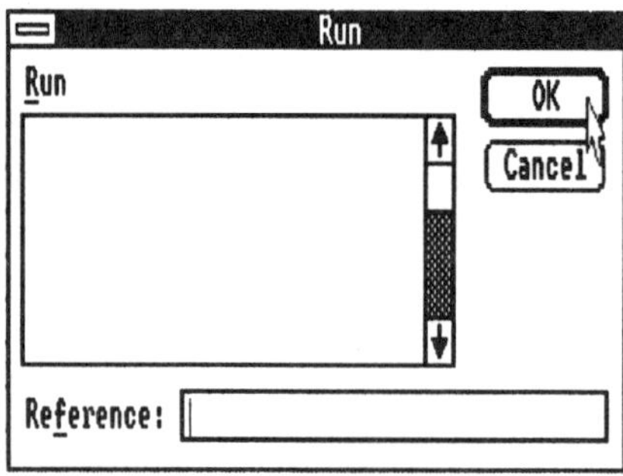

Each available macro is listed, together with its shortcut key.

APPLICATIONS

Use the Run command to perform the operations in a macro. Additionally, use the Run command to see a listing of the available macros and their shortcut keys.

TYPICAL OPERATION

In this session you activate the sales summary macro that you created in the Record module.

1. Start Excel.
2. Open the SUMMARY.XLM macro sheet.

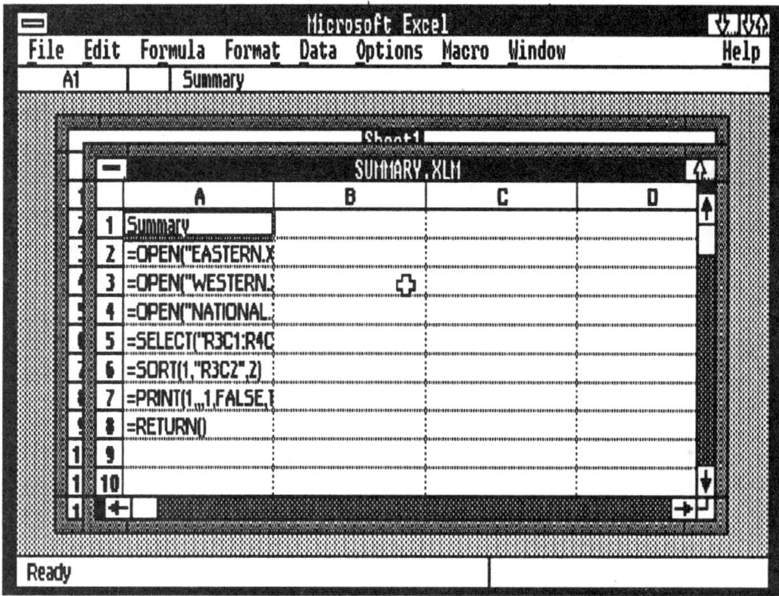

3. Pick **Run** from the Macro menu.

4. Pick the macro **SUMMARY.XLM!Summary**.

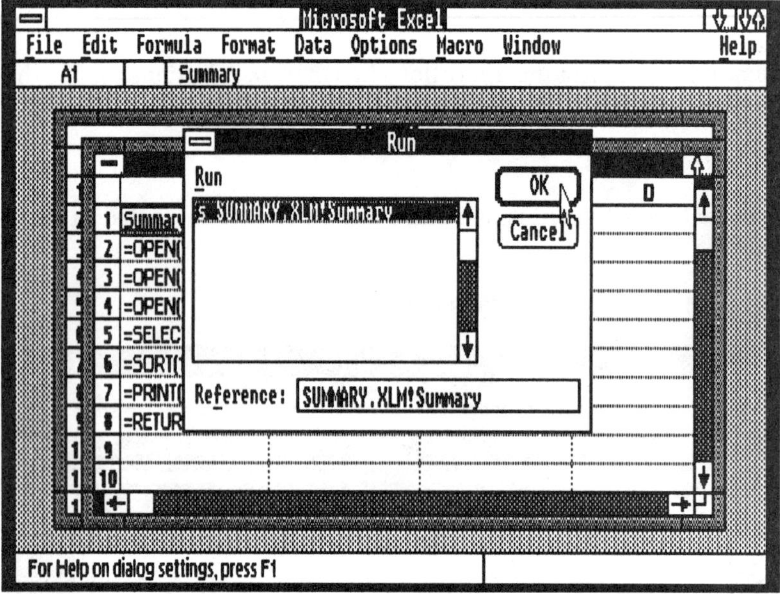

5. Pick **OK**.

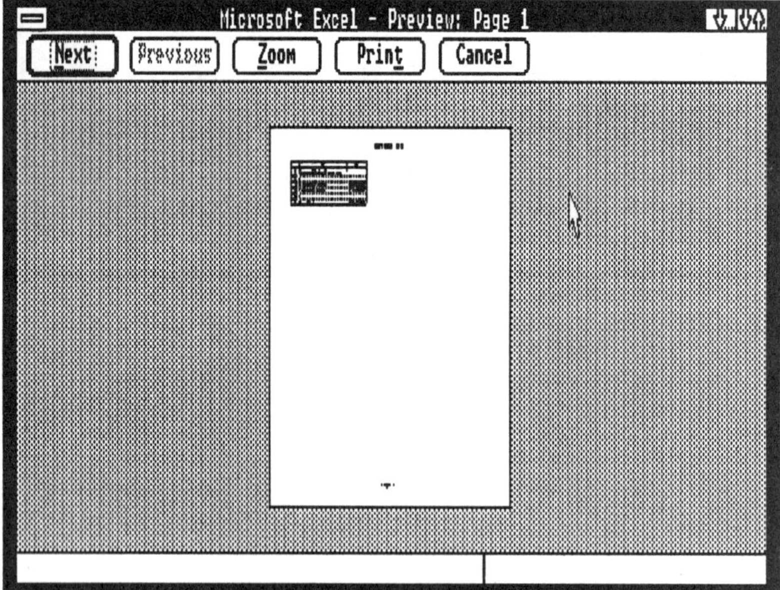

6. Pick **Cancel**.

7. Close the worksheets and exit Excel.

This concludes the learning sequence.

Module 58

SAVE, SAVE AS, SAVE WORKSPACE

DESCRIPTION

The Save commands are crucial to the use of any software application. You must be able to keep the work that is done at one session so that you can recall it and continue to work with it in future sessions. These three commands are located on the File menu. To access them with a mouse, click on File in the menu bar, then click on the desired command. To access them from the keyboard, press Alt-F and S (Save), A (Save As), W (Save Workspace). The first time you save a document, both Save and Save As permit you to assign the worksheet a particular name. Once a document has been saved under a particular name, the Save command will continue to save it under that name.

The Save As command will always permit you to change the name of a document before it is saved. The Save As command will also permit you to save a worksheet in a format different than Excel. If you select the Options option from the Save As dialog box, you see the following screen.

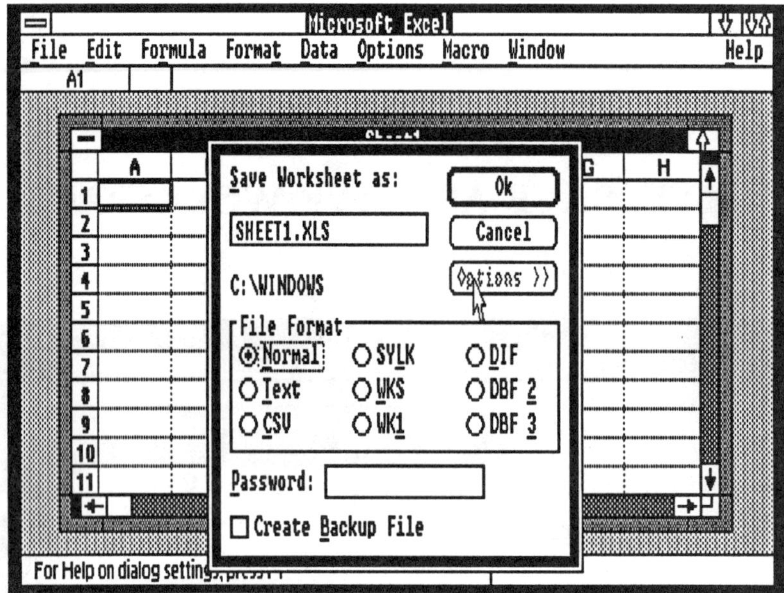

You can save it as Normal for Excel format. Text refers to an ASCII file and CSV is comma-separated values. SYLK is for symbolic-link format that can be used by other Microsoft programs; WKS is for release 1A of Lotus 1-2-3, WK1 for release 2 of Lotus 1-2-3, DIF for data interchange format, DBF 2 for dBASE II format, and DBF 3 for dBASE III format.

The Save Workspace permits you to save several worksheets as one document, under one name. When you retrieve that document, all of the associated worksheets are retrieved at the same time. When the dialog box appears, you can save the workspace under any name you want. If you don't name it, Excel will give it a default name. The name assigned to the Workspace will end in XLW to differentiate it from a worksheet.

Finally, Excel permits you to save a worksheet without ending your work session. When you specify that a document is to be saved, Excel performs the function and returns you to the point you were when you asked for it to be saved.

CAUTION

A workspace file does *not* contain the documents
themselves. If you change or delete an individual
document, the original version is not retained in
the workspace file.

APPLICATIONS

In order to save a document, Excel must know the name it will be called. Documents are stored by their name so that they can be recalled by name. If you don't want to name a document, Excel will name it for you, using the default name of "Sheet" or "Chart" or "Resume" followed by an extension. It is much easier to recall a particular document if you give the document a name that describes the kind of information that it contains. You should get in the habit of giving each document you save a descriptive name.

The "Save" and "Save As" commands in Excel permit you to write the document you have been using on either a hard disk or a floppy disk for recall at a later time. In this way you can do your work on a hard disk, and when you save it, you can specify that Excel write it on a floppy so that you will have a backup copy for an emergency.

A significant advantage of the "Save Workspace" command is the time you will save when you have many documents that are related in some way. By having Excel bundle them together as one large document, you can retrieve them all together. In this way all of the documents you might need to perform a certain task will be opened and ready for you to work with them. You won't need to go look for that one missing piece of information that you might need to complete your work.

TYPICAL OPERATION

In this operation you use the save commands to write documents on disk for future use. Since the Save command is quite a simple command and was demonstrated in Module 3, Sample Session, this operation focuses on the Save As and Save Workspace commands. Begin the session by saving the worksheet created in the previous module.

1.   Select **Save As** from the File menu.

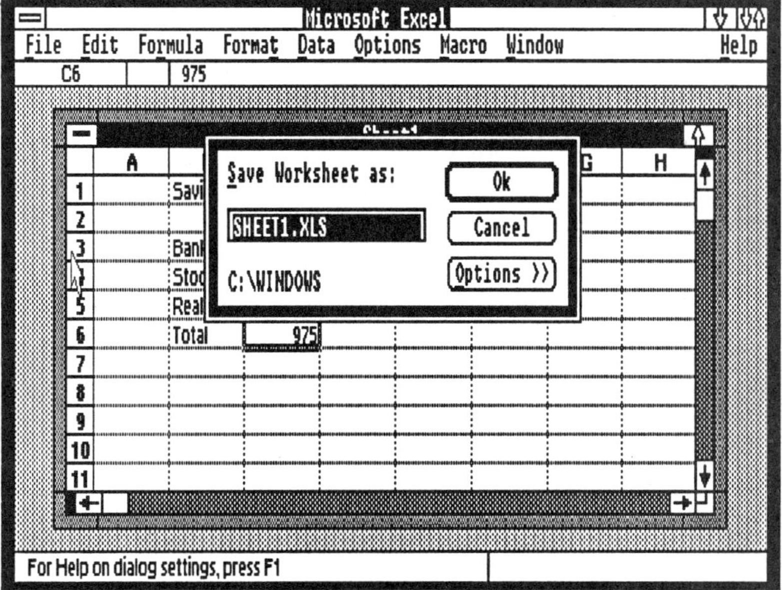

2.   Type **SAVINGS** and press **Enter**. The worksheet is saved as SAVINGS.XLS.

3.   Select **Open** from the File menu.

4.   Select SHEET1.XLS as the desired worksheet.

```
┌─────────────────────────────────────────────────────────────────────────┐
│ ▬                        Microsoft Excel                          ▼▐▼▲▌   │
│  File  Edit  Formula  Format  Data  Options  Macro  Window          Help  │
│    E8          =B3*0.2                                                     │
│ ┌─────────────────────────────────────────────────────────────────────┐ │
│ │ ▬                        SHEET1.XLS                               ▲  │ │
│ │      A      B      C      D      E      F  ┿  G      H            ▲  │ │
│ │  1 │Income│      │      │Expenses│      │      │      │           │ │
│ │  2 │      │      │      │      │      │      │      │      │           │ │
│ │  3 │Salary│$3,500│      │Mortgage│$625 │      │      │      │         │ │
│ │  4 │      │      │      │Food  │$250 │      │      │      │             │ │
│ │  5 │      │      │      │Auto  │$300 │      │      │      │             │ │
│ │  6 │      │      │      │Clothes│$200│      │      │      │             │ │
│ │  7 │      │      │      │Savings│1425│      │      │      │             │ │
│ │  8 │      │      │      │Taxes │ 700│      │      │      │             │ │
│ │  9 │      │      │      │      │      │      │      │      │           │ │
│ │ 10 │      │      │      │      │      │      │      │      │           │ │
│ │ 11 │      │      │      │      │      │      │      │      │ ▼         │ │
│ │ ◄ │                                                         ► │         │ │
│ └─────────────────────────────────────────────────────────────────────┘ │
│  Ready                                       │                            │
└─────────────────────────────────────────────────────────────────────────┘
```

SHEET1.XLS is retrieved from the disk and is now the active worksheet. It occupies the same space that it did when it was saved.

5.   Select **Save As** from the File menu.

6.   Type **BUDGET1** as the name of this worksheet and press **Enter**.

Now you have two worksheets that refer to the same general activity. It is likely that you will want to use them both whenever you work with your budget. You now save them together.

7.   Select **Save Workspace** from the File menu.

NOTE

If Save Workspace is not on your File menu, it is because your system has only displayed the short menu. Open the Options menu and select Full Menus.

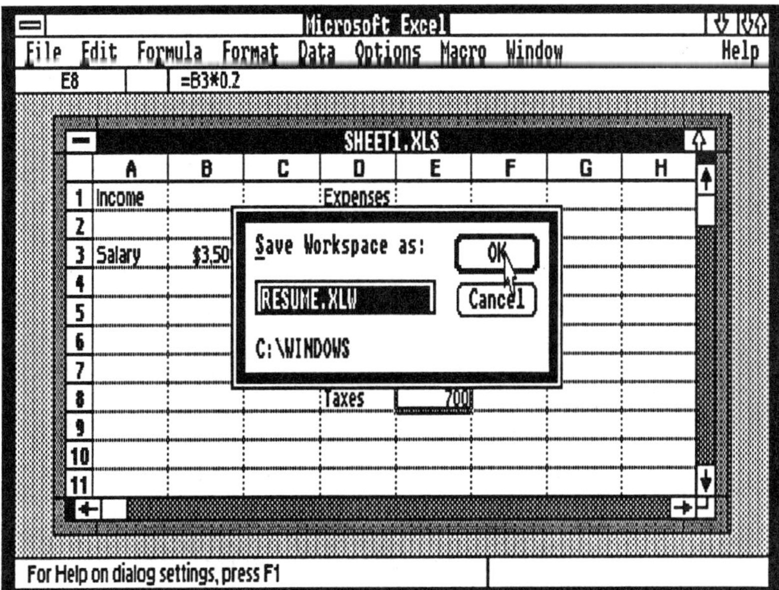

The dialog box gives you the opportunity to assign a name to this workspace. If you choose not to, Excel assigns it the name "RESUME.XLW."

8. Type **BUDGET** as the name of the workspace in which to save all the active screens at this time. This includes both BUDGET1 and SAVINGS (and any others that you may have opened in the process of working through this module).

9. Press **Enter**.

10. Select **Open** from the File menu.

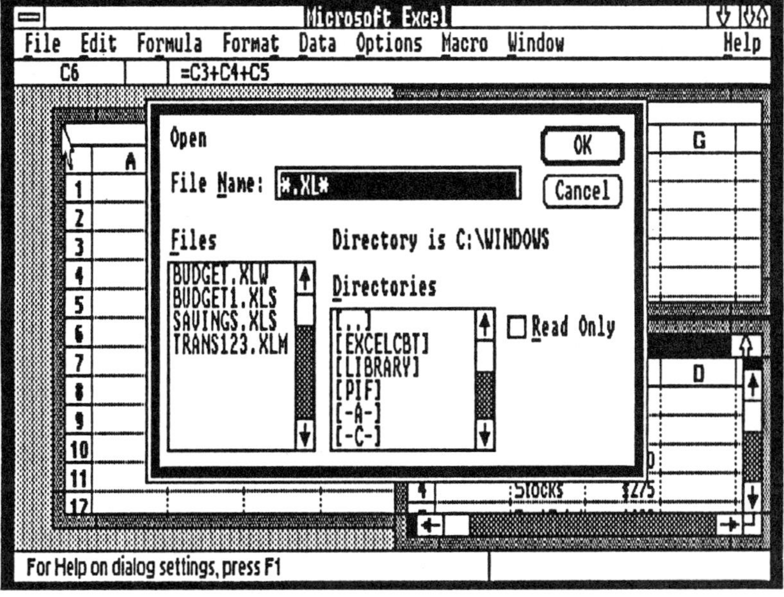

You now have all of the documents saved individually and as a group. Notice that the workspace document ends in "XLW" to differentiate it from a worksheet which ends in "XLS." If you want to change one of the names of the other documents, you need only open them and save them, using the "Save As" command. You will be asked to give the name under which you want them saved.

NOTE

In each Typical Operation you have been instructed to start Excel at the beginning of the session and exit Excel at the end of the session. By following this procedure exactly, your screen always matches the display in the book. However, now that you have learned to use the New command to create a new worksheet, you may choose to continue your work session directly from one module to the next in the learning sequence without exiting and restarting Excel. To continue directly from one module to the next, close the active worksheet(s) at the end of the module, then select New to create a fresh worksheet for the subsequent module. When continuing directly from one module to the next, the default worksheet name continues to increment, but this should not affect your ability to complete the activities. The screen illustrations, however, assume that Excel is restarted at the beginning of each module.

11. Press **Esc** or select **Cancel**.

12. Exit Excel, or close each worksheet and continue your work session.

13. Turn to Module 32 to continue the learning sequence.

SELECT SPECIAL

[Screenshot of Microsoft Excel showing the Formula menu open with options: Paste Name..., Paste Function..., Reference, Define Name..., Create Names..., Apply Names..., Note..., Goto..., Find..., Replace..., Select Special... (highlighted). Status bar reads "Select cells of specified type".]

DESCRIPTION

Use the Select Special command on the Formula menu to identify only certain types of cells from a worksheet or a region of the worksheet containing several types of cells. Begin the operation by selecting the desired region. To select the entire worksheet, select a single cell. To select from a range, highlight the desired range. When you pick Select Special, the following dialog box appears.

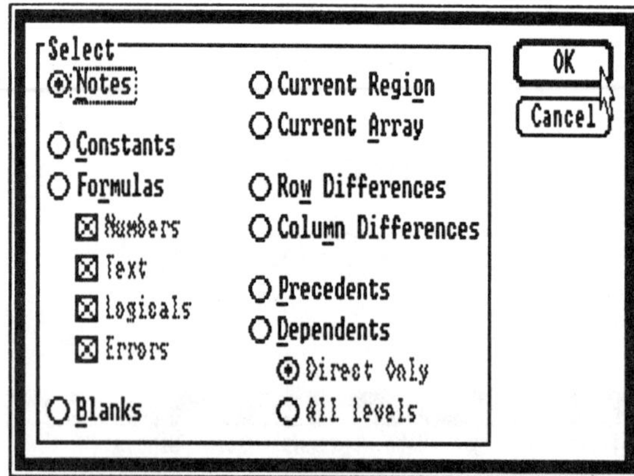

You may select cells by the kind of information they contain. You may select Notes, Constants, Formulas, and Blanks. Within formulas, you may select Numbers, Text, Logicals, and Errors. You may choose to examine the current region, or the current array.

You may look for differences between rows of cells or columns of cells, selecting only those cells that are different from their counterparts. You may also select cells based on their precedent/dependent relationships with other cells.

Most of the selections are exclusionary. You can, in general, select only one category of cell within a single Select Special operation.

Once the cells are selected, you can perform any valid Excel command with the selected cells including modifying their format, moving them, or copying them.

APPLICATIONS

When examining a worksheet, especially one that someone else created, examining the worksheet notes is an excellent method for understanding the strategies involved. In preparing a worksheet for others to examine, it is helpful to call attention to the cells' specific classes of information. One way to do this is to display cells of different types in distinctive fonts. You might, for example, display cells containing notes in an italic font to alert a co-worker that there is additional information there to examine.

When making business decisions based on the contents of a worksheet, it is imperative that you examine the worksheet carefully to catch logic errors. You can use the *precedents* feature to highlight the cells that are referenced elsewhere in the worksheet. Information in a worksheet that is not referenced elsewhere is an indicator of possible logic errors. For example, in examining a worksheet used for preparing a bid proposal, if the value of a cell labeled "Overhead Rate" is not referenced anywhere else in the worksheet, the final bid amount may not provide any profit. You would want to examine the worksheet in detail to see how the final bid price was determined.

TYPICAL OPERATION

In this session you use the Select Special command to select cells that are prescendents for other cells.

1. Start Excel, or continue your work session from the previous module by creating a new worksheet.

2. Type **Plant**, **Labor**, **Materials**, **Variable**, and **Total** in cells A1 through A5.

3. Type **150**, **291**, **141**, and **75** in cells B1 through B4.

4. Highlight the region A1 through B4, then pick **Create Names** from the Formula menu. In the dialog box, pick **Left Column** then pick **OK**.

5. Select cell B5 and type **= Plant + Materials + Variable** and press **Enter**.

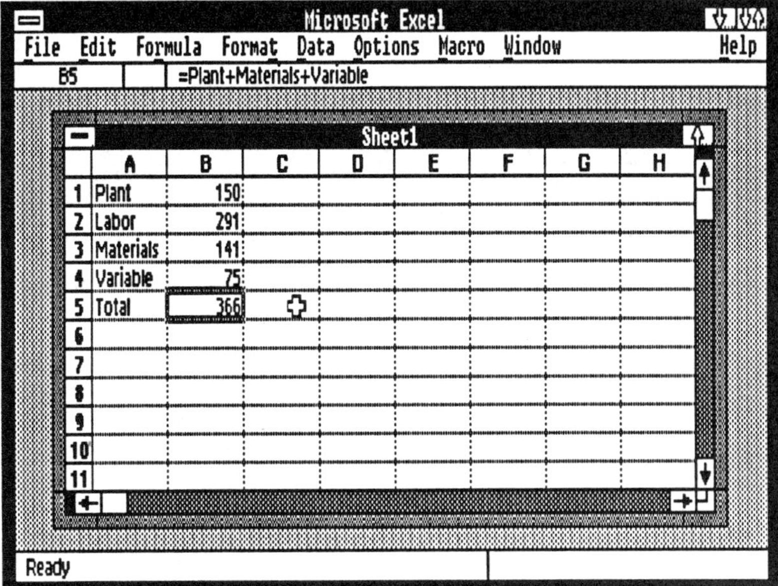

6. Pick **Select Special** from the Formula menu. Pick **Precedents** from the dialog box.

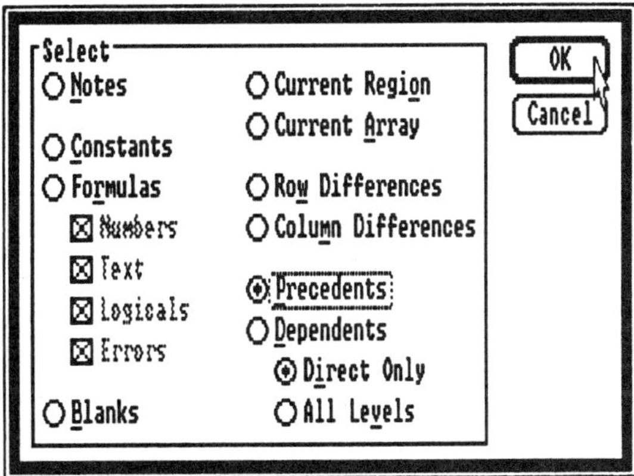

7. Pick **OK**.

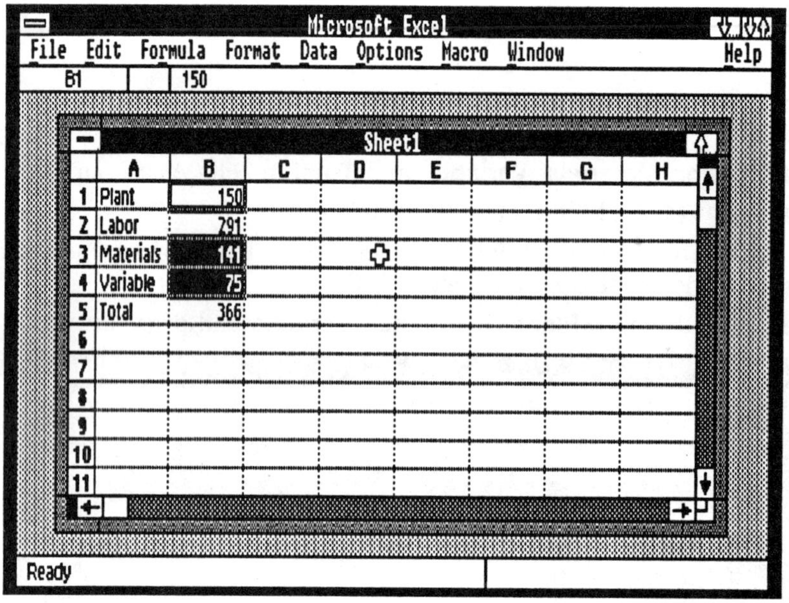

Notice that the cell ajacent to labor is not selected. This indicates that the value is not referenced in the worksheet.

8. Close the worksheet, there is no need to save it. Exit Excel, or continue your work session without an active worksheet on the screen.

9. Turn to Module 62 to continue the learning sequence.

Module 60

SERIES

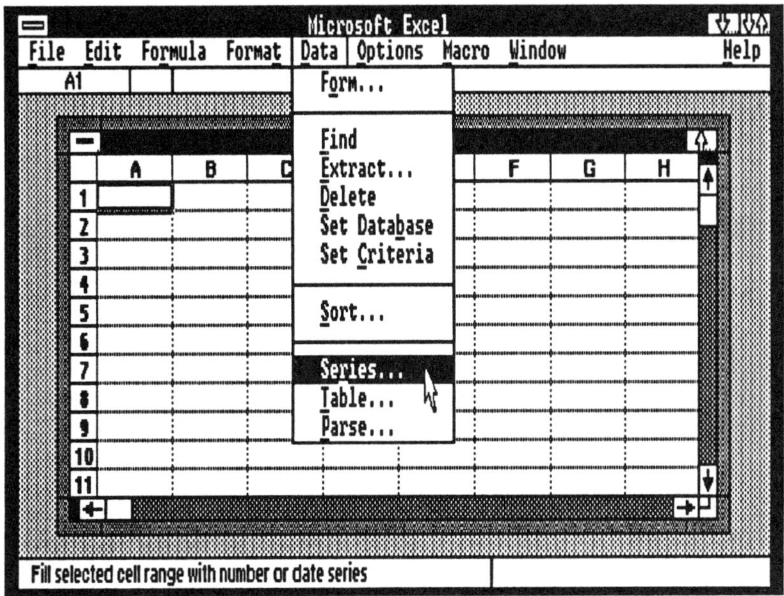

DESCRIPTION

The Series command creates a row or column of numbers or dates in a worksheet. Although the Series command is located on the Data menu, it is a general-purpose command that operates on any range of a worksheet.

First, place the starting value in the first cell of the row or column where you want the series to begin. If you want the series to occupy a specific range of cells, highlight the start value and all cells in the range, then select Series from the Data menu. If you want to define the series over a specific range of values, such as 1..100, 12 months, 90 days, etc., highlight only the starting value; then select Series from the Data menu. (Use the mouse to make your selection from the menu or press Alt-D R.)

When you pick Series, the following dialog box appears on the screen.

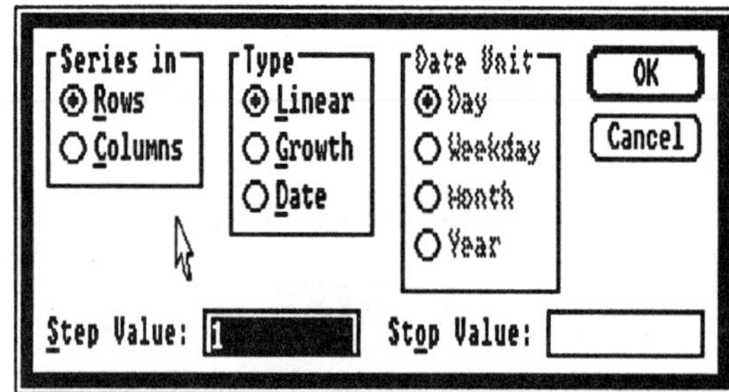

First, pick whether you want a series of rows or a series of columns. Second, select the *Type* of increment you want between each value in the series. A *Linear* type adds the Step Value to create each subsequent value in the series. A *Growth* type multiplies the Step Value to create each subsequent value. A *Date* type requires you to additionally specify the date units (day, weekday, month, or year) for incrementing the starting date, and a Step Value to determine the number of those date units in each increment.

If you specified a range on the worksheet for the series to occupy, pick OK with the mouse or press Enter on the keyboard. If you want the series created over a range of values, taking whatever portion of the worksheet necessary to contain the series, place the ending value for the series in the Stop Value box, then pick OK or press Enter to carry out the Series command instructions.

APPLICATIONS

When working with a database, it is frequently useful to have a unique record number for each record in the database. To create record numbers in a database, first add a column to the range of the database with the Set Database command; then place a descriptive name, such as "Record," as the field name. Highlight the first cell of the field and type 1. Continue highlighting the column to the bottom of the database. Pick the Series command from the Data menu to actually create the record numbers.

When creating worksheets for financial projections, it is frequently necessary to place a series of dates across the top row of a range of the worksheet. The Series command is an excellent way to produce such a row of headings. In this application, you might make use of the Stop Value to create a series of dates covering a single fiscal period: a month, a quarter, or a year.

TYPICAL OPERATION

In this session you create an 11-year population/city services projections worksheet incorporating several series, using the series data both as worksheet headings and as data.

First, you create a series of dates covering the 11-year period from 1990 to 2000. You could treat this as a linear numeric series starting at 1990, and incrementing by 1 to 2000. However, in this case, you instruct Excel to treat the data as dates, incrementing by years from 1990 to 2000.

1. Start Excel, or continue your work session by creating a new worksheet.
2. Expand the default worksheet to occupy the full screen.
3. Type **Year** in cell A3.

4. Type **1/1/90** in cell B3 and press **Enter**.

5. Select **Series** from the Data menu.

Excel recognizes the data format of the current cell as a date and defaults to a Date-type series.

6. Select **Year** as the Date Unit, and type **1/1/2000** as the Stop Value.

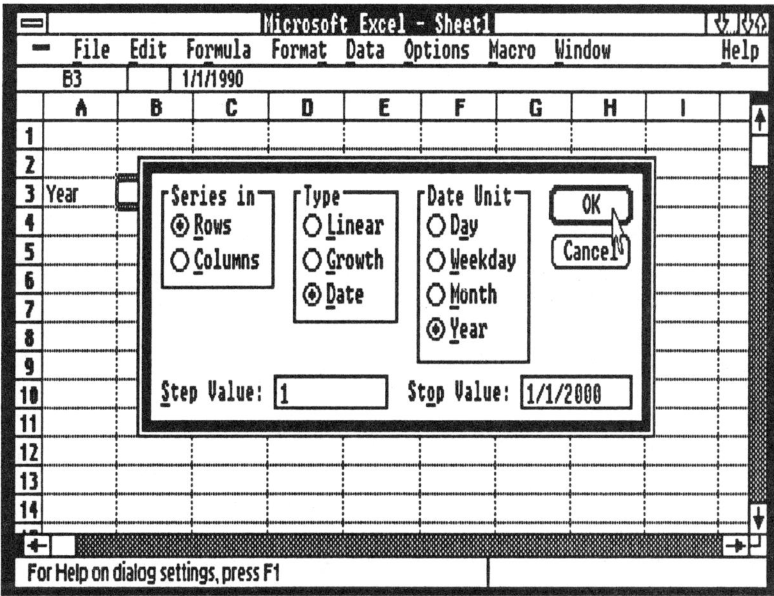

7. The default Step Value of 1 is correct. Select **OK**.

8. Type **Population** in cell A4.

9. Type **24155** in cell B4 and press **Enter**.

10. Adjust the width of column A to reveal the complete text of the labels.

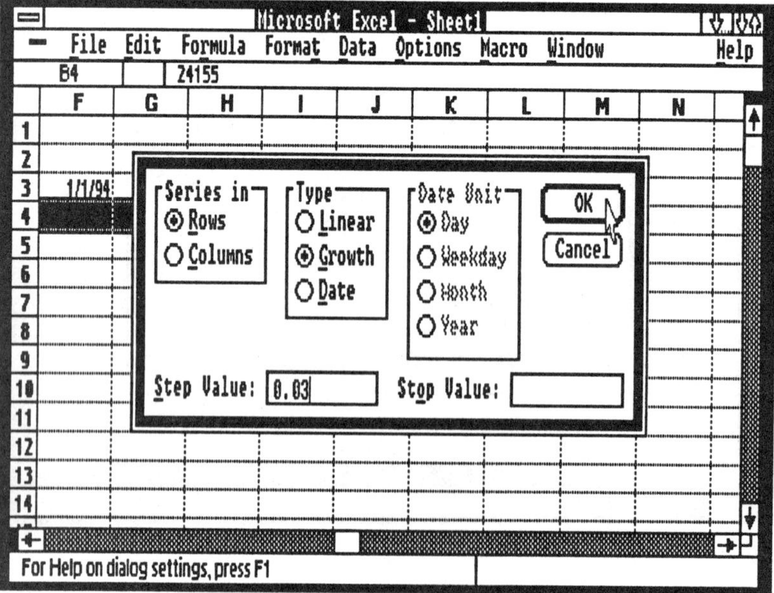

11. Type **Children** in cell A5 and type **4822** in cell B5.

12. Highlight the row of cells B4 through L4, then select **Series** from the Data menu. Select **Growth** for Type and type **0.03** for Step Value (3% growth).

13. Select **OK**.

14. Now select the row of cells B5 through I5, then select **Series** from the Data menu. Select **Linear** for Type and type **25** for Step Value. Then select **OK**.

15. To avoid working with fractional people, select rows 4 and 5, then select **Number** from the Format menu. Select whole number format.

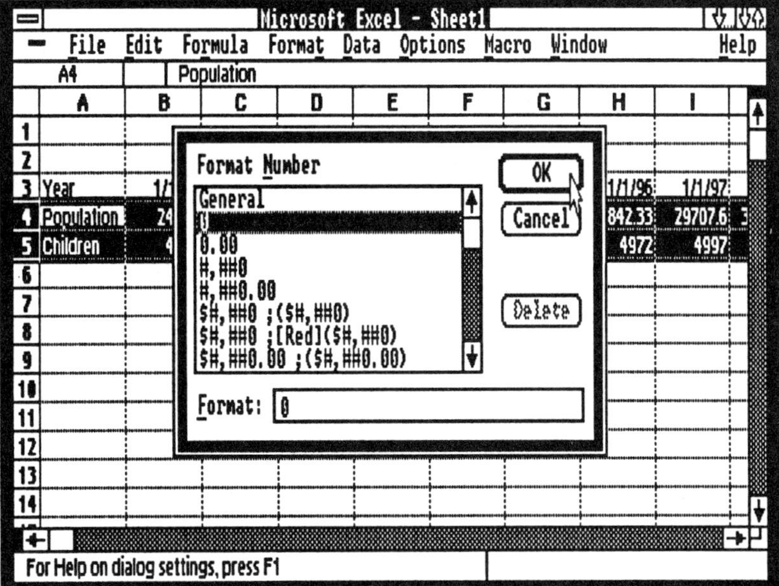

16. Pick **OK**.

17. Select an empty cell to remove the reverse video, and observe the finished set of projections.

The first row of data is a series of date data. The second row of data is a growth-type series showing a 3% increase each year. The third row of data is a linear-type series showing an increment of 25 each year.

18. Close the worksheet without saving it.

19. Exit Excel, or continue your work session without an active worksheet on the screen.

20. Turn to Module 70 to continue the learning sequence.

Module 61

SET CRITERIA

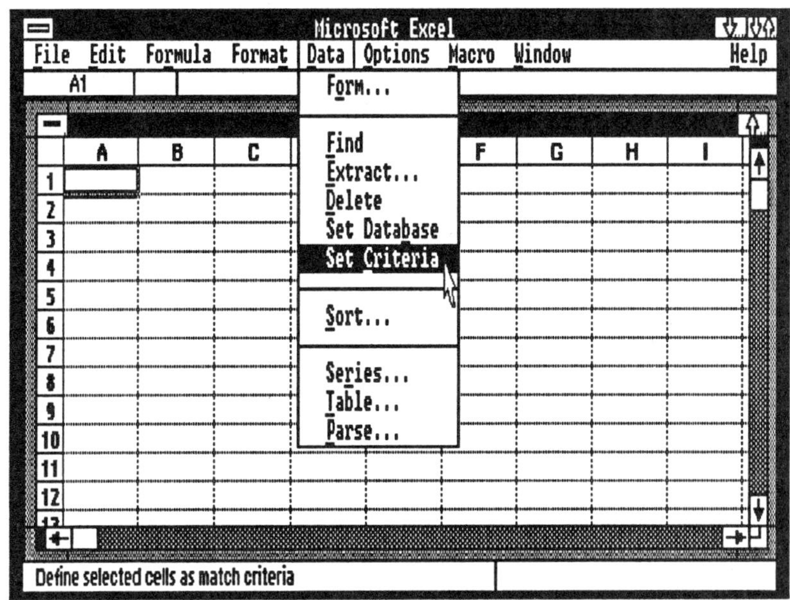

DESCRIPTION

The Set Criteria command on the Data menu allows you to select specific database records for use with the Delete, Find, and Extract commands. There are numerous criteria combinations you can use. Consider the following examples based on the camping store inventory created in the Set Database module.

1. You may select a single criteria for a single field (column). For example, you could set a criteria to select all items in the inventory costing more than $50.00.

2. You can set multiple criteria for a single field, such as selecting items that cost more than $50.00 but less than $100.00.

3. You can set criteria for multiple fields, for example, finding all inventory in the Fishing department costing more than $50.00, or more than $50.00 and less than $100.00. You can also define a criterion that uses a formula.

When you define a database, you commonly leave several blank rows above the start of the database for defining selection criteria. If you do not leave the space when you define the database, use the Insert command (see Module 33, Insert) to insert several blank rows above your database range. It is possible to place the selection criteria in a separate area of the worksheet, although the common practice of experienced Excel users is to place the criteria definition area immediately above the database.

You use the Set Criteria command to define a rectangular area of the worksheet as the selection criteria definition area. You enter the field names for the criteria in the first row of the range and the selection values beneath the field names. The names (column titles) in the selection area must be identical to the names in the database, although Excel does not differentiate between uppercase and lowercase letters in this context. The easiest way to guarantee that all column headings are exact is to use the Copy command to duplicate the database field names to the top row of the criteria area. If a field (column) name is not needed for selection, it does not have to be included in the first row of the selection criteria area. It is sometimes, however, easiest to copy the entire name line from the database area, including the extra fields.

In the columns below the field names you type the selection requirements for that field. Excel uses the logical "and" operation to combine criteria on a single row and the logical "or" operation to combine operations on a single row. For example, the criteria set

City	Sales
Dallas	> 1000
Atlanta	

selects Dallas sales over $1000 and Atlanta sales regardless of amount.

The criteria set

City	Sales
Dallas	> 1000
Atlanta	> 1000

selects Dallas sales over $1000 and Atlanta sales over $1000. To select sales from Dallas that are over $1000 but less than $10,000, it is necessary to add a new column in the selection criteria range. You may have more than one column with the same name in a single criteria selection set. The required definition is as follows:

City	Sales	Sales
Dallas	> 1000	< 10000

The specification selects only sales in Dallas between $1000 and $10,000. The following specification

City	Sales
Dallas	> 1000
	< 10000

selects sales in Dallas greater than $1000 but includes all sales under $10,000 regardless of location. Specifically, a Dallas sale under $1,000 does not match the first criterion, but because the rows of the selection criteria are combined with a logical "or" operation, these sales are selected by the second criteria. The preceeding specification is actually equivalent to

City	Sales
Dallas	
	< 10000

because it selects all Dallas sales and sales from other locations that are less than $10,000.

The steps in defining selection criteria are:

1. Type or copy the required field (column) names onto a row of the worksheet.
2. In the columns immediately under each name, specify the criteria for that field. Do not leave any blank rows between the names and the first row containing criteria.
3. Highlight the rectangular region of the worksheet containing the name row and the rows beneath it containing the specifications. Be careful not to highlight extra empty rows beneath the selection criteria range.
4. Select Set Criteria from the Data menu. Make the selection with the mouse, or press Alt-D C.

NOTE

Excel interprets a blank row in the selection criteria range as a "wildcard" that matches all values. If the area you highlight as your criteria range contains any blank rows, the selection set includes all records (rows) in the database.

COMPARISONS Excel provides a set of comparison operators that work with numeric values, dates and times, and with alphabetic data. The meaning of the operators is consistent across each data type as shown in the following chart.

Data Type

Operator	Numbers	Aphabetic	Time/Date
<	Less than	Before	Before
>	Greater than	After	After
=	Equal to	Match	Same time/date
< =	Less than or equal to	Before or match	Before or match
> =	Greater than or equal to	Match or after	Match or later
< >	Not equal to	Not matching	Different time

CONTROLLING MATCHES   An alphabetic search does not require a whole-field match. For example the search criterion Washington matches both Washington D.C. and Washington. When you must limit the search to exact matches, you enclose the criterion in quotation marks and enclose the beginning quotation mark with equal signs. For example, an exact match on Washington (excluding Washington D.C.) is specified as = " = Washington."

When you need a flexible match, the wildcard characters ? and * are invaluable. The character ? matches any single character. For example the match criterion C?tfish selects both Catfish and Codfish. The match criterion ???fish matches Catfish, Codfish, and Redfish. Notice that each occurrence of the character ? corresponds to exactly one character in the target field. When you need a more general match, the character * is the answer. A search criterion of *fish not only matches Catfish, Codfish, and Redfish; it also matches Whitefish, Swordfish, and Fish. The asterisk wildcard replaces any combination of characters, including no characters at all.

COMPUTING SELECTION CRITERIA   Sometimes you need to select database records based on a value that is not in the field, but can be computed from values in the database. In a retail inventory you might have fields for "Cost" and "Retail." If you want to identify the products you sell that have low profit margins, you have two choices.

The first choice is to add a computed field to the database containing margin information. When you need to examine the information on a frequent basis, adding a computed field to the database can be an excellent idea. However, adding computed fields to your database has a down side as well. First, if the information is not important as an end result, but only as a means to an end, it can clutter your screen display with trivial information not related to the decision-making process. Second, computed fields add to the memory required by your database, limiting its size and decreasing performance.

The second choice for selecting database records based on a computed value is to place the computation in the selection criteria portion of the worksheet instead of in the database itself. This technique decreases the storage requirements for your worksheet and helps improve performance. The method you use is to redefine the Set Criteria area of the worksheet to include an additional column. Naming this column is optional. You can provide a name or leave the name field blank. If you provide a name, you must make sure that the name does not duplicate an existing field name in the database. In the retail inventory example it would make sense to name the computed field "Margin." Then, in the cell(s) below the heading, you place the computed criteria. For example you might use the formula

    = Retail/Cost < = 0.10

to identify inventory items with low profit margins.

APPLICATIONS

The Set Criteria command does not perform any operations by itself, but it controls the operation of the Delete, Extract, and Find commands. In fact, selecting the Find, Extract, or Delete commands prior to creating a criterion definition and using the Set Criteria command produces the error message "Criteria range is not valid."

If you frequently switch between multiple sets of criteria, you may find it useful to set up several criteria ranges in your worksheet. Of course, Excel allows only one criteria area to be active at a time; but there is no problem with having several sets of criteria set up and ready to go.

TYPICAL OPERATION

In this session you use the camping equipment inventory worksheet that you used most recently in the Sort module. You establish criteria definitions and use the Set Criteria command to define the selection criteria area of the worksheet.

1. Start Excel. Open the INVENT.XLS worksheet and maximize the sheet.

	A	B	C	D	E	F
9						
10	Dept	Description	Quantity	Cost	Value	
11	Camping	Mountain Tent	6	$330.21	$1,981.26	
12	Clothing	Rain Jacket	12	$45.50	$546.00	
13	Clothing	Red Bandana	144	$0.96	$138.24	
14	Clothing	Blue Bandana	71	$0.96	$68.16	
15	Fishing	Spinning Rod	3	$14.32	$42.96	
16						
17						
18						
19						
20						
21						
22						

2. Use the side scroll bar to reposition the worksheet, allowing you to view the first ten rows of the worksheet.

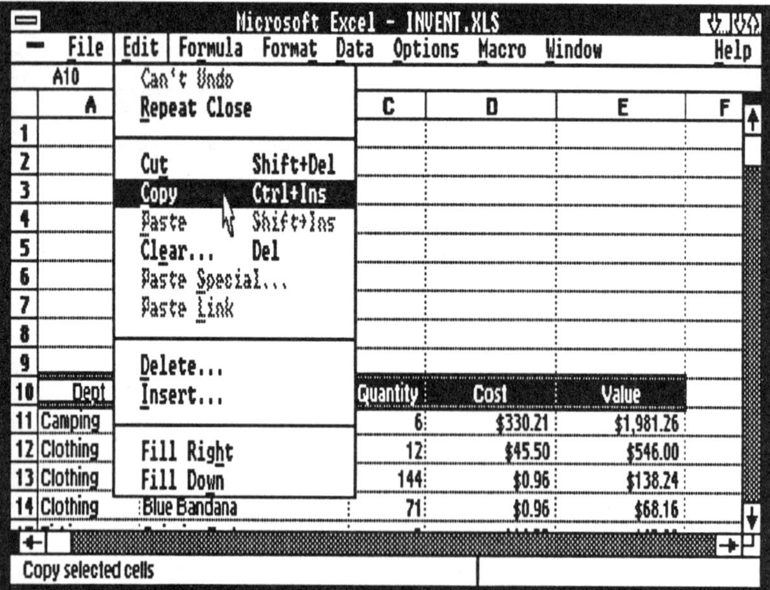

3. Highlight the field headings for the database, then select **Copy** from the Edit menu (or press **Ctrl-Ins**).

4. Place the cursor in cell A1, then choose **Paste** from the Edit menu (or press **Shift-Ins**).

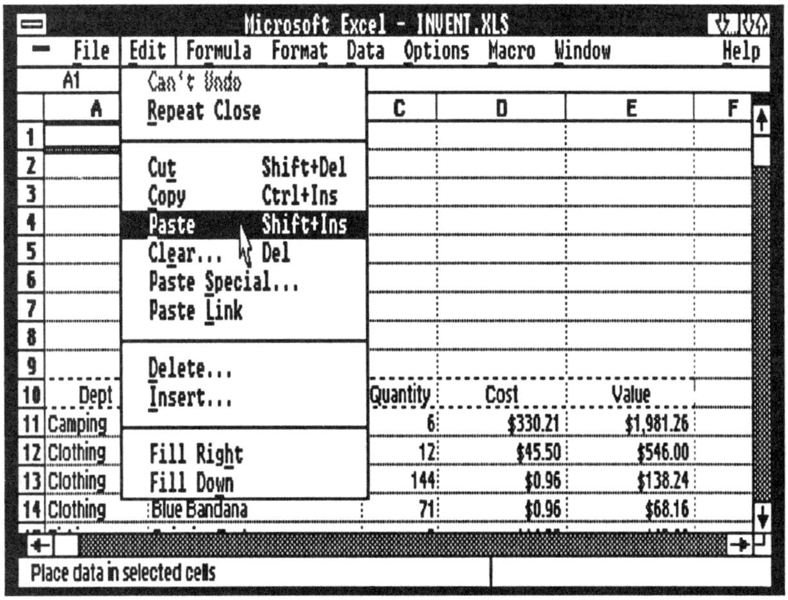

5. Move to cell A2, type **Camping**, and press **Enter**.
6. Move to cell A3, type **Fishing**, and press **Enter**.
7. Select the region A1 through E3.

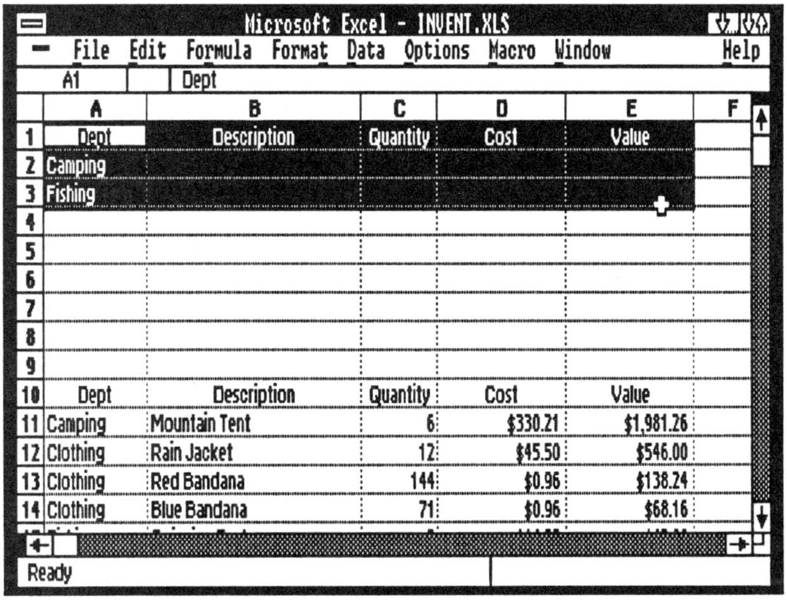

8. Select **Set Criteria** from the Data menu.

Like the Set Database command, the Set Criteria command produces no visible change in the worksheet. However, the region A1 through E3 is now defined as the current set of selection criteria.

9. Save the worksheet. You use these criteria to find the selected records in the Find (Database) module.

10. Exit Excel, or continue your work session with the active worksheet displayed on the screen.

11. Turn to Module 24 to continue the learning sequence.

Module 62

SET DATABASE

DESCRIPTION

You must define an area of the worksheet as a database before using any of Excel's data managment commands. To do this, use the Set Database command. First you select the area of the worksheet to hold the required data, then you select Set Database from the Data menu.

When defining small areas of the worksheet as a database, visual selection of the area, through moving the mouse or cursor control keys, is acceptable. However, moving the cursor over a large area of the worksheet is cumbersome. To define a large area of the spreadsheet as a database, move the cursor to one corner, press the GOTO key (F5), type the coordinates of the diagonally opposite corner, and press Shift-Enter. Then select the Set Database command from the Data menu.

APPLICATIONS

Excel's data management features allow you to treat areas of the worksheet as a database. Each record of the database is placed on a row of the worksheet, and each field of the record occupies a column. The Set Database command tells Excel to group together a particular area of the worksheet for use with data management.

Using Excel's data management features, you can extract records that meet specific criteria: sales regions with sales over $100,000, interest rates below 9 percent, or addresses in the 76201 zip code. You can use the Sort command to arrange the database in either ascending or descending order, based on the value of either a numeric or alphabetic field.

When working with databases, it is convenient to provide several empty rows above and below the data range. The rows above the database are convenient for specifying selection criteria as described in the Set Criteria module. The rows below the database are useful for adding and inserting records. This allows you to insert records anywhere in the database without redefining the database range.

TYPICAL OPERATION

In this typical operation you construct an inventory system for a camping equipment store. You then label the fields and enter data using the standard Excel data entry techniques. You then save the worksheet on disk. In the modules that follow in the recommended learning sequence you create a data entry form, sort the database, find specific entries from the database, and extract subsets from the database.

1. Start Excel and use the default worksheet SHEET1.XLS, or continue your work session by creating a new worksheet with the **New** command from the File menu.
2. Move the cursor to row 10 and type column headings **Dept**, **Description**, **Quantity**, **Cost**, and **Value** as labels for columns A through E.
3. Select cell A10, then select **Column Width..** from the Format menu. Type **12** as the column width and pick **OK**.
4. Select cell B10. Use the same technique to set the column width at 25.
5. Select cells D10 through E10 and set the column width at 15.
6. Select A10 through E10, then select **Alignment** from the Format menu.
7. Select **Center** and **OK** from the dialog box.

8. Type the inventory data into the worksheet as shown on the following screen. Depending on your graphics display, you may need to scroll the worksheet to make additional rows visible on the screen.

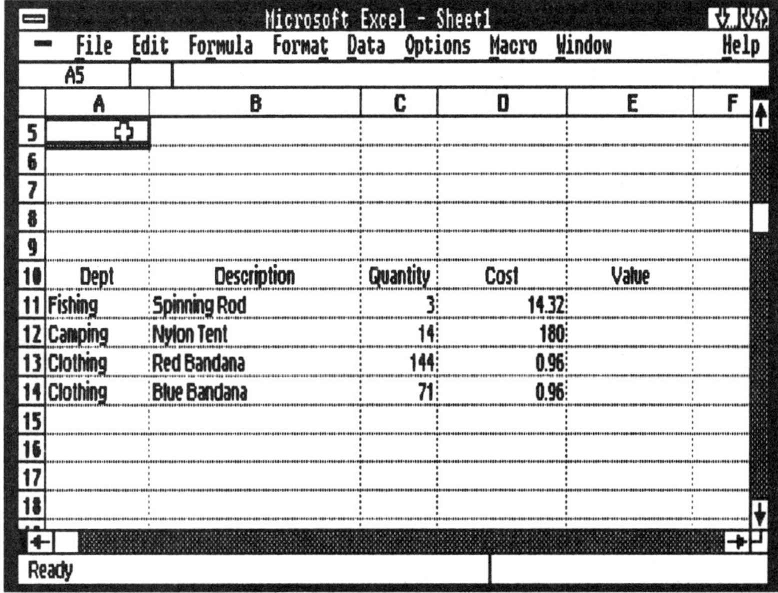

9. Select columns D and E, then select **Number** from the Format menu.

10. Select dollars and cents format **$#,##0.00 ;($#,##0.00)** as shown in the following screen.

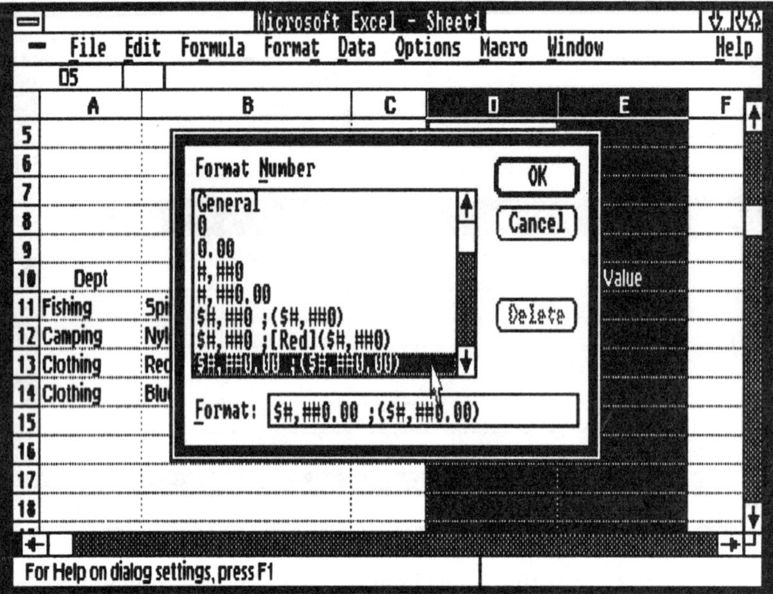

11. Pick **OK** from the Format Number dialog box.

12. Pick in an unused portion of the worksheet to remove the highlighting. Your screen appears as follows.

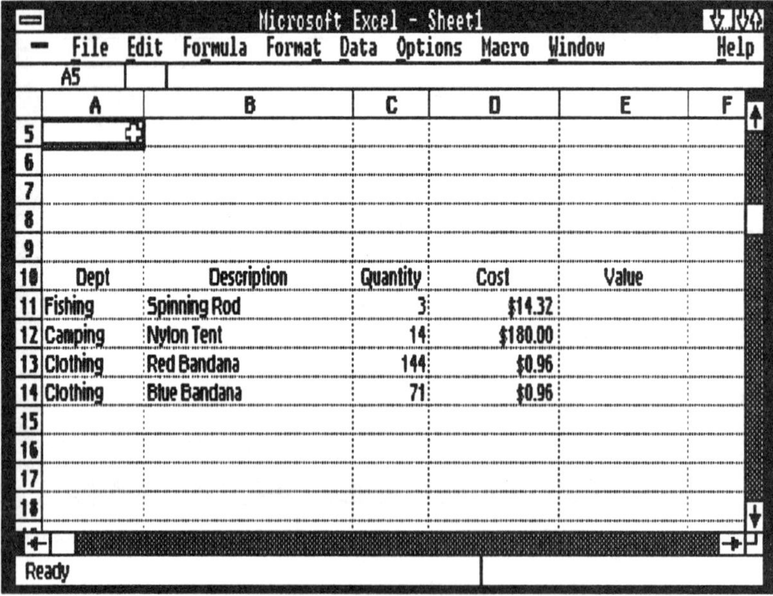

13. Select cell E11, type the formula **=C11*D11**, and press **Enter**.

14. Select the column range E11 through E14, then select **Fill Down** from the Edit menu.

15. Highlight the range with the upper left corner in A10 and the lower right corner in E20.

    Mouse: Position the cursor in A10. Press and hold the left mouse button, drag the cursor to E20, and release the mouse button.

    Keyboard: Position the cursor in A10. Press F5 to open the GOTO dialog box. Type E20 and press Shift-Enter.

16. Select **Set Database** from the Data menu, as shown in the following screen.

```
┌─────────────────────────────────────────────────────────────────────┐
│ ═        Microsoft Excel - Sheet1                                     │
│  ─   File  Edit  Formula  Format │ Data │ Options  Macro  Window  Help│
│      A10         │    Dept       │  Form...                           │
│          A       │      B        │              D          E       F  │
│   9                              │  Find                              │
│  10    Dept          Description │  Extract...    ost      Value      │
│  11 Fishing       Spinning Rod   │  Delete        $14.32   $42.96     │
│  12 Camping       Nylon Tent     │  Set Database  $180.00  $2,520.00  │
│  13 Clothing      Red Bandana    │  Set Criteria  $0.96    $138.24    │
│  14 Clothing      Blue Bandana   │                $0.96    $68.16     │
│  15                              │  Sort...                $0.00      │
│  16                              │                         $0.00      │
│  17                              │  Series...              $0.00      │
│  18                              │  Table...               $0.00      │
│  19                              │  Parse...               $0.00      │
│  20                              │                         $0.00      │
│  21                              │                                    │
│  22                              │                                    │
│  Define selected cells as database                                    │
└─────────────────────────────────────────────────────────────────────┘
```

Although no visible change takes place on the worksheet, the highlighted region is now defined as the current Excel database.

17. Select **Save As...** from the File menu. Type **INVENT** as the worksheet name, then pick **OK**.

18. Exit Excel, or continue your work session with the active worksheet on the screen.

19. Turn to Module 27 to continue the learning sequence.

Module 63

SET PAGE BREAK/REMOVE PAGE BREAK

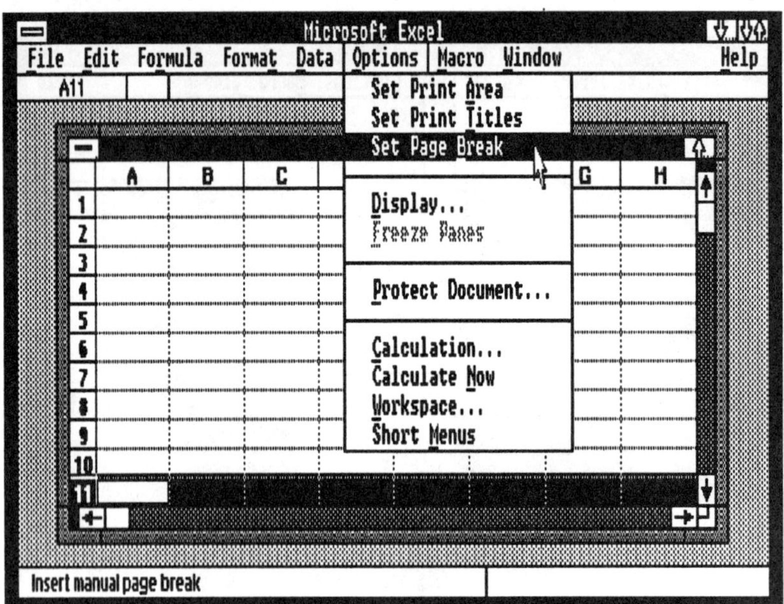

DESCRIPTION

Use the Set Page Break command on the Options menu to force either a horizontal or vertical page break when printing an Excel worksheet. When you print a worksheet, Excel automatically inserts page breaks both horizontally and vertically on the worksheet. If these breaks do not occur where you want them, use the Set Page Break command to move them. First select the row or column where the page break should be inserted. Then select Set Page Break from the Options menu with the mouse or press Alt-O B. Then select Print from the File menu to perform the print operation.

When you change your mind about a page break that you insert, select the row or column with the page break, then select Remove Page Break with the mouse from the Options menu or press Alt-O B.

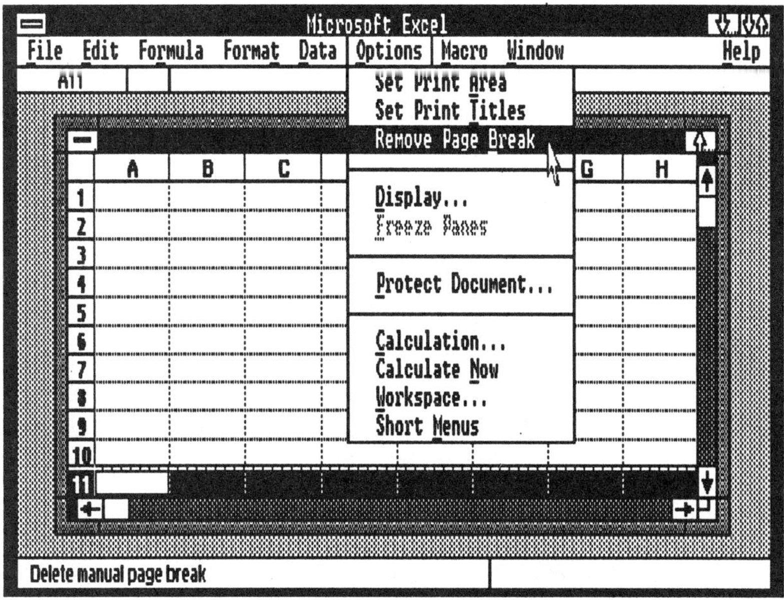

APPLICATIONS

Excel divides a large worksheet into pages according to how much information fits on a page, not how much information makes sense to place together on a page. You may want to insert page breaks between departments to print individual department reports on separate pages; you may want to place a page break between income and expenses on an accounting report.

The Excel Set Page Break command works both horizontally and vertically. You may use the Set Page Break repetitively in your document to create page breaks.

TYPICAL OPERATION

In this session you insert a page break into the BUDGET1.XLS worksheet you used most recently in the Page Setup module.

1. Start Excel and open the worksheet BUDGET1.XLS, or continue your work session from the previous module.

2. Select column C, then select **Set Page Break** from the Options menu.

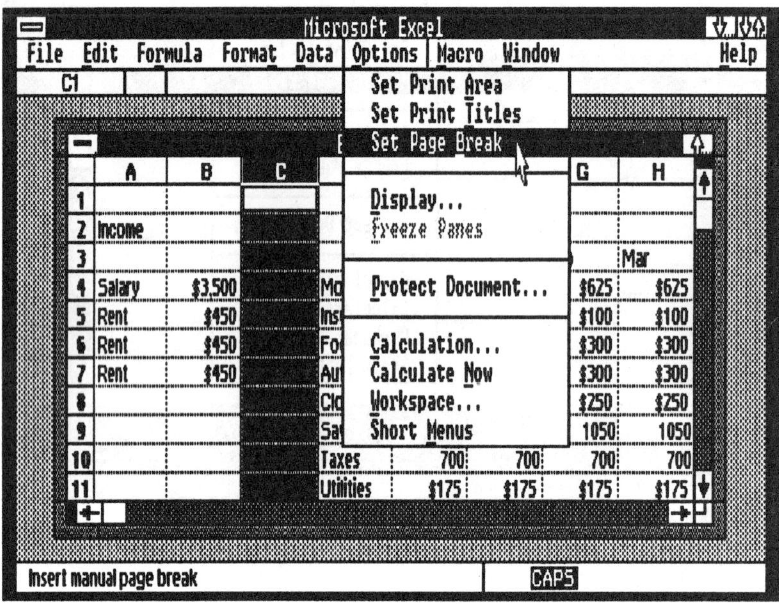

3. Pick cell A1. Notice the page-break line between columns B and C as shown in the following screen.

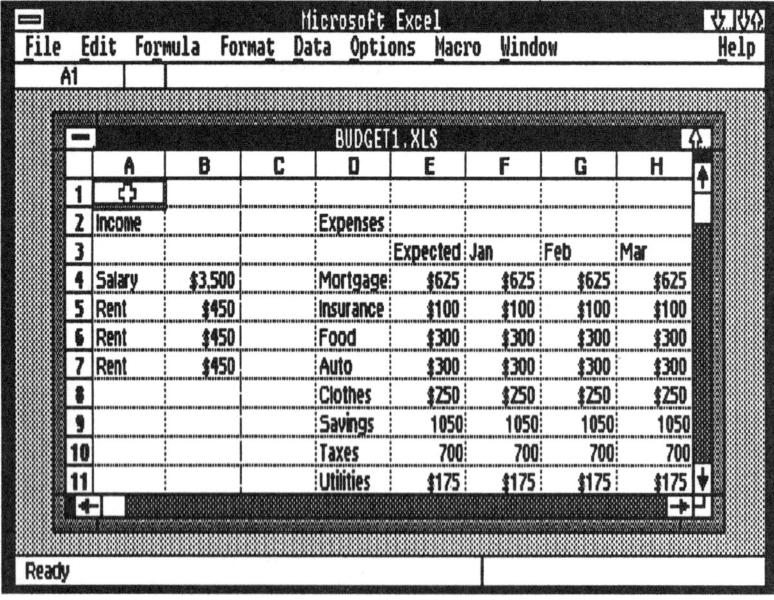

4. Select **Print** from the File menu. Verify that **Preview** is selected, then pick **OK**.

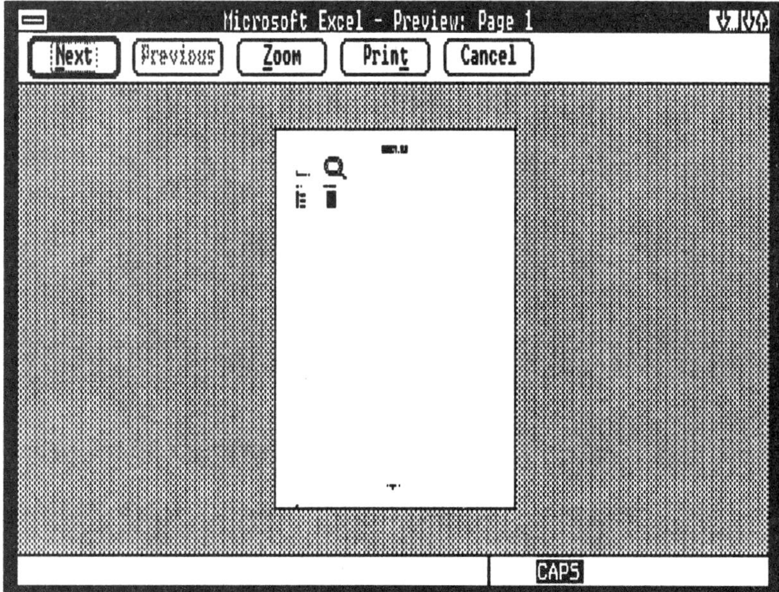

5. Move the cursor to the upper left corner of the print image and click the mouse.

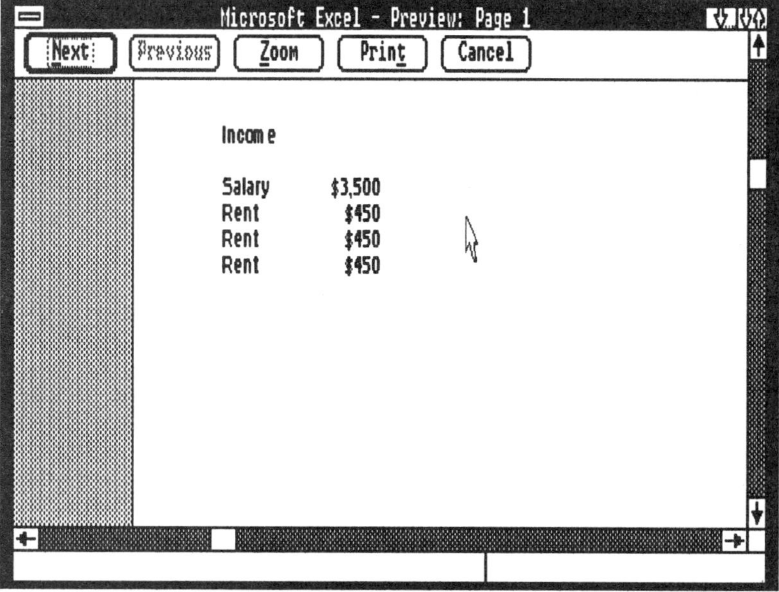

6. Pick **Next**. Notice that the expenses are shown on a second print preview page.

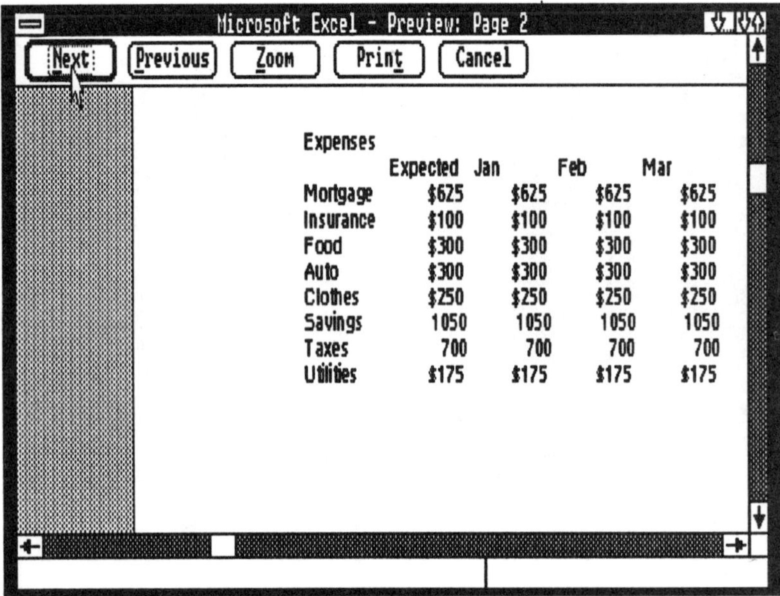

7. Pick **Cancel** to end the print preview operation.
8. Close the worksheet without saving it.
9. Turn to Module 64 to continue the learning sequence.

Module 64
SET PRINT AREA

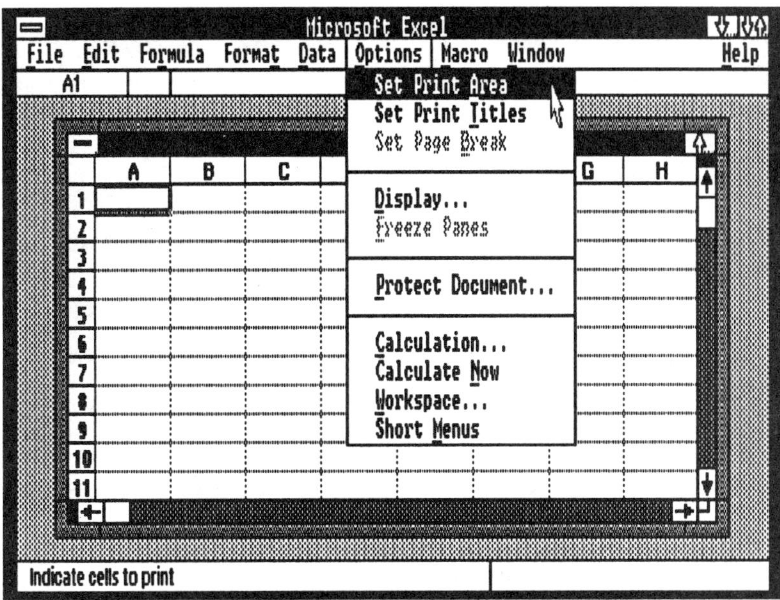

DESCRIPTION

The Set Print Area command on the Options menu allows you to select the portion of the worksheet you want to print. When you select Print, Excel assumes that you want to print the entire portion of the worksheet containing data, unless you instruct otherwise with the Set Print Area command. To print a worksheet region smaller than the entire area in use, first, select the region on the screen. Second, select Set Print Area from the Options menu or press Alt-O A. Then, select Print from the File menu to perform the print operation.

APPLICATIONS

Most worksheets contain confidential, irrelevant, or other data that may not be important for a summary report. You may want to produce departmental reports without producing a report for the company as a whole. Use the Set Print Area command any time you want to restrict the region of the worksheet printed on a report.

TYPICAL OPERATION

In this session you print only the income information on the BUDGET1.XLS worksheet, most recently accessed in the Set Page Break/Remove Page Break module.

1. Start Excel. Open the worksheet BUDGET1.XLS.

2. Select the region A1 through B7 as shown on the following screen.

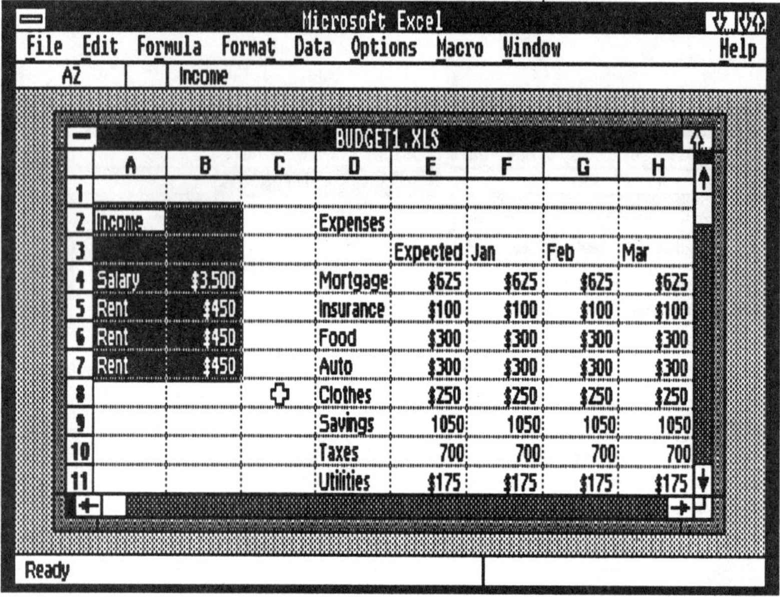

3. Select **Set Print Area** on the Options menu.

4. Select **Print** from the File menu, verify that **Preview** is already picked on the dialog box, then pick **OK**.

5. Move the cursor to the upper left portion of the page image and click the left mouse button. Notice that the selected region is the only portion of the worksheet that is printed.

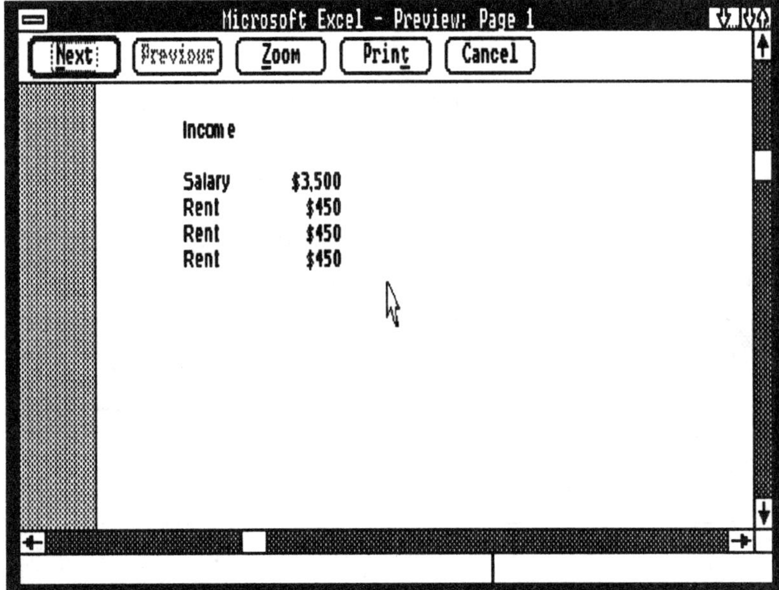

6. Select **Cancel** to leave the page preview.
7. Close the worksheet without saving it.
8. Turn to Module 65 to continue the learning sequence.

Module 65

SET PRINT TITLES

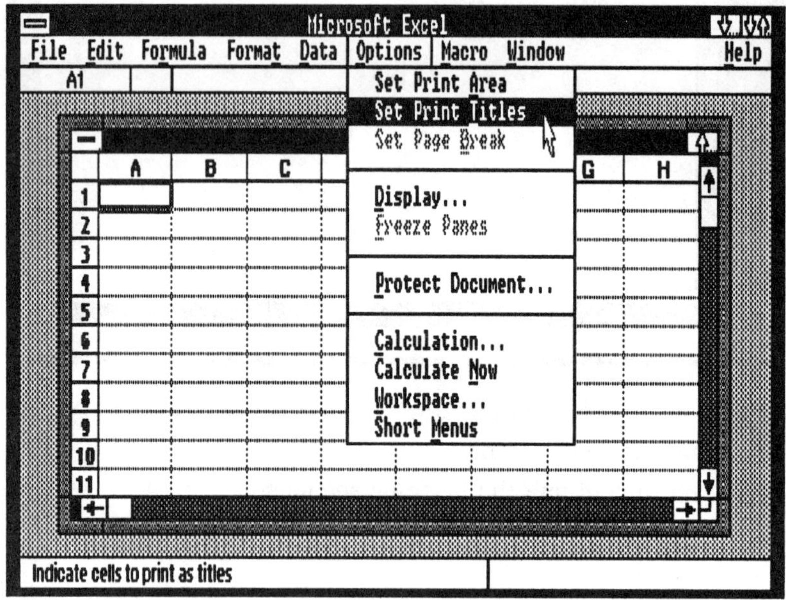

DESCRIPTION

Use the Set Print Titles command on the Options menu to specify one or more rows or columns to appear as titles on every page of a worksheet printout. Selected row titles appear at the top of every printout page, column titles appear along the left edge of every printout page. First, select the row or rows containing the title information. Second, pick Print Titles from the Options menu. Finally, pick Print from the File menu to perform the print operation.

To remove titles, select Define Name from the Formula menu. Pick Print_Titles, pick Delete, then pick OK. The title information is deleted.

APPLICATIONS

Placing title information on printed worksheets, especially multi-page worksheets adds greatly to keeping your work organized. Set Print Titles allows you to place a multi-line and/or multi-column heading on your printout. Compare this to the Heading option of the Page Setup command that allows only a single line of text at the top of each page.

Use the Set Print Area command on the Options window to exclude the rows and columns containing the title specifications from the printout. Otherwise the first page of the printout contains double titles.

TYPICAL OPERATION

In this session you place column titles at the top of each page of a printout of the BUDGET1.XLS worksheet that you accessed most recently in the Set Print Area module.

1. Start Excel. Open the BUDGET1.XLS worksheet and select row 2.

2. Select **Set Print Titles** from the Options menu.
3. Select row 6, then select **Set Page Break** from the Options menu to force the printout onto two pages.
4. Highlight the region A3 through I11, then select **Set Print Area** from the Options menu.

5. Select **Print** from the File menu. Verify that the **Preview** option is set, then pick **OK**.

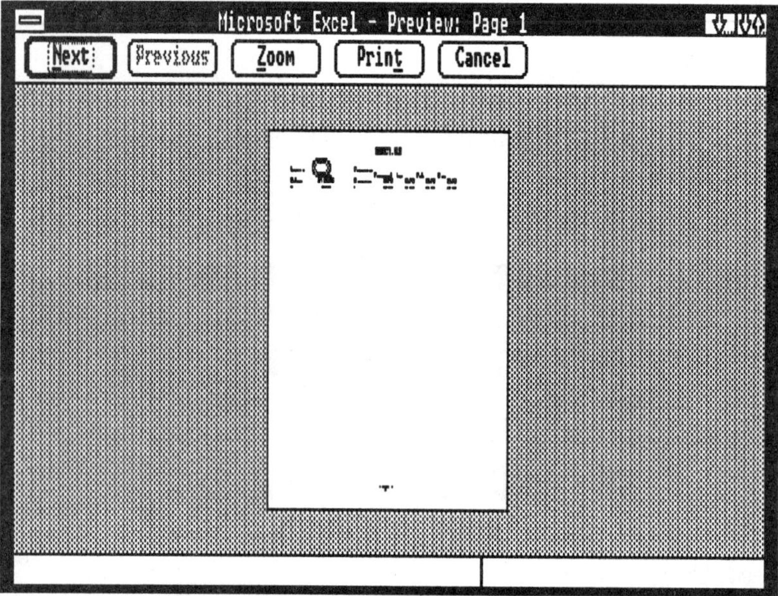

6. Move the mouse to the upper left region of the print image and click the left mouse button. Notice the titles on the preview.

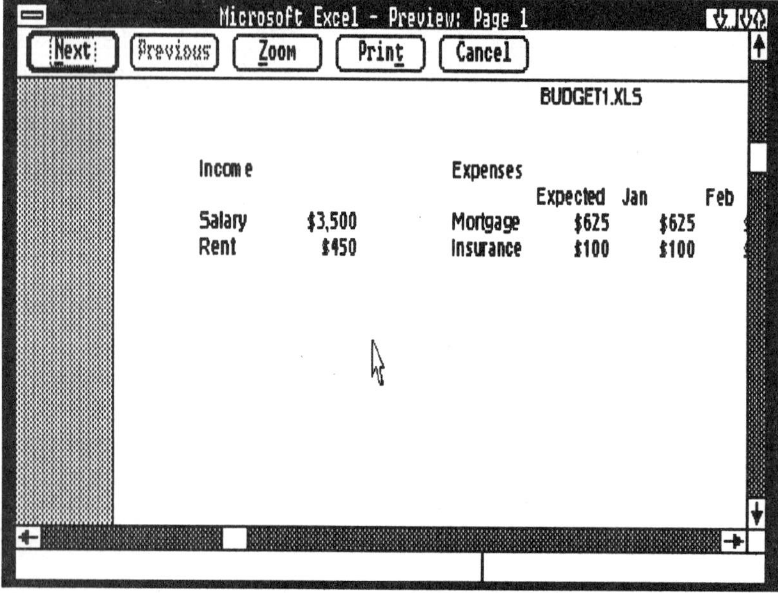

7. Select **Next**. Notice that the titles carry forward onto the second page.

```
Microsoft Excel - Preview: Page 2
Next    Previous    Zoom    Print    Cancel

                                    BUDGET1.XLS

        Income              Expenses
        Rent      $450      Food      $300   $300
        Rent      $450      Auto      $300   $300
                            Clothes   $250   $250
                            Savings   1050   1050
                            Taxes      700    700
                            Utilities $175   $175
```

8. Select **Cancel** to end the page preview.
9. Close the worksheet without saving it.
10. Turn to Module 25 to continue the learning sequence.

Module 66

SHOW INFO/SHOW DOCUMENT

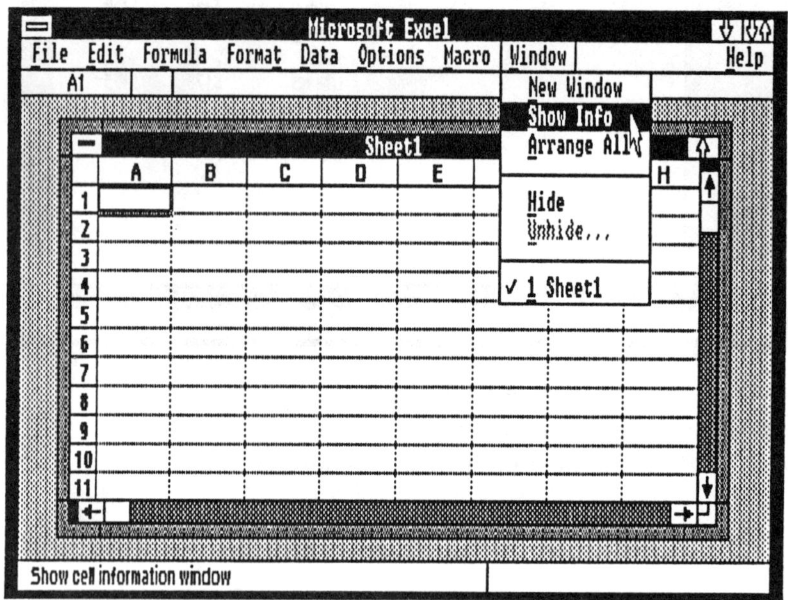

DESCRIPTION

The Show Info command is located on the Window menu. You may select it with the mouse or by pressing Alt-W S. When activated, it displays selected information about the cells in the active worksheet. By default, the Show Info window provides you information indicating the cell address, any formulas in the cell, and any notes you may have made associated with the cell.

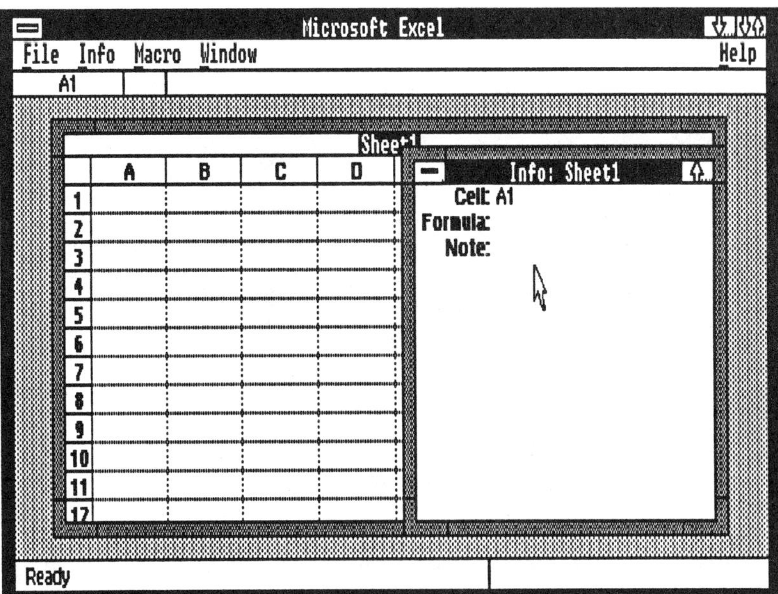

Once selected, Show Info also modifies the Excel menu system. The Window menu, shown in the following screen display, is modified by the substitution of Show Document for Show Info, as shown in the following display.

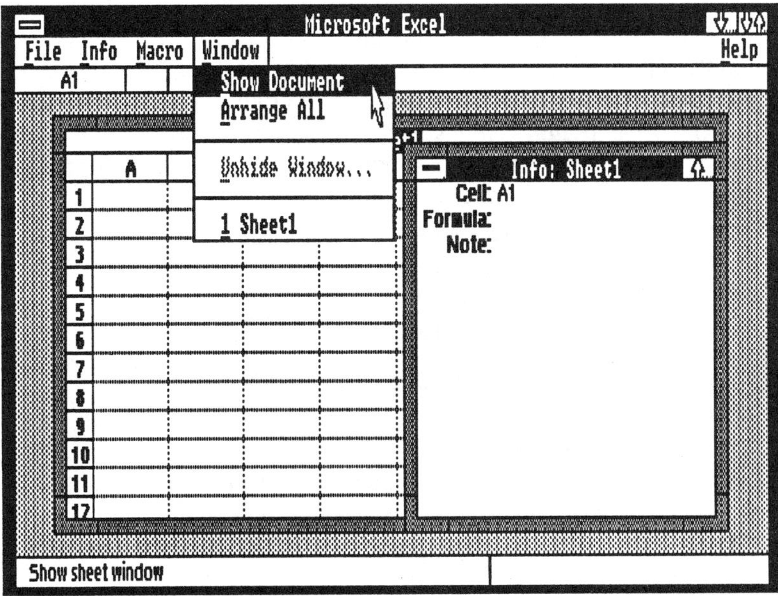

Selecting Show Document reactivates the current worksheet and toggles to the standard Excel menu system. You may also move between the worksheet window and the Show Info window by moving the mouse cursor into the desired window and clicking the left mouse button. As you change the active cell on the worksheet, information about the cell is displayed in the Show Info window.

The Show Info menu bar adds an Info menu as shown in the following screen display.

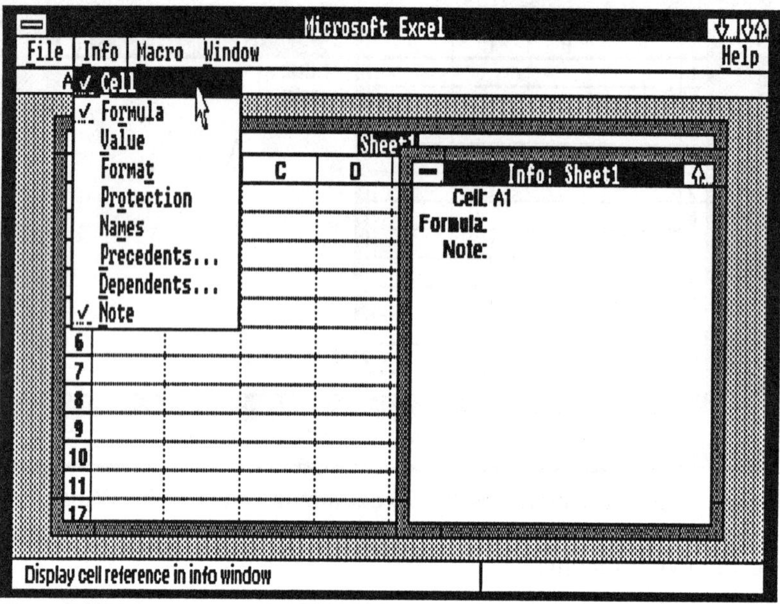

Notice that the default information of Cell, Formula, and Note are checked on the Info menu. Each item on the menu operates as a toggle, determining whether that category of information is displayed. You may selectively add the display of the cell's value, format, protection status, names, precedents, and dependents. When you select either precedent or dependent information, a dialog box appears that requires you to specify whether you are interested in only direct precedents and dependents or indirect relationships as well.

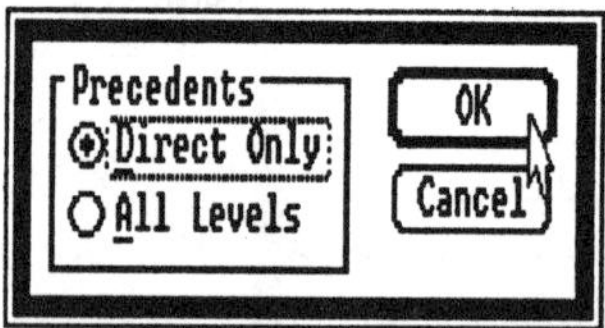

If the Show Info window covers a portion of the worksheet that you need to view, you may either move the Show Info window (it moves like any other Excel window) or resize by pointing to any corner of the window, pressing the left mouse button, and dragging the window to the desired size. You may also select Arrange All from the Window menu to arrange both the worksheet and the information display on the screen, as shown in the following display.

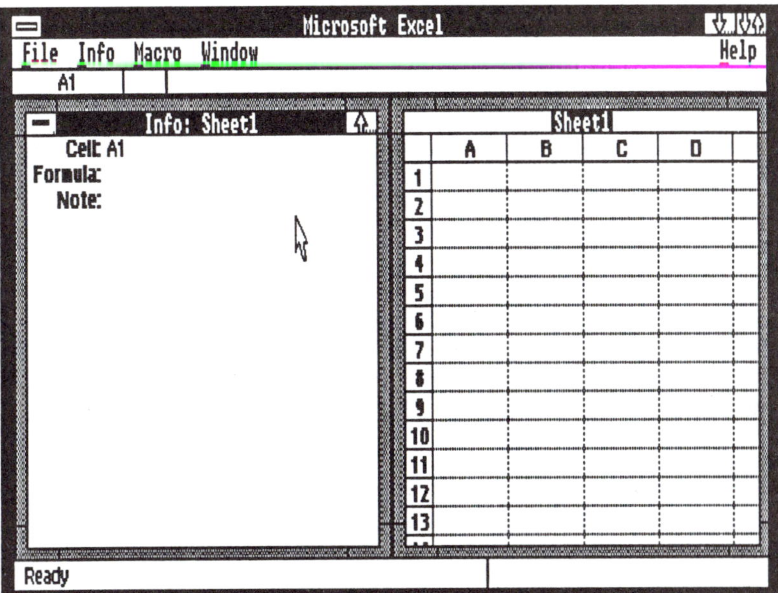

To eliminate the Show Info window, press Ctrl-F4 or select Close from the Control menu of the Show Info window as shown in the following display.

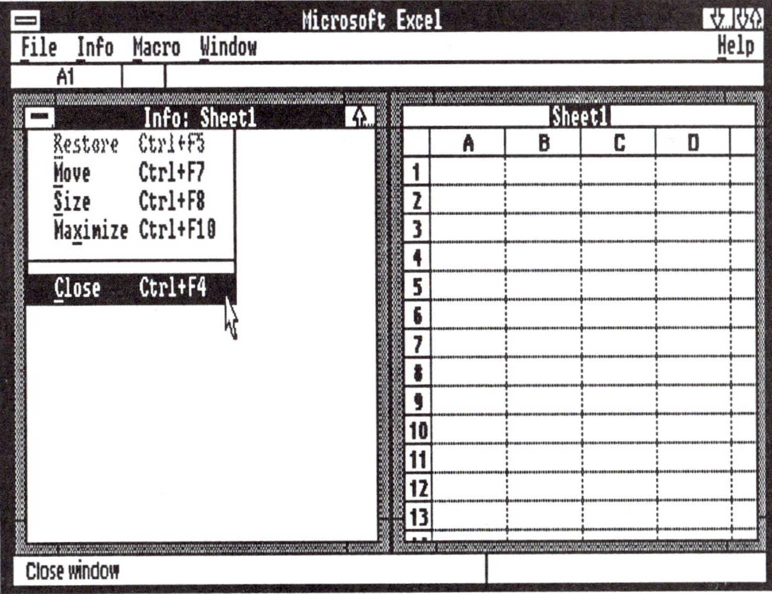

APPLICATIONS

If you change the workspace to remove the formula bar from the screen, the Show Info command can be used to see what formulas you may have in a particular cell.

Since Excel permits you the option of making notes associated with a particular cell (see Module 40, Note), it also provides you a way of seeing the notes.

One of the most powerful features of the Show Info command is its ability to display information about precedent and dependent worksheet cells. When you make critical business decisions based on the values in a worksheet, it is important to review your work. Displaying information about precedent cells allows you to trace your final result back through your chain of calculation and logic to its fundamental assumptions. When you need to change part of a worksheet, displaying the dependent information about the changed cells allows you to identify the cells that depend on the information you are about to change, so that you can anticipate problems before they occur.

TYPICAL OPERATION

In this session you activate a Show Info window to examine the GOLD worksheet created in Module 16 and modified in Module 15.

1. Start Excel and close SHEET1.XLS, or continue your work session from the previous module.
2. Open the GOLD.XLS worksheet.
3. Select cell E8 if it is not already selected.

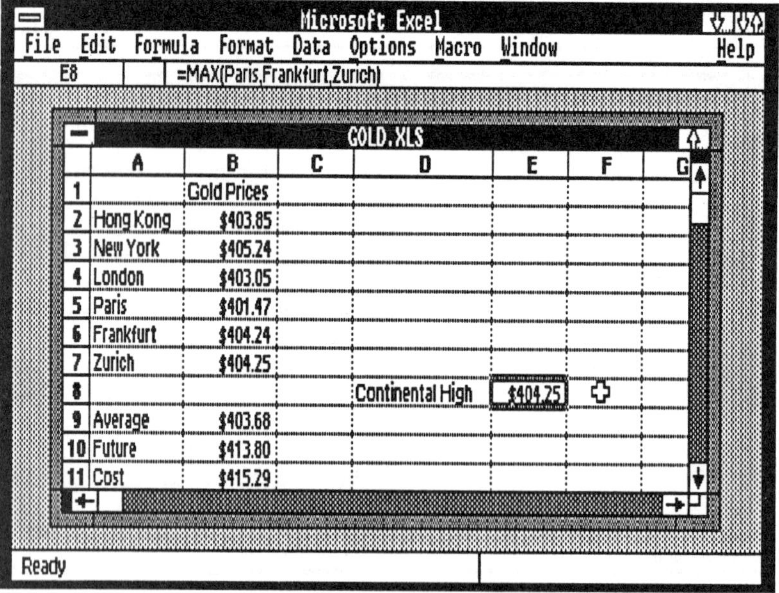

4. Pick **Show Info** from the Window menu.

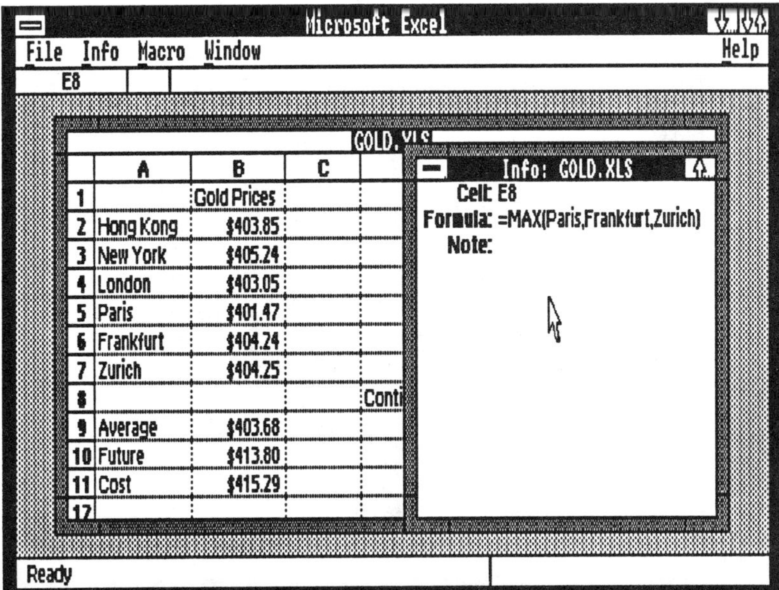

5. Select **Arrange All** from the Window menu.

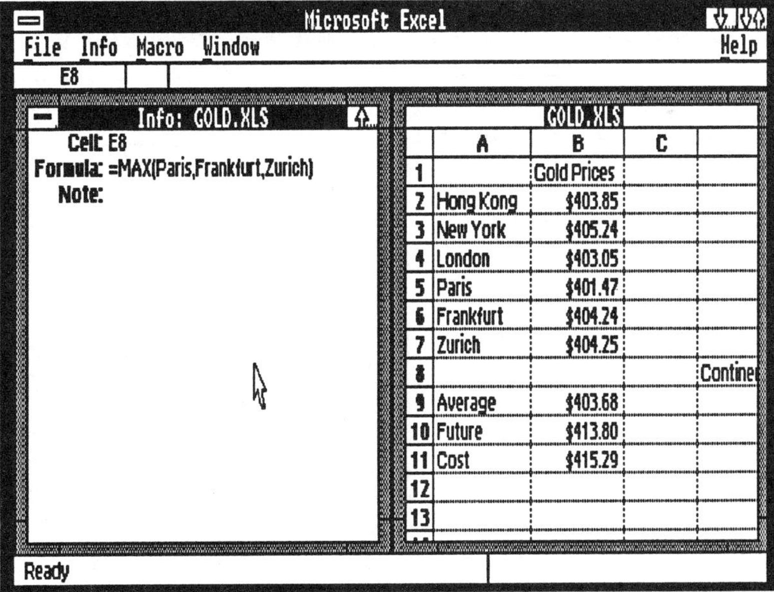

6. Pick **Precedents** from the Info menu.

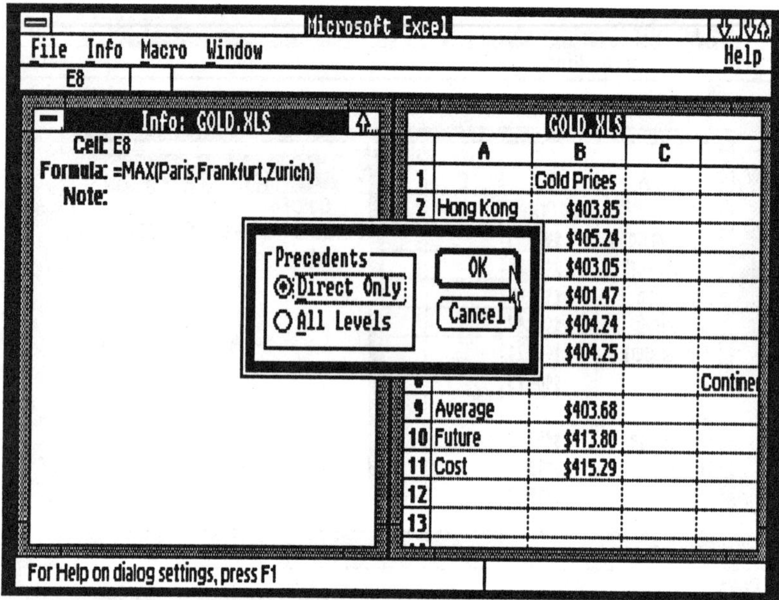

7. Verify the selection of **Direct Only** and pick **OK**.

The Show Info window displays the fact that the cell range B5:B7 serves as a precedent to cell E8.

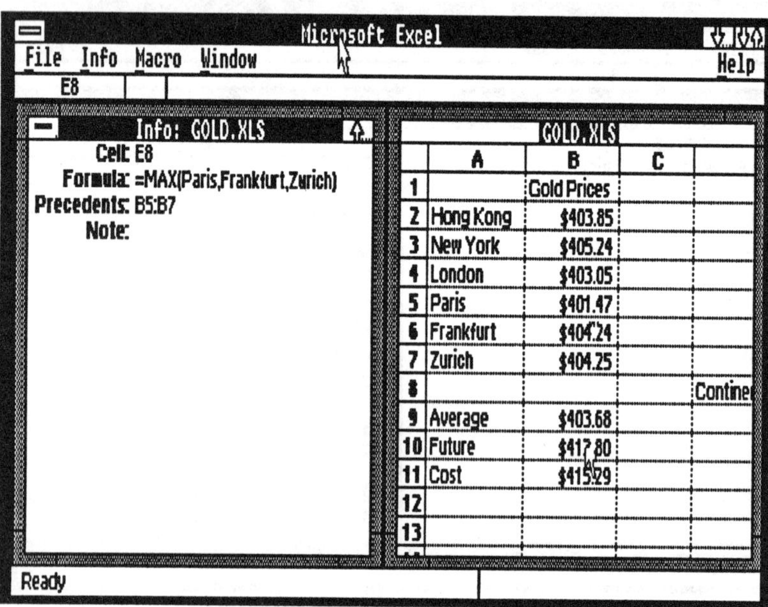

8. Pick in the worksheet to make it the current window. Then pick cell B3. Notice the following display, including the text of the cell note.

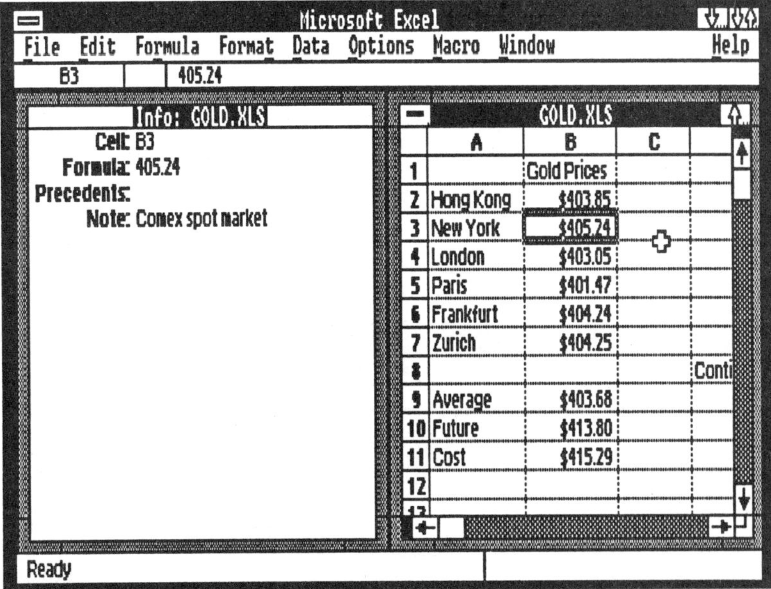

9. Pick in the Show Info window to make it the current window. Then pick the Control icon for the Show Info window.

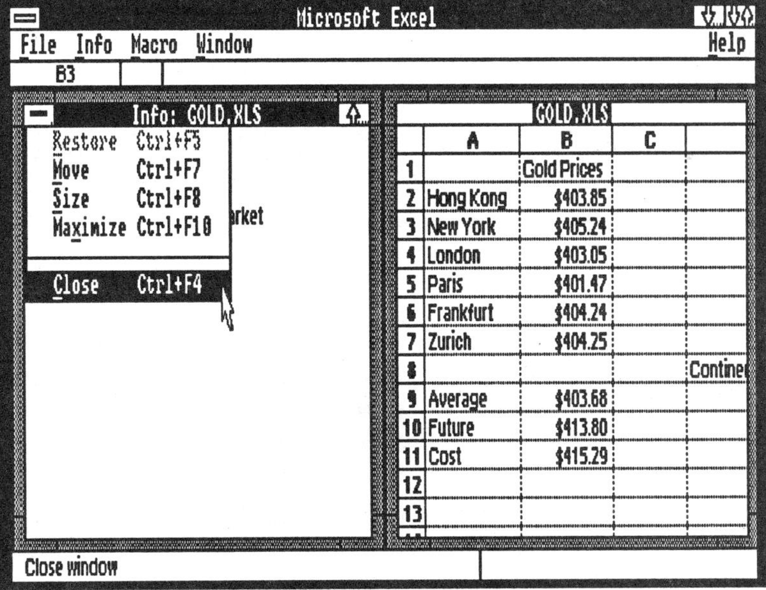

10. Select **Close**. The Show Info window disappears.

11. Close the worksheet without saving it.

12. Exit Excel, or continue your work session without an active worksheet on the screen.

13. Turn to Module 20 to continue the learning sequence.

Module 67

SIZE

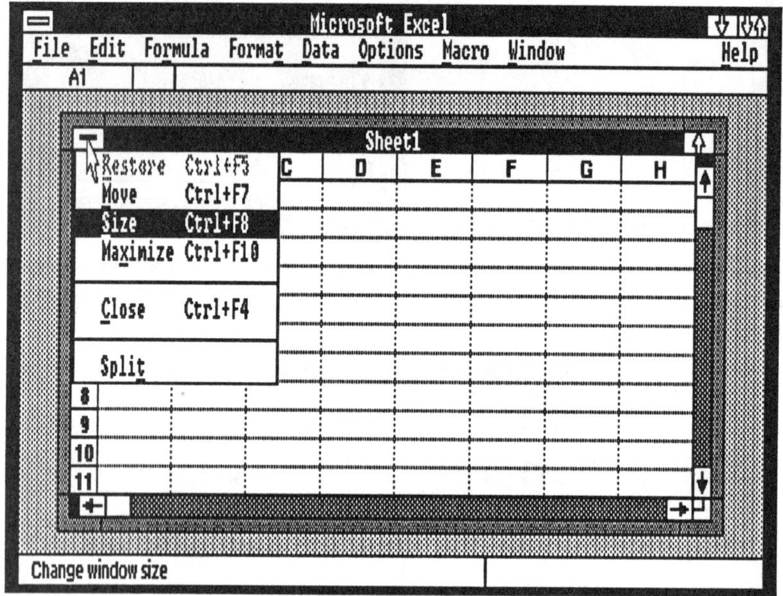

DESCRIPTION

Changing the size of the active window can be done in several ways. Pressing Ctrl-F8 is one method. Accessing the Size command from the Control menu of the active window is another. Using the mouse cursor to drag the corners of sides of the window is a third. Once you access the Size command or use Ctrl-F8, you are then able to use the arrow keys to change the size of the window.

If you use a mouse, position the cursor at the side of the worksheet until it changes to a "double-headed" arrow. Press the left button and hold it while you drag the side of the worksheet across the screen.

At the bottom right corner of the worksheet is an icon shaped like a corner. Placing the mouse cursor on that icon and holding the left button will permit you to size the worksheet by dragging the corner to the location desired.

APPLICATIONS

The ability to size active windows permits you to reduce the space they occupy on the screen. This operation allows you to see the window that is behind the one you sized. Using this technique, you can arrange several windows on the screen at the same time. This is helpful if the work you are doing requires you to examine the data on more then one window.

Once you have reduced the size of the windows, you can activate any of them by simply clicking on any portion of the desired window with the mouse. If you don't use a mouse, the keystrokes of Ctrl-F6 will do the same thing.

TYPICAL OPERATION

In this operation you change the size of available windows. You should continue this activity from the New Window module. If you need to, open BUDGET1 and then open a new window using the New Window command. You should have three windows available to you. BUDGET1, Sheet1, and a new window associated with BUDGET1. Begin this module with Sheet1 as the active window.

1. Press **Ctrl-F8** or access **Size** from the Control menu.

NOTE

When using the corner icon to maximize the worksheet, it is not uncommon for you to expand the worksheet to the extent that the scroll bars and the corner icon are almost off the screen. There will, however, always be a small portion visible and to adjust the worksheet, you need only place the mouse pointer in the visible area.

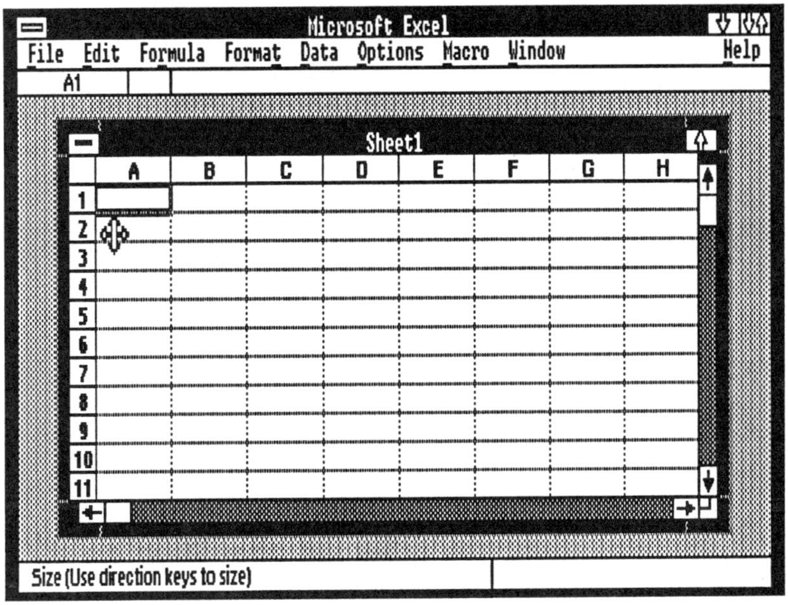

Microsoft Excel
File   Edit   Formula   Format   Data   Options   Macro   Window   Help
A1
Sheet1
A   B   C   D   E   F   G   H
1
2
3
4
5
6
7
8
9
10
11
Size (Use direction keys to size)

The borders of the screen have changed color or shading.

NOTE

The first arrow key pressed after making this selection dictates which border of the window is be adjusted. For example the Up Arrow pulls the top up or down, the Left Arrow pulls the left side one way or the other. Once the border is selected, the appropriate direction arrow moves the border.

2. Press the **Left Arrow** once.

3. Press the **Right Arrow** 27 times and press **Enter**.

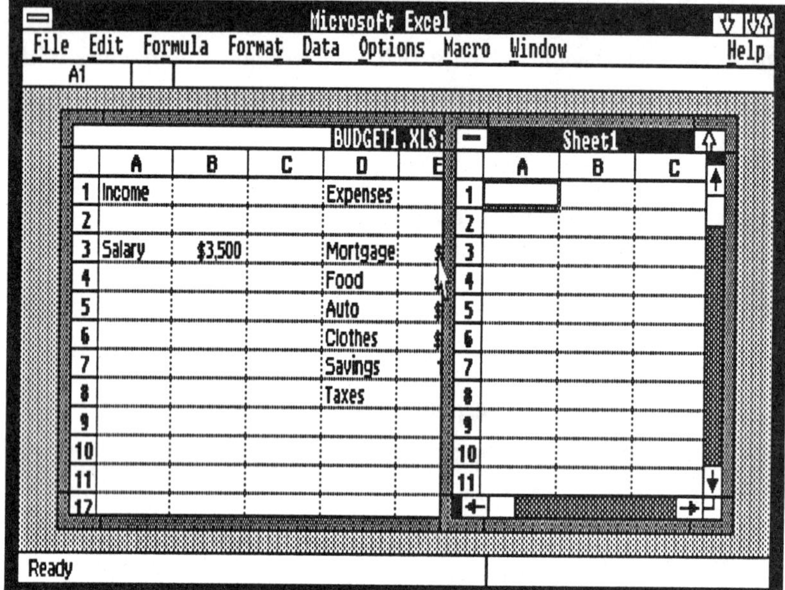

4. Click on BUDGET1 or press **Ctrl-F6**.

5. Access **Size** from the Control menu of this worksheet.

6. Press **Up Arrow** once.

7. Press **Down Arrow** 10 times and press **Enter**.

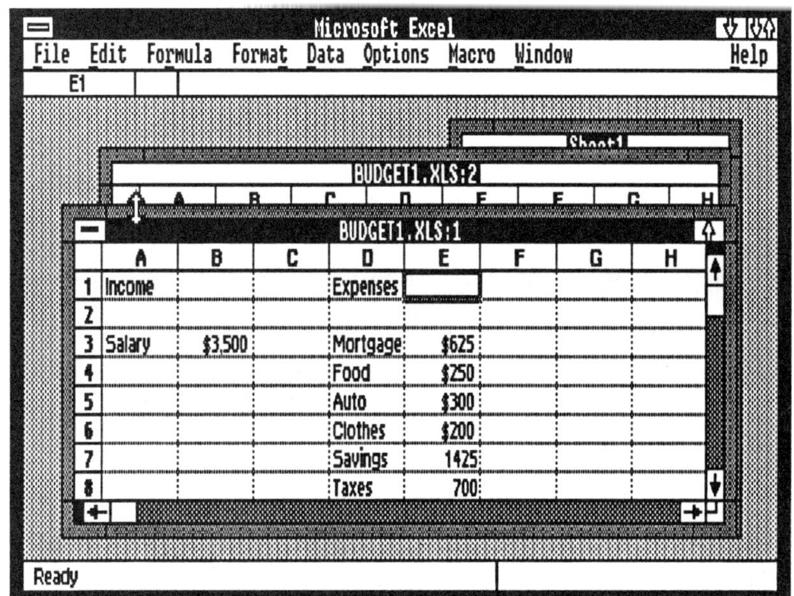

You must use the same procedures to restore the windows to their original size as you used to change them.

NOTE

If you use the Maximize and Minimize commands from the Control menu or the Maximize and Minimize arrows in the upper right corner of the active window, you can use the Restore command on the Control menu or Ctrl-F5 to return the worksheets to their original size.

8. If you are unable to continue your work session, use the Save Workspace command to save your work, then exit Excel.

9. Turn to Module 37 to continue the learning sequence.

Module 68
SORT

DESCRIPTION

The Sort command arranges a rectangular region of the worksheet in either ascending or descending order, based on the values in one, two, or three fields, in a single operation. Although the command appears on the Data menu, and its most common application is sorting databases, its function is more general. Specifically, the Sort command can sort a worksheet region either by rows or by columns.

Before you select the Sort command you must first select an active region of the worksheet for sorting. The region arranged by the Sort command is the region of the worksheet that is selected (highlighted) when you initiate the Sort command. The sort region is completely independent from the region identified as a database with the Set Database command. In the case of a database (the normal situation) this means that you must select the region of the database containing data, excluding the top row containing the field names. If the database definition contains the row with the field names when you issue the Sort command, the field names are sorted as a record and end up somewhere in the middle of the database.

When you select Sort from the Data menu, the Sort dialog box appears.

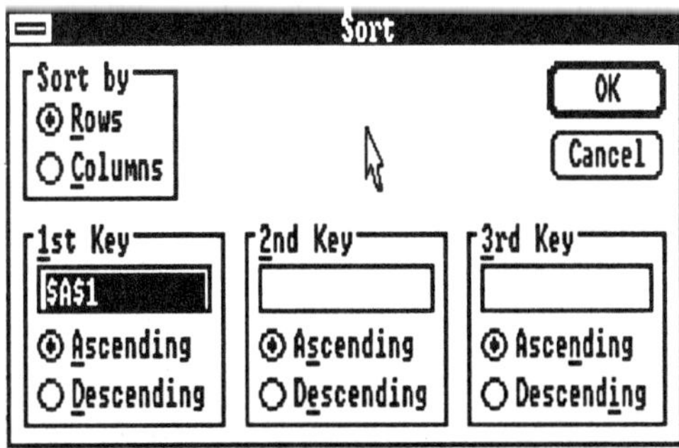

By default, the sort is performed by rows. However, Excel also allows you to sort by columns when needed. The column sort capability is for general worksheet sorting applications; you should not create a database where each record occupies a column. The Form, Find, Delete, and Extract commands work only on a database created with columns corresponding to fields and rows corresponding to records.

There is space provided in the dialog box for a maximum of three keys. The keys are the fields used for sorting and are used in priority order. For example, in sorting an address list, specifying the state as the first key, the city as the second key, and the last name as the third key produces a sorted database that first sorts the state names, then arranges the cities alphabetically within the states, then arranges the individuals alphabetically within each city by name. It is not necessary to use all three available keys; use one, two, or three keys as required by your application. By default, the position of the cursor when you select Sort is copied into the space for the first key.

You specify the sort keys by placing the location of the field names in the spaces provided for each key. You can type the location of the field names in the spaces provided or pick them on the screen with the mouse. First, place the mouse cursor in the key field and pick it. The text cursor appears in the field. Then move the mouse cursor to the field name on the screen and pick it. The location appears in the sort window. This method of selecting the sort keys is less likely to result in errors from incorrect typing.

NOTE
When you select the Sort command, the Sort dialog box may cover the required fields on the screen, preventing you from picking the fields with the mouse. If this happens, move the mouse to the title bar of the Sort dialog box, press the left mouse button, and drag the dialog box to a more convenient location.

Each key allows you to specify either an ascending or descending sort. An ascending sort places character information in normal alphabetical order, numerical information in order from smallest to largest, and time/date information in order from oldest to newest. The descending sort reverses this ordering. Excel uses an ascending sort as the default setting. If the database range (established with the Set Database command) includes any blank lines, they are placed at the end of the database, regardless of the settings for ascending and descending.

APPLICATIONS

There are many reasons to change the order that information is stored. Although storing a set of names and addresses alphabetically by last name is highly useful, you may want to sort the database by zip code when it is time to prepare a presorted mailing. Arranging a database of purchase orders by P.O. number is excellent for use by the receiving dock, but sorting by account number may be more appropriate for budget calculations.

Sorting a database only arranges the placement of existing records in the database. It has no effect on records that are added after Excel finishes the sort. To incorporate newly added records in the properly sorted order, you must direct Excel to again perform the sort operation.

The three-key limitation of Excel is easily bypassed. When you need to sort your data on more than three keys, perform multiple sort operations. First, sort the data on the least important keys. Then sort the data on successively more important keys. Continue the process as many times as necessary to sort the data on any number of desired keys.

TYPICAL OPERATION

In this operation you use the Sort command to rearrange the camping store inventory created in the Set Database module, using both a single key and multiple keys. You place the inventory in alphabetical order by item description within department, and then sort the database again by inventory value.

1. Start Excel and open the INVENT.XLS worksheet, or continue your work session from the previous module.

	A	B	C	D	E	F
9						
10	Dept	Description	Quantity	Cost	Value	
11	Fishing	Spinning Rod	3	$14.32	$42.96	
12	Clothing	Blue Bandana	71	$0.96	$68.16	
13	Clothing	Red Bandana	144	$0.96	$138.24	
14	Camping	Mountain Tent	6	$330.21	$1,981.26	
15	Clothing	Rain Jacket	12	$45.50	$546.00	
16						
17						
18						
19						
20						
21						
22						

The database definition established in previous modules defined the database as the region bounded by A10 and E20. The Sort command does not respect the database definition, but requires you to highlight the region you want to sort.

2. Highlight the region bounded by A11 and E15.

NOTE
Excel does not "forget" your database definition simply because you changed the active selection area of the screen. The active database region is still defined, it simply is no longer highlighted.

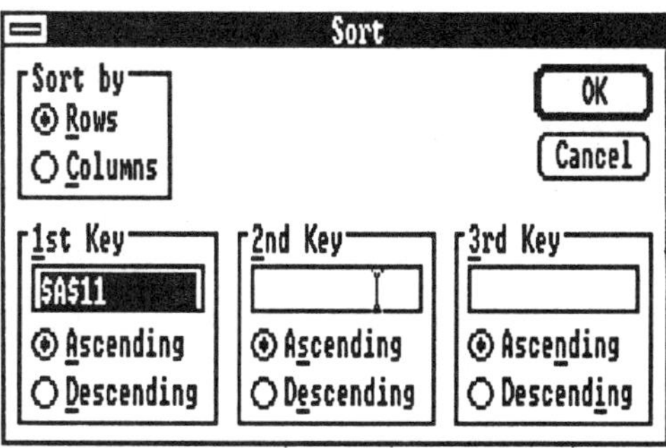

	A	B	C	D	E	F
9						
10	Dept	Description	Quantity	Cost	Value	
11	Fishing	Spinning Rod	3	$14.32	$42.96	
12	Clothing	Blue Bandana	71	$0.96	$68.16	
13	Clothing	Red Bandana	144	$0.96	$138.24	
14	Camping	Mountain Tent	6	$330.21	$1,981.26	
15	Clothing	Rain Jacket	12	$45.50	$546.00	
16						
17						
18						
19						
20						
21						
22						

In the first sort operation, you sort the inventory alphabetically by item within each department.

3. Pick **Sort** from the Data menu.

The Sort dialog box appears on the screen.

Because this is a standard database sort, you accept the default arrangement by rows. For this sort operation you need to use the first two key fields in the dialog box. The first key will specify sorting by department, the second key will specify sorting by item. The default value of "ascending" is used for both keys, as that specifies standard A to Z ordering.

Because cell A11 was highlighted when the Sort command started, its reference is automatically placed in the field for the first key. Since this is the desired value, move on to consideration of the second key.

4. Move the typing cursor to the field for the second key, either by clicking on the second key field with the mouse or by pressing **Tab** twice.

At this point, you could type the reference for the second field "$B$11" into the space provided, or pick the position from the screen. In this session you pick the position from the screen.

The Sort dialog box covers the item description field.

5. Move the Sort dialog box to a position lower on the screen, revealing at least the top row of database data. (With the mouse, point to the dialog box title bar, press the left mouse button, drag the box to the position shown, and release the mouse button. With the keyboard, press **Alt-Spacebar**, type **M**, press **Down Arrow** repeatedly until the box moves to the desired position, then press **Enter**.)

6. Move the mouse pointer to cell B11 (Spinning Rod) and pick it.

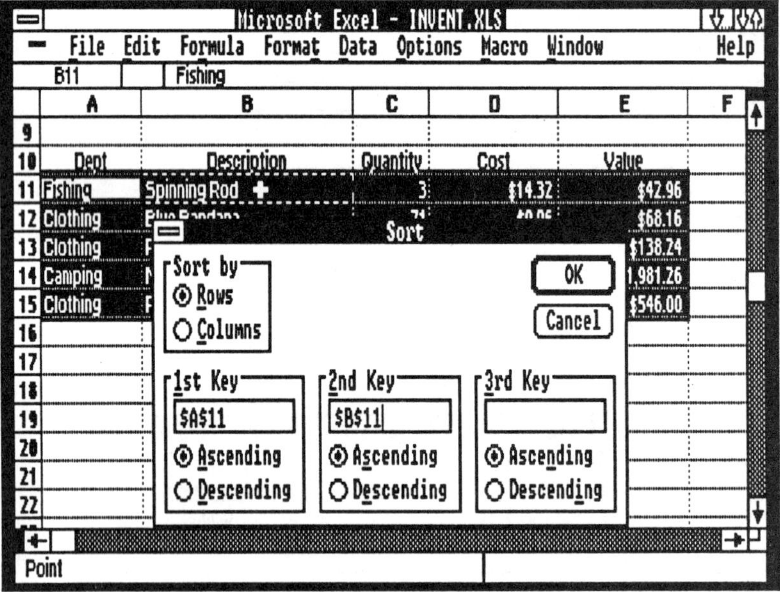

The coordinates $B$11 appear in the second sort key field. The specification of this sort operation is now complete.

7. Click on **OK** or press **Enter** to perform the sort.

The data is rearranged in alphabetical order, first by department name, then by the item description within the department.

In the next sort operation, you sort the inventory by value, placing the items tying up the most capital at the top of the list.

8. Pick **Sort** from the Data menu.

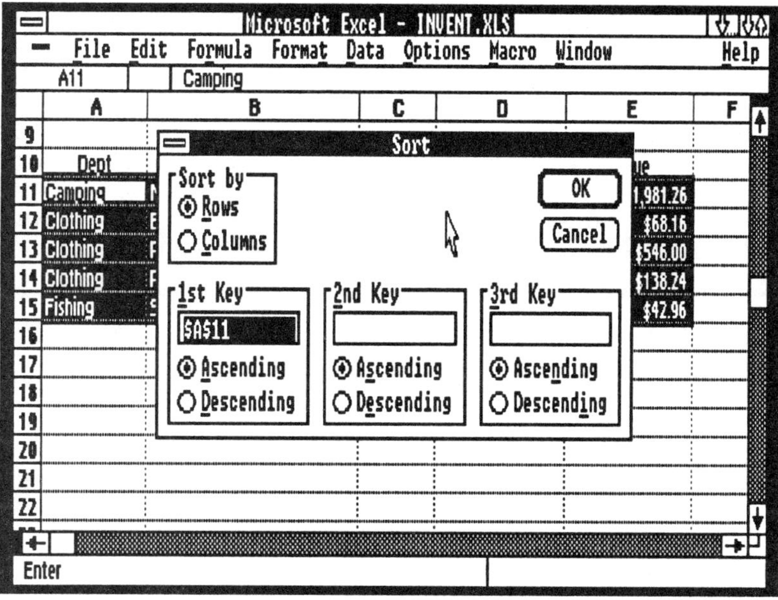

9. Pick **E11** with the mouse, (move the dialog box if necessary) or type **$E$11** in the 1st Key field of the Sort dialog box.

10. Pick the **Descending** option for the first sort key.

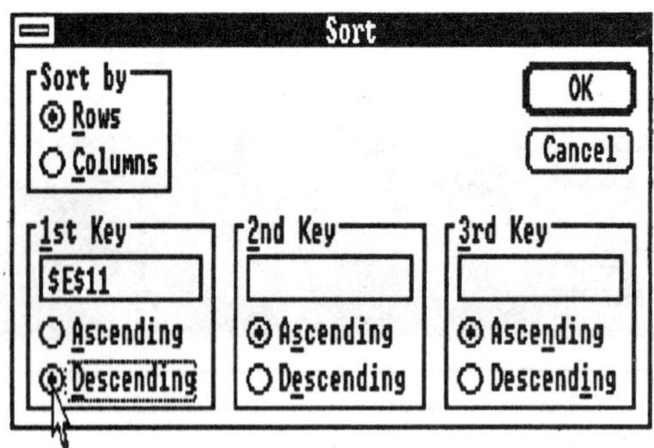

11. Pick **OK** or press **Enter** to perform the sort.

The data is arranged in descending order by value.

Dept	Description	Quantity	Cost	Value
Camping	Mountain Tent	6	$330.21	$1,981.26
Clothing	Rain Jacket	12	$45.50	$546.00
Clothing	Red Bandana	144	$0.96	$138.24
Clothing	Blue Bandana	71	$0.96	$68.16
Fishing	Spinning Rod	3	$14.32	$42.96

12. Select **Save** from the File menu. You need this worksheet again in the Set Criteria module.

13. Exit Excel, or continue your work session with the active worksheet on the screen.

14. Turn to Module 61 to continue the learning sequence.

Module 69

SPLIT

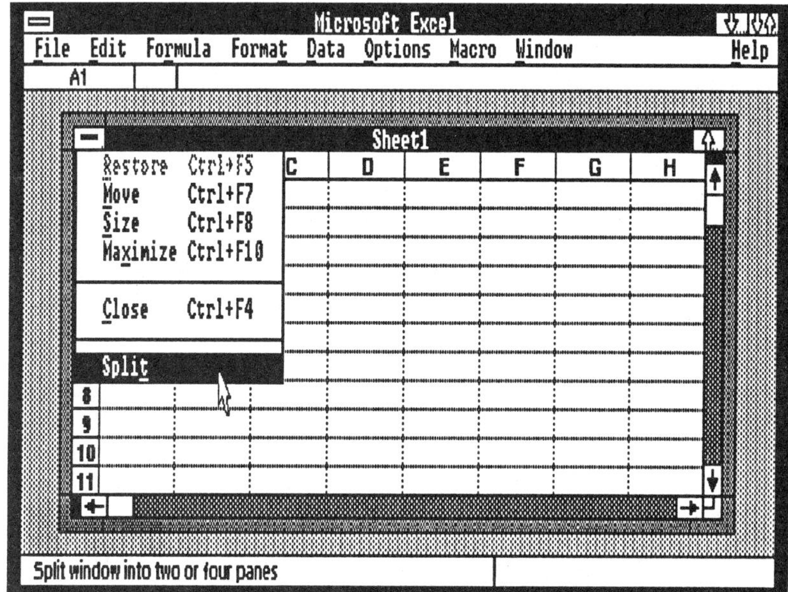

DESCRIPTION

The Split command allows you to divide your view of a worksheet into two or four regions or *panes*. The Split command is located on the Control menu for each worksheet. To select it with the mouse, click on the Control menu icon (a short horizontal bar in the upper left corner of the worksheet), then click on Split. To select it with the keyboard, press Alt-hyphen T.

When you select Split, horizontal and vertical markers appear on the screen as shown.

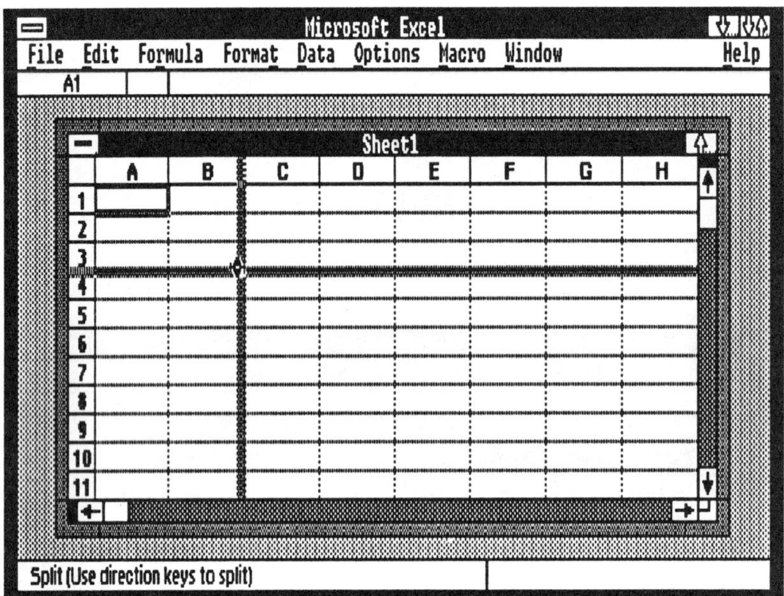

Move the markers, using either the mouse or the cursor control keys to specify the desired division of the worksheet.

You can split the worksheet into two or four sections. To split the worksheet into two sections, place one of the markers at the extreme edge, top, or bottom of the worksheet. To split the worksheet into four sections, place the markers at the division point. When the markers are located in the desired position, either click the left mouse button or press Enter. Excel divides the worksheet according to your specification.

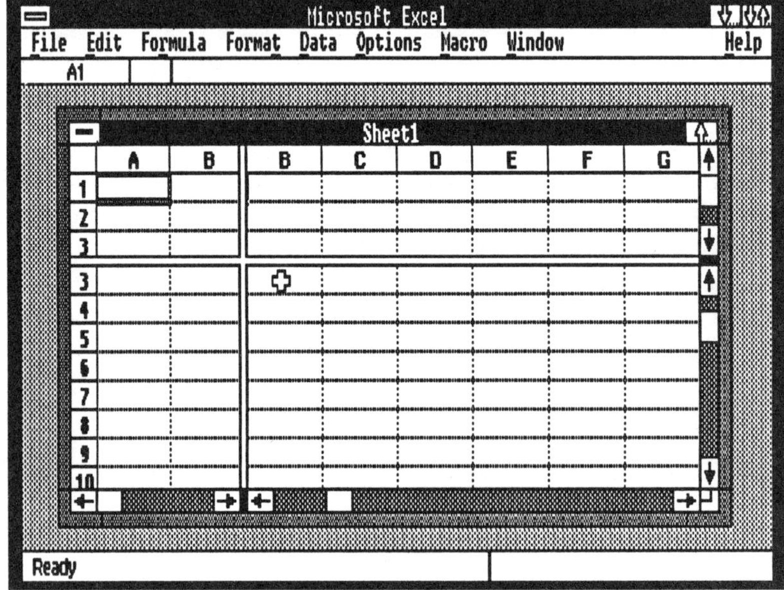

Each section gives a separate view of the worksheet. When you scroll horizontally or vertically, the corresponding sections of the worksheet scroll in parallel with the active section.

To reverse the split operation, returning to a single view of the worksheet, select the Split command again from the Control menu, move the markers to any corner of the worksheet, and click the mouse or press Enter.

APPLICATIONS

Use Split to view data in different locations on the worksheet at the same time. A typical worksheet model may have assumptions in one portion of the sheet, an analysis section in a second area of the sheet, and summary data in a third area of the sheet. Use the Split command to view both the assumptions and the summary data at the same time, eliminating the need to scroll through the analysis for comparison. The Split command is excellent for performing side-by-side comparisons. For example, you might compare budgeted amounts in one portion of the worksheet side-by-side with actual expenses located many columns away.

Additionally, you can use the Split command in combination with the Freeze Panes command to freeze row and column titles on the screen.

TYPICAL OPERATION

The use of the Split command is demonstrated in the Typical Operation session for Freeze Panes/Unfreeze Panes.

Turn to Module 29 to continue the learning sequence.

Module 70

TABLE

DESCRIPTION

The Table command on the Data menu provides a convenient method for substituting a series of values into a formula. The table can contain either a row of data values for substitution, a column of data values, or both a row and a column of values to create a large rectangular table. The table consists of a rectangular range of the worksheet containing the formula, the values to use, and a place for Excel to put the results. The Table command substitutes each table value, or pair of values, into the formula and displays the result in the corresponding worksheet cell.

In developing the table, you can arrange it either as a row-oriented table with the values for substitution going across the worksheet, a column-oriented table with the values for substitution going down a column of the worksheet, or a rectangular worksheet with substitution values going both down and across. First, place the formula in the upper left cell of the table. The formula must be based on the value of cells *outside* the range of the table. The value of the "substitution cells" could be blank, but that can cause the formula result to appear strange on the worksheet.

A better method is to place a reasonable value for the data in the substitution cell(s). This method helps assure you of the validity of your formula, helping to reduce errors. If a single value is to be subsituted into the table, place the values either extending in the column below the formula, or in the row extending to the right of the formula. The choice of a row table or column table depends on what makes the most sense for your worksheet. If you want to explore the effect of two varying values, place one set of values in the column and one in the row.

After the formula and values are entered on the worksheet, highlight the rectangular region of the worksheet containing the formula, the substitution values, and the row, column, or region for the formula results, then pick the Table command from the Data menu. (Use the mouse or press Alt-D T.) The following dialog box appears.

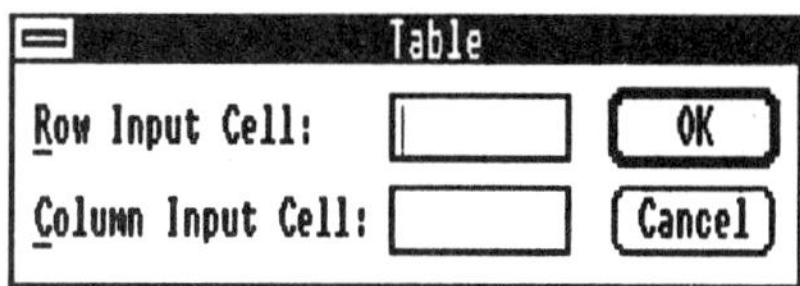

The dialog box has fields for both a row input cell and a column input cell. If you are constructing a row-oriented table, place a cell reference only in the Row Input Cell field. If you are constructing a column-oriented table, place a cell reference only in the Column Input Cell field. When constructing a two-dimensional table, place a cell reference in both fields. The cell references for the row input and column input cells are the cells in the worksheet for which you are substituting values. They are *not* cells in the range of the table.

You can specify the input cell either by typing its location in the field, or by picking the location with the mouse. If the dialog box is in the way, you can move it by grabbing the title bar with the mouse and dragging the box to a better location, or by pressing Alt-Spacebar M, pressing the cursor control keys to move it, and pressing Enter to accept the new position.

After you specify the input cells and click OK, Excel calculates the values and fills in the table.

APPLICATIONS

In performing a what-if analysis of a business projection you may need to explore the effects of a range of values on the bottom line. This is especially true when the cost of a key commodity may be difficult to predict, or when you lack absolute confidence in projections of sales volume.

One way of exploring the effect of a range of values on a formula is to repeatedly run the analysis, substituting varying values for the number in question. However, this method can be tedious. For projections containing long, involved calculations, waiting for the worksheet to recalculate between entries may be inconvienient.

Excel provides the Table command to allow you to explore the effect of a range of values on a calculation. For projections involving complex calculations over a wide range of values, Excel can calculate the full range of projections as one projection, allowing you to go out to lunch instead of changing a single value and recalculating the worksheet every few minutes.

If you create a worksheet containing several large tables, allowing Excel to recalculate all table values after every worksheet entry (Excel's default setting) may produce tedious delays in your work. Use the Calculation command on the Options drop-down menu to set calculation at "Automatic except Tables" during worksheet development to suppress the recalculation of tables after every worksheet entry. When the worksheet is complete, use Calculate Now to recalculate all worksheet values.

The Tables command is used to explore a range of values surrounding an expected value to try to determine a best-case and a worst-case scenario in performing forecasting activities, or for simply exploring options in the decision-making process. A classic example is a two-value table exploring the varying effects of interest rates and payment terms on the payment amount in loan calculations. A single-variable table can be used to explore a range of wages on the profitability of a manufacturing operation. A table makes sense for computing the potential cost of a refrigeration or air conditioning system across varying electrical rates. Anytime you need to look at a range of values, a table can be an excellent tool.

TYPICAL OPERATION

In this session you create a table to help analyze the cost of owning a new car. The table shows the cost of driving a thousand miles as a function of the cost of gasoline and the fuel efficiency of the car.

1. Start Excel, or continue your work session from the previous module by creating a new worksheet.
2. Expand Sheet1, or the newly created default worksheet, to fill the screen.
3. Type **Cost of Gasoline** in cell A1.
4. Type **Miles Per Gallon** in cell A2.
5. Type **Thousand-Mile Cost** in cell A3 and press **Enter**.

6. Adjust the width of column A to hold the labels.

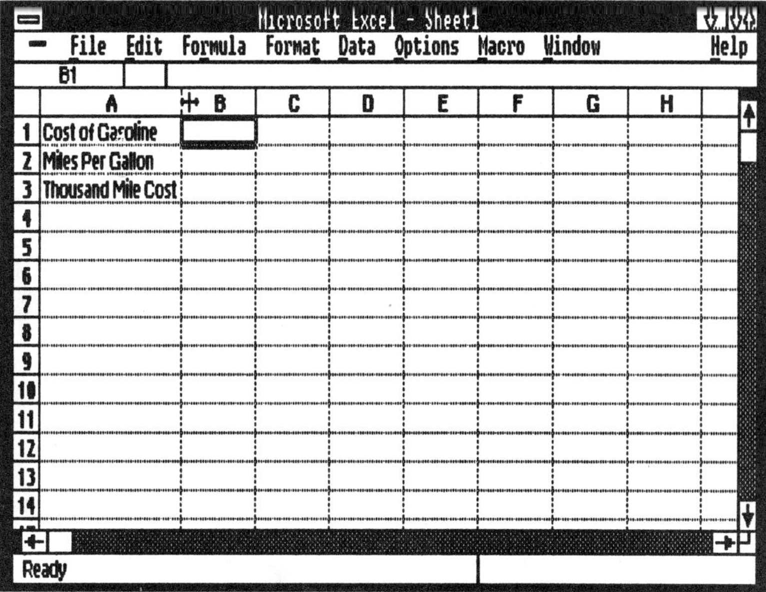

7. Select column B; set its format to **#,##0.00** using the **Number** command on the Format menu.

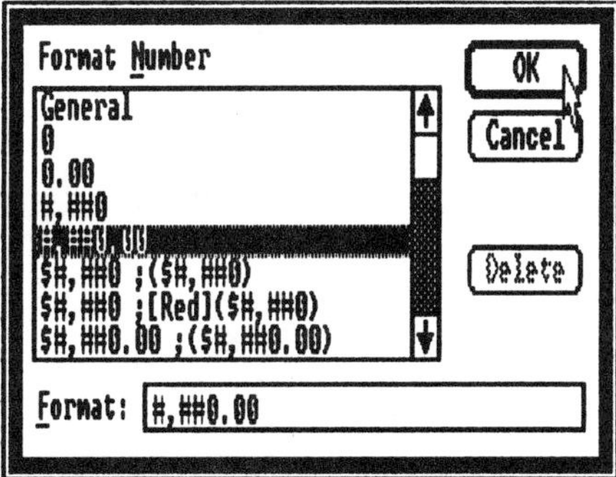

8. Click on **OK**.

9. Type **1.00** in cell B1, representing the cost of gasoline.

10. Type **25** in cell B2, representing the number of miles per gallon.

11. Type **=1000/B2∗B1** in cell B3 and press **Enter**. Notice that $40.00 is the correct cost for gasoline to drive 1000 miles at 25 miles per gallon with $1.00 per gallon gasoline.

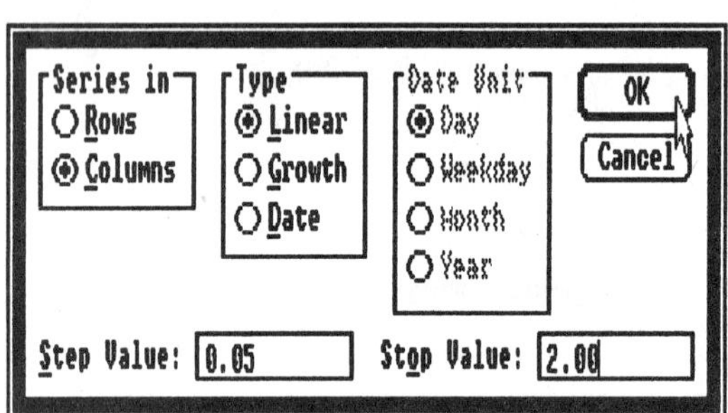

12. Type **0.70** in cell B4 and press **Enter**, establishing the minimum cost per gallon of gasoline.

13. With cell B4 highlighted, pick **Series** from the Data menu.

14. Select **Columns** as the series direction. Accept the default setting of a linear series. Type **0.05** as the Step Value and **2.00** as the Stop Value.

15. Pick **OK**.

16. Type **14** in cell C3 and press **Enter**, establishing the minimum number of miles per gallon in the analysis table.

17. With C3 highlighted, select **Series** from the Data menu. Accept the default values of "Rows" and "Linear." Type **2** as the Step Value and type **30** as the Stop Value.

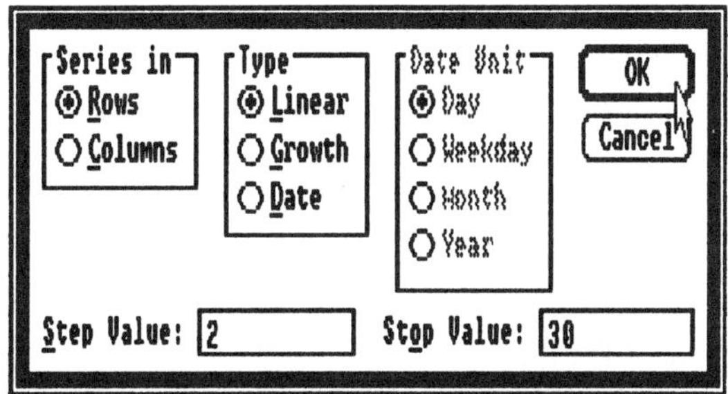

18. Select **OK**.
19. Select cell B3, the cell that forms the upper left corner of the developing table. Press **F5** (Goto), type **K30** as the Reference, and press **Shift-Enter**.
20. Select **Table** from the Data menu.

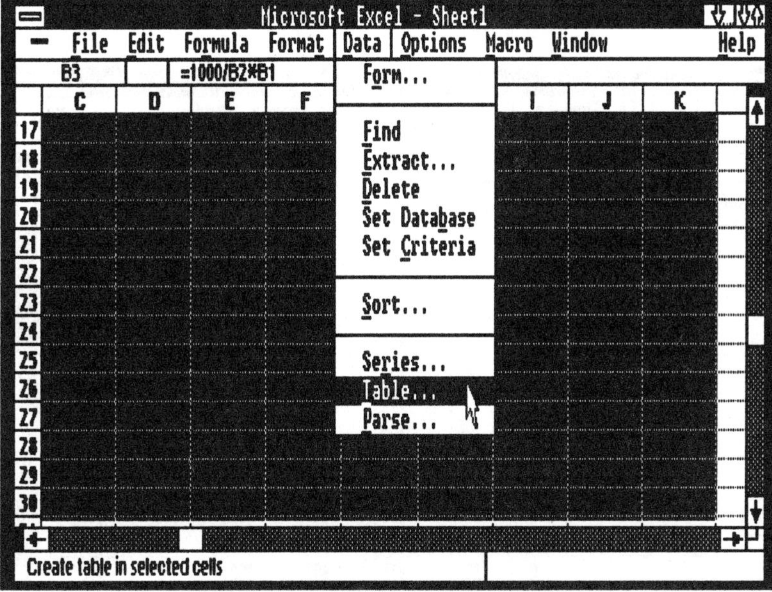

21. Type **B2** as the Row Input Cell, press **Tab**, and type **B1** as the Column Input Cell.

22. Pick **OK**.

Excel fills in the values for the table but does not format them in a desirable fashion.

23. Select cell K30; press **F5** (Goto), type **C4** as the Reference, then press **Shift-Enter**.

24. Select a dollars without cents numeric format (Use the Number command on the Format menu.) for the table data range.

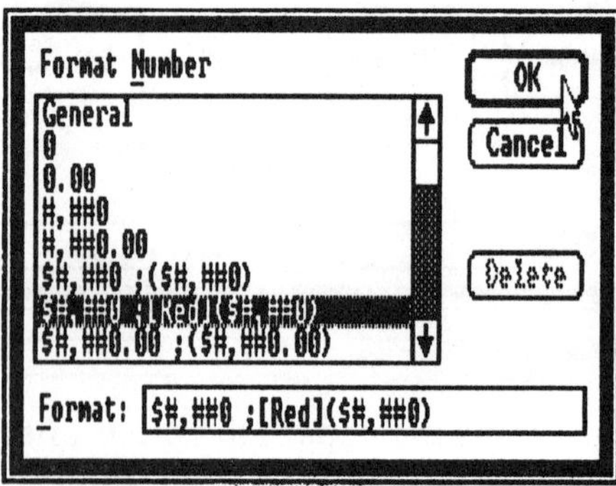

25. Pick **OK**.

26. Press **F5** (Goto), type **A1**, then pick **OK** or press **Enter** to position the worksheet display at the upper left corner of the sheet.

Microsoft Excel - Sheet1
File Edit Formula Format Data Options Macro Window Help

A1		Cost of Gasoline					
A	**B**	**C**	**D**	**E**	**F**	**G**	**H**
1 Cost of Gasoline	1.00						
2 Miles Per Gallon	25.00						
3 Thousand Mile Cost	40.00	14	16	18	20	22	24
4	0.70	$50	$44	$39	$35	$32	$29
5	0.75	$54	$47	$42	$38	$34	$31
6	0.80	$57	$50	$44	$40	$36	$33
7	0.85	$61	$53	$47	$43	$39	$35
8	0.90	$64	$56	$50	$45	$41	$38
9	0.95	$68	$59	$53	$48	$43	$40
10	1.00	$71	$63	$56	$50	$45	$42
11	1.05	$75	$66	$58	$53	$48	$44
12	1.10	$79	$69	$61	$55	$50	$46
13	1.15	$82	$72	$64	$58	$52	$48
14	1.20	$86	$75	$67	$60	$55	$50

Ready

27. Save the worksheet as GASOLINE.XLS. You need this worksheet again in the Freeze Panes/Unfreeze Panes module.

28. Close the worksheet.

29. Exit Excel, or continue your work session without an active worksheet on the screen.

30. Turn to Module 44 to continue the learning sequence.

Module 71
UNDO

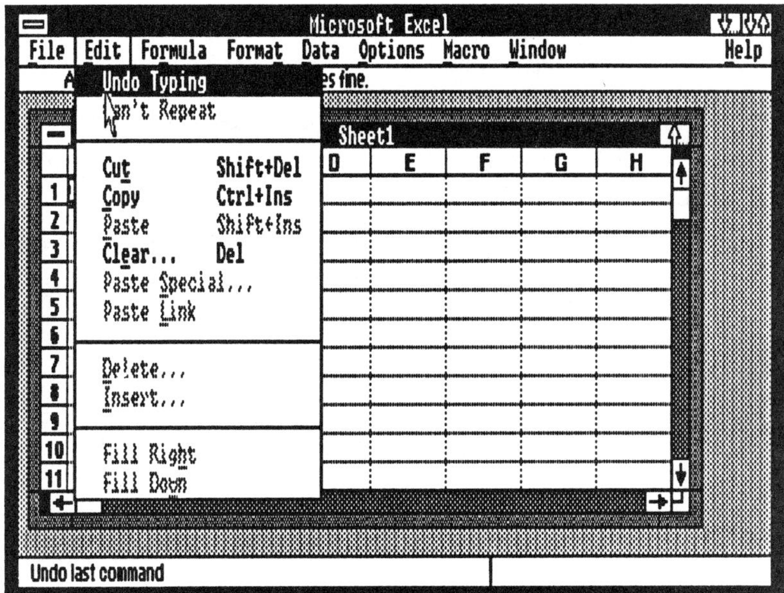

DESCRIPTION

The Undo command is available to you from the Edit menu whenever you add or delete some information from a worksheet. It is accessed with Alt-E U. It is available to you immediately after you perform a function that can be undone. Undo can't be used to recall a file that has been deleted, nor can it be used to cancel the Sort command of an Excel database. You can undo any of the commands on the Edit menu and you can reverse the Apply Names, Replace, and Paste List commands from the Formula menu.

APPLICATIONS

Use the Undo command to help recover from mistakes. When you make a mistake, immediately check the Edit drop-down menu to determine whether or not the Undo command is available. If it is available, use it to recover from the mistake. The Undo command is not accessible until you perform some function that can be undone. If you don't use the Undo command immediately after a particular action, it will not be available to you. For instance, if you delete some text from a worksheet, "Undo Delete" will be active for you to use. If you perform another function, you will not be able to go back and undo the delete. You can undo the Undo command, since the command works on itself.

The Undo command is additionally useful in combination with the List option of the Paste Names command. When you want to examine a list of name definitions, you can paste the list onto your worksheet, examine the list, then use the Undo command to erase the list.

TYPICAL OPERATION

In this module you enter some text and then remove it using the Undo command.

1. Start Excel. Use the default worksheet for your work.
2. Press **Alt-E** or click on the Edit menu.

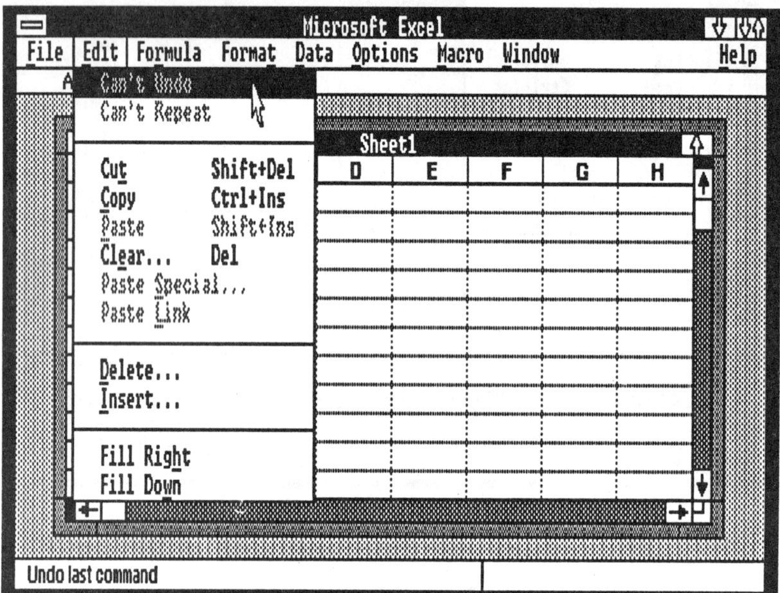

The drop-down menu shows the Undo command. The Undo command, in its current position, is not active. This is because you have not yet done anything that can be undone.

3. Press **Esc** to leave the menu.
4. Type **Every good boy does fine.** in cell A1.
5. Open the Edit menu.

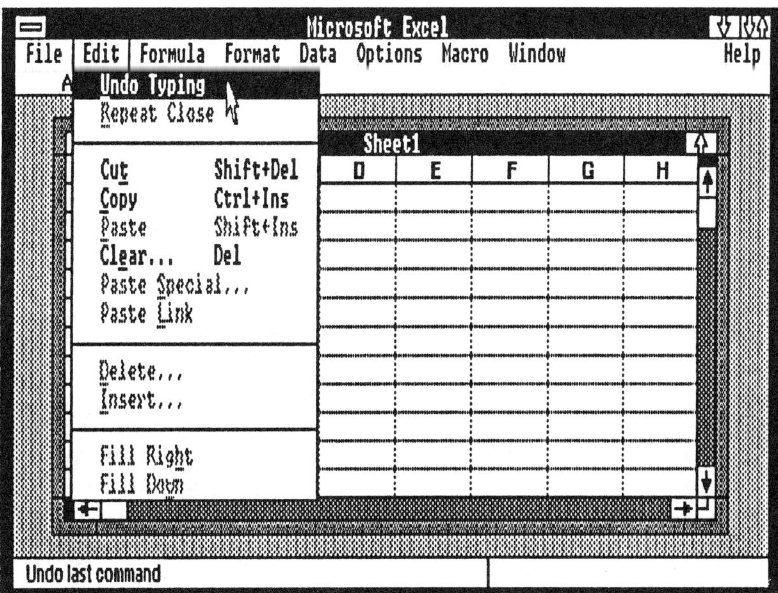

The Undo command is now active.

6. Type **U** or click on **Undo Typing**. The material you entered is deleted.

7. Open the Edit menu once more.

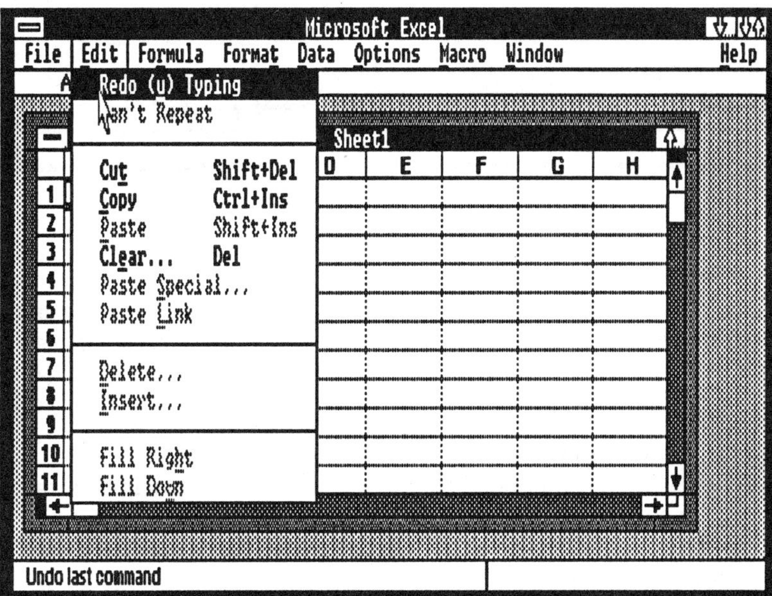

8. Type **u** or click on **Redo (u) Typing**. The text is returned to its original location.

9. Select **Exit** from the File menu to return to the DOS prompt or the MS-DOS Executive. There is no reason to save the worksheet.

10. Continue the learning sequence with Module 12.

Module 72
WORKSPACE

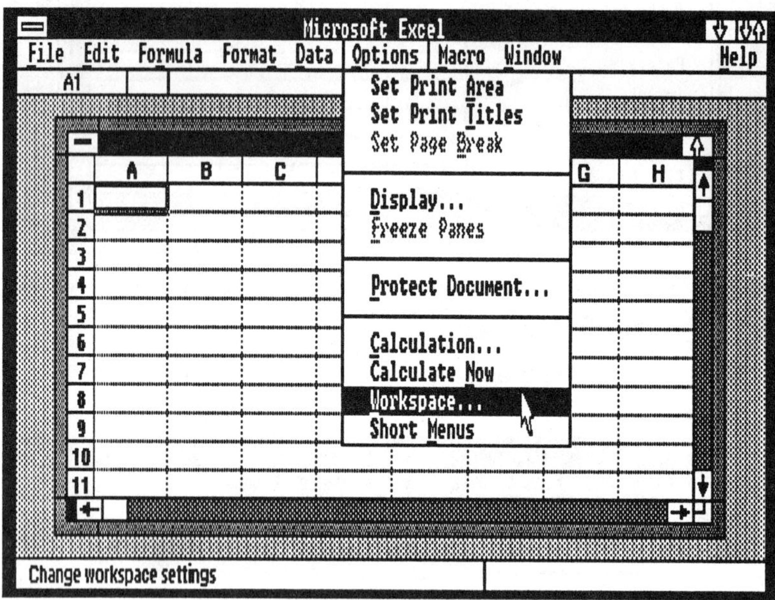

DESCRIPTION

The workspace is the area that appears on the screen. The Workspace command is accessed through the Options menu with the mouse or by pressing Alt-O W. This command permits you to change the default settings for the way the workspace appears on the screen. With this command you can:

1. Change the style of the rows and columns in the worksheet;
2. Hide the Status, Scroll, and Formula bars;
3. Change the setting for the number of decimal places in numerical data;
4. Change the key used to access the menu bar from the keyboard;
5. Instruct Excel to ignore any requests for information from outside Excel. This will only affect you if you are using the full version of Windows.

APPLICATIONS

The reasons a person might want to change the appearance of the workspace are practical as well as personal. When working with numerical data that needs to be displayed in a particular manner, it would be easy to change the default setting so that the data was automatically entered in that way.

Excel displays numerical data according to where you place the decimal. For example, if you type 45.20, Excel will display 45.2. If you are working with data that requires a specified number of place values, you can direct that Excel always display the data in that format. For example, suppose you were working with numbers that were all to be displayed as decimal numbers of a set length, say 2 or 3. Rather than typing them as decimal numbers, you could preset the default to be the desired decimal size and type the numbers as whole numbers, and Excel would enter them and display them in the appropriate format.

Being able to change the format for the rows and columns makes the Excel worksheet look like other worksheet software that you may have used before.

Hiding the Scroll, Formula, and Status bars will provide you with more working space in the worksheet. If you hide the Status, Scroll, and Formula bars, you can still use them, and the information you enter will be displayed, but only while it is being entered. Thus, if you type in a formula, it will be displayed while you are typing.

TYPICAL OPERATION

In this operation you change the default settings on the Excel worksheet to see how they are different. Begin this operation with a blank worksheet on the screen.

1. Start Excel, or continue your work session by selecting **New** from the File menu to create a new worksheet.

2. Select **Workspace** from the Options menu.

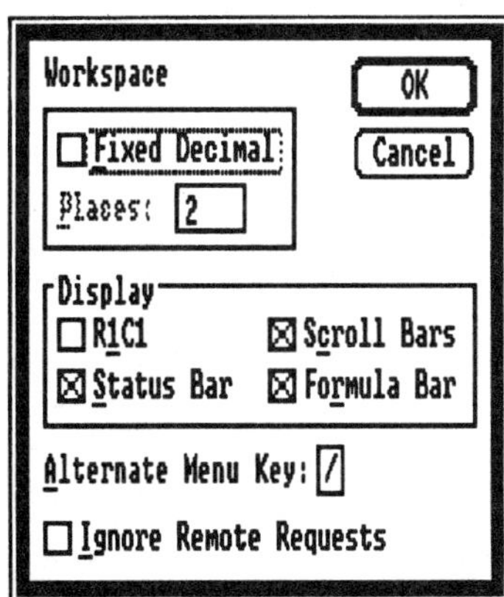

The dialog box indicates the different ways you can change the default settings for your workspace. To change any of the settings, simply mark or remove a mark in the box associated with what you want to change.

3. Use the mouse or press **Tab** once to activate the R1C1 option.

4. Press **Spacebar** once to change this setting.

5. Press **Tab** and **Spacebar** three more times to change the settings on Scroll Bars, Status Bar, and Formula Bar.

NOTE

You can use the mouse to accomplish the same action by clicking on each box to change the setting.

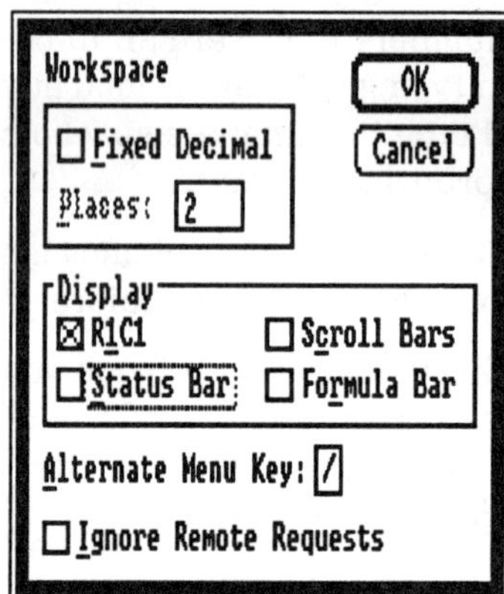

6. Press **Enter**.

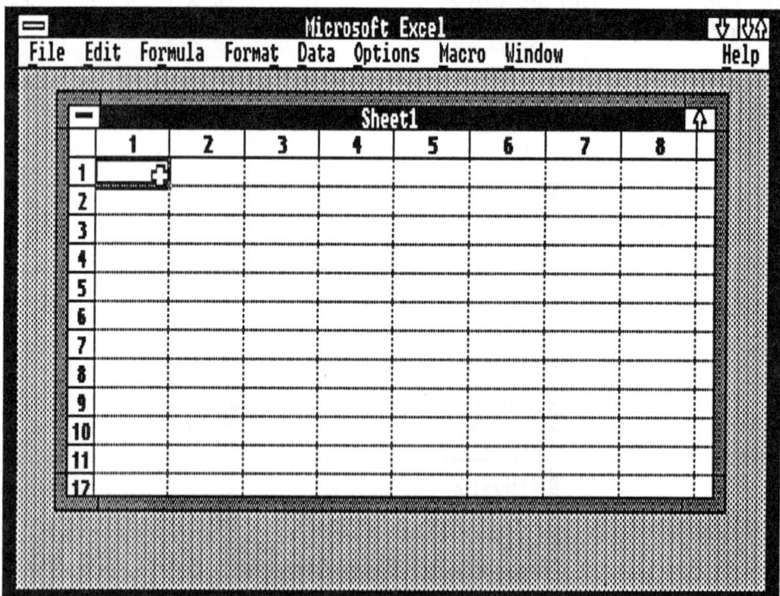

Notice the differences between this screen display and the earlier ones. The Scroll, Status, and Formula bars are gone and the columns are numbered.

7. Type **45** in cell 11 and press **Enter**.

8. Type **45.50** in cell 22 and press **Enter**.

9. Type **45.55** in cell 33 and press **Enter**.

10. Select **Workspace** from the Options menu again.

11. Activate **Fixed Decimal**. You must do this in order to change the value of the decimal. If you choose to do so, you can now press Tab or use the cursor to change the value of the decimal.

12. Press **Enter**.

13. Type **45** in cell 44, **45.50** in cell 55, and **45.55** in cell 66 and press **Enter**.

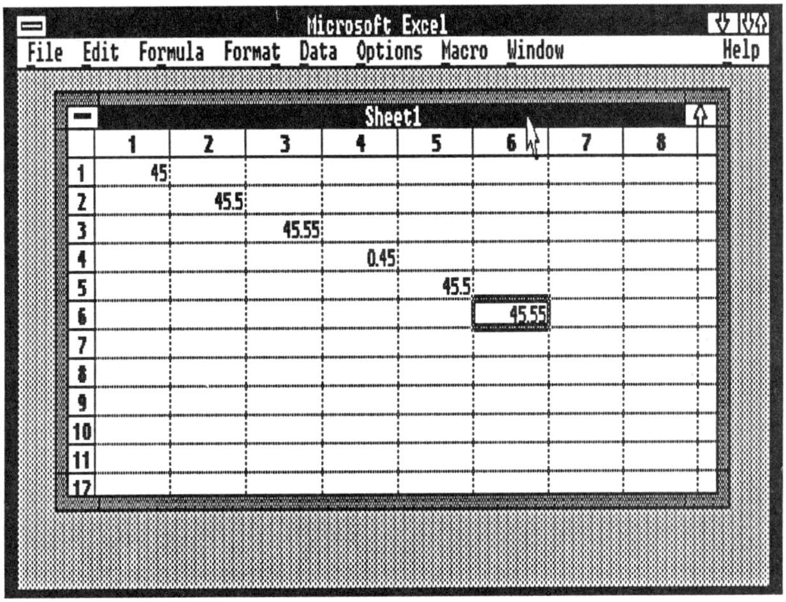

The only change in the data from imposing a fixed decimal on the system is in the number you typed and no decimal was specified. You may want to experiment with these settings.

14. Abandon Sheet1 and exit Excel to prevent unwanted workspace settings from carrying forward to the next module.

15. Turn to Module 30 to continue the learning sequence.

Appendix A
TERMS AND DEFINITIONS

Terms	Definitions
1904 Date System	A serial-number system for keeping track of dates in the Macintosh version of Excel. To maintain compatibility with Macintosh dates you must change to the 1904 date system with the Calculate dialog box from the Options menu.
Active Worksheet	Designated by a solid title bar and scroll bars, commands you give are carried out on the active worksheet.
Argument	The variables used with a function formula. For example, in the formula = COUNT(A1:A29) the argument is the range of values contained in cells A1 through A29.
ASCII	The American Standard Code for Information Interchange. The character set used by Excel to represent letters, numerals, and special symbols.
Cell contents	The information contained in a worksheet cell.
Cell format	The appearance of the data in the cell. Includes the font, the height, alignment, and in the case of numeric data, the number of decimal places used.
Cell name	The row and column address, such as A1, used by default to refer to a specific worksheet cell. Also, any name assigned to a cell through the use of the Create Names or Define Name commands.
Chart	A specialized Excel worksheet that displays information in chart form rather than in rows and columns.
Clipboard	A temporary storage location provided by Windows. Contains the information copied or cut from the most recent copy or cut operation.
Column	All the cells in a single vertical line.
Current cell	The highlighted cell in the active worksheet.
Field	A database management term. As implemented in Excel, each column of a spreadsheet contains the data for a field.
File	The data saved on the disk.
Function	An expression that takes as its input 0 or more arguments and returns a single value.
Label	A cell containing text.
Link	A reference from a cell in one worksheet to a cell or cells in another worksheet.

Terms	Definitions
Macro	A set of Excel commands and functions that are carried out in a particular order.
Macro Sheet	A specialized Excel worksheet for recording and editing macros.
Mouse cursor	The pointer that moves in response to mouse movements.
Open	The action performed when loading a worksheet, chart, or macro sheet from the disk into the active workspace.
Parameters	Another word for argument.
Path	Terminology used by DOS to describe the location of files on the disk. The full path of a file contains a drive letter, followed by a list of the subdirectories used to access the file.
Range	A rectangular region of cells in a single worksheet.
Record	A term used in database management. When developing a database in Excel, each row of the database corresponds to a record in the database.
Row	All the cells in a single horizontal row.
Windows	A multi-tasking, graphics based set of operating system extensions that provide extensions to MS-DOS that are necessary for using Excel.
Worksheet	Other software companies call them spreadsheets. The rectangular region of rows and columns that form the foundation for Excel.

Appendix B
KEYSTROKE COMMANDS AND FUNCTIONS

The most common keystrokes are included in this appendix. You can use them to access menus and perform various functions. They are listed in alphebetical order to facilitate access. These keystrokes are explained in the various modules of this book.

Command	Keystroke Combination
About	(ALT-H A)
Absolute Record/Relative Record	(ALT-M A)
Activate Application Menu	(ALT-F10)
Add	(SHIFT-F8)
Add Arrow	(ALT-C R)
Add Legend	(ALT-C L)
Add Overlay	(ALT-C O)
Alignment	(ALT-T A)
Application Menu Activation	(ALT-F2)
Apply Names	(ALT-R A)
Area	(ALT-G A)
Arrange All	(ALT-W A)
Attach Text	(ALT-C T)
Axes	(ALT-C X)
Bar	(ALT-G B)
Border	(ALT-T B)
Calculate Now	(F9)
Calculate Now from Chart Menu	(ALT-C N)
Calculate Now from Options Menu	(F9) or (ALT-O N)
Calculate Document	(SHIFT-F9)
Calculation	(ALT-O C)
Cancel	(ESC)
Cell Protection	(ALT-T P)
Clear	(DEL or ALT-E E)
Close	(ALT-F C) (ALT-SPACE-C) or (ALT-F4)
Close Application Window	(ALT-F4)
Close Document Window	(CTRL-F4)
Column	(ALT-G C)
Column Width	(ALT-T C)
Combination	(ALT-G M)
Context Help	(SHIFT-F1)
Copy	(CTRL-INS) or (ALT-E C)
Create Names	(SHIFT-CTRL-F3) or (ALT-R C)
Cut Selection	(SHIFT-DEL)
Cut	(SHIFT-DEL) or (ALT-E T)

Command	Keystroke
Define Names	(ALT-R D) or (CTRL-F3)
Delete	(ALT-F D)
Delete Character	(DEL)
Delete End of Line	(CTRL-DEL)
Delete from Data Menu	(ALT-D D)
Delete from Edit Menu	(ALT-E D)
Display	(ALT-O D)
Edit Formula	(F2)
Enter Array	(SHIFT-CTRL-ENTER)
Enter Data and Move to Next Cell	(ENTER)
Enter Data and Move to Prior Cell	(SHIFT-ENTER)
Exit	(ALT-F X)
Extend	(F8)
Extend Selection	(SHIFT-LEFT/RIGHT/UP/DOWN ARROW)
Extend Selection Down One Window	(SHIFT-PAGE DOWN)
Extend Selection Up One Window	(SHIFT-PAGE UP)
Extend to End of Control	(CTRL-SHIFT-END)
Extend to End of Line	(SHIFT-END)
Extend to Start of Data	(CTRL-SHIFT-HOME)
Extend to Start of Line	(SHIFT-HOME)
Extract	(ALT-D E)
Feature Guide	(ALT-H F)
Fill Down	(ALT-E W)
Fill Enter	(CTRL-ENTER)
Fill Right	(ALT-E H)
Find	(ALT-D F) (SHIFT-F5) or (ALT-R F)
Find Formula	(SHIFT-F5)
Find Next Data/Formula	(F7)
Find Previous Data/Formula	(SHIFT-F7)
Font	(ALT-T F)
Form	(ALT-D O)
Formula Note	(SHIFT-F2)
Freeze Panes	(ALT-O F)
Full Menus/Short Menus from Chart Menu	(ALT-C M)
Full Menus/Short Menus from Options Menu	(ALT-O M)
GoTo	(F5) or (ALT-R G)
Gridlines	(ALT-C G)
Help	(F1)
Hide	(ALT-W H)
Index	(F1) or (ALT-H I)
Insert	(ALT-E I)
Justify	(ALT-T J)
Keyboard	(ALT-H K)
Legend	(ALT-T L)
Line	(ALT-G L)
Linked	(ALT-F L)
Lotus 1-2-3	(ALT-H L)
Main Chart	(ALT-T M)
Maximize	(ALT-SPACE-X) or (ALT-F10)
Maximize Application Window	(ALT-F10)
Maximize Document Window	(CTRL-F10)
Minimize	(ALT-SPACE-N) or (ALT-F9)

Command	Keystroke
Minimize Application Window	(ALT-F9)
Move Application Window	(ALT-F7)
Move Document Window	(CTRL-F7)
Move Down One Window	(PAGE DOWN)
Move from Chart Format Menu	(ALT-T V)
Move from Ctrl Menu	(ALT-SPACE-M) or (ALT-F7)
Move in Direction of Arrow	(LEFT, RIGHT, UP, DOWN ARROW)
Move to End of Control	(CTRL-END)
Move to End of Line	(END)
Move to Start of Data	(CTRL-HOME)
Move to Start of Line	(HOME)
Move up One Window	(PAGE UP)
Multiplan	(ALT-H M)
New	(ALT-F N)
New Chart	(F11)
New Macro Sheet	(CTRL-F11)
New Window	(ALT-W N)
New Worksheet	(SHIFT-F11)
Next Application Window	(ALT-ESC) or (ALT-F6)
Next Area	(CTRL-TAB)
Next Cell Right	(TAB)
Next Document Window	(CTRL-F6)
Next Pane	(F6)
Note	(ALT-R N)
Number	(ALT-T N)
Open	(ALT-F O)
Open File	(CTRL-F12)
Overlay Chart	(ALT-T O)
Page Setup	(ALT-F T)
Parse	(ALT-D P)
Paste	(SHIFT-INS) or (ALT-E P)
Paste Function	(SHIFT-F3) or (ALT-R T)
Paste Function	(SHIFT-F3)
Paste Link	(ALT-E L)
Paste Name	(F3) or (ALT-R P)
Paste Name	(F3)
Paste Special	(ALT-E S)
Patterns	(ALT-T P)
Pie	(ALT-G P)
Preferred	(ALT-G R)
Previous Application Window	(ALT-SHIFT-ESC) or (ALT-SHIFT-F6)
Previous Area	(SHIFT-CTRL-TAB)
Previous Cell Left	(SHIFT-TAB)
Previous Document Window	(SHIFT-CTRL-F6)
Previous Pane	(SHIFT-F6)
Print	(ALT-F P)
Print File	(SHIFT-CTRL-F12)
Printer Setup	(ALT-F R)
Protect Document from Chart Menu	(ALT-C P)
Protect Document from Options Menu	(ALT-O P)
Record	(ALT-M C)
Reference	(F4) or (ALT-R R)

Command	Keystroke
Repeat	(ALT-E R) (ALT-ENTER) or (ALT-F1)
Replace	(ALT-R E)
Restore	(ALT-SPACE-R) or (ALT-F5)
Restore Application Window	(ALT-F5)
Restore Document Window	(CTRL-F5)
Rotate to Next Reference	(F4)
Rotate to Previous Reference	(SHIFT-F4)
Row Height	(ALT-T R)
Run	(ALT-M R) or (ALT-SPACE-U)
Save	(ALT-F S)
Save As	(ALT-F A)
Save As from File Menu	(F12)
Save from File Menu	(SHIFT-F12)
Save Workspace	(ALT-F W)
Scale	(ALT-T S)
Scatter	(ALT-G S)
Select Chart	(ALT-C C)
Select Column	(CTRL-SPACE)
Select Plot Area	(ALT-C A)
Select Row	(SHIFT-SPACE)
Select Special	(ALT-R S)
Select Worksheet	(SHIFT-CTRL-SPACE)
Series	(ALT-D R)
Set Criteria	(ALT-D C)
Set Database	(ALT-D B)
Set Page Break	(ALT-O B)
Set Preferred	(ALT-G T)
Set Print Area	(ALT-O A)
Set Print Titles	(ALT-O T)
Set Recorder	(ALT-M T)
Show Info	(ALT-W S) or (CTRL-F2)
Size Application Window	(ALT-F8)
Size Document Window	(CTRL-F8)
Size from Chart Format Menu	(ALT-T Z)
Size from Ctrl Menu	(ALT-SPACE-S) or (ALT-F8)
Sort	(ALT-D S)
Space Character	(SPACE)
Split	(ALT-HYPHEN-T)
Start Recorder	(ALT-M S)
Table	(ALT-D T)
Text	(ALT-T T)
Tutorial	(ALT-H T)
Undo	(ALT-E U)
Unhide	(ALT-W U)
Workspace	(ALT-O W)

Appendix C
ERROR MESSAGES

Message	Description
#DIV/0!	Division by zero is not defined.
#NAME	There is a problem with text that you typed in a formula. You may have misspelled a function name or omitted the colon from a range.
#N/A!	You have referenced a value that is not available.
#NULL	You have specified the intersection of two areas that don't intersect.
#NUM	You have used a number that is outside the available range (either too large or too small). You may also have used a mathematical function incorrectly, such as $SQRT(-1)$.
#REF	You have referred to a cell that is not on the worksheet. Typically, you have created a complex link to a supporting worksheet that is not open.
#VALUE	You have used the wrong type of argument for a function. You either used text where a number was expected, or a number where text was expected.

Appendix D
EXERCISES

1. About This Book
   a. What kind of information is presented in paragraph form?
   b. What kind of information is presented in numbered steps?
   c. What is the significance of information printed in bold type?

2. Overview
   a. How many windows can be opened at the same time when using Excel?
   b. How do you recognize when a window is active?
   c. How many rows and columns are in an Excel worksheet?
   d. How do you access the menus?

3. Sample Session
   a. What function does Ctrl-Right Arrow and Ctrl-Down Arrow perform?
   b. How can you scroll the worksheet?
   c. How can you recognize the active cell in a worksheet?
   d. How can you delete text you may be entering into the worksheet?

4. Alignment
   a. What types of alignment are available in Excel?
   b. How do you center text?
   c. How do you change an inappropriate alignment specification?

5. Apply Names
   a. What must happen before the Apply Names command is available as a menu choice?
   b. How do you restrict the operation of the Apply Names command to a particular region of the worksheet?
   c. How to you perform the Apply Names operation on the entire worksheet using a single command?
   d. Why would you want to use the Apply Names command?
   e. How do you control which names are applied in the worksheet?

6. Arrange All
   a. What happens when you use Arrange All?
   b. How can you change the arrangement of the worksheets once you have used Arrange All?
   c. Which available worksheets will be arranged in the workspace when you use Arrange All?

7. Border
   a. How do you draw a vertical line extending across multiple cells?
   b. How do you put a box around a cell?
   c. What does the Shade option accomplish?

8. Calculation, Calculate Now
   a. What does Excel do to any referenced cell contents when you change a formula anywhere in the worksheet?
   b. What are the options available to you once you access the Calculation command?
   c. How do you make calculations once you activate the manual mode?
   d. What is meant by "circular definition"?
   e. What options are available to you when working with calculations of circular definitions?

9. Cell Protection
   a. What two operations can you perform from the Cell Protection command?
   b. Cell Protection will only work when what other command is activated?
   c. In what menu is the Cell Protection command located?

10. Chart
    a. What is the purpose of a legend?
    b. What is the plot area?
    c. What is Attached Text?
    d. How do you attach text to a data point?
    e. How do you move text around the chart?

11. Clear
    a. What is the purpose of Clear?
    b. How can you recover from an inappropriately cleared worksheet?
    c. On what types of data does Clear work?
    d. What data will be cleared if you use the Formula option?
    e. What type(s) of data will be cleared if you use Format option?

12. Close
    a. What does the Close command do?
    b. Where is Close located?
    c. How is Close different from Exit?
    d. What happens when you select Close after working with a worksheet?

13. Column Width
    a. What are two ways to adjust the width of a column?
    b. How can you hide the information in a column?
    c. Once hidden, how do you restore a column to view?

14. Copy, Cut, Paste
    a. Which command does not adjust formulas for the new locations?
    b. How do you copy information to a new worksheet?
    c. Which command moves the data to a new location?
    d. How can you tell what portion of the worksheet is marked to be copied or cut?

15. Create Names
    a. When should you use Create Names instead of Define Name?
    b. Where can data names be placed with respect to the information to take advantage of the Create Names command?
    c. Is there a difference between names created with Define Name and names created with Create Names?

16. Define Name
    a. Why should you use the Define Name command?
    b. What prevents you from using the same name twice in a worksheet?
    c. Is it necessary that the name refer to a worksheet cell?

17. Delete (Database)
  a . What is the difference between the Delete command on the Data menu and the Delete command on the Edit menu?
  b . Why is the Delete command on the Data menu more approprite for working with Database information?
  c . What steps do you take to protect yourself from disaster through inadventent deletion?

18. Delete (Edit)
  a . What is the purpose of the Delete command from the Edit menu?
  b . What determines the amount of memory Excel assigns to a worksheet?
  c . What does it mean if you are given this error message "#REF!" when you try to delete a row or column?
  d . How can you mark an entire row or column in the worksheet?

19. Delete (File)
  a . What is the function of the Delete command on the File menu?
  b . What are the two methods of deleting a file from the dialog box associated with the Delete command on the File menu?
  c . How can you retrieve an inappropriately deleted file?

20. Display
  a . How do display the text of the formulas in the worksheet instead of the results?
  b . How do you force the display of zero-values as blanks?
  c . What effect does the Display command have on the appearance of printed output?

21. Exit
  a . When would you likely use the Exit command?
  b . What two outcomes will occur if you use Exit?
  c . Are you permitted to save changes when using Exit?

22. Extract
  a . What is the difference between the Extract command and the Delete command?
  b . What is the difference between the Extract command and the Copy command?
  c . What happens to information stored below the extract range when the extract range contains only the field titles?
  d . Is it necessary to include all fields when performing a database Extract operation?

23. Fill Right, Fill Down
  a . What is the purpose of Fill?
  b . Where can duplicate data be inserted using Fill?
  c . What are the restrictions on the area designated to receive the duplicate data?

24. Find
  a . What will Excel search for when you select Find?
  b . Where will Excel search for the desired information?
  c . If you select the Formula option, where will Excel concentrate the search?
  d . How do you indicate to Excel that you only know part of the string?
  e . What is critical to be done if you select the Whole option?

25. Find (Database)
  a . What is the difference between the Find command and the Find option of the Form command?
  b . How do you define the criteria used for the Find command?
  c . Can you perform a "replace" operation in conjunction with the Find command?

26. Font
    a. How many fonts can you use on a worksheet?
    b. What is the special significance of font number 1?
    c. When you change the definition of a font number, what happens to information displayed under the old font definition?

27. Form
    a. What actions must you perform before using the Form command?
    b. How does Excel determine the length of the fields on the form?
    c. How do you move between records when finding them with the Form command?
    d. How do you add additional records with the Form command?
    e. How do you get out of a database form once you are in it?

28. Format
    a. Specify at least three types of changes you can make to a chart from this menu.
    b. How does the Font option affect text? numbers?
    c. What does the Pattern command allow you to do?
    d. What options are available to you from the Text command?
    e. What options are available to you from the Scale command?
    f. What is Unattached Text?

29. Freeze Panes/Unfreeze Panes
    a. What must you do prior to using the Freeze Panes command?
    b. How do you determine which pane or panes are frozen?
    c. Once you have frozen panes on the screen, how do you change them?

30. Gallery
    a. What function does the Gallery menu serve?
    b. How do you change the preferred chart type?
    c. What is the default chart type in Excel?
    d. How many different types of charts are available in Excel?

31. Goto
    a. What purpose is served with Goto?
    b. On which menu is Goto located?
    c. What appears in the listing on the Goto dialog box?
    d. How do you use the Goto command?

32. Hide/Unhide
    a. What is the purpose of Hide?
    b. How can you keep track of the windows you may have hidden?
    c. How can you hide specific information and leave the worksheet on the screen?

33. Insert
    a. What is inserted using the Insert command?
    b. If you insert a new column, where does the data located in the designated column go?
    c. If you insert a new row, where does the data located in the designated row go?
    d. What must you do before selecting Insert if you want to insert four cells in a worksheet?

34. Number
    a. What kinds of values can you control the format of with the Number command?
    b. How do you specify a numeric format that does not appear as one of the menu selections?

35. Links
    a. When you select Links, what files are displayed in the Links dialog box?
    b. What procedure must you follow when you rearrange worksheet files on your hard disk?
    c. How can you determine what the supporting worksheets are for the active worksheet?

36. Menus
    a. How can you change between short and full menus?
    b. How do you know which options of a menu are not available to you at any specific time?
    c. How do you open a menu with the mouse?
    d. How do you open a menu from the keyboard?
    e. How do you move around a dialog box?

37. Move
    a. How can you access Move?
    b. When is Move used?
    c How do you designate which side of the window will be moved when using Move?

38. New
    a. What type of document can be opened with New?
    b. What is the advantage of being able to open a new document?
    c. How many documents can you open at one time?

39. New Window
    a. When would you use New Window?
    b. How do you know how many windows are open at one time?
    c. How can you move between available windows?

42. Open
    a. What is the purpose of the Open command?
    b. What types of objects or documents can Excel open?
    c. What happens if you try to open a worksheet created with Lotus 1-2-3?
    d. What is the purpose of the Open command?
    e. What are the procedures for designating a file to open?
    f. What is purpose of the TRANS123.XLM file?

43. Page Setup
    a. What effect does the Page Setup command have on the appearance of your screen?
    b. How do you change the printout heading using Page Setup?
    c. How do you specify the placement of the page number on the printed output?
    d. What happens when you change the Gridlines option on the Page Setup dialog box?

44. Parse
    a. When you read an ASCII file into a worsheet, how does Excel treat the file?
    b. What is the function of the Guess option on the Parse dialog box?
    c. What if the Guess option is confused by your ASCII data? What do you do next?

45. Paste Function
    a. What is a function?
    b. What the the purpose of the Paste Arguments option of the Paste Function command?
    c. In addition to using the Paste Function command, what other technique is available to use functions in your worksheet?

46. Paste Link
    a. What is a simple link?
    b. What is a complex link, and how is it different from a simple link?
    c. What alternative is there to using the Paste Link command to create links between worksheets?
    d. What type of error is generated when a complex link refers to a worksheet that is not open in the workspace?

47. Paste Name
    a. What must you do in your worksheet before the Paste Name command is available?
    b. How do you examine the definitions of selected names in a worksheet?
    c. What two ways are available to examine the definitions of all the names in a worksheet?

48. Paste Special
    a. What is the difference between the Paste command and the Paste Special command?
    b. What types of Excel documents can Paste Special move information between?
    c. Will Paste Special work in conjunction with the Cut command?
    d. What is the function of the Transpose option on the Paste Special dialog box?

49. Print
    a. What types of document windows can you print with the Print command in Excel?
    b. What is the advantage of the Preview option on the Print dialog box?
    c. What is the difference between Draft quality printing and the default printing?
    d. What is the purpose of the Zoom option in the preview?
    e. What is the meaning of the heavy dotted lines that appear on the document after you have previewed it?

50. Printer Setup
    a. How do you switch between available printers?
    b. Why would you want to print your output at a graphics resolution less than the maximum available?
    c. How do you add another printer to the list of those that are available?

51. Protect Document
    a. Why would you want to use the Protect Document command?
    b. How do you reverse the operation of the Protect Document command?
    c. What protection command is closely related to Protect Document?
    d. How do you hide the contents of cells by using Protect Document?
    e. What two aspects of a document can be protected?
    f. What is one disadvantage of using a password in protecting a document?
    g. How can a document be protected if you choose not to use a password?

52. Record
    a. How is the Record command different from the Repeat command?
    b. How do you stop recording a macro definition?
    c. How do you examine a macro definition?
    d. Where are macro definitions stored?
    e. What commands can be included in macros?

53. Reference
    a. What is a relative reference?
    b. What is an absolute reference?
    c. What is a mixed reference?
    d. What symbol do you use to specify that a reference is absolute?

54. Replace
    a. How do you instruct Excel to only search a particular portion of the worksheet?
    b. What is accomplished with the "Replace All" option?
    c. If you only wish to replace a particular type of string in the worksheet, how do you so indicate to Excel?

55. Repeat
    a. When you select the Repeat command, what command is repeated?
    b. Why is the Repeat command useful?

56. Row Height
    a. What three methods are available for changing the height of a row?
    b. What impact does changing fonts have on the row height?
    c. How can you use the Row Height command to hide the contents of a row?
    d. Once hidden, how do you return a row to its "normal" height?

57. Run
    a. What command must be used before you use the Run command?
    b. What option does Excel provide with the Run command?
    c. What is the required status of the macro sheet when you use the Run command?

58. Save, Save As, Save Workspace
    a. Which of the save commands permit you to change the name of an existing document?
    b. When can you use the Save command to name a document?
    c. What does Save Workspace do?
    d. Where are the original documents stored when you use Save Workspace?
    e. Which of the save commands permits you to write the document to floppy disk?

59. Select Special
    a. What types of cells may be selected with the Select Special command?
    b. How do you perform the Select Special command on the entire worksheet?
    c. How do you limit the Select Special command to a specific portion of a worksheet?
    d. What types of prescedents are used by the Select Special command?

60. Series
    a. What are the two types of series?
    b. How do you limit the number of entries in the series?
    c. How do you restrict the range of the series, without regard to the number of worksheet cells that are occupied?

61. Set Criteria
    a. Does using the Set Criteria command produce any visible change on the screen?
    b. What commands are dependent on the Set Criteria command?
    c. What is the effect of an empty row in the Set Criteria area?
    d. What operators are available to specify the selection criteria?

62. Set Database
    a. What Excel commands are dependent upon the Set Database command?
    b. What must you do before selecting the Set Database command?
    c. The rows of the worksheet correspond to database __________ (fields/records).
    d. The columns of the worksheet correspond to database __________ (fields/records).

63. Set Page Break/Remove Page Break
    a. What are the two available types of page breaks?
    b. What determines whether Set Page Break or Remove Page Break is available on the menu?
    c. How can you examine the location of page breaks without using the Print command?

64. Set Print Area
    a. If you do not use the Set Print Area command, what portion of the worksheet is printed by the Print command?
    b. Must the print area be set every time you print a worksheet?

65. Set Print Titles
    a. What is the difference between Set Print Titles and specifying a header with the Page Setup command?
    b. What must you do before using the Set Print Titles command?

66. Show Info/Show Document
    a. What determines whether Show Info or Show Document is available from the Screen menu?
    b. What advantage is there to working in the Show Info mode?
    c. What disadvantage is there to working in the Show Info mode?

67. Size
    a. What are the methods you can use to size a window?
    b. If you use Size to reduce the size of a window, what will you see behind it?
    c. How can you use the mouse to make a window active?
    d. What keys do you use to identify the side to be moved after selecting Size?
    e. When is it appropriate to use the Restore command or Ctrl-F5 to return a window to its original size?

68. Sort
    a. What is the relationship between the database defined with Set Database and the operation of the Sort command?
    b. How do you sort by rows?
    c. How do you sort by columns?
    d. How do you sort by more than three sort keys?

69. Split
    a. How do you split a worksheet into multiple panes?
    b. Once split, how do you return a worksheet to a single pane?

70. Table
    a. What is the advantage of providing a "reasonable" value in the table substitution cell?
    b. How can you prevent table recalculation from degrading the performance of every worksheet recalculation?

71. Undo
    a. What will the Undo command accomplish?
    b. What operation will Undo not apply to?
    c. When does Undo become accessible?

72. Workspace
    a. What is meant by workspace?
    b. What aspects of the workspace are you able to modify with Workspace?
    c. What does deactivating the formula bar accomplish?

Index

Absolute names, 15
Absolute record, 255
Absolute reference, 15, 157
ACOS, 207
Active worksheet, 4
Add Arrow, 32
Add Legend, 32
Address, 5
After, 299
Alignment, 11
Align text, 123
Alphabetic search, 300
AM, 181
AND, 202
Apply Names, 14
AREAS, 200
Arrange All, 19
Array, 268
Arrows, 32
Ascending sort, 334-335
ASCII text file, 193
ASIN, 207
ATAN, 207
Attach text, 32
Automatic calculation, 25
Automatic page break, 240
Automatic text, 123
AVERAGE, 205
Axis, 32

Background shading, 23
Backup file, 282
Before, 299
Border, 22

C-prompt, 82
Calculate Now, 25
Calculation, 25
Categories, 227
Category axis, 124
CELL, 200
Cell address, 143
Cell note, 176
Cell protection, 29, 250
Change, 354
Change Links, 156
CHAR, 205
Chart, 118, 137
Chart title, 32
CHOOSE, 202
Circular definitions, 25
CLEAN, 205

Clear, 39
Close, 42
Co-processor, 2
CODE, 205
COLUMN, 201
Column Differences, 268
Column Row, 15
Comma delimited, 181
Complex link, 213
Compuserve, 194
Computed field, 84
Control menu icon, 165-166, 341
Control panel, 240
Copy, 50
COS, 207
COUNT, COUNTA, 205
Create Names, 56, 222
Criteria, 297
Cross cursor, 272
CSV file, 281
Cut, 50

Database, 305
Database sort, 338
Data Point, 36
DATE, 199
DATEVALUE, 199
DAVERAGE, 198
DAY, 199
DBF, 2 file, 3 file, 282
DCOUNT, DCOUNTA, 198
DMAX, 198
DDB, 199
Define Name, 56, 59, 222
Delete, 39, 65, 71, 74
Dependents, 268
Dependent worksheet, 214
Descending sort, 334
Device driver, 240
Dialog box, 162
DIF file, 281
Display, 77
Division point, 342
DMIN, 198
DOLLAR, 205
Dollar amounts, 182
Dollar sign, 262
DPRODUCT, 198
Drop-down menus, 161
DSTDEV, DSTDEVP, 198
DSUM, DVAR, DVARP, 198

EXACT, 205
Exit, 81
EXP, 203
Expanded memory, 2
External reference, 158, 214
Extract, 83

FACT, 203
FALSE, 202
Field names, 84
File format, 281
Filenames, 156
Fill down, right, 91
Fill justification, 12
FIND, 205
Find, 95, 102
Find Next, Prev, 112
FIXED, 205
Fixed decimal, 355
Font, 105, 118
Font size, 275
Footer, 188-189
Form, 95, 111
Format, 118, 137, 180
Format pattern, 181
Formulas checkbox, 78
Freeze Panes, 130
Full Menus, 162
FV, 199

Gallery, 137
General alignment, 11
General format, 182
General-purpose deleting, 65
Goto, 143
Gridlines, 32, 77, 188-189
GROWTH, 205
Growth series, 292
Guess, 194

Hardware, 2
Header, 188-189
Header file, 243
Height, 275
Help, 6
Hide, 29, 145
Hide Formula bar, Scroll bars, 354
Hide row, 275
Hide Status, 354
HLOOKUP, 202
Horizontal text, 123
HOUR, 199

Icon, 3
IF, 202
Ignore Remote Requests, 355

INDEX, 203
INDIRECT, 201
Insert, 150
Installed printers, 240
INT, 203
Interactive delete, 66
Invisible, 122
IPMT, 199
IRR, 200
ISBLANK, 201
ISERR, ISERROR, 201
ISLOGICAL, 201
ISNA, 201
ISNONTEXT, ISTEXT, 201
ISNUMBER, 201
ISREF, 201
Iterations, 25

Justify, 152

Keyboard, 5
Keyboard scrolling, 8

Landscape orientation, 240
LEFT, 205
Legend, 32, 129
LEN, 205
Linear series, 292
LINEST, 205
Links, 156
LN, 203
Locking titles, 133
LOG, LOG10, 203
LOGEST, 205
LOOKUP, 203
LOWER, 205

Macro, 255, 278
Manual calculation, 26
Margin, 188-189
MATCH, 203
Match or after, 299
MAX, 205
Maximize, 5, 165
MDETERM, 204
Menu bar, 4, 161, 165
Menus, 161
MID, 205
Miltiple criteria, 297
MIN, 205
Minimize, 5, 165
MINUTE, 199
MINVERSE, 204
MIRR, 200
Mixed names, references, 15
MMULT, 204

MOD, 204
MONTH, 199
Move, 118, 143, 166
MS-DOS Executive, 44, 82

N, NA, 201
Named cell, reference, 157
Names in sheet, 60
Names reference, 144
New, 137, 169
New printer, 245
New window, 173
New worksheet, 170
NOT, 202
Note, 176
NOW, 199
NPER, NPV, 200
Number, 180
Numeric co-processor, 2
Numeric format, 180

Omit column name, row name, 15
Open, 185
Open Links, 156
Optional digit, 181
Options, 162
OR, 202
Outline, 23
Overlay, 32, 127

Page setup, 188
Pane, 130, 341
Parse, 193
Password, 282
Paste, 50
Paste Function, 197
Paste Link, 213
Paste Name, 222
Paste Range, 226
Paste Special, 226
Patterns, 118
PI, 204
Plot area, 32
PM, 181
PMT, PPMT, 200
Point, 271
Portrait orientation, 240
PostScript, 243
Precedents, 268
Precision as displayed, 182
Preview, 240
Print, 237
Print Area, 315
Print Titles, 318
Printer setup, 240
PRODUCT, 204

PROPER, 205
Protect document, 29, 250
PV, 200

R1C1, 355
RAND, 204
Range reference, 60
RATE, 200
Rearrange text, 152
Recall worksheet, 186
Reference, 15, 261
Refers to, 59-60
Region, 268
Relative, 15
Relative record, 255
Remove page break, 310
Reorganize, 19
Repeat, 256, 265
Replace, 268
REPLACE, 205
Replace existing categories, 227
REPT, 205
Restore row, 273
Reverse, 351
RIGHT, 207
ROUND, 204
ROW, 201
Row & Column Headings, 77, 188-189
Row Height, 271
ROWS, 202
Ruling lines, 23
Run, 278

Save, 281
Save As, 281
Save workspace, 157, 281
Scale, 118
Script, 121
Scroll bars, 5
SEARCH, 207
Search criteria, 95
SECOND, 199
Select special, 287
Selection criteria, 90, 306
Series, 36, 291
Series names, 227
Set criteria, 65, 95, 297
Set database, 65, 95, 305
Set page break, 310
Set print area, 315
Set print titles, 318
Shading, 23
Sheet1, 169
Short Menus, 162
Shortcut key, 278

Show Document, 322, 323
Show Info, 322
SIGN, 204
Simple link, 213
SIN, 207
Size, 118, 330
Skip blanks, 227
SLN, 200
SLYK file, 281
Sort, 306, 334
Split, 130, 341
SQRT, 204
Standard height, 271
Standard width, 45
STDEV, STDEVP, 205
Step value, Stop value, 292
Subsets, 84
SUBSTITUTE, 207
Substitution cells, 344
SUM, 205
Supporting worksheet, 157, 214
SYD, 200

T, 202
Table, 344
TAN, 207
TEXT, 207
Text file, 281
TIME, 199
Timeout, 243
TIMEVALUE, 199

TRANSPOSE, 204
Transpose, 227
TREND, 205
TRIM, 207
TRUE, 202
TRUNC, 204
TYPE, 202
Typefaces, 105

Undo, 39, 351
Unhide, 145
Unlock, 29
UPPER, 207

VALUE, 207
Value axis, 32, 124
VAR, VARP, 205
Vertical marker, 341
Vertical text, 123
View Links, 156
VLOOKUP, 203

WEEKDAY, 199
Width, 45
Wildcard characters, 300
Windows, 3
WK1 file, WKS file, 281
Worksheet, 4
Workspace, 354

YEAR, 199

Zero values, 77

Other Books from Wordware Publishing, Inc.

Artificial Intelligence
Artificial Ingelligence Programming
    Techniques in BASIC
Illustrated Turbo Prolog 2.0
Illustrated VP-Expert

Computer-Aided Drafting
Illustrated AutoCAD (Release 9)
Illustrated AutoCAD (Release 10)
Illustrated AutoSketch 1.04
Illustrated GenericCADD

Database Management
The DataFlex Developer's Handbook
Illustrated dBASE II (2nd Ed.)
Illustrated dBASE III Plus
Illustrated dBASE IV
Illustrated Paradox Volume II 1.2
Illustrated Paradox Volume II 3.0
Illustrated VP-Info 1.4

Desktop Publishing
Desktop Publisher's Dictionary
Desktop Publisher's Thesaurus
Graphics Impact with Ventura 2.0
Handbook of Desktop Publishing
Illustrated PageMaker 3.0
Illustrated Ready, Set, Go! 4.5
    (Macintosh)
Illustrated Ventura 2.0
pfs: First Publisher
Ventura Troubleshooting Guide

General Advanced Topics
The Complete Communications
    Handbook
Consulting Handbook for the
    High-Tech Professional
Illustrated Dac Easy Accounting 2.0
Illustrated Dac Easy Accounting 3.0
Illustrated Novell NetWare

Programming Languages
Advanced Graphic Programming with
    Turbo Pascal 5.0
Illustrated C Programming (ANSI)
The FOCUS Developer's Handbook
From BASIC to 8086/8088 Assembly
    Language
Library of Turbo Pascal Programs
    2nd Edition
Illustrated QuickBASIC 4.0
Illustrated RM/COBOL

Programming Languages cont.
Illustrated Turbo C
Illustrated Turbo Pascal 4.0
Illustrated Turbo Pascal 5.0

Spreadsheet/Integrated
Illustrated Framework II
Illustrated Framework III
Illustrated Lotus 1-2-3 2.01
Illustrated Microsoft Excel 2.10 (IBM)
Illustrated Microsoft Excel 1.5
    (Macintosh)
Illustrated Multiplan 2.0
Illustrated Q & A
Illustrated Quattro
Illustrated Symphony 1.2

Systems and Operating Guides
Illustrated Microsoft Windows 2.0
Illustrated MS/PC-DOS 3.3
Illustrated MS/PC-DOS 4.0
Illustrated OS/2

Word Processing
Illustrated DisplayWrite 4
Illustrated Microsoft Word 5.0
Illustrated Sprint 1.01
Illustrated WordPerfect 1.0
    (Macintosh)
Illustrated WordPerfect 4.2
Illustrated WordPerfect 5.0
Illustrated WordStar Professional (Rel. 4)
Illustrated WordStar Professional (Rel. 5)
The New WordStar Customizing Guide 4.0
WordPerfect: Advanced Applications
    Handbook

Business-Professional Books
Business Emotions
How to Win Pageants
Innovation, Inc.
Investor Beware
MegaTraits
Occupying the Summit
Steps to Strategic Management

Regional
This Dog'll Hunt
100 Days in Texas — The Alamo Letters
Exploring the Alamo Legends
Wit and Wisdom
Forget the Alamo
Rainy Day Workbook, Texas Edition

Call Wordware Publishing, Inc. for names of the bookstores in your area.
(214) 423-0090